The University of Alberta Press

CKUA

Radio Worth Fighting For

MARYLU WALTERS

With research assistance by Sharon Sinclair

Published by
The University of Alberta Press
Ring House 2
Edmonton, Alberta T6G 2E1

NATIONAL LIBRARY OF CANADA CATALOGUING IN PUBLICATION DATA

Walters, Marylu.
    CKUA : radio worth fighting for

    Includes bibliographical references and index.
    ISBN 0-88864-395-0

    1. CKUA (Radio station : Edmonton, Alta.)—History. I. Title.
HE8699.C2W34 2002   384.54'0971'2334   C2002-910981-7

The University of Alberta Press has made every effort to identify correctly the sources of photographs used in
this book. If we have misidentified a rights holder, please let us know and and we will correct the error in any
subsequent printings. Photos on pages 80 and 260 are courtesy of CKUA; photo on page 260 by Brian
Dunsmore. Photo on page 368 is courtesy of the Provincial Archives of Alberta PA 1631/5.

Printed and bound in Canada by Houghton Boston, Saskatoon, Saskatchewan.
Photos scanned by Screaming Color Inc., Edmonton, Alberta.
∞Printed on acid-free paper.
Copyediting by Jill Fallis.
Book design by Alan Brownoff.
Publication assistance by Tara Taylor and Lisa LaFramboise.

The University of Alberta Press acknowledges the financial support of the Government of Canada through
the Book Publishing Industry Development Program for its publishing activities. The Press also gratefully
acknowledges the support received for its program from the Canada Council for the Arts.

THE CANADA COUNCIL | LE CONSEIL DES ARTS
FOR THE ARTS | DU CANADA
SINCE 1957 | DEPUIS 1957

Canadä

*Inside covers: For decades musicians and other entertainment personalities visiting the CKUA studio have been asked to sign
the cloth cover of the station's grand piano. These images suggest the variety and number of visitors over the years.*

To my mother, Lucy Ray

CONTENTS

PREFACE

This book is the first comprehensive history of CKUA ever undertaken. Two previous histories—celebratory booklets published on CKUA's fortieth and sixtieth anniversaries—sketched the story up to 1987. So much had happened since then—privatization of the station, its closing and stunning rebirth—that I worried the last decade would far outweigh, in sheer *eventfulness*, all that had come before, making for a very unbalanced narrative. It turns out CKUA had been through other political conflicts and near-death experiences equally as dramatic—and equally undocumented.

As research progressed it also became obvious CKUA was a player in a story much larger than itself. This was no simple tale of the quirky little radio station that could and the personalities that drove it. To be properly understood and appreciated, CKUA's story needed to be put into the political and cultural context of its times. It's true, CKUA rarely turns up in the indexes of Canadian broadcast histories. But cross-referencing events in CKUA's history with what was going on nationally at the same time makes clear that the station's fortunes were affected by political battles waged far beyond Alberta's borders; and in turn, CKUA's existence had a bearing on major national broadcast policy decisions.

CKUA's influence within Alberta's borders has been profound—in stark contrast to the pittance it represented on the provincial government's budget ledgers during the sixty-seven or so years before it was privatized. From its start, CKUA has been a platform for Albertan and Canadian talent and ideas. But as evidenced by the intense loyalty it has consistently inspired in its listeners, CKUA is also much more. In fact, some people consider the station an Alberta cultural institution in itself. For all these reasons, CKUA's history needed to be set down.

This book is by no means the whole CKUA story, nor is it the "authorized biography." While many people generously contributed their stories and other information to this effort, I take full responsibility for what was selected and what was left out. For every person named or quoted within, countless others deserve equal attention. To them, I apologize. I hope they will be motivated to contribute their own CKUA stories to the station's "archives," there to be mined for a future history—perhaps to mark CKUA's hundredth anniversary.

ACKNOWLEDGEMENTS

I am indebted to the many people who committed their time, memories, photographs, personal papers and unique knowledge to this effort. Sharon Sinclair deserves special credit. A former CKUA/ACCESS employee who worked for many years at the station in various capacities, Sharon was an invaluable research ally. To borrow an expression from Tommy Banks, she "knew where the ketchup was." She opened many doors through her extensive contacts and friendships, called on former colleagues to lend anecdotes and photographs for the book and interviewed others, assisted in a survey of CKUA's vast "archives," contributed her own stories and files, and cast a critical eye on the manuscript.

My warmest appreciation goes to the late Percy Brown and his wife Shirley for their hospitality and intimate perspectives on H.P. Brown and CKUA's early years.

Special thanks also to Jack Hagerman and the late Larry Shorter for trusting me with their personal files and drawing the big picture; to Fil Fraser for encouraging me to expand the scope of the book; to Jim Shaw for providing a bridge to University of Alberta Faculty of Extension history; and to Tony Cashman for sharing his knowledge of early radio history in Edmonton. Joe McCallum deserves credit for his booklet *CKUA and 40 Wondrous Years of Radio*; George Duffield, for his histories of Canadian radio stations on the Canadian Communications Foundation website; and Mary Vipond, Ralph Clark and Ron Faris, for their excellent histories, from which I have borrowed.

I am most grateful to CKUA's staff, management and board for their cooperation—especially to Bill Coull for allowing his image to be used on the cover—and to everyone who graciously agreed to be interviewed with no guarantee they would like the result. Thanks are also due to Frank Gasparik, who generously allowed the use of his photos in this book.

Raymond Frogner and Sarah Kelly at the University of Alberta Archives and Wendy McGee at the Provincial Archives of Alberta were most helpful. I wish to acknowledge the Alberta Foundation for the Arts for providing funding assistance.

I am also indebted to Grant Dunlop, Gail Helgason and John Dodd for taking the time to vet my manuscript.

Finally, I want to thank my friends for their encouragement over the five years this book was in the making—and my son, Mark Antonelli, for the music.

PROLOGUE
The Last Radio Show

By one measure, radio station CKUA's "Night Music" program for Thursday, March 20, 1997, was every listener's dream—at least for those who didn't know what was going on. For probably the first time in the station's almost seventy-year history—the big anniversary was coming up in November—its programmers were putting their heads together and picking the music for a single show.

"Radio Radio" by Elvis Costello, Mercedes Sosa's "Gracias a la vida," Shirley Horn's "Here's to Life," some Miles Davis, Fred Astaire singing "You Can't Take That Away From Me." How good does it get? It was an eclectic mix of the type CKUA had pioneered and was best known for. But, to listeners who were plugged in to the grapevine, there was a sad, defiant subtext.

Bob Remington, the Edmonton Journal's entertainment editor, knew what was coming down. "I sat alone in front of the stereo ... with the lights dimmed and the radio tuned to 94.9 FM listening intently, wondering what the staff at CKUA would have up their sleeve before the plug was pulled on nearly 70 years of broadcast history," he wrote.

He wasn't disappointed: "It was radio programmed from the heart, and it was done in trademark CKUA style—subdued, with material that was intelligent, thoughtful and creative. On-air staffers got in their parting shots, but they did it with dignity, letting the music speak for them."

With ten minutes left to go, Calgary band Seanachie came on with "Go To Hell," a song written by Gordon McCulloch about his civil servant father's forced retirement. Then, finally, "The Last Waltz," by The Band.

"Musically, it was a great show," the program's host, Chris Martin, said in retrospect. With just two years at the station, Martin, at thirty-one, was the junior member of the CKUA family, paying his dues filling in for regular on-air staff who called in sick or were on holidays. So he didn't think twice when operations manager Ken Davis called him in that afternoon to do the "Night Music" show for Tony Dillon-Davis, a thirty-year CKUA veteran.

And Dillon-Davis didn't think much of it when Davis called that day to suggest he'd been working too hard and might like to take the evening off. But, unbeknownst to his boss, Dillon-Davis had to go in to the station anyway to tape his "Play It Again" show for Sunday. So when he appeared, Davis had to let him in on what was happening: after seventy years as one of Alberta's cultural landmarks, Canada's oldest public radio station would be shut down at midnight.

Three years earlier, a deficit-slashing Alberta government, which had owned CKUA for fifty years—arguably for its whole life—had cut the station loose, selling it for ten dollars to a private, not-for-profit charitable foundation. Staff knew money was tight, but there had been some new hiring recently, themes were being discussed for the upcoming seventieth anniversary, and the station was gearing up for its spring fundraiser.

"Nobody was more surprised than I when I was called at ten or eleven o'clock one morning to be told that I could have the privilege later that day of telling everybody that they were being let go and the station was being shut down," Davis said. "There was no sense from myself on down that we were about to be shut off. Not a clue. Literally we were forward looking, forward planning. We thought we were in business."

Martin figured Davis had called him in to do the deed that day because, as the relative newcomer, he was the staff member least likely to get emotional or say something untoward while hosting CKUA's final hour. "Ken called me

◆ Chris Martin, host of "the last radio show."

Courtesy of CKUA; photo by Frank Gasparik.

into his office ... and said, 'At midnight we're off the air.' I thought, 'I know. We're off the air every night at midnight.' And he said, 'This is it. We're shutting down at midnight.' I caught the gist of what he meant, but it still had to sink in for a moment."

Martin was told not to tell anybody else what he knew. Davis said he would get the news out to each staff member personally. "He said, 'Do a normal show as if it were any other show you would do—as if theoretically we were going back on the air the next day—but don't answer the phone and don't talk to any media.'

"He thought that I should be the last one on the air because I had been around here the least. To expect Tony Dillon-Davis, who had been here for thirty-odd years, to have basically his entire life taken away from him and have him be the last bang ... Tony's a complete professional, and I don't doubt that he would have done the show as a complete professional. From the viewpoint of the people handing down the message, they probably had the worst-case scenario in mind, just in case."

They needn't have worried, Dillon-Davis said. "My gut feeling is that, in fact, if what he was trying to do was to quietly go into that dark night with the radio station with Chris Martin piloting, he chose the wrong person to do the piloting. If he'd chosen me, I would have just done an ordinary evening, said good night and left. I kinda suspected it was going to happen anyway. I felt the place was pretty well doomed." So he turned around and went home.

As for Martin: "I was just walking around in a daze, thinking this is crazy.... And I started to think about what the heck I was going to play. You know, it was theoretically the last show that CKUA was ever going to have. So I went up to the record library and I thought, 'Well, you should promote the whole idea of thanking Alberta,' so I started to pull out all the Alberta artists that I could think of. And I thought, 'Maybe I'll just play all Alberta artists and say thanks to those people for providing us with great music over the years.'"

Leaving the library and still wandering around in disbelief, Martin passed the studio where Cathy Ennis was putting together her "Passport" world music program for Saturday night. "The whole time I kept walking past the studio thinking, 'Well, that's kind of futile.' Mark [Antonelli] was on the air. Ken asked me not to mention it to Mark—particularly not to Mark—because he was on the air at the time and it would be rather disturbing to someone in mid-program.... But I did actually go and tell Cathy before she heard from Ken, because it just seemed idiotic for me to watch her put all this time and energy into a project that would never come to fruition. So I interrupted her while she was doing her taped programming and said, 'Don't bother. We're finished at midnight.... You're just wasting your time.' She was about as stunned as I was."

People who were at the station that afternoon were told the news first-hand. Some heard by phone. Those who weren't home to receive the calls found out when they played back their answering machines.

By the time the BBC news came on at 10:00 p.m., half an hour before Martin's show, CKUA's four phone lines had started ringing non-stop.

Martin had heard that programmer Lee Onisko was gathering stunned staff at her house "to chat, grieve, gripe, whatever.... After I'd picked out all the Alberta music, I thought, 'Well, maybe some of the other DJs would like to have a hand in what's going on over the air for the final show.' So I called over to Lee's and said, 'You people start thinking about what you want to hear and I'll call back periodically....'

"By the time I went on, I was just shaking like a leaf, uncertain as to what I was going to say. I don't remember what I said. But I started off with 'Radio Radio' by Elvis Costello, particularly because of the line 'Radio is a sound salvation.' I thought that was a good line to start off the last program of seventy years with.

"I do remember that I said things that were rather pointed perhaps in a *double entendre* way, or metaphorical way. I was sort of making statements that essentially alluded to the fact that we were done. But I never at any point came out and said, 'This is our last broadcast....' I was actually instructed not to even allude to it in any means, but I thought, 'What are they going to do, fire me?'"

Outside the on-air booth, the station was deserted and the doors were locked. The combinations had already been changed and, according to Martin, "some punk kid working for some local security company" had been hired to man the front desk. Martin could see by the studio video camera, trained on the front door six floors below, that the television media were milling around waiting to capture the story of CKUA's demise as it happened.

"I felt I should go down and say, 'Listen, I'm not coming out till the end of the show and I've been instructed not to say anything, so you might as well go home.' I felt badly they were hanging out there for the night."

Whenever he had a long piece playing or two queued up in a row, Martin would phone Onisko's house for requests. It was Onisko who came up with the idea of closing with "The Last Waltz."

But when it came to last words, Martin said he was totally unprepared. "I used to have a bad sarcastic sense of humour, and I thought I should say something mildly sarcastic. And to some degree, I thought, 'I bet this isn't the last of CKUA....' The whole time during the show, in the back of my mind I thought, 'What if ...?'

"I knew everyone was over at Lee's house, and I wanted to get over there as quickly as possible.... So I was putting some CDs away while 'The Last Waltz' was playing and then I realized the song had ended, so I ran back to the on-air booth. I was literally running down the hall, and then when I got on the air, I was kind of out of breath, so it sounded as though I was all choked up. But really, I was just trying to catch my breath. For dramatic purposes, it sounded a lot better over the air than it was intended to."

What does one say when closing down a seventy-year-old institution?

"We'll be back ... after this."

Taking the University to the People

1

CKUA was born on November 21, 1927, the offspring of a marriage between the hot new technology of radio and the passion for rural adult education that was sweeping North America at the time. The station survived radio's tumultuous early years—when the mortality rate for new stations was almost as high as their birth rate—thanks to nurturing by some remarkable people who brought a potent combination of vision and energy to this bold experiment in university extension programming.

When CKUA began broadcasting, more than a quarter of a century had passed since Guglielmo Marconi picked up the first transatlantic wireless signal—Morse code for the letter *s*, transmitted from Cornwall, England, to a receiver attached to a kite at Signal Hill in St. John's, Newfoundland. *The Globe* pronounced Marconi's feat of December 12, 1901 "the most wonderful scientific discovery of modern times." A year earlier, Canadian-born engineer Reginald Fessenden had already demonstrated to a largely disinterested business community that wireless technology could be used to transmit the sound of the human voice. From his laboratory near Washington, DC, he transmitted the first intelligible speech by electromagnetic waves—"One, two, three, four, is it snowing where you are, Mr. Thiessen?"—and received a reply from his assistant a mile away.

But, for practical purposes, wireless technology was considered useful only as a way to transmit Morse code—that is, for wireless *telegraphy*. Fessenden, a prolific inventor, persisted with his experiments, and on Christmas Eve 1906 he topped his earlier coup with a feat of wireless *telephony* that opened the door for radio as we know it. Broadcasting from Brant Rock, Massachusetts, he surprised wireless operators onboard ships in the Atlantic with a rendition of "O Holy Night" on his violin and a reading of the Christmas story from the New Testament, wishing them a merry Christmas as he signed off.

Despite Fessenden's revolutionary demonstrations, radio's potential as a mass medium was slow to catch on. Until the First World War, radio was primarily a maritime medium, used for point-to-point communication, in code, between ships or from ship to shore. It was adapted for military use during the war and only began to be used as a broadcast medium when experienced wireless operators returned from duty and amateur operators began to appear on the scene.

One of these amateurs was Frank Conrad, an assistant chief engineer at Westinghouse Electric and Manufacturing Company in Pittsburgh. Working out of a laboratory in his garage, Conrad had designed and tested transmitters and receivers for the US Signal Corps. After the war he continued his garage experiments, attracting the attention of other radio enthusiasts in the area who picked up his signal on their home-built crystal radio sets. Conrad sometimes played phonograph records on his station and soon started getting requests from his listeners.

In the winter of 1919 he began broadcasting regular weekly concerts, sometimes with his sons as announcers. When he exhausted his own record collection, he struck up a deal with a music store to borrow records in exchange for mentioning the store on the air. Thus, within a short time during the early months of 1920, Conrad had pioneered the basic concepts of modern commercial radio: a broadcast audience, regular scheduled programming and advertising to pay for it.

It didn't take long for news of Conrad's programs to pique the interest of the general public. Soon they wanted to know how they could get in on this new medium of entertainment. A local department store ran a newspaper ad offering radio sets that could pick up Conrad's broadcasts. The idea wasn't wasted on Westinghouse. The company had manufactured radio equipment for the government during the war, but the Radio Corporation of America (RCA) had managed to create a virtual monopoly in commercial radiotelegraphy in the United States. Westinghouse was casting about for a viable commercial enterprise for its radio manufacturing plant. When company vice-president Harry P. Davis saw the newspaper ad, a light bulb went on over his head: Westinghouse would produce radio receivers for the general public and set up its own radio station to create a market for the product.

Radio station KDKA went on the air on November 2, 1920, broadcasting returns of the US presidential election as reported over the phone from the *Pittsburgh Post*. Between reports, the station filled in with a banjo player and some phonograph records. After the election KDKA returned to the air with a regular one-hour nightly broadcast, going down in history as the first station to broadcast regularly in the US and possibly the world.

"When the year 1920 began, the only people who thought about radio thought of it as an art that could be understood and enjoyed only by the expert or the electronics whiz," writes George H. Douglas in *The Early Days of Radio Broadcasting*. "When the year 1920 was over there were few who failed to see that radio was calling out to everybody. Now it just might be that the radio receiver could be a household utility like the stove, the phonograph and the electric light."

By early 1922, Douglas adds, "scores of new stations would seek and receive licenses, and the broadcasting idea would then spread like wildfire around the country." Westinghouse's Davis said he recognized radio telephony at the time for being "the only means of collective communication ever devised."

In Canada the wireless industry evolved at a similar pace. In 1902 Marconi's Wireless Telegraph Company, headquartered in England, registered a subsidiary in Ontario, as it did in a number of countries. The Marconi group built and operated wireless telegraph stations in marine settings for navigational and commercial purposes, including a number for the Canadian government. The company also manufactured wireless equipment.

Following a move by the British government in 1904 to license wireless transmission, the Canadian government passed the Wireless Telegraphy Act in 1905, giving the minister of marine and fisheries authority over licensing the operation of wireless transmitters and receivers. The more comprehensive Radiotelegraph Act of 1913 gave the federal government far-reaching authority over the development of radio broadcasting, even though the concept of radio as a popular medium was still only the daydream of a few visionaries. The earliest private commercial licensees were companies, including some in Alberta's oil and lumber industries, that used telegraph for communications between branches or between field operations and head office. Meanwhile, a growing community of hobbyists was building crystal sets for listening in on shipping signals and communicating with one another in code.

By 1919 the Marconi Wireless Telegraph Company of Canada was experimenting with speech transmission between Glace Bay, Nova Scotia, and Clifden, Ireland. The company had an experimental licence to operate a station with the call letters XWA from its Montreal laboratory and was programming speech and music. The station is credited with being the first broadcasting station in the world and with what some argue was the first regularly scheduled radio broadcast ever. On May 20, 1920 XWA broadcast a concert performed by Dorothy Lutton singing in a room in the Marconi factory in Montreal to members of the Royal Society of Canada assembled in the ballroom of the Chateau Laurier hotel in Ottawa. Around that time, the station secured a formal broadcast licence with the call letters CFCF. The first commercials were quick to follow as the station borrowed records from a music store in return for mention on the air. Like Westinghouse, Marconi of Canada used its broadcast enterprise to create a market for the receiving sets it manufactured.

In the early 1920s radio stations "blossomed like spring crocuses, from Nanaimo, BC, to St. John's, Newfoundland," according to Canadian radio historian Kenneth Bambrick. On April 1, 1922 the Radio Branch of the Department of Naval Service began issuing licences, including one for owners of radio receivers, who had to pay one dollar per year for the privilege. Broadcasters could apply for "private commercial" licences, which allowed stations to broadcast commercials from their owners, or "public commercial" licences, authorizing them to sell commercial time to other businesses.

Within a month, twenty-one stations had been licensed from Halifax to Vancouver. Sixteen of those licences went to electrical manufacturers, news-papers and department stores, including the T. Eaton Company. This reflected the interests that drove early radio. Department stores and other electrical retailers needed programs for their salespeople to tune in to when demonstrating their radios. Newspapers, which accounted for the largest group of early radio enterprises, saw the new medium as a natural extension of their communication role and a potential weapon in their circulation wars. First off the mark was the *Toronto Star*, which launched station CFCA on April 10, 1922. The *Calgary Herald*'s CQCA (soon to become CFAC) began broadcasting on May 2 of that year.

Two notable public corporations got into the Canadian radio business on the ground floor. In late 1923 Canadian National Railways (CNR) equipped a number of its parlour cars with receiving sets to entertain passengers as the trains passed through areas with broadcasting stations. Before long the rail-road had decided to set up broadcast facilities of its own in key cities. Over the next decade, CNR acquired thirteen licences, three for stations of its own and ten for "phantom stations," which rented facilities owned and operated by others. The second publicly owned broadcasting station was CKY Winnipeg, owned and operated by the Manitoba Telephone System (MTS), a provincial government organization. Under a unique arrangement with the Radio Branch in 1923, MTS was granted a monopoly situation in Manitoba whereby it received half of all receiving licence fees collected in that province as well as the power to veto any other radio broadcast licences in Manitoba. CKY was also allowed to operate commercially, selling ads to make a profit.

The general public embraced the new medium of radio with a sense of awe. Newspaper commentators heralded it as miraculous, perhaps even the greatest invention of the century. Some saw radio's potential as a community builder and the glue to bind a vast, unwieldy country. Others extolled radio as a cure for any number of social ills. It would ease the loneliness of shut-ins, housebound women and isolated rural Canadians, keep teenage boys off the streets, and bond families around home-based entertainment.

Crowds heard demonstrations of this modern wonder over loudspeakers at the Canadian National Exhibition and at theatres and cinemas prior to the main show. Demand for home receivers outstripped the industry's ability to

◆ *E.A. Corbett in a special speaking studio, 1934.*
University of Alberta Archives; used by permission.

supply them, even though what passed for regular scheduled programming at the time consisted of as little as one or two hours of concerts or lectures a couple of nights a week. Most listeners had to build their own receivers— simple crystal sets and, later, more sophisticated vacuum tube sets.

As the decade progressed, according to Canadian radio historian Mary Vipond, "all those involved in broadcasting, from the big corporate manufacturers to the Radio Branch bureaucrats, from the pioneer broadcasters to the ordinary listeners, had a strong sense that they were participating in a new era in history."

For listeners, the idea that something happening far away could be experienced immediately in the privacy of their living rooms lent a special air of excitement. Vipond says they also were fascinated by the sense that "they were part of a vast unseen audience, all sharing a single experience simultaneously." She suggests this combination of intimacy and community was a powerful draw in a post-war era that was "increasingly impersonal and alienating. Ironically, the new mass medium perhaps most appealed because it helped the anonymous individual feel more like a person and the mass more like a community."

By early 1923 Canada had forty-four broadcasting stations with the combined potential to provide service to virtually every home in the country. Their audience included the holders of the nearly ten thousand radio-receiving licences issued by that point.

Approximately 450 of those licensed radio receivers were in Alberta, where, according to radio pioneer T.J. "Jim" Allard, "radiomania" had infected people more intensely than anywhere else in Canada. The population of the young prairie province was just over half a million, with three-quarters of the residents spread out among small towns and farms. Most rural Albertans had come from Ontario and northern Europe before the war to homestead. The province's economy was dominated by the price of wheat and its politics by the United Farmers of Alberta, which had scored a coup in the 1921 election by wresting power from the Liberals, throwing Alberta's former two-party system offside for decades to come.

Outside the cities, travel was difficult and in winter often impossible, and luxuries such as electricity, telephones, cinema and other forms of mass entertainment were for the most part inaccessible. No wonder, then, Allard writes, "People would travel 50 miles through the bitter cold of a northern Alberta winter to huddle about a crystal set in the hope of picking up a few faint squawks from a far distant radio station. Earphones were passed around eagerly from hand to hand so that each in turn might hear."

The first broadcasts heard in Alberta came from a station set up for tele-graph communication for Canadian Forestry Patrol aircraft. The operator was W.W. "Bill" Grant, who provided radio services for the Allies during the war and was considered a genius by his contemporaries. In 1922 Grant was operating forestry patrol stations in High River and Morley, and decided to fill in the evenings with an hour of music. His broadcasts were received as far away as Honolulu. Grant set up a licensed broadcasting station for himself in High River that same year and then moved it to Calgary, where he established it as CFCN. The station eventually became known as "The Voice of the Prairies." Grant built and installed transmitters for numerous other Alberta stations, the *Calgary Herald*'s station among them.

Meanwhile, radio clubs were popping up all over, including several in Edmonton with names like the Night Fliers and the Radio Ramblers. The *Edmonton Journal*, in preparation for the launch of its own radio station, ran articles throughout the spring of 1922 on how to build home receivers for as little as three dollars. The Edmonton Radio Club secured an amateur broadcasting licence in 1922. According to Allard, the club's first broadcast drew a complaint from a nearby listener that it was interfering with his efforts to pick up station KOA Denver. Similar responses to Canadian broadcasts were received often in the 1920s as Canadians discovered they could listen in to more entertaining and more regularly available programming from higher-powered, better-financed American stations.

The Edmonton Radio Club was getting technical advice from George Richard Agar (Dick) Rice, a young newcomer to Canada, barely out of his teens. Rice had joined the Marconi Admiralty Wireless Service in 1916 at the age of fifteen and served until the end of the war. He settled in Edmonton in 1920. On May 1, 1922, when the Edmonton Journal launched the city's first private commercial broadcasting station, CJCA, Dick Rice was manager and chief announcer. The transmitter operated at 580 kilohertz, a frequency CJCA would be required to share with other stations to come in the city. Sharing of frequencies was common at the time, since few stations had the resources to program a full schedule.

Like newspaper owners, educators and religious evangelists immediately grasped radio's power to reach people. Paying particular attention were a Calgary high school principal and Baptist preacher named William Aberhart and two members of the University of Alberta Department of Extension— Albert Edward Ottewell, director of the department, and Harold Purcey ("H.P.") Brown, director of visual instruction.

Aberhart had moved to Alberta from Ontario in 1910. He became principal of Calgary's Crescent Heights High School in 1915 and around the same time started building a reputation as a Bible teacher and preacher. His Sunday afternoon classes in biblical prophecy grew into the Calgary Prophetic Bible Conference, which in the mid 1920s established the Prophetic Bible Institute with Aberhart as dean. By that time his meetings were so popular they had to be moved to the Palace Theatre. In 1925 he began broadcasting his Sunday afternoon sermons on CFCN radio. Aberhart's dramatic oratory struck a chord with a huge listening audience, and his programs were eventually carried by stations across western Canada and the adjacent states.

Ottewell, a former miner, lumberjack and farmer from Clover Bar, had enrolled in the new University of Alberta (U of A) in 1908 at the age of twenty-seven, becoming a member of its first graduating class in 1912. That same year U of A president Henry Marshall Tory, inspired by the pioneering extension work of the University of Wisconsin, organized a Department of Extension to "carry the University to the people." Given Ottewell's background and experience as a youth on an Alberta homestead, he was the logical choice to head up the new department.

For the first few years, Ottewell was a one-person department, drawing lecturers in from other departments and sending them out into the countryside to bring enlightenment to isolated rural Albertans. Those early adult educators travelled by rail, Model T, and horse (or even mule!) and buggy, meeting their audiences in schoolhouses, churches and community halls. To spice up their lectures, they came armed with the state-of-the-art in educational technology, the "magic lantern," an early form of slide projector. Brown paints a vivid picture of a typical extension foray into the Alberta countryside before rural electrification:

> Mr. Ottewell was a great believer in visual forms of education and early took to the road in a Model T Ford with a lantern and set of slides. The lantern was illuminated with acetylene gas. When the schoolhouse windows were covered with tar-paper shutting out the light and also the ventilation, audiences were often treated to a mixture of tar and gas which had a more potent effect than the driest of lectures. It was not long before a small electric generator of 30 volts was mounted under the hood of the Model T Ford and driven by its engine to provide light for the lantern and later on a running-board generator of 1000 watts at 110 volts was obtained. Mr. Ottewell carried many gadgets in his little car, one of the most useful (and necessary in those days of dirt roads), was for the purpose of getting out of mudholes. This consisted of a flange attached to the rear driving wheel which, when the engine was started, coiled up a steel cable the other end of which was hooked on to a convenient fence post or telephone pole. The car then proceeded to pull itself out of the mud by its own "bootstraps."

Hungry for learning and entertainment, rural audiences welcomed presentations on topics ranging from agriculture and economics to Shakespeare and evolution, often as a prelude to an evening of music and dance. A familiar face on the extension circuit was Dr. Edward Annand (Ned) Corbett, another

◆ CKUA's first studio director, H.P. Brown, also served as announcer, disc jockey, sound-effects man and lecturer.

Canadian adult education pioneer. Corbett originally studied for the ministry and had "a burning social conscience ... a ready wit, and a gift of language which placed him among Canada's greatest raconteurs," according to historian Ron Faris.

In Corbett's account of those bracing days, *We Have with Us Tonight*, he described a night that epitomized the hardships endured by extension lecturers. Corbett had journeyed to Edgerton by train on a winter evening to be met at the station by the brothers Herbert and Henry Spencer (Henry later to become a member of Parliament and one of the famous independent Ginger Group) with their mule-and-pony-drawn cutter. On the nine-mile trek to the schoolhouse where the lecture would be held, the cutter tipped, tossing Corbett's moving picture machine, films, projector and slides into a snowbank. The party arrived an hour late for the lecture only to find some of the gear missing, presumably still buried in the snow.

H.P. Brown, who changed careers to join the extension department in 1915 as supervisor of the newly formed Division of Visual Instruction, described himself as "an accountant with many hobbies." This was an understatement. Brown had arrived in Edmonton from London in 1909, settling in the Jasper Place district to raise his family. He had a lively interest in visual technologies, and almost from the minute he set foot in the city took an active part in the community.

During his first year in Edmonton, he hung a canvas screen over the front of the King Edward Hotel and tried to project a moving picture onto it from the Edmonton Journal office in the Tegler Building, but a high wind came up and blew the screen four blocks away. In the 1920s he rigged up a magic lantern to flash up-to-the-minute election results from the second floor of the Journal building on 101 Street onto a huge sheet draped over the entrance to McDougall United Church across the way. According to the Journal, "No election night in The Journal was complete without H.P. and his magic lantern.... Excitement often reigned high as the downfall of one government and the election of another was recorded on the 'slides'." Brown—who was always known as "H.P."—also operated the magic lantern for visiting explorers, including Sir Ernest Shackleton, Robert Peary and Roald Amundsen, who took to the lecture circuit after their triumphs.

Brown was a natural "doer." He organized Edmonton's first community league—in 1917 in Jasper Place—to lobby to get utilities to that area. He was one of the founders of the Edmonton Film Council, precursor to the Edmonton Film Society; he started the Edmonton Safety Council and launched the local Red Cross water safety program. A lay reader, he also organized the building of what is now St. Paul's Anglican Church in Edmonton's west end. According to Lawrence Twigge, who was hired as Brown's assistant in the extension department and found himself shanghaied into volunteer service on the church construction, Brown had a way of drawing people into his pet projects. "He was always busy. He was always into something." One of Brown's sons, Percy, recalled his father inviting the neighbourhood children into the family home—always a centre of activity—for monthly silent movies with live piano accompaniment.

While taking a photography course in Chicago in 1921, Brown heard radio for the first time and was fascinated. Back home, he built a crystal set and later a tube radio so he could tune in to some of the American stations.

Always resourceful, he even hooked up a wire to the top of the Anglican church next door to improve reception, his son Percy told the *Edmonton Journal*. "We would sit around the table with ear plugs until they came up with a loudspeaker.... It was wonderful. In the early years you could get all the U.S. stations; we would sit up all night and get Chicago and New York and Los Angeles."

It didn't take long for Brown to see the superiority of radio over mules and Model Ts in the dead of winter for taking the university to the people. Ottewell and Tory were thinking along the same lines. But they figured it would be foolhardy to buy equipment that would soon be outdated, as usually happens with a rapidly developing technology.

Instead, Ottewell arranged with Dick Rice at CJCA for the extension department to broadcast a series of Monday evening lectures beginning in November 1925. The lectures were heavily weighted towards agricultural topics—Professor R.D. Sinclair, assistant professor of animal husbandry, on "Care of the Brood Sows and Fall Pigs"; Professor E.H. Strickland on "The Wheat Stem Sawfly." But there were also general-interest programs: A.E. Ottewell on "Alberta's Early Homesteaders"; music by the University Orchestra and Glee Club; Dr. R.T. Washburn, superintendent of the University of Alberta Hospital, on "Orthopaedic Work in a Modern Hospital."

CJCA provided the time at no cost to the university. Initially, the professors had to travel across the river to the *Journal* building. Then Ottewell had a microphone and amplifier installed in a corner of his office with a telephone hookup to the station. In October 1926 the Division of Visual Instruction created a rudimentary studio on the upper floor of the extension department's quarters in the Power Plant by moving some partitions and hanging burlap drapes from overhead crossbeams to muffle outside noise.

Within a year, the university had expanded its radio program to over two hours a week. Dr. A.S. Tuttle of St. Stephen's College and Rev. Brother Rogation Boulton of St. Joseph's College delivered ten lectures on evolution, which was a hot topic in those days, as Darwin's theories were being used to justify a Canadian immigration policy that peopled the Prairies primarily with white northern and eastern Europeans. Ottewell organized national evenings of songs, poetry and stories by English, Scottish, Irish, Welsh, French and Ukrainian artists for homesick newcomers. The university produced several radio plays, including one for Alberta's francophone community.

The radio programs found an audience. Tory wrote to Premier John E. Brownlee in October 1926: "We are receiving letters of commendation by the hundreds." The department's 1926 annual report said letters of appreciation were coming "from all parts of the province and from different parts of Canada and the United States."

By December, Tory and Ottewell were lobbying for funding to enable the department to set up a station of its own. They wanted to expand and knew they couldn't expect CJCA to provide more free time. The universities of Wisconsin and Minnesota and the Latter Day Saints University in Salt Lake City had pioneered the concept of university-owned radio stations in 1922— a year that ultimately saw seventy-three American educational institutions receive radio licences. In Canada, two universities, Queen's and Montreal, owned and operated their own stations.

Tory made his case to the executive committee of the university's board of governors, suggesting the university could have a station for about five thousand dollars. On January 22, 1927 the board allocated an additional four thousand dollars to the department's budget for "broadcast extension." That same month Ottewell applied to the Department of Marine and Fisheries in Ottawa for a broadcast licence but was turned down on the grounds that three licences had already been granted for Edmonton, more than a sufficient number for a city of its size, in the regulator's opinion.

At that time, the Radio Branch was allocating each city only one frequency, or at most two, to be time-shared by up to three stations. This policy was driven by the regulator's determination to satisfy the listening public, the majority of whom still owned primitive receivers, either crystal sets that couldn't separate stations within 100 kilohertz of each other or non-selective one-tube sets. Listeners often let it be known they didn't want two stations on the air at once and also resented local stations interfering with their reception of their favourite American programs. In his rejection letter, the deputy minister of marine and fisheries suggested the university might purchase one of the existing licences.

By March, Tory and Ottewell had arranged to buy the licence and the 100-watt transmitter of radio station CFCK, owned by Jim Taylor and Hugh

Pearson's Radio Supply Company, for six hundred dollars. The station had been broadcasting from a studio on the top floor of the Royal George Hotel, sharing the 580 frequency with CJCA. In a letter requesting the transfer of the licence, Tory explained the situation in Edmonton to the deputy minister in words that would later come back to haunt the university:

> The work carried on by us will be of a purely educational character, the only organization here doing that sort of work. The "Edmonton Journal" has a station with which we have had some connection and have been giving them one programme a week of an educational character. The other station is one devoted entirely to religious propaganda of a rather peculiar type.

He was probably referring to CHYC, the station of the International Federation of Bible Students. Another religious station, CHMA, shortly began broadcasting from the Beulah Tabernacle on the same frequency under a licence held by the Christian and Missionary Alliance.

On May 7 the University of Alberta Senate established a committee on university broadcasting with Ottewell and Corbett as chairman and secretary, respectively. The committee met that same day and decided the university should build its own station.

Tory's five-thousand-dollar estimate for the task was modest for the time. According to Vipond,

> In the very early 20s one could open a station with little more than a licence ($50 per annum), some used parts, an ingenious engineer cum announcer (often seconded from other duties), and a stack of records. But that soon changed. In 1923 the minister of marine and fisheries estimated that it cost anywhere from seven to twenty thousand dollars to set up a good broadcasting station and between two and six thousand a year to maintain it.

Vipond quotes "a well-informed observer" who estimated that by the end of the decade it would take a total investment of $54,100 to build a 500-watt station, and another expert who calculated it would cost $7,500 a year to operate that station.

◆ *The University of Alberta's electrical engineering class of 1928 had a hand in building and operating CKUA. Professor Hector J. MacLeod appears at left.*
Courtesy of Clarence Laverty.

Ottewell had told the senate radio committee that the proposed station could operate on an annual budget of one thousand dollars. Brown, who would assume the day-to-day responsibility for operating the station, said the station was constructed "on a shoe-string." He wrote, "We had very little money but lots of vision and zeal." That zeal rubbed off on many others who would provide services and talent to the new undertaking.

One of them was W.W. Grant. According to Brown, "Enquiries as to the cost of building a transmitter with a station building to house it and the accompanying towers and antenna were not encouraging and it was decided to seek the assistance of a radio engineer to build the transmitter as a public service. Mr. W.W. Grant, then operating Radio Station CFCN at Calgary undertook to build a transmitter of 500 watts...."

Grant built the transmitter using "the two tallest farm windmill towers that could be obtained (80 feet topped by 20' masts)," on a knoll immediately south of Pembina Hall on campus. Professor Hector J. MacLeod and two assistants from the electrical engineering department, W.E. Cornish and J. Wardlaw "Ward" Porteous, provided technical assistance. (Cornish and

◆ The original CKUA
radio towers outside
Pembina Hall, 1927.
University of Alberta Archives
69–97–699a; used by permission.

Porteous would earn their master's degrees in 1933 based on this work.) Dick Rice, of CJCA, also "lent a willing hand" in setting up the studio equipment, according to Guy Vaughan.

Including a small station house, the whole lot was constructed for under five thousand dollars. Equipment for the studio—amplifiers, microphones, gramophone turntables and accessories—came to about twelve hundred dollars. Burlap draperies, by some accounts purchased from a brewery for $25, and some simple furnishings, including a second-hand grand piano for about $1,500, brought the total cost of setting up the station in at $7,316.96.

There is another, widely published but unsubstantiated account of how the extension department got funding for its radio station. According to one version of the story, CKUA owes its existence to "a certain amount of sleight-of-hand" by Brown to overcome an obstacle posed by a shortage of funds at the university. "The university's 1927 budget included a request for $7,000 for a new lecturer in the Department of Extension. The extra money was granted but the new lecturer never arrived. Mysteriously, a group of electrical engineering students were busy at a course project, hand-building their own radio transmitter and antenna."

◆ The engineering graduates of 1928, some of whom helped build CKUA's transmitter.
Courtesy of Clarence Laverty.

◆ University of Alberta promotional postcard, ca. 1926. Before launching CKUA, the
university broadcast music and lectures over the Edmonton Journal's station CJCA.
University of Alberta Archives 68–9; used by permission.

Jack Hagerman, who was station manager from the mid 1950s to the early 1970s, thinks this story is suspect.

"H.P. loved a good story. But H.P. was not in a position to tinker with the books. He used to tell the story about having put in seven thousand dollars to hire a new assistant. And then they didn't hire a new assistant. What they did was build a radio station. Now, A.E. Ottewell, who would have been able to tinker with the books, it seems to me, at some point or another denied that story. But then, if he was the one who tinkered with the books, maybe he would deny it. So, who knows?"

In any event, a salary of seven thousand dollars for a lecturer would have been way out of line for the times.

The university asked to have the call letters on its licence changed to CUOA (for U of A), but the CU prefix was not available, according to Brown. "CK sounded pretty good to us because k is a pretty easy letter to pronounce," and UA was close enough. The new radio station was set to go on the air on November 21, 1927.

The first broadcast began with "God Save the King," played on the aging grand piano by Emma Newton, a young faculty wife who was destined to play a unique, largely undocumented role in the life of the station. Then, with the words "Good evening, friends of the radio audience," Tory began the first radio talk. There were messages from university and provincial dignitaries, and Mrs. Newton played Chopin's "Revolutionary" étude.

There was also a glitch or two. It turned out CKUA couldn't be heard on its own frequency. So Grant called Calgary and took his own station, which used a nearby frequency, off the air. CKUA came in beautifully on Grant's frequency. Meanwhile, Brown had his camera set up in the studio to take pictures of the historic occasion. Flash bulbs not having been invented yet, he used magnesium powder to set off his flash and inadvertently set fire to the nap of the studio's burlap curtains. "A sheet of flame went up the whiskers of the burlap," he recalled.

And CKUA was launched with a bang.

Buffalo Robes, Gunny Sacks and
Monday Evening Folk-Dancing | 2

"Good evening, everybody. This is your university station CKUA—
HPB announcing."

An Albertan tuning in to the 580 frequency Monday and Thursday nights
in 1928 would likely hear this greeting in H.P. Brown's chipper British accent.
Brown served as studio director and announcer for the new station in addition to his regular extension department duties. He was also disc jockey,
sound-effects man, mechanic and occasional lecturer, putting in eighteen-
hour days on his exciting new project.

From the start, CKUA concentrated on programming for the rural audience, partly because the need was greater outside urban centres but also
because, in Ned Corbett's words, "people who live in the country are more
disposed and have more time, particularly in the long winter evenings, to
listen to programs of a sound educational character."

The program guide for January through June of 1928 shows broadcasts on
Mondays from 4:45 to 7:00 p.m. and 8:00 to 10:15 p.m., and on Thursdays
from 3:00 to 4:00 p.m. and 8:30 to 10:15 p.m. Mondays started with a one-

hour organ recital from Convocation Hall, followed by a forty-five-minute music program from the CKUA studio. Miss J.F. Montgomery, the extension librarian, presented a half-hour "Children's Program" and a twenty-minute "Young People's Program." Affiliated colleges—St. Stephen's and St. Joseph's—had from 8:20 to 8:45 p.m. for their programming. Then the main "Studio Program" came on with a varied menu that could include a fifteen-minute lecture, music, plays or debates, and a weekly news bulletin.

On Thursdays CKUA offered a one-hour "Women's Program" in the afternoon under the direction of Miss Mabel Patrick, head of household economics. This was later expanded to Mondays as well, offering "music, and talks on Favourite Poets and Prose Writers, Travel talks, Current Events, Book Reviews, Music and Musicians, etc." for the "many women throughout the country districts who are cut off from the educational facilities that they have been accustomed to."

By 1932 CKUA was running three days a week, with the "Homemakers' Hour" offering features such as "A Union of the Arts—Drama and Music," "Style vs. Fashion," "What You Should Know Concerning Mouth Hygiene," and during the spring months, a regular gardening segment by "men and women who have made gardening their hobby, not experts ... but busy people like many of our listeners, who consider that 'A garden is a lovesome thing.'"

In the evening listeners would hear a "Farm Program" from the studio including lectures, music and the "Question Box," a feature that invited them to send in questions, generally of a scientific nature, to be answered by the university's experts. Lectures ranged from university librarian D.E. Cameron on "Robert Burns" to Dr. A.W. Henry, professor of plant pathology, on "The Menace of Cereal Root Rots" and Dr. Karl Clark, research professor, road materials, on "Alberta's Tar Sands" (Alberta's oilsands deposits were once valued mainly for their potential use as road-paving material).

CKUA listeners also learned about "Bee Keeping," "Early Canadian Literature," "The Home," "Weedless Lawns," "The Story of Measurement" (from a math professor), "Why We Study Classics," "The Greek Idea of Democracy," and "Plows—Their Operation and Adjustment," to name just a few of the lecture topics over those first six months.

During CKUA's first year, the extension department received hundreds of letters of appreciation, some from as far away as Saskatchewan, British Columbia, Yukon and Texas. An editorial in the *Manitoba Free Press* for February

◆ *The Rainbow Toddle Orchestra in the CKUA studio, 1928.*
University of Alberta Archives 69–97–770; used by permission.

13, 1928 noted CKUA's arrival on the scene and commented on the popularity of the University of Manitoba's own "radio evenings" on the station operated by Manitoba's telephone company:

> It begins to look as though the "dreaming towers" of the modern university were the radio spirals.... Providing that the lone homesteader does not weaken, and the rhythm of the wolf's howl—or the polar bear's—does not interfere with the wave length, by the time the season is over he will be by way of achieving a university culture of no mean order. And he should be a better farmer.... The university of today has a new ally and the boundaries of its day are no longer physical to any degree, but conditioned only by the mentality of the receiver. The university has left her dreaming towers and becomes a house by the side of the road—perhaps she has taken her dreams with her.

Not everyone in the extension department was as enthusiastic about radio as A.E. Ottewell and Brown at the start. Corbett later wrote that he had his reservations about "the new gadget":

◆ The CKUA radio booth at the Edmonton Exhibition, 1928 or 1929.
University of Alberta Archives 69–97–761; used by permission.

I, as Assistant Director of the department, was sceptical and slightly contemptuous of the whole undertaking. Those were the days when bug-eyed enthusiasts would sit up half the night glued to their crystal sets, listening to the crash, bang, whistle, wheeze, of remote signals and report breathlessly to their bored acquaintances next morning "last night I got Texas."

Not a radio-owner himself, Corbett said he had occasion, when stranded in a farmhouse by a snowstorm, to listen "in nervous irritation to the evangelical bellowing of Mr. Aberhart and had caught distorted, tortured bits of organ music from the Mormon Temple in Salt Lake City. I could see no use for such a treacherous medium."

Corbett admitted it was not until 1928, when he became director of the extension department, "that H.P. Brown was able to enlist my support for

◆ CKUA's sound effects
department in the late
1920s. Dick MacDonald,
seated, is holding a pistol.
University of Alberta Archives
74–152–6; used by permission.

the expenditure of funds from our overworked budget to build a studio, install new equipment, and generally take an interest in what he rightly believed to be one of the most important educational instruments of all time." Corbett said he came to appreciate "the tremendous possibilities of radio" through hearing weekly radio plays produced by Tyrone Guthrie over the CNR network in 1928–29.

"I shall never forget the dramatized story of Henry Hudson adrift in an open boat in Hudson's Bay and the sound effects of the ice-floes, the groaning oarlocks, the howling of the wind, the very feel of the cold and the despair of Hudson."

Technical difficulties often arose in CKUA's shoe-string operation. On one occasion Corbett enlisted British actor Maurice Colborne, who was in town for a theatre performance, to give a radio lecture. Just as Colborne started his talk, Brown rushed into Corbett's office: "Holy smoke, we're off the air. I think we've blown a tube. What do we do now?"

"Just let him go on. What he doesn't know won't hurt him," Corbett replied. Colborne gave his talk without ever knowing "that he had been pouring out his soul to a dead microphone."

Sometimes the microphone went dead simply because the speaker's voice was too high-pitched or an announcer with a lisp accidentally created a

◆ *Clarence Laverty, an electrical engineering student who was involved in building and sometimes operating CKUA, 1928.*
Courtesy of Clarence Laverty.

whistling sound. Clarence Laverty, one of Hector MacLeod's electrical engineering students who was involved in building the station and occasionally served as operator, recalled, "We had trouble with carbon microphones—they were very poor when compared with the present-day microphone. They had inconsistencies.

"For instance, they would not broadcast a high-pitched voice if you put them anywhere close to it. We used to turn them backwards for a high-pitched voice, and then we could handle that. But if you turned them around so that a person was singing into it, well, the set would go crazy and you had to take it off the air.

"That happened one night. An Edmonton woman was singing, and I had to cut her off the air and flip the switch over and take a gramophone record. And when she got through, she called somebody and found out she'd been off the air, and she came in and raised the devil with me.... But I told her unfortunately she'd cut herself off the air, not me. And she said, 'How did I do that?'

"'Well,' I said, 'did you turn the microphone around when you went into the room?'

"'Sure,' she said. 'I wasn't going to sing into the back of a microphone.'"

This woman was probably not a crooner. From the very first days of radio, the tendency for female singers' voices to cause mayhem with radio equipment had been a problem. But the first woman whose singing voice was ever heard on the air, Vaughn De Leath, had already figured it out. De Leath developed a low, soft, lullabying style of singing which she used to render "Swanee River" over a New York City wireless telephone station in early 1920. Her style caught on in a big way and later influenced Bing Crosby and Rudy Vallee. But at CKUA there was no interest in crooners.

Instead, Edward Jordan, who had been a workroom boy in Brown's division, solved the problem for radio stations everywhere. Jordan took the job as CKUA control operator and became so intrigued by radio technology that he enrolled in electrical engineering. In the course of his studies, Jordan invented a device that would control the modulation and prevent the station from being shifted off frequency or knocked off the air entirely by loud noises, lisps or sopranos hitting high notes. Called a "peak limiter," it earned him his master's degree and became standard equipment for all radio stations in North America. Jordan developed a reputation as an international expert in the field of radio and eventually became head of the University of Illinois electrical engineering department.

Ward Porteous, who became dean of the U of A electrical engineering department, recalled the logistics of sharing the 580 frequency with CJCA in CKUA's first year: "We had only been on the air I think for two or three days when the old CJCA station had a fire and we had to take over their programs…. When we went on the air for our own program, we used to listen on a crystal set until CJCA went off the air, at which time we'd turn our transmitter on and sail away."

The International Bible Students Association wasn't so gentlemanly. One evening CJCA was carrying a prize fight between Jack Dempsey and Gene Tunney that went into overtime and beyond CJCA's allocated time. The Bible students, whose station CHCY shared the 580 frequency for a short time, simply started broadcasting over the fight, much to the ire of CJCA fight fans.

Throughout CKUA's first decade, the Department of Electrical Engineering was responsible for the care and operation of the station. During 1933–34 the engineers rebuilt the transmitter with the result that CKUA was picked up sometimes as far away as Honolulu and Long Island Sound. But by the standards of the times, CKUA was still a crude operation. Porteous later said, "I well remember around that time Dr. MacLeod and the late Professor Cornish and myself being up at the station and having it completely apart and spread out all over the floor at four o'clock and having to have it back together again by six to go on the air.

"Believe me, there were times when it was quite a struggle and, no doubt, times when we were a few minutes late."

The federal government used to send inspectors—better known as "ether cops"—to make sure stations were keeping their equipment properly maintained. Porteous recalled one inspector who kindly looked the other way when CKUA's facilities were found wanting—for example, when the government decided stations should have a crystal monitor so they could tell whether or not they were on the right frequency:

> The radio inspector would come in when I'd be sitting there operating. He'd open the door—not a word would be said. He'd look under the table, in the wastebasket, in the back room, behind the transmitter. Finally, he'd come out and say, "No monitor?" And I'd say, "No monitor." Then we'd carry on with our normal conversation and that would happen every time....
>
> Until the time he died, whenever I'd run into him, he'd remark about CKUA's old transmitter. It was a gem.

The studio was just as makeshift, according to Corbett. "Equipment for the station was crude enough, but the studio itself looked like an Arab's tent. It was all flapping burlap." Brown recalled the reaction of one government inspector to the scene: "This chief engineer came into our studio, took one look around, took a look at our burlap drapes and said, 'Well, for goodness sakes, I've only seen one studio like this before and that's in a Montreal brewery.'"

Brown's memory of the conversation may have substituted "Montreal brewery" for "Toronto distillery." The Gooderham and Worts distillery operated radio station CKGW from its headquarters in the King Edward Hotel in Toronto at the time, supposedly to advertise the distillery's product in the United States, which was then under prohibition.

In addition to the old grand piano, the studio boasted two or three potted ferns, some folding chairs and a floral carpet Brown had "picked up for a song" from the lieutenant-governor. The buffalo robe came courtesy of a happy listener. According to Brown, "One night Louis Trudeau, who was a furrier in the city, phoned me up and said, 'I liked your program so much tonight, I'm going to send you a buffalo robe.' We didn't know what to do with a buffalo robe, but we thought a little more dampening of the sound was advisable so we just hung it in the studio."

Most people involved with CKUA cheerfully made do with the primitive studio arrangements, but Laverty recalled one lecturer who expected better:

We had Dr. Boyle [R.W., dean of the Faculty of Applied Science] one night giving a talk. He was a very good speaker, and everybody liked to listen to him.... All we could give him was an ordinary card table with the thing draped around with gunny sacks so that he wouldn't be getting interference from outside. And he went in there and gave his talk, and he came out and he was swearing mad!

He said, "To sit in there, a bunch of gunny sacks, and nothing but a table to look at and a glass of water." He said, "That's enough for me."

Not that the gunny sacks helped much. "Every passing car or barking dog penetrated the walls of the canvas studio and went on the air," Corbett wrote. Brown's son Percy recalled for the *Strathcona Plaindealer* one instance of unfortunate timing: "CKUA was broadcasting a story of the relief of Lucknow during the Indian mutiny and the besieged heroine called out 'Hark, I Hear the Bagpipes Coming.'" The control operator had mislaid the bagpipe recording and as he scrambled to find it, a train whistled its approach to the nearby High Level Bridge—"two longs and three shorts, clearly audible on the air."

Lawrence Twigge, Brown's assistant, said part of his job was to stand guard to keep unwanted noise out of the studio: "There was a musician named [Percy] Humphrey, who was well known in Edmonton—he had a music store on 97th Street and sold musical instruments.... He played cello.... He

◆ Sheila Marryat,
CKUA's first program
manager and first full-time
paid staff member.
University of Alberta Archives
81–117; used by permission.

would come in about once a month ... over the winter season and bring a
string trio or string quartet.... Every time they would play—I think it was an
hour—I had to stand at the bottom of the stairs ... and not let anybody go up
the stairs. Everyone had to be quiet."

The extension department's 1932 annual report complains, "Sixteen
plays and dramatic sketches, including five French plays, have been broadcast during the year, but this work is greatly handicapped by lack of funds for
royalties and insufficient studio facilities. One play was almost ruined at its
commencement by the power-house steam blowing off for five minutes.
Undoubtedly many listeners tune out when this happens, as it does
frequently."

Brown sometimes used the lack of soundproofing to advantage. "In one
of our early plays, we had to have the sound of a plane coming in. There were
no records for sound effects in those days, and we were wondering what to
do. One of the players said, 'I have a friend who works at the airport who can

bring a plane over any time we want.' We had to synchronize our watches between the studio and the airport, and it came over quite well. The sound came over beautifully."

CKUA's only full-time paid employee was radio secretary Sheila Marryat, a perfectionist with a keen interest in drama and a firm belief in the value of adult education. Marryat did most of the work in the early years, serving as program director, dramatist, lecturer, scriptwriter and studio hostess—obviously well worth her salary of $110 per month.

Dorothy Sheila Marryat was the youngest of nine children of Colonel Ernest Lindsay Marryat, an English engineer who built railroads in Egypt and India. The Marryats were an affluent, lively, artistic lot, who often put on plays for family and friends. The eldest child, Mary Irene, came to Alberta to visit a friend in the Buffalo Lake district in 1896 and ended up marrying Walter Parlby, one of the first white settlers east of Lacombe. Sheila received her early education at a girls' school in London, and in 1905, when she was sixteen, the colonel moved the whole family to Alberta.

The Marryats built a seventeen-room mansion on the shore of Haunted Lakes near what would become the village of Alix. Nicknamed "Marryat's Folly" by the neighbours, the house resembled a French chateau and had an open fireplace in every room. The Marryat home was the centre of social life in the area, and the family often put on plays for the benefit of the local church. Irene became president of Local 1 of the United Farm Women of Alberta and won the seat in Lacombe when the United Farmers of Alberta (UFA) swept to power in 1921. She became known across Canada as one of the "Famous Five" in the 1929 Persons Case.

Sheila led a less public but equally accomplished life. Before the war, she and a cousin ran a successful chicken ranch, supplying eggs and dressed poultry to the Canadian Pacific Railway for their dining cars. She volunteered in the fields when local men went to war and later graduated from the Olds School of Agriculture. In 1923 she became the University of Alberta's first female agriculture grad. The class of 1923 yearbook lists her as president of the dramatic society and an officer of the literary association and describes her as "one of the boys." Her stated ambition was "to improve our educational system." In a letter to The Gateway student newspaper, she wrote, "The aim of education is, as I understand it, to develop the highest type of man or woman, not merely to cram him with a definite number of facts which must

◆ The University Radio Orchestra performed in the late 1920s and early 1930s. Mrs. J.B. Carmichael, near the centre, wearing a necklace, was the conductor.

University of Alberta Archives 69–97–54b; used by permission.

be kept as near the surface as possible so as to be regurgitated at the final exam."

Marryat's great-niece, Eve Keates, of Alix, described her as "a gentle lady, but slightly on the mannish side because she was doing things most women didn't." After graduation Marryat returned to the Buffalo Lake area, where she lived with her close friend and companion Jean Reid, a suffragette from Scotland who had been the family housekeeper at the Haunted Lakes mansion. The two women were very active in the community, leading Camp Fire Girls and organizing plays and literary events. Marryat had a reputation for being an earnest and strict director who expected the best performance. The two friends adopted an orphan boy, and in the late 1920s they moved to Edmonton, where Sheila took the position of radio secretary at CKUA and began applying her high standards there.

Professor MacLeod, a Harvard Ph.D., served as station director and made CKUA a special project for his electrical engineering students, who received a dollar an hour as student operators and disc jockeys. None of the artists or outside lecturers received any payment for their services beyond taxi fare. Yet CKUA boasted its own twenty-piece orchestra and its own drama group.

"CKUA was very, very fortunate in having available a wide range of talent who just loved to be on the radio," Jordan recalled. "All the best musicians in town and the university lecturers—it was quite a thrill for them to be on radio and be talking to listeners all over the province."

Mrs. J.B. Carmichael, for many years director of the Edmonton Civic Opera, organized and conducted the CKUA Radio Orchestra, which eventually grew to thirty-five members ranging from professors to the campus messenger. The orchestra regularly squeezed into the studio to present live programs of opera, symphony and concert music. Sometimes Mrs. Carmichael hosted a music circle in her home, which was wired for remote broadcasts. CKUA also broadcast recitals on the Memorial Organ in Convocation Hall by Professor Lawrence H. Nichols, a lecturer in physics who was also the university organist and mixed chorus conductor. The station picked up other organ recitals from city churches, including many by Vernon Barford at All Saints Cathedral. Barford's granddaughter, Pat Barford, would be employed at CKUA decades later.

There seemed no end to the talented volunteers available to the station and no limit to the time and effort they were ready to commit in their enthusiasm at being involved in this new medium. A typical example was the special program Brown arranged late one night for some American radio hobbyists, or "DXers." (These keen listeners try to pick up faraway radio stations, then write to the stations reporting the details and quality of reception. In return, stations send cards or letters to the DXers to verify their experience.) According to Brown, CKUA received letters from DXers in the southern United States asking the station to put on programs for them. Brown decided the best time would be late at night after other stations went off the air.

"We thought we would really do this thing up in style. So we got Professor Nichols to come on the job and we got Mrs. Carmichael and the orchestra, and at two in the morning we went on the air with this slap-up program." Letters poured in from astonished DXers. "Some suggested perhaps we had overdone it a little putting on such a glorious program at that time in the morning and we could in the future use records."

In 1933 Barford hosted a series of music appreciation lecture-recitals on Sunday afternoons. The series attracted the attention of the Carnegie Foundation, which decided to finance the continuation of the program and

◆ The CKUA Radio Players gather to perform "The Building of Canada" by Elsie Park Gowan. Sheila Marryat is at the extreme left; Dick MacDonald is at the extreme right, behind the piano. University of Alberta Archives 74–116–4; used by permission.

presented the university with a collection of 824 classical records. Before the arrival of the Carnegie collection, CKUA had depended on the generosity of a local man, Albert Neil, whose record collection was described by Brown as "one of the finest in Canada."

Marryat wrote of Barford's programs, "The response to these recitals far exceeded expectation—hundreds of people of all types expressed their appreciation ... and stated that they learned more about music in those lectures than they had gained in a lifetime." A rural listener wrote,

> A course such as this was something I never expected having in my experience. I thought that such a course would be kept for the specialist in musical circles. To have the opportunity of a series of this nature come into your own home week by week was a joy and marvelous privilege.

Marryat organized the CKUA Radio Players, who had originally come together under the direction of Professor James Adam. The group attracted many prominent members of Edmonton's active drama community including, among others, Sid Lancaster, Harry Taylor, Elizabeth Sterling Hayes, Farnham Howarth, H.E. Bronson, Charles Sweetlove, Les Pilcher, Maxine Webber, Jack Wilson and Dick MacDonald.

Jack Delany recalled for the Edmonton Journal the sense of purpose that drove them: "[CKUA] really was a light in the darkness. The plays produced on air here were the only culture a lot of people had access to." He described Marryat, fondly, as "a slave driver. We used to work until three in the morning trying to get things right." Taylor said of Marryat, also with fondness, "She was a wonderful woman, and she was really devoted to the work. Nothing was too much trouble, and time meant nothing to her. And sometimes it seemed our time also meant nothing to her."

Another CKUA Players alumnus underscored the dedication the group brought to the project: "I remember one time Harry Taylor showed up for rehearsal a little subdued and not as genial as he usually was. We found out later, accidentally, that his wife had died of cancer earlier in the evening. But he came rather than let everyone down."

In 1931 the players put on a series called "Famous Conversations," consisting of imaginary conversations between well-known historic figures. They also dramatized scenes from famous books. Local theatre troupes, including the Edmonton Little Theatre Players and the University Dramatic Society, gave guest performances.

During the 1934 season, a grant from the Carnegie Trust Fund financed the writing of a series of historical sketches on great Canadian personalities. According to the extension department's 1934 annual report, "These plays were given week by week in connection with Mr. Corbett's talks on the same subject, and evidently this form of presentation was greatly appreciated by listeners.... As well as the 20 Canadian Sketches, the Players have to their credit four other plays ... over 90 different players were used ... and this does not include many extra people used for crowd effects."

The CKUA Radio Players performed a number of plays by a leading British radio playwright, L. du Garde Peach, made available by the BBC in England for educational purposes. In 1936 Marryat commissioned the local talents of Elsie Park Gowan and Gwen Pharis Ringwood to write a series of radio plays on famous historical figures. Gowan had taught school in rural Alberta before marrying U of A physics professor Ted Gowan. Married women weren't

◆ *One of the many groups that performed live on CKUA, 1928.*
University of Alberta Archives 69–97–26; used by permission.

allowed to teach, so she turned to writing. However, she said Marryat "twisted my arm.... I knew nothing about radio writing then." Gowan and Ringwood wrote ten thirty-minute scripts each for the series "New Lamps for Old" and were paid five dollars per script. Subjects ranged from Mary Wollstonecraft to Madame Curie and Elizabeth Fry. For Gowan, the assignment was the beginning of a long and successful career that would bring her national acclaim and many awards as a radio dramatist. The CBC Western Network picked up the series in 1937.

Following that success, Marryat commissioned another historical series from Gowan, the twenty-part "The Building of Canada," which prompted W.S. Milne to write in the 1937 *Letters in Canada*:

> There have been written in Canada during 1937, some radio scripts of a very high order. Especially notable is the series "New Lamps for Old" by Elsie Park Gowan.... The same author has another capital series, "The Building of Canada," grand stuff. One has to confess that the

eastern stations have not yet discovered as brilliant a script writer as has CKUA, the station of the University of Alberta.

The CBC ran the series nationally in 1938–39. Gowan wrote numerous other dramas for the CBC, beginning CKUA's long tradition of serving as a *de facto* "farm team" for the national broadcaster.

The CKUA Radio Players and various musical groups often performed at the Red Cross recreation "hut," an extension of the University Hospital for veterans of the First World War. CKUA had a line to the hut and broadcast "hut concerts" regularly.

The use of so much live programming seems unusual by today's standards, but in those days live broadcasts were the norm. In fact, most stations had their own "house bands." While the earliest radio programs in North America consisted mostly of phonograph records, by 1925 the Radio Branch had ruled that stations could not use "mechanically operated musical instruments"—that is, phonographs or player pianos— between 7:30 p.m. and midnight without permission. However, they could play records during the daytime hours. According to Mary Vipond, "This restriction seems to have been motivated by the belief that excessive recorded music would harm the growth of broadcasting because listeners did not want their radios simply to duplicate their phonographs, because such programming was of lower quality, and because it constituted a deception of the public."

In 1926 the Radio Branch altered the rule to accommodate marginal stations that couldn't afford live talent. But in the later part of the decade, a new kind of recording came on the scene to complicate the picture: American advertising agencies had started to produce fairly sophisticated programs on pre-recorded sixteen-inch discs packaged with advertisements, which they made available to radio stations. Canadian broadcasters wanted to use these recordings, too, forcing the Radio Branch to reconsider its policy in 1930. At the same time, Canadian musicians' unions began to lobby to protect their interests against the incursion of recorded music on radio, especially recorded music from the United States.

In 1931 the Radio Branch issued new regulations prohibiting the use of phonograph records during the prime time between 7:30 p.m. and midnight, with some provisions for smaller stations. Pre-recorded electrical transcriptions were permitted only in non-prime hours, with the exception of one half-hour each evening, and could be broadcast only once. They also had to be produced and manufactured in Canada.

"This last provision, of course, was to protect musicians' jobs," Vipond writes. "It constituted the first Canadian content requirement ever in Canadian broadcasting." The branch made a special exception for CKUA and another university station—CKIC at Acadia University in Wolfville, Nova Scotia— allowing them to use recorded educational material, no matter its source, for up to seven hours a week during prime time.

While classical music, lectures and historical drama predominated, CKUA's programming wasn't all highbrow. On October 13, 1928 CKUA carried the first play-by-play radio broadcast of a football game in Canada— the Edmonton Eskimos versus the U of A Golden Bears. A brother from St. Joseph's College who had once played for Notre Dame phoned in a running commentary from CKUA's table at centre line. The brothers of St. Joseph's and St. Stephen's colleges regularly served as commentators for the popular inter-varsity football games. The station also had lines to the varsity rink and main gym.

CKUA's microphones turned up in the strangest places to bring listeners live educational programming. Brown recalled an unusual zoology program by Professor William Rowan: "Dr. Rowan ... was experimenting in bird migration, and he had this open-front cage down at the bottom of his garden. He had very brilliant lighting which he could switch on at a moment's notice and a number of canaries, and these lights could be switched on almost any time in the night and the canaries would start to sing.

"So we put a mike in there. I think it must have been twenty below zero that night—it was very cold and just before Christmas—and the lights were switched on and the canaries started to sing brilliantly. We had those old mikes—those old carbon button mikes—and the mike finally froze up, but the canaries didn't. They continued singing."

CKUA transmitted Alberta's first school broadcast to much fanfare in May 1929. According to Brown,

We thought we'd try to broadcast to schools, which had never been done before. The first one was on May 23, 1929. There were no receivers in the schools at all. The Department of Education got behind us—we persuaded the radio dealers to put sets in the schools for Empire Day. And our station and a station in Calgary were tied in together. The Department of Education was very impressed with the result of that.

I remember being in the studio that afternoon, and we had a number of high officials standing around listening to a part of the program coming in from an Edmonton school—the old McCauley School—another part of it from Calgary, and telegrams began to come in, and telephone messages. It was like election night at the Journal. It was really exciting to find out that our little 500-watt station was being heard from Jasper to Lloydminster and places that we'd never reached before.

When schools were kept closed in September 1936 due to an epidemic, the Department of Education used CKUA to broadcast lessons to children in their homes. By the end of its first decade, CKUA's school broadcasts were reaching five hundred schools. The department started a formal school broadcast program using CKUA's facilities in 1939.

Throughout the 1930s, CKUA gradually expanded its programming, experimenting with all the possibilities radio had to offer. In 1930 CKUA carried inter-varsity debates broadcast in Alberta, Saskatchewan and Manitoba by arrangement with the three provincial governments' telephone systems. During the 1930–31 academic year, CKUA became affiliated with the CNR's "chain," becoming the first Edmonton outlet for a national network broadcast. The first CNR network broadcast from Edmonton featured Vernon Barford's choir performing in CKUA's studio.

In 1930 the extension department began broadcasting "definite courses" in English literature and Canadian history on Tuesday evenings. According to the department's annual report for that year, "The reports received on these broadcasts have fully justified the experiment and we are planning to continue this work next season as we are fully convinced ... that broadcasting is likely to take a more and more important place as one of the greatest agencies in adult education." The following year, in conjunction with the Canadian history course, the department sent maps showing the routes of early explorers to listeners who requested them. The audience for that program was estimated to number between eight hundred and one thousand.

The year 1930 also found groups of children meeting at private houses on Monday evenings to learn folk-dancing by radio, taught by "an enthusiast in

◆ *The CKUA studio in 1929. University of Alberta Archives 69–97–779; used by permission.*

this work," Mrs. Roy McKeen Wiles. "Not only has this experiment shown us the feasibility of teaching folk-dancing by radio, but it has opened up a tremendous field, at present untouched in Alberta, for teaching of special subjects to the school children of Alberta by radio," the extension department said in its 1930 annual report. The station also experimented with art appreciation lectures, sending listeners sets of prints donated by the National Gallery in Ottawa.

In the 1931–32 academic year, the department offered an experimental course in French phonetics given by Professor Hector Allard. The course—originally intended for teachers and high school students—was wildly successful. The department was inundated with requests for the lesson materials and ended up sending out fourteen hundred mimeographed copies. The program apparently met a long-standing need in rural Alberta, with fifty-seven percent of the French students at Vegreville High School alone taking the course and, according to a letter from their teacher, "showing considerable enthusiasm." The department later added German lessons.

CKUA was a valuable resource for poorly paid, ill-equipped rural school-teachers at a time when a high school education outside the major cities was a luxury. At the request of the School Festival Committee for Northern and

Central Alberta, Barford presented a series of Saturday morning lessons, with the assistance of young boy choristers, to help rural teachers train their pupils in group singing. Children throughout the province tuned in to "The Singing Hour" and sang to Barford's direction.

Following Barford's program, Mrs. N.W. Haynes advised teachers on how to direct a school play. "Last Saturday's talk by Mrs. Haynes on the 'business' of the play was a revelation to one who has had to direct children's plays without having had the benefit of any instruction on this phase of the work," a grateful teacher wrote.

Other programs were less formally "educational." Indeed, the department had closed its 1931 annual report with a statement that foreshadowed a debate over the definition of "education" that would arise decades later when CKUA's existence was threatened: "We have continued to stress the educational side, and have arranged and broadcast other programs of a varied nature, many of them having a distinctly educational value though presumably being for entertainment."

Contemplative listeners appreciated the Sunday afternoon "Quiet Half Hour," an inspirational program consisting of a short talk or reading "of some beautiful piece of literature with music appropriate to the central idea," with the names of the speakers and musicians not given. "The endeavour has been to obtain a certain atmosphere of reticence and reverence about this Quiet Half Hour." In 1931 the provincial Department of Health presented a series of talks on the "Homemakers' Hour." One of CKUA's most popular programs was the nightly "Symphony Hour," a recorded music feature described by one happy listener as "next only to the incomparable programs which reach us from New York."

Listeners also loved the "Dinner Hour of Music," which featured popular light classics usually selected by Marryat. Jordan told *New Trail* that one time as a young operator he was left to select the recordings for the program when the key people were all on holidays.

"I was told that the lady in the Record Shop on Jasper Avenue would help make the selection of records as she had always done. Alas, when I showed up on the first morning of the vacation period to pick up the records for that day, it was to find that the record lady herself was also on vacation, leaving in charge a 'sweet young thing' who knew even less than I about what constituted a suitable selection."

Jordan and the young woman picked out several records that appealed to them, and then she mentioned a new hit called "Two Black Crows." "So we played it and delighted in the banter and repartee of the Black Crows, with exchanges such as, 'Status Quo? What's dat?'—'Oh dat's Latin for the mess we's in'." Jordan added it to his selections.

That evening everything went well (that is, there were no calls in to the station during or after the dinner hour), but next morning word came down that the boss (Mr. E.A. Corbett) had listened to the program and immediately issued orders that henceforth for the duration of the vacation period, the record selection would be made by Miss Montgomery, long-time librarian for the Extension Division. But even now [1987] ... I cannot help but feel that that evening's program was one of the best "Dinner Hours of Music" ever aired over CKUA.

The "Science Question Box," hosted by Professor Ted Gowan, was a hit with the rural audience. Gowan kept a scrapbook of questions sent in by inquiring minds from Bawlf to Pakan. Beside them, in a tidy longhand, he entered detailed notes for the answers he would provide on air. A letter dated October 21, 1935 asks,

Dear Sir,

Would you, if convenient tell us over the air to-morrow Tuesday.
1. <u>Does the Moon affect the weather?</u> For instance it is generally thought that frost is apt to come on the full Moon in June.
2. <u>Has the Moon any effect on seeds planted at any period of the Moon?</u> Old world people tell us some wonderful stories along these lines, you have heard them no doubt. Make it as clear as possible please because none of us have had much in the way of educational advantages.
Thanking you in anticipation.

Yours truly,
Wondering

"Wondering" received a detailed answer on the October 29 program.

A listener from Duhamel provides insight into what conversations might have been like on cold winter nights in prairie farmhouses:

Dear Sir,

We are almost daily listeners to the afternoon talks from the University over C.K.U.A. We find these talks very instructive and interesting. Would you kindly answer the following, perhaps seemingly, very foolish question, which has nevertheless been a subject of controversy in our home for more than a year;—

Supposing it was possible to drill a hole to the centre of the earth and right through to the opposite side. If an object was dropped into this hole, at what point would it stop falling? Would not centrifugal force caused by the rotating motion of the earth stop the downward acceleration of the object?

Would the action be different if the hole was drilled from pole to pole?

Thanking you very much for this favor,

Yours truly,
Huldah B. Franklin

Huldah Franklin learned from CKUA that the dropped object would oscillate back and forth and then come to rest in the centre of the earth.

Early Radio Politics | 3

Shortly after CKUA signed on, the Great Depression settled over Alberta like a lead blanket. Between 1929 and 1933, Premier John E. Brownlee, a fiscal conservative, cut the province's budget in half with disastrous effects in all areas, including education. Hurting badly and disillusioned with the United Farmers of Alberta, many Albertans embraced the Social Credit theories of an English economist, Major C.H. Douglas, and were demanding total reform of the economic and fiscal order. Among them was William Aberhart, who had his own interpretation of Douglas' theories and began incorporating Social Credit into his radio evangelism.

Masterfully using the power of radio, Aberhart urged his followers to wrest control of credit from the "50 big shots in eastern Canada" who he claimed were running the country's financial system. The prairie preacher's new Social Credit party swept the 1935 election, beginning a thirty-five-year reign of another non-traditional party in Alberta, one based on a peculiar combination of religion and political theory that sharpened the line between western and eastern Canadian interests.

Other movements were afoot in the regulatory arena during CKUA's early years. Throughout the 1920s, the Radiotelegraph Branch of the Department of Marine and Fisheries had mainly concerned itself with technical matters such as licensing, inspection, eliminating interference, and assigning power and frequencies. The radio bureaucrats took a limited interest in content, concentrating mostly on monitoring the use of inappropriate or recorded material and the wording of advertisements (no "direct" advertisements, mentioning price or money, were allowed). Major policy issues concerning broadcasting and its role in Canadian culture were not yet a matter of public or political interest. The Radio Branch essentially made policy on the fly with its ear tuned to what it perceived to be the wishes of the listening public.

By 1928 numerous religious organizations had gained access to the airways, either by setting up licensed stations of their own or by taking out phantom licences. The International Bible Students Association (IBSA)—forerunners of the Jehovah's Witnesses—owned four stations across Canada, including one in Toronto and one that shared the 580 frequency with CKUA and CJCA in Edmonton. The IBSA used its stations to preach a strident, intolerant brand of evangelism that drew numerous listener complaints. As a result, the Radio Branch refused to renew any of its licences for 1928–29. At the same time, the branch reshuffled the Toronto stations, leaving a station owned by the Toronto Star, a Liberal paper, in a favoured position. This raised a storm of protest from a number of quarters, including the IBSA, accusing Mackenzie King's Liberal government of political interference in the licensing situation.

The controversy prompted the government to appoint a Royal Commission on Radio Broadcasting in 1928. The commission quickly came to be known as the Aird Commission after its chairman, Sir John Aird, president of the Canadian Bank of Commerce. Its terms of reference were "To examine into the broadcasting situation in the Dominion of Canada and to make recommendations to the Government as to the future administration, management, control and financing thereof."

At the time, there was also simmering concern over the increasing domination of radio frequencies by the more powerful American stations and the difficulties faced by private Canadian broadcasters trying to finance improvements to their operations, given the constraints on advertising and their limited reach. Even before the Aird Commission began its cross-country hearings, the minister of marine and fisheries, P.J.A. Cardin, suggested the preferred solution was likely to be to nationalize Canadian radio broadcasting. A model already existed in England, where radio broadcasting had been placed under control of a crown corporation funded by licence fees and advertising was not allowed.

The commissioners looked at various models for ownership and regulation in New York, London and several European countries and then conducted hearings in twenty-five Canadian cities. Ned Corbett and Hector MacLeod prepared the University of Alberta's submission, which called for a system of high-powered stations across Canada under federal control but with allowances made for provincial and regional requirements.

Some historians suggest the Aird Commission exercise was stacked from the start in favour of nationalizing the broadcasting medium. According to Roger Bird,

> The Aird Commission had tended to hear from the organized intellectual, social, or financial elite. By its very nature, a royal commission attracts the opinions of committed public spirits among citizens, corporations and clubs. Many not heard from by the Commission were at home, happily listening to music and comedy shows on the US stations whose signals reached them, or on Canadian stations linked by land lines or recording to the US source.

The commissioners presented their report on September 11, 1929. It said Canada's far-flung population could not be adequately served by the existing system of privately owned broadcast stations with their limited resources. The commission believed that Canada's youth were being increasingly influenced by American ideas coming in over the more powerful American stations. It contended that radio plays such an important educational and national role that broadcasting should come under national control. In short, "Canadian radio listeners want Canadian broadcasting," the commission concluded.

The report recommended the creation of a national radio broadcasting company that would own and operate all broadcasting stations in the country. This body would be governed by a board with three members representing the federal government and one member from each of the nine provinces. The provinces would have full control over the programs broadcast in their areas. The existing patchwork of privately owned stations would be replaced by a national system of seven high-powered stations supplemented by smaller stations as needed to ensure coverage in all areas of the country. The system would be supported by an increased annual licence fee for radio receivers, an initial subsidy by the federal government, and a limited amount of indirect advertising. The new national system would ensure that religious and political broadcasts remained within acceptable bounds, would allow Canadian listeners to continue receiving good programs from outside Canada, and would reserve time for educational programs.

Regarding educational programming, the Aird report said, "The potentialities of broadcasting as an instrument of education have been impressed upon us; education in the broad sense, not only as it is conducted in the schools and colleges, but in providing entertainment and of informing the public on questions of national interest."

The prime minister ordered legislation incorporating most of the commission's recommendations, but before the new act could come before the House, he called an election. King's government was defeated by the Conservatives under R.B. Bennett in July 1930. The Aird report was temporarily sidelined while the Bennett government got up to speed.

Control of radio broadcasting was now a hot public issue. One group in particular was determined to keep up the momentum in favour of a national publicly owned broadcasting system. Formed in October 1930 by Graham Spry and Alan Plaunt, the Canadian Radio League consisted of intellectuals and members of traditional voluntary groups such as the Canadian Club and the Canadian League. Its primary goal was to protect Canada from domination by American culture beamed north from powerful American radio stations controlled by private corporate interests.

The Canadian Radio League's very spirited—and single-minded—campaign is described in detail by Mary Vipond in her history *Listening In: The First Decade of Canadian Broadcasting, 1922–1932* and Ron Faris in his book *The Passionate Educators: Voluntary Associations and the Struggle for Control of Adult Educational Broadcasting in Canada, 1919–1952*. Jim Allard, a former CJCA Edmonton announcer who became an ardent spokesperson for the Canadian

Association of Broadcasters, covers the story in his book from the viewpoint of private broadcasters, who he felt were vastly outmanoeuvred by the Radio League: "Within thirty days the League had managed to create, in the political world, the impression that implementation of the Aird Report was the most urgent desire of nearly all Canadians—when many of them were drought-stricken, or unemployed, or wondering how soon they would be."

Corbett, the original educational radio skeptic, had been actively promoting the Aird Commission recommendations and educational broadcasting in general as a way to create a national Canadian consciousness. In June 1930 he and Professor C.H. Mercer of Dalhousie University participated in the first conference of the Institute for Education by Radio at Ohio State University. At the conference, Corbett talked of

> the desire on the part of the Canadian people to establish a system of radio broadcasting which will enable us throughout Canada to enjoy distinctly Canadian programs, to establish in our children Canadian ideals of education and of conduct, and to bring up the future citizens of Canada united in their consciousness of national unity and independence.... We want to provide them with Canadian programs which will equal in quality the best that we get from the United States, and we want also to have a system sufficiently powerful to shut out the cheaper and shoddier programs with which we are constantly flooded by stations in the United States. We cannot do this in a commercial way. We have not the money to compete with the highly commercialized system already well established in the United States. The only way in which we can achieve this ideal is through the government ownership and administration of our complete radio system.

Mercer spoke on the state of Canadian educational broadcasting and said that CKUA's programs were "by far the most ambitious and successful."

Corbett became the western representative of the Radio League and drummed up support for the Aird report among farm organizations, women's institutes and church groups across Alberta.

Throughout 1930 and 1931 groups on both sides of the public versus private control of broadcasting issue lobbied government and tried to swing popular opinion over to their views. Meanwhile, a new, related issue surfaced.

In April 1931 Quebec challenged the federal government's jurisdiction over broadcasting by passing an act giving the Quebec government complete licensing authority within the province. The Judicial Committee of the Privy Council, in London, resolved the case in favour of the federal government.

In spring 1932 the Bennett government appointed a special Commons committee on radio broadcasting to hear submissions leading to a new radio act. Corbett appeared before the committee to promote a national public system, citing CKUA's experience in educational broadcasting.

The Canadian Radio Broadcasting Act, passed in May 1932, was a compromise that both sides could live with. It created the Canadian Radio Broadcasting Commission (CRBC), which would be responsible for regulating and controlling all broadcasting in Canada, but kept licensing with the minister of marine. The commission could determine the power of stations, allot frequencies and make recommendations to the minister regarding licensing. It could set limits on the amount of time devoted to advertising and define acceptable advertising. It could also prohibit private networks.

The CRBC was authorized to "carry on the business of broadcasting in Canada" by purchasing or leasing existing stations, constructing new stations, or even taking over all broadcasting in Canada. Only leasing was not subject to the approval of Parliament. The commission could also originate or purchase programs. Parliament would allocate funding for the commission solely from the sale of broadcasting and receiving licences, and income from advertising and sale of programs.

The CRBC would be administered by three government-appointed commissioners in Ottawa who would be advised by nine assistant commissioners appointed from the provinces. Analyzing the act, Vipond concluded, "Although not recognized by all at the time, it is evident that ... the drafters of the act intended that the move toward nationalization would be slow and gradual and perhaps never completed." Further, she wrote, "The 1932 Radio Broadcasting Act gave the country public broadcasting if necessary but not necessarily public broadcasting." Early in 1933 the CRBC purchased the CNR chain, which would later form the backbone of the CBC.

The great public radio debate was prompted in part by concerns over encroachment by more powerful American stations into Canadian airwaves. By 1930 CKUA was already receiving complaints of interference; its effective coverage had been reduced to within a 125-mile radius of Edmonton. In

October of that year CKUA struck a deal with station CKLC Red Deer, owned by the Alberta Pacific Grain Company, to extend its reach. CKLC carried simultaneous broadcasts of CKUA's lecture program and paid for the telephone line charges.

The extension department's 1930–31 annual report said, "If CKLC (1000 watts) had not co-operated with us in this way it is likely that our audience would have been very much reduced owing to the fact that a great many stations in the United States have increased their power enormously.... A number of letters from various points in the province have been received complaining that they cannot get the University clearly this year owing to this interference." A couple of years later, listeners outside the Edmonton area were having trouble receiving CKUA in the evenings due to interference from a new Mexican station.

A 1930 article in the *Edmonton Journal* reported that the inspector of radio for northern Alberta from the Department of Marine and Fisheries had "traced 265 interference troubles to their sources" and eliminated 246 of them. Practically all were caused by streetcars and transmission lines, especially in damp weather. A good number were caused by doctors using medical equipment. The *Journal* was pleased to report "in almost every instance" the offending doctors "have agreed to avoid broadcast hours." According to Vipond, dentists' drills were also a major cause of radio interference in those days.

Complaints about interference continued to plague CKUA, along with budgetary constraints. Ralph Clark, in A History of the Department of Extension at the University of Alberta, 1912–1956, tells how Corbett and University of Alberta president R.C. Wallace tried to deal with these problems and preserve CKUA while navigating the murky waters of radio politics. The university's Senate Committee on Radio Broadcasting had considered taking fees for broadcasts in order to raise funds to upgrade the station's power. A potential sponsor, the National Loan Corporation, had even stepped forward with an offer. But the committee decided that paid advertising of any sort would put the station in danger of being accused of commercialism. It was also concerned that if CKUA became commercialized it would have to start paying its contributors.

The station had received permission in 1931 from the Radio Branch to accept reimbursement for expenses incurred in putting on special broadcasts for various organizations and government departments, but it was still hard-pressed. The university's financial situation became so dire that in December 1932 Wallace wrote to Hector Charlesworth, chairman of the CRBC, suggesting that the commission take over CKUA as its station in northern Alberta. The commission had already entered into this type of arrangement with stations elsewhere in Canada. Wallace cited the valuable contribution CKUA had made to community life in Alberta and argued that "any curtailment of this particular aspect of our extension activities would be very regrettable." No reply was forthcoming.

Normally, CKUA broadcast during the academic year from September through June. But in 1933 cutbacks forced the station to stop broadcasting in mid May. Wallace wrote again to Charlesworth, and Premier Brownlee added his support to the proposal.

The broadcast commissioners visited Edmonton in September and told Corbett that CKUA needed certain technical upgrades to meet CRBC standards. Apparently under the impression the commission was smiling favourably on his proposal, Wallace secured sixteen hundred dollars from the provincial government to make the improvements, and CKUA resumed broadcasting in November. That same month, Corbett received a telegram informing him that the CRBC had selected CJCA as its station in northern Alberta. No reasons were given. According to Clark, there was speculation that the commissioners might have been influenced by Prime Minister Bennett, who held a long-standing grudge against Henry Marshall Tory and the University of Alberta. But he says a more likely explanation is "the general ineptitude of the Commission and its lack of interest in educational broadcasting." Allard's account of the CRBC's activities would support this:

There was little consultation between the Commissioners. Their inability to distinguish between policy and administration resulted in total lack of planning and co-ordination.

In its first year of operation, the Commission succeeded in antagonizing virtually every segment of the Canadian population. Within that period Prime Minister Bennett was grumbling that nothing gave himself and his Cabinet colleagues more trouble or provoked more exasperation.

The commission came under blistering attack during 1934 hearings of a special committee of the House which Bennett had appointed to review its work. E.A. Weir, formerly of the CNR radio department and soon-to-be-dismissed director of programs for the commission, was angry that CKUA wasn't allowed to carry the commission's programs and said in his presentation to the hearings,

Had the Commission's interest in educational broadcasting been as great as it would have us believe, its program service would have been extended to such stations as CKUA of the University of Alberta (which under the greatest of difficulties and direct economizing manages to carry on an educational program infinitely superior to that of any other station in Canada). The excuse that the Commission must limit its programs to one key station in each city in such an instance as this is puerile.

Corbett, too, was critical of the commission's programming, judging from this comment: "The sort of people who delight in crooners, cowboy yodellers, jazz orchestras, old-time fiddlers and red-hot mammy torch songs are well supplied by local commercial stations and the Radio Commission and are therefore no part of our concern."

Wallace finally received a response from the CRBC in February 1934 notifying him that his proposal was being considered. But by that time, CKUA had found another way to extend its broadcast reach. The station collaborated with CFAC Calgary and CJOC Lethbridge to establish the Foothills Network, using the network to disseminate its agricultural lectures and the agricultural news flashes prepared twice a week by the provincial government. Alberta Government Telephones supplied the lines to connect the stations.

CKUA used the new connection to set up a citizens' forum, called the "Round Table," which Brown later said was the first program of its type and the forerunner of the "Citizens' Forum" of the national CBC public radio network.

"A lot of the things they [CBC] are doing today [1957], we did for the first time…. A citizens' forum—it was called a 'Round Table.' It started in Calgary. We picked up some businessmen in Calgary and broadcast them over our station as well as the Calgary station. Later on, that program alternated between Edmonton and Calgary. We had some very wonderful discussions from some of the leaders in the two cities....

"A lot of things the CBC does today which are quite commonplace, we did as just things that were ready-made for an educational station to develop."

Later, a "Farm Radio Forum" on CKUA involved 108 listening groups with fifteen hundred members. This pioneering concept predated a CBC farm forum series which became the model for adult education projects in India, Pakistan and Japan.

In 1934 CKUA won the 580 frequency all to itself as a result of changes that would set the scene for Edmonton radio for the next decade. Jim Taylor and Hugh Pearson, who had sold their first station to CKUA, took over the Christian and Missionary Alliance station CHMA, changed the call letters to CFTP and obtained use of the 1260 frequency, allowing the alliance airtime on Sundays as part of the deal. Later that same year, the *Edmonton Journal* invited them to submit a proposal to manage and operate CJCA, which had changed to the 930 frequency in 1928. They succeeded over a competing bid by CJCA's manager Dick Rice and his partner Hans Nielsen. Rice and Nielsen subsequently formed Sunwapta Broadcasting, bought CFTP from Taylor & Pearson Ltd., and obtained a licence with the call letters CFRN (for "Rice" and "Nielsen").

On November 1, 1934 the two organizations essentially swapped radio stations. CJCA had been assigned its own frequency, 730, the previous year. In 1936 CFRN, by then owned solely by Rice, moved down to 960. More changes in 1941 brought CJCA up to 930 and CFRN to 1260. In the decades to follow, Rice and his competitors, Taylor and Pearson (with a third partner, Harold Carson), would be major players in Canadian broadcasting.

By 1936 Mackenzie King was back in power. In June of that year he replaced the CRBC with the Canadian Broadcasting Corporation (CBC). The CBC had the same regulatory powers and program responsibilities as the CRBC but had financial autonomy and was responsible to a nine-member board of governors. Major Gladstone Murray, a friend of the Radio League and former director of public relations with England's public radio network, the BBC, was hired as general manager. According to Allard, the CRBC's demise was due in part to vigorous campaigning by the Radio League, which was disappointed in the commission's failure to get into educational broadcasting.

When the CBC was formed, CKUA was still strapped for funds and was broadcasting fifty hours a week between October and May with coverage within only a sixty-mile radius of Edmonton. Through its commercial partners over the Foothills Network, CKUA managed to reach a province-wide audience with ten hours of lectures a week. In Corbett's words, the station was just "marking time."

In 1936 Corbett left to become director of the recently formed Canadian Association for Adult Education, and Donald Cameron took over the helm of the extension department. The Foothills Network came to an end that same year. Cameron cobbled together a tenuous Alberta Educational Network with CFCN in Calgary—and later CJCJ—which lasted until 1940. But ultimately, neither of these networks, dependent as they were on the largesse of commercial broadcasters, met CKUA's needs for province-wide educational broadcasting. In March 1937 University of Alberta president W.A.R. Kerr approached Murray of the CBC and worked out an agreement whereby CKUA would carry CBC programs not broadcast by CJCA. The CBC would also pay CKUA two hundred dollars to broadcast a drama series produced by the CKUA Players. Cameron saw CKUA's role over the next decade as "expansion and close co-operation with our national system, especially in its broadcasting for the Western Region [System]."

On CKUA's tenth anniversary the Edmonton Journal carried a two-page feature, complete with congratulatory ads from community businesses. The feature appeared to be a platform for the university to lobby for more money from the province and increased support from the national broadcaster. Corbett contributed an article in which he said that CKUA "has undoubtedly led the way so far as Canada is concerned in exploring and developing the adaptation of this new science [broadcasting] to the entertainment and educational demands of community life."

He said that radio was now "accepted as one of the most powerful constructive forces for mass education that science has yet given to the world." The CBC had "a long way to go" to compete with the giant American networks in terms of high-class entertainment, but Canada might soon pull ahead of the United States in the use of radio in the schools and in adult education "because it is a nationally-controlled system, and not subject to the necessities of a commercial system."

Corbett suggested that if the CBC was going to take the lead in developing new techniques in radio education, it should have "one or more experimental stations endowed for this specific purpose." And CKUA could perform that service. "A few thousands of dollars a year from the national organization would enable CKUA to lead the way in the future, as she has done in the past, in educational broadcasting for Canada.

"CKUA has done a great work for the people of Alberta," he concluded. "If the people of Alberta rally to its support and demand that the provincial government enlarge its appropriation so as to enable the station to have a decent margin for successful operation, it can do still greater things than it has done. It is not likely that any 500-watt station in the world carries on its work on so small a subsidy as that which supports the programs of CKUA."

A retrospective article by A.E. Ottewell summed up the station's philosophy:

The idea consistently followed in university radio work has been to provide a "different" program from those commonly available. That this result has been achieved in the main is abundantly evident from the response of listeners who have repeatedly emphasized the unique character of our broadcasts.... It is safe to say that in its own field this station has made and is making a definite contribution to the educational and cultural life of the community and it is hoped that the ideals with which it set out can be steadily maintained, and that its services can be expanded in the future.

How powerful a lobby CKUA listeners might have been at the time is difficult to determine. One clue might be found in the congratulatory ads in the *Journal*'s anniversary feature. They included one from the Northern Hardware Company featuring a General Electric 1938 radio for sale on "easy terms, small down payments" and a Jones & Cross advertisement offering five different automatic-tuning Philco radios—"A glance ... a flick of your fingers ... there's your station"—priced at $149.50 to $310 "on terms that you can easily afford." A radio was still a pricey appliance—especially compared to family income. In 1937 the average annual wage of industrial workers was $965.

Nevertheless, eighty percent of homes in Edmonton had radios at the time, according to the *Edmonton Journal*. The newspaper reported that Alberta ranked fourth in Canada in the number of receiver licences, with 62,000 licences issued for the nine months ended December 31, 1936. Edmonton accounted for more than 15,000 of those licences. Since a significant segment of the population didn't bother to license their radios, the actual numbers would have been considerably higher. By 1943, seventy-nine percent of all Alberta homes had radios.

Not long after CKUA's tenth anniversary, the two strong, hands-on personalities who had nurtured the station over its first decade—H.P. Brown and Sheila Marryat—moved on to other pursuits. Marryat left in 1939 to join the CBC in Winnipeg as talks producer for the prairie region. At the time, the *Edmonton Journal* acknowledged her departure with a major story, noting that "her name has been synonymous with the development of radio in this province." Marryat told the *Journal* that the reward in her work with CKUA came from the knowledge that she was "doing a little something" for the women in rural Alberta. "I grew up in the country myself, and I know its loneliness. I feel that the radio programs must be some compensation to the women who have been plunged into country life, leaving their music, drama and friends behind them."

In 1940 Marryat retired to Vancouver Island, where she lived until her death in 1962. Years later, Elsie Park Gowan said of her, "I can't speak strongly enough about the leadership Sheila Marryat gave. She was an Englishwoman of the upper classes—using the word in its best sense. She was gentry—an aristocrat, if you like. She had high standards of every-thing—in drama, in music. Nothing shoddy or cheap ever got on the air when she was there."

Brown, who had fuelled the station with his enthusiasm and resourceful-ness, relinquished his post as chief announcer and studio supervisor to devote full time to his responsibilities as head of visual instruction for the Department of Extension. Bill Pinko, who worked for CKUA starting in the early 1940s, recalled Brown's presence in the department: "My memories of Brown are of a very effervescent person with a ready smile and laugh. He was full of ideas ... and when he was doing anything it was usually at high gear and he was always ready to help if asked."

Commenting upon Brown's death in 1965, Gowan said he was "a prince of a man ... a man dedicated unselfishly to the enlargement of the human spirit."

Flies in the Ointment | 4

When CKUA first began broadcasting, something as trifling as a lecturer's lisp could knock the station off the air. Even after Edward Jordan invented the peak limiter and Ward Porteous rebuilt the transmitter, the technical operation of the station was still a delicate business. In fact, a mere fly could shut the equipment down, according to Arthur Craig, who was transmitter operator in 1939.

At that time, federal regulations required that someone be on duty at the transmitter while a radio station was on the air. Because of this, transmitter operators and their families often lived on the premises where transmitters were located, much the way lighthouse keepers lived in lighthouses. Craig, a young radio buff just out of high school, had already worked a couple of summers relieving the transmitter operators at CJCA and CFRN. He said the CFRN job, which had him working in a small house in Edmonton's west end, often entailed babysitting for the children of the household as well as minding the transmitter, which was housed in a spare bedroom.

Commercial radio stations generally purchased their transmitters. These came "in metal boxes like a refrigerator, only larger," Craig recalled. "They were large and noisy and had to have ventilating fans. Radio tubes generated a lot of heat—there were no transistors then—and as a result, you had to move a lot of air to keep these tubes cool." When a tube failed, the transmitter would have to be shut down—perhaps for as long as fifteen minutes or even an hour—while the operator replaced it. "It could happen once a month or it could happen twice a day. You never knew."

The transmitter built by Porteous and his students was a homemade affair housed in a small wooden shed, about sixteen feet square, just south of Pembina Hall on campus.

"It was not a state-of-the-art transmitter," Craig said. "It was a good, serviceable old workhorse.... It was what used to be called a 'rack and panel' job—metal posts and sheet metal front with meters and dials. It was fairly rugged, fairly rough, nothing very sophisticated about it, but it worked.... It had two very large metal towers between which the antenna was strung, and a lead-in from the antenna came directly down to this little wooden shed."

The shed was furnished with a desk or table, chair, gas heater, turntable and microphone. Craig recalled arriving to begin the broadcast day:

> In the winter-time, the shack was very cold when I went in there in the morning and turned the gas heater up. Sometimes you had to start broadcasting from the shack instead of the studio, which was in one of the buildings on campus, because there wasn't anyone there at that time. We had a phone, and you could phone and see if there was anybody home. We had a little library of 78 records, and I would play three or four of those until somebody showed up at the studio. But you had to hand-turn the turntable on. It would just grind itself around, frozen stiff practically. It was still pretty cool in there—the place hadn't warmed up, so you turned the turntable by hand until it warmed up, and then you put a record on which, of course, had to be a symphonic record—no popular stuff of any kind was allowed. It had to be pretty much classical stuff.

After Craig played a few records, the phone would ring and a plummy English voice would say, "We are here." Dick MacDonald, who was appointed

◆ Dick MacDonald,
a member of the CKUA
Players, was appointed
studio director in 1939.
University of Alberta Archives
69–97; used by permission.

studio director in 1939, had a background in theatre. He had been with the university for ten years and was a member of the CKUA Players. MacDonald was an authority "on all things classical," according to Craig. "He was an English gentleman with a marvelous mellifluous voice and beautiful, beautiful diction." MacDonald himself said he had been turned down by the CBC for sounding "too English." However, at CKUA, "he had a long, long following of faithful listeners, and he got lots of phone calls and letters and requests," Craig said. MacDonald's dexterity left a particular impression on Craig. "He was a chain smoker and the only man I knew who could change a disc—turn it right over—with one hand while smoking a cigarette."

MacDonald would sign the station on and start the day with his morning classical program. At night when it was time to close the station down, Craig would get a call out in the shack telling him to play a few more records and then sign off. Sometimes Craig was enlisted to play a part in one of the radio plays. "It was like a family thing," he said. "They were nice people, a lot of fun."

The young Craig enjoyed a little autonomy alone out there in the shack and often tacked a "Good night, Mother" to his standard sign-off. But he didn't think much of CKUA's musical fare, which he considered rather high-brow. Asked if CKUA was as popular as Edmonton's other two stations, he said, "If you were suitably old." Setting out to correct this perceived deficiency, Craig brought one of his own records to work one day.

"I had a couple of band records at home that I was particularly fond of, and they were fairly racy records. They didn't have them at CKUA, so I took one over there—I wasn't supposed to do this—but I took it over there anyway, and I played it as a sign-off record.... It was not the thing to do, and the dear old transmitter didn't like it and one of the tubes gave in. I took quite a razzing about that."

But what Craig remembered most was the challenge of operating CKUA's outdated equipment.

"There was a homemade thing, a big 'variable condenser,' ... that we used to tune the antenna—[it was] part of the antenna circuit—and it was ... made out of big sheets of galvanized iron ... fixed ones and some moveable ones. And the moveable ones were ganged together with a wooden strip, and you'd pull the sliding ones back and forth and tune the antenna and get it exactly right. And these metal plates were separated by maybe three-eighths of an inch, a quarter of an inch, half an inch.

"The problem was, the flies used to get in there—it acted like a bug killer. The flies would zip in there and—*zap, zap*. And sometimes that would just trip the old transmitter right off the air. So we had to build a little screen out of window screen and enclose this thing to keep the flies out of the transmitter."

This was no way to run a radio station. Not only was the equipment unstable, but CKUA's mission was also increasingly compromised by its low power and dependence on network arrangements with commercial broadcasters. The commercial parties to the Foothills Network, and later the Alberta Educational Network, were originally generous in providing time. But it became difficult for the university to get time that coincided with the needs of its audience. Noon-time suited farmers best. But "each year the difficulty of getting suitable time has increased until the time when the C.B.C.'s soap programmes went on CFCN [CKUA's partner in the Alberta Educational Network], when it became impossible to get noon-day time that was of any value," extension department director Donald Cameron lamented in a brief to the CBC in 1941. He said commercial stations complained that educational programming drove their audiences away and cited a 1941 audience survey for CFCN showing that educational talks rated as low as 2.3 compared to 56.7 for "Fibber McGee and Molly" and 57.0 for "Charlie McCarthy," two popular American programs.

According to a history put together by the university around that time, CKUA was in dire condition:

> During the last two years the station has operated with steadily decreasing transmitting efficiency and by the winter of 1939–40 breakdowns were coming with such increasing frequency that there could be no satisfaction in operating the station and no guarantee that it could be operated for another term without major repairs. Furthermore, the station no longer met the requirements established by law as the minimum standard necessary for broadcasting.

Porteous and Cameron had advised U of A president W.A.R. Kerr of the situation in November 1939. Kerr took the issue up with the university's board of governors, saying that the station needed capital improvements of at least fourteen thousand dollars or it would "have to carry on in an unsatisfactory manner in a developing field until such time as it is forced off the air." The board instructed him to seek funding from the provincial government, setting the stage for a political tug-of-war that would last more than a decade and profoundly change the character of CKUA.

Kerr took his case to the provincial treasurer, using a more realistic figure of twenty-five thousand dollars, but got no immediate response. Meanwhile, Cameron went east on an information-gathering trip in early 1940. He visited the Manitoba government station CKY in Winnipeg and met with CBC general manager Gladstone Murray in Ottawa. In his report on the trip, he said Murray had indicated there should be no problem if CKUA wanted to go commercial as long as its licence was in order and had pointed out that, indeed, CKUA already had a commercial licence. That would be the "private commercial" licence the university had transferred from Jim Taylor and Hugh Pearson in 1927. However, the university had been paying a reduced fee because it was using the licence solely for educational purposes. University officials assumed they would only have to pay the higher fee to exercise the commercial option, and Murray's comments to Cameron seemed to support that assumption.

◆ Premier William "Bible Bill" Aberhart was eager to have the province take over CKUA in the early 1940s. *Provincial Archives of Alberta A.2043; used by permission.*

In June 1940 Cameron found himself in a meeting in Premier William Aberhart's office on another matter, along with the deputy minister of education and R.S. Lambert, who was head of school broadcasts for the CBC:

> As we were getting up to leave, Mr. Aberhart said to me: "What about this radio situation at the University?" I replied that I was most anxious to know just what the situation was, my understanding being that the President [Kerr] was under the impression that the first word concerning future developments was to come from the government.... The Premier then said that he was anxious to have the matter attended to right away, and said that the government was willing to put up $25,000 for the provision of a new transmitter, subject to conditions:
>   1. That the station should be on a semi-commercial basis;
>   2. That the government should have control.

Cameron told the premier he had no trouble with the first condition, but in his opinion, "government requirements could be satisfactorily taken care of with the station on a semi-commercial basis under University auspices." He suggested "the new station" might be operated under a board of governors appointed partly by the university and partly by the provincial government.

According to Cameron, Aberhart replied, "You fellows over there don't want to be bothered with the details of running a commercial radio station and it had much better be done under the Department of Public Works." Further, Cameron said, "Mr. Aberhart stated ... that if the government took the station over we would be given all the time we would require in any case and he could not see why we would want to be bothered with it at all."

Aberhart then cited the example of station CKY, owned by the Manitoba government through its telephone company. That situation, unique in the country, had been quietly in effect since the early 1920s.

Aberhart "finally said that he was sorry that I didn't see eye to eye with him on the question of control of the station." Cameron noted that the CBC's Lambert was in the room during part of this exchange.

The next day J.A. Weir, who was serving as acting president while Kerr was away, sent Kerr a confidential memo outlining the situation: "The insistence of the Premier upon immediate action suggests the government has its heart set upon gaining control of a wave length which is, I understand, a very desirable one." Indeed, according to Edmonton historian and one-time CKUA program director Tony Cashman, CKUA's 580 frequency was much coveted at the time because of the tremendous reach of ground waves at that frequency.

Kerr immediately consulted the CBC's Gladstone Murray to sound him out "in strictest confidence" as to how the CBC would receive a proposal to turn CKUA over to the provincial government. He reported that Murray was encouraging, although the CBC official did point out that the CBC board of governors would have to approve the proposal. Kerr then met with Aberhart and his cabinet on August 6, 1949 "in order to discuss the problem arising from the wearing out of our radio station."

Later, Kerr wrote, "University opinion, of course, would be opposed to complete surrendering of our station. I had been giving the matter thought and had come to the conclusion that possibly a compromise might be arrived at which would appeal to both parties concerned." He proposed to Cabinet an arrangement similar to the joint government-university board

◆ Dick Rice, owner of CFRN (Sunwapta Broadcasting Co. Ltd.), was both friend and competitor of CKUA.

City of Edmonton Archives
EA–160–662; used by permission.

that governed the University Hospital. They reached an "agreement in principle" whereby the government would put up between $20,000 and $25,000 to rebuild CKUA as a 1,000-watt station. The new station would be governed by a joint board and operate on a semi-commercial basis.

Kerr outlined this proposal for joint operation of the station to Murray and received an encouraging reply: "My own feeling is that your revised proposal is a sound solution of the problem." Murray followed up with a telegram on September 6:

EXCELLENT PROGRESS SO FAR EXCEPT REGARDING POWER STOP
BELIEVE OFFICIAL APPROVAL FORTHCOMING EARLY NEXT WEEK.

Boosting CKUA's power to 1,000 watts was not just a matter of CBC approval but was subject to terms of an international agreement regarding radio frequencies and power. It should be noted that the question of operating commercially was not mentioned in Kerr's outline to Murray.

Around this time, Dick Rice, manager of the Sunwapta Broadcasting station CFRN—which operated at the 960 frequency and which was upgrading to 1,000 watts—approached the university with two proposals. In the first, Rice offered to have CFRN remodel and modernize CKUA's 500-watt transmitter at no cost to CKUA except for parts. The transmitter would be installed at CFRN's transmitting station, and CFRN would operate and maintain it, again at no cost to the university other than for parts.

The second proposal was an offer to take over the prized 580 frequency after CFRN had upgraded to 1,000 watts. In exchange, CFRN would give the university a minimum of two and a half hours of broadcast time a day under its own call letters. CKUA would be able to sell any part of that time and keep the revenue. Rice outlined the benefits and drawbacks of each proposal, with a clear bias towards the second. He warned that with the first proposal, CKUA would have to compete for audience share and advertising in the Edmonton market:

> It is recognized by Eastern Advertising Agencies, that Edmonton is the home of two of the most highly competitive radio stations in Canada.... Experience has definitely proven that a third station entering into competition with two established broadcasting units has an exceedingly difficult "row to hoe."

Proposal number two, Rice stressed, would have the advantage to the university of dividing the local audience only two ways instead of three and give it the benefit of CFRN's sales and promotion force.

The university rejected Rice's overtures. At a meeting of the executive committee of the university's board of governors on October 10, Kerr presented a draft of a letter to Aberhart approving the compromise arrangement he had proposed with the government. "It was sent with the unanimous approval of those present including the Chairman of the Board, though the latter said he was not very enthusiastic about the arrangement and would like to have kept the Government out of the negotiations altogether," Kerr wrote.

The Alberta government agreed to the terms. But its motives became a matter of controversy when the agreement was made public. In mid November a group of independent MLAs attacked the government's move, passing a resolution stating that while the nation was financing its World War Two effort, "the government should not spend such a large sum of money on something which may very well be dispensed with." The group further accused the government of attempting "to introduce Hitler methods into Alberta."

Aberhart had already tried to exercise control over the media in 1937 by ramming through the Accurate News and Information Act, which was successfully challenged by the *Edmonton Journal* as unconstitutional. The "progressive, independent" newspaper *The Spotlight* asked,

> Will Mr. Manning [acting premier Ernest Manning] state definitely whether it is the plan to broadcast Premier Aberhart's Sunday night Bible Conference programme over CKUA when the rebuilding of the station is complete? ... If there is no intention of using the University radio station for propaganda purposes or for the Bible Conference broadcasts, why should the station be taken away from the control of the board of governors of the University?

An Order in Council, dated November 25, 1940, approved a loan guarantee of $30,000 "to modernize the station and provide for the transfer of the station to a new site outside the limits of the City of Edmonton, as required by the Department of Transport, Ottawa." Among the *whereases* in the formal document is one stating "whereas it is anticipated that revenues from the Station will over a period of years repay this capital outlay."

With the government-backed loan in place, the university planned to have its new station up and running by April 1, 1941. In January it advertised for a commercial manager. But Kerr sensed something was amiss in Ottawa. On January 13 he wrote to Gladstone Murray:

> As you are probably aware, we have gotten along quite satisfactorily with our proposals for the rehabilitation of our university station, C.K.U.A. Indeed, the majority of our serious difficulties are now in full process of solution and really the only remaining matter that bothers us is the fact that we have not yet received official authorization to raise our power from the present 500 watts to the suggested 1,000....
>
> ... There are already indications that we shall not want for customers for time at the new station.

Kerr closed with an invitation to Murray to visit. Murray's reply of January 17 lacked any assurance:

> As I explained to Mr. Cameron, this is a matter with which only the Board of Governors can deal and it will be considered at their next meeting, the date of which is not settled as yet.
>
> I, too, hope that I shall be able to visit Edmonton and see the work you are doing in the near future but with the changing picture from day to day, it is extremely hard for me to get away from my base of operations.

The "changing picture" may refer to machinations in Ottawa and within the CBC having partly to do with political differences over the role the national broadcaster should play with respect to the war. (The details are covered by Frank W. Peers in *The Politics of Canadian Broadcasting: 1920–1951*.) Around the time of CKUA's application, Murray's position in the organization was being undermined, and his authority, as well as his travelling budget, was reduced in early 1941.

Kerr wrote again on February 10:

> I don't like bothering you about C.K.U.A. and its affairs but our construction program is well forward and we hope to begin broadcasting in about a month from now....
>
> We note that C.F.R.N. has been raised from 100 watts to 1000 watts, whereas no action as yet seems to have been taken on our petition to your Board though the matter has been under negotiation since last summer.
>
> I do not like to press the question unduly, nor embarrass you in any way, but we have already spent $30,000 on the rehabilitation of C.K.U.A. and our public is expecting the new station to go on the air in early spring.

Murray responded merely that the board's next meeting was tentatively set for March 24. A night letter sent on February 18 from Kerr to Murray reflects Kerr's increasing consternation:

University anxious to appoint commercial manager this week and start commercial broadcasting March 29th....

From your letter of Sept. 3 and wire of Sept. 10th stating that you considered proposed expansion programme in the public interest, and your verbal assurance to Cameron in Ottawa on September 10th that we have necessary commercial license, we assume there is no obstacle to our going ahead as planned....

Murray's reply by telegram on February 19 did nothing to relieve Kerr's anxiety:

RETEL EIGHTEENTH YOUR APPLICATION FOR THOUSAND WATTS WILL HAVE TO BE CONSIDERED BY NEXT MEETING BOARD BEFORE RECOMMENDATION CAN BE MADE MINISTER STOP ALSO IT MAY BE NECESSARY CONSIDER COMMERCIAL ASPECT AT SAME TIME AS TRANSPORT DEPARTMENT INDICATES PRESENT LICENSE PERMITS ONLY EDUCATIONAL PROGRAMMES STOP SUGGEST YOU COMMUNI-CATE DIRECT WITH DEPARTMENT IN THIS CONNECTION.

Something was definitely awry in Ottawa. Cameron immediately drafted a letter to Walter Rush, the controller of radio in the Department of Transport, outlining the university's dealings with Murray leading up to the rapidly developing crisis:

1. On January 29th, 1940, I interviewed Major Murray in his office for the purpose of discussing radio matters.... Major Murray stated that there was no objection to our going commercial as long as our license was O.K. He further pointed out that we already had a private commercial license even if we were not using it as such. From this I assumed that there would be no difficulty if and when the time came for us to consider entering the commercial field. The reason I recall this now is to draw your attention to the fact that the possibility of CKUA being forced, in order to remain on the air, to go commercial is not a new element in our negotiations.

2. On July 20th President Kerr wrote to Major Murray outlining the University's plans for re-building the station, and on August 21st

(Approximate date, as I have not the President's file before me.) received a letter saying that he approved of the plans for re-building and was taking it up with the Board. On September 3rd Major Murray wired the President to go ahead and confirmed this by letter on September 10th.

3. On September 10th, 1940, I had another interview with Major Murray for the purpose of discussing a number of matters pertaining to CKUA. At that time I raised the matter of CKUA operating on a commercial basis and asked Major Murray if he could give me any advice with respect to a commercial manager. His advice was that we should "get a local man if possible."... That same day I wrote to you ... making formal application for an increase in power to 1000 watts.

4. On November 21st I wrote to you inquiring as to what action had been taken about our application for an increase in power, and at the same time said that we hoped to operate our station on at least a semi-commercial basis from about March 1st, 1941.

   You replied under date of November 28th ... that before we could operate on a commercial basis we would have to get the approval of the Minister of Munitions and Supply and to pay a much higher license fee.

5. On receipt of your communication of November 28th, I wrote under date of December 7th to the Hon. C.D. Howe [Minister of Munitions and Supply] making formal application to operate CKUA on a commercial basis as from March 1st, 1941. I wrote to you on the same date advising you that I had made application to Mr. Howe for approval of our plans to go commercial and asking you to advise me what the new fee would be.

6. On December 13th, you acknowledged the application and stated that it was being referred to the Canadian Broadcasting Corporation for their recommendation to the Minister.

Cameron then outlined the financial commitments the university had made as a result of these communications:

Acting on Major Murray's permission to proceed as given in his wire of September 3rd, 1940, we proceeded to purchase a site, erect a transmitter house, install the ground system, run a private telephone line from our studios to the transmitter and to order new transmitting equipment. These developments have involved the university in expenditures amounting to over $30,000 to date. We are therefore naturally anxious that our plans should be carried out as our negotiations led us to believe they would be....

With further reference to the matter of our license ... we have only paid the non-commercial fee since 1927 because we were not using our commercial privilege. We now wish to use that privilege and are prepared to pay the commercial fee.

Any refusal to grant this permission at this time would result in unfair discrimination against our station in relation to the other local stations....

What he didn't mention is that the university had also committed to hiring a commercial manager and was busy negotiating a five-year contract. So certain was everyone of a positive outcome with Ottawa, Bill Rea had already given notice to the Vancouver radio station where he was employed, sold his home and bought a new car to use in his work selling advertising in Edmonton for CKUA. What's more, Rea and Cameron were busy drawing up a detailed advertising rate card for the station.

Cameron and Kerr presented a brief at the March 24 meeting of the CBC board of governors. With it they provided letters of support from the United Farmers of Alberta and the United Farm Women of Alberta expressing appreciation for "the excellent services given over CKUA" to farmers within its broadcast area. They said the primary function of the station would continue to be educational. They stressed that the station was still owned by the university and that "there is no question of the station becoming a private station for any government." These points addressed certain political realities of the day without spelling them out. First, there was no love lost between the Aberhart government and the Liberal government of Mackenzie King. Second, the CBC, as it was constituted at the time, was subject to political manipulation. And third, Aberhart was a master at using radio to stoke his political following.

The brief ended with two arguments that would seem to clinch the university's case. One, a precedent had already been set in the case of the Manitoba Government Telephone Commission, which had been operating CKY Winnipeg and CKX Brandon commercially for years. And two, to counter Rice's argument that a third commercial station would squeeze the Edmonton market, the brief cited the example of Calgary, where three private commercial stations had been operating for some time in a primary coverage area smaller than Edmonton's.

The arguments made no impact. "Mr. Cameron and I did not have very good luck with the C.B.C. Board in Ottawa," Kerr lamented in a "personal and confidential" letter to H.H. Parlee, chairman of the university's board of governors. The main stumbling block seemed to be Aberhart:

I felt the atmosphere not perhaps hostile but chilly, when we presented ourselves to the Board.... The answer to our request obviously depended on the attitude they had towards the Premier of Alberta. The question of his getting control of the radio emerged at once and formed the background of our interview. We have as yet no official reply to our petition, but from semi-official sources I do not doubt that it will consist of granting us the request for 1000 watts but refusing our request for a commercial licence without which, of course, we are at a complete standstill.

Kerr described reactions of individual board members. René Morin was "cool, but not overtly hostile," while Nathan Nathanson "led the attack and was not to be convinced." These two men were known to be particularly influential and close to the minister, C.D. Howe. A member of the board from Quebec, who was not in Howe's inner circle, "was frankly in favour." A fourth board member present at the meeting was Dr. James S. Thomson, president of the University of Saskatchewan. Although Cameron had petitioned him in advance for support, Kerr noted that "Dr. Thomson was inert after promising all support."

CKUA's "private commercial licence" was renewed for the year April 1, 1941 to March 31, 1942, with a sentence typed in at the bottom saying "This licence is issued subject to the condition that this station be operated on a non-commercial basis only." No CKUA licence prior to that date had carried any restriction.

Walter Rush, the government's controller of radio, informed the university that it had permission to increase its power to 1,000 watts, but the CBC's board of governors did not recommend that CKUA be allowed to operate commercially. However, there seems to have been some miscommunication, again from Murray. Cameron claimed the CBC general manager had advised him verbally after the March 24 meeting that the application had simply been deferred and that the university should submit further information with figures proving it couldn't operate without going commercial and showing there was room for three commercial stations in Edmonton. The university submitted the additional information, but on June 10, Cameron received a telegram from Morin:

AFTER CAREFUL DELIBERATION BOARD UNABLE TO ACCEDE REQUEST COMMERCIAL LICENCE.

Thomson, who later succeeded Murray as CBC general manager, conceded "there was a good deal of concern in Ottawa about the possibility of the new station becoming a private station for Mr. Aberhart's political purposes," according to Ralph J. Clark. Murray had censured CFCN Calgary more than once for carrying "dramatized political broadcasts" by Aberhart, and the Alberta premier had often complained to the CBC and Mackenzie King that the federal government was using the national public broadcaster for partisan political ends. Aberhart questioned the CBC's decision in a letter to King, to which the prime minister replied, "No one will appreciate better than yourself how important it is, if the confidence of the public in the independence of the Canadian Broadcasting Corporation is to be maintained, that it should be kept free from any suspicions of political interference."

Aberhart replied that he saw nothing wrong with broadcasting a political address from a public platform:

I think the rule of the Corporation [CBC] is against free speech.... It is surely most ridiculous that I should be compelled to leave the public platform and go to the studio to give my Sunday afternoon broadcast while the leader of the opposition and other members of the governments throughout Canada are continuously broadcasting from a public platform political addresses. May I also respectfully suggest that you have not the full facts in connection with Station CKUA.... If you are satisfied to accept the information that you refer to as accurate, I have no way of proving to you that there is an injustice being done.

The licence issue didn't end there. Indeed, it was just heating up. On June 21 Cameron wrote to Murray demanding in detail the reasons for the CBC board's denial of a commercial licence. Murray replied on July 8: "It was the Board's feeling that two commercial stations in the city of Edmonton are entirely adequate and that public interest, convenience and necessity would not be served by establishing a third commercial station."

In February 1942 the university's radio board turned down a purchase offer from CJCA and rejected the possibility of joint operation with CFRN or CFCN. Following instructions from Aberhart to find a solution to the station's financial situation, Robert Newton, chairman of the Administrative Board of the University Radio Station, reported to the premier that there were only two courses open to the university: sell the station or continue to operate it on the current basis.

"The first of these alternatives could only be offered as a counsel of despair. The station has already proved its educational value, and has attained great popularity throughout the Province. We believe it is on the threshold of still greater things."

Newton noted that the provincial departments of health, education and agriculture were already using two thousand dollars per year worth of time on CKUA and that the university hoped to expand the educational and informational services it could provide to government departments.

CKUA was costing the provincial government about $10,400 per year, including $6,200 in operating costs, $3,000 in capital charges (towards liquidating the bank loan) and $1,200 interest. Even though the operating budget had nearly doubled since 1932, it was a standing-still budget. The university needed an infusion of new funding just to keep up with a maturing radio industry. The new transmitter had greatly extended CKUA's coverage, from Peace River in the north to High River and Vulcan in the south. But to meet CBC requirements, it had to be built outside Edmonton city limits, and the university now had to keep a resident engineer on the site year-round.

The station had always shut down for five months in the summer, but increasing competition from other stations was making it difficult for CKUA to win back its listening audience each fall. The university wanted to increase to year-round operation. Also, dependent on volunteer amateur talent, the station was finding it difficult to compete in a market where the general quality of programming was becoming more professional each year. The university's efforts to keep CKUA afloat seemed to be thwarted at every turn.

During this time some of the key players in the CKUA licence issue changed. In 1942 university president Walter Kerr had offered Aberhart an honorary degree based on a go-ahead he had received from the executive committee of the university senate. But the full senate subsequently twice vetoed the offer by one vote. Kerr resigned over the embarrassing affair, and Robert Newton succeeded him. Continuing political turmoil in the federal government over the operation of the CBC led to Gladstone Murray's resignation in February 1943. Thomson (the man Kerr had described as "inert" in the CBC board meeting) took over as general manager of the CBC for a year starting in the fall of 1942.

H.H. Parlee, chairman of the university's board of governors, visited Thomson in Ottawa in November and reported back to Newton: "He was cordial and frank. Also he is a politician—Think he has guessed our feeling that we would prefer a grant to a commercial license."

Around this time, the CBC moved its weekly Metropolitan Opera broadcast from CKUA to one of its local commercial outlets. This did not sit well with the university radio board. Parlee conveyed their displeasure to Thomson in a letter advising him of a resolution "that the Administrative Board of the University Radio Station insists upon the right to continue releasing the Metropolitan Opera Programme over CKUA."

Thomson replied with a lesson in public relations:

I am rather anxious to help CKUA all I can. I am very anxious to use it particularly for purposes which are clearly associated with its University character, namely that of being an educational centre.... I think all these matters can be helpfully reconciled, but if I may respectfully suggest it they will not be advanced too well if your Board uses the language of insisting upon rights.... [W]hile I appreciate strength of language, sometimes it is not too helpful.

Thomson went out to Alberta and met with the university's radio board in December. They hammered out a "working agreement" whereby CKUA "might enter into a special relationship with the CBC ... to make CKUA an educational center for the Prairie provinces." CKUA would become a "subsidiary station" for the CBC and would rent its facilities to the CBC for $8,000 per year. The CBC would pay CKUA "at regular rates" for all programs originating with CKUA and would provide part of the salaries for a station manager and other staff. The total value of the agreement to CKUA would be $22,600.

The university understood the agreement needed only rubber-stamping by the CBC board of governors. But Thomson wrote to Cameron on February 10, 1943 that although "the Board of Governors are very sympathetic with the predicament in which station CKUA finds itself" and "are very desirous of seeing it placed on a satisfactory basis," they had resolved "that the method which was discussed between us ... could hardly be accepted." The CBC didn't want to create a precedent, he explained. Other universities in Canada were waiting to set up stations and might expect the same treatment. Parlee called the CBC's attitude "shocking."

The CBC suggested two counter-proposals: (1) that CKUA be allowed to undertake just enough commercial work to let it carry on as an educational station, or (2) that the CBC acquire CKUA as one of its own stations and let the university use the facilities to develop its educational programs. The board unanimously rejected the idea of selling the station to the CBC.

On April 8, 1943 the Edmonton Journal reported that the CBC was going to consider granting a commercial licence to CKUA at an upcoming meeting and that Newton had left for Ottawa to attend. It noted that the university had applied for the licence after meeting with Thomson "some weeks ago" in Edmonton. Cameron attached a clipping of the article to an urgent letter posted on April 9 to Newton, who was now ensconced at the Chateau Laurier in Ottawa:

I must say that I was amazed that such a story broke at this time because no word of any of our negotiations had gone from this office. The first inkling I had that rumors were going around was about 6 o'clock on Wednesday evening when Gordon Henry of CJCA telephoned me and asked me point blank whether CKUA had applied for a commercial license.... I hedged on the question and said CKUA did not want to go into commercial operation and that we were pressing to have the C.B.C. accept our memorandum of December 28th with which he was partly familiar as a result of his discussions with Dr. Thomson. I told him that the C.B.C. had rejected our proposal ... and had countered with two proposals of their own, one of which was to take the station over. I told him that I did not feel I was at liberty to disclose what the other alternative was, but I could assure him that we were anxious to operate the station on a non-commercial basis if we could.

You can imagine how I felt when I was informed of the story in yesterday afternoon's *Journal*. I have been in touch with both Dick Rice and Gordon Henry since then, and they feel that Thomson has double-crossed them because he had discussed our December proposal with them and they had both agreed to support it; and they feel that if he is giving us a commercial licence now he has gone back on his word to them. They are both naturally going to make every move they can to prevent our getting a commercial license, and Rice was going to take the plane last night to Ottawa. I told them both that in view of the story which was now out, that the C.B.C. had offered us a commercial license as an alternative to our proposal....

I think it is most unfortunate ... that the story should have got out at this time.

Trusting that your negotiations will be successful in any event....

Newton later described his doomed mission in a 1959 letter to his successor, Walter Johns: "I went to Ottawa and appealed to the CBC Board of Governors for the privilege of limited advertising in support of an improved programme over the new transmitter we had built on the Calgary Trail. Dick Rice followed by the next train, and apparently persuaded them there was no room for a third commercial station in Edmonton."

The university was offered a commercial licence, but under terms it couldn't swallow. On May 22, Walter Rush wrote to Cameron that the minister of transport had agreed with the recommendation of the CBC board of governors:

that a licence for commercial operation be granted provided that the gross advertising revenue be limited to $25,000 per annum, exclusive of commissions deducted by advertising agencies, and that the gross revenue figure be subject to review at intervals of not more than one year and further provided that if CKUA takes any existing business from CFRN the commercial licence of CKUA may be cancelled.

Newton challenged the decision in a letter to Rush on June 10:

The [Radio] Board finds itself unable to accept the conditions quoted in your letter.... Your Act and Regulations do not appear to make provision for restrictions of this sort on commercial licences, and they seem therefore to be illegal.

In a letter to the CBC Board of Governors, dated 12 April, I offered ... to limit our commercial operation to $25,000, a restriction imposed by the CBC Board before they would consider our application.... It was, however, a private arrangement with the Board which, since it was not made in compliance with any act or regulation, does not appear to have a necessary place in your letter. The second restriction ... came as a surprise, and seems to us wholly improper as well as illegal and unworkable.

Newton asked whether the department "still insists upon" the conditions. He copied the letter to Transport Minister C.D. Howe. The minister evaded responsibility for the decision, informing Newton that "the conditions to which you take objection were laid down by the Board of Governors of the Canadian Broadcasting Corporation."

The university's radio board rejected the conditions, expressing their "unanimous resentment." There would be no commercial licence. However, in September the CBC offered the university a one-time grant of $2,500 for the 1943–44 school year to apply to its "problem" and to make amends for the apparent miscommunication.

In the midst of this licence battle, Aberhart died suddenly, on May 23, 1943. He was succeeded as premier by his protégé Ernest Manning, who had learned well the potential of radio for mass communication.

But as the CKUA story unfolded, it became clear that Aberhart wasn't the only obstacle to saving the university's radio station.

A Frustrated Government | 5

While the drama over CKUA's licence played out behind the scenes, it didn't affect what listeners heard. But other influences were gradually changing CKUA.

The CKUA Players continued for a few years after Sheila Marryat's departure in 1939 and then disbanded. Lectures and recorded music, particularly symphonic music, became the station's mainstays for lack of money to finance more ambitious programs. As World War Two began, many lectures and panels focussed on the issues behind the conflict.

The evening "Symphony Hour" of "good music," hosted by Dick MacDonald, continued to be popular. At some point, MacDonald decided to devote Friday's hour to listeners' requests, a move that proved so successful that he never had time to satisfy them all. In 1941 MacDonald took leave from CKUA to serve in the Canadian army. On his last night he announced he would stay on the air until he had played all requests.

"By nine o'clock, all the phones were jammed and the telegrams were coming in from all over—even from across the border from Utah and

Montana," MacDonald recalled. "At midnight they were still coming in. We finally signed off at 3:00 a.m. For us, it was concrete proof of the listening audience CKUA had built over the years for programs of good music. And not all requests were filled that night, by any means."

In 1943, for the first time, CKUA did not shut down over the summer months. But by then, the university was producing only three live programs a week—on science, home economics and agriculture—and recorded music accounted for two-thirds of the programs originating at the station. A program schedule for November 1943 shows a series on the credit union movement and a series on "plays, acting, stagecraft and directing" called "Curtain Going Up" presented by Sydney Risk, supervisor of dramatics for the extension department. U of A students provided a weekly news program.

The electrical engineering department was becoming less involved in the station. The new manufactured transmitter held little interest for the department as a teaching tool because, unlike the earlier homemade equipment, it came housed in a box and "we couldn't tear it apart anymore," Ward Porteous said.

Starting in 1939, the provincial Department of Education regularly used CKUA to produce and broadcast educational programs for in-school listening. The first school broadcasts were created primarily to help isolated rural teachers, but eventually the programs were designed for use by all Alberta teachers. Among the school broadcasts in 1940 was a series of eleven high school programs on drama and playwriting. There were also study groups on current affairs and news commentaries for high school students. By 1943 other provincial government departments, including health, agriculture, trade and industry, as well as the Department of Education's Correspondence School Branch, were contributing the lion's share of live broadcasts on the station.

Although CKUA wasn't the CBC's "basic" outlet in Edmonton (that was CJCA), the station carried an increasing number of programs from the national broadcaster. In 1943 CBC-produced programs, including dramas and agricultural talks, made up more than forty percent of CKUA's offerings. CKUA, however, was receiving just one hundred dollars per month from the CBC.

From its start, the CBC, like its predecessor, had been embroiled in controversy regarding its role and powers. The main issue was the corporation's function as both regulator and station-owner/provider of national broadcasting services. This rankled private broadcasters, who were often in competition with the CBC for listeners and advertisers.

Funding was another issue. The government expected the CBC to be supported primarily by receiver licence fees and to a lesser extent by advertising, with a minimum amount of taxpayer money in the form of loans. The stated ultimate goal of broadcast legislation was total public ownership of Canadian broadcasting in order to further a sense of national identity. But the financial realities of the time and the existence of a private broadcast industry made total public ownership a distant ideal. In the meantime, the CBC would cobble together a national network by leasing, purchasing or even expropriating existing stations and building new stations.

The majority of CBC programs were advertising-free. A small number were American commercial programs; however, they often occupied prime hours. Canadians loved American network programs, and the CBC dared not alienate its audiences by shutting out the most popular American shows. So, in addition to symphonic, chamber and choral music, original Canadian plays, and Canadian public affairs, sports and news, the CBC ran American programs such as the Metropolitan Opera broadcasts, "Charlie McCarthy" and the "Lux Radio Theater." Advertising sales not only helped support the CBC but were deemed to be in the national interest because they provided a national advertising outlet for Canadian businesses to counteract American competition. When the CBC broadcast commercial programs through its network of basic private stations, it split the advertising dollars with the affiliated stations. This arrangement proved lucrative for the private stations even while CKUA received next to nothing for running the CBC's sustaining programs, which the private broadcasters were reluctant to run for fear of losing their audiences.

CKUA's partner in the Alberta Educational Network, CFCN Calgary, was one of those private stations. In late 1943 the CBC demanded more prime time from CFCN for its commercial programs. This resulted in CFCN bumping CKUA's fifteen-minute "Farm and Home Forum" from 9:00 p.m. to 9:15 p.m. Donald Cameron resented this and wrote to CFCN's commercial manager. It seems farmers went to bed early, and 9:15 was pushing things.

I must say that both the Government and the University are very much concerned about the fact that when any entertainment programme of a commercial nature comes along it is considered the thing to do to bounce the educational programme. I think this is an entirely wrong policy and that it is neither in the interests of ourselves or of a private station like yours that this should be done....

I must say frankly that the assumption that commercial shows must have priority on all the best listening times is not one that is warranted on any other grounds than that the sponsors have more money than the educational institutions.... Our Board feels that ... if private radio stations are going to continually give in to this they are going a long way towards surrendering the right to any consideration which they should have at the hands of the national radio authority.

As far as CFCN president H.G. Love was concerned, Cameron was biting the hand that fed CKUA, and Love immediately shot back a scathing rebuke to U of A president Robert Newton, copied to Premier Ernest Manning:

I have spent many years dealing with an ungrateful public but, without doubt, after taking all the circumstances into consideration this, to my mind, is tops. For many years I have endeavored to co-operate and assist your Department of Extension in the broadcasting of their messages and discussions, even though many were of a decidedly "pinkish" tinge, and more often than otherwise they were poorly presented and by speakers horrible to listen to.

Love pointed out that this arrangement came at "a tremendous cost" to his station and drove his listening audience to a "minimum":

Now to have the "commercialism" cry thrown at me is uncalled for, inconsiderate, discourteous, inaccurate and, when the circumstances are considered, can only be classed as the ravings of one who has come to believe that he is entitled to demand that which has, heretofore, come to him on a silver platter.

In fact, Love said, commercial programs were what made it possible for his station to donate time to the university:

> Is it not commercialism (and farmers are commercial if anything) that makes it possible for institutions such as the University to exist in our present civilization? But perhaps the Director of your Department of Extension, who, once a number of years ago, proudly stated to the writer he was a Communist, looks forward to that Utopian state where totalitarianism exists, as his letter reeks with the stench of such a situation.

Love closed with the threat that "the whole matter of continuing to carry these programs is having our present consideration."

Newton went into damage-control mode, suggesting to Love that Cameron felt "his close friendly relations with you had seemed to justify speaking in the more or less casual way one would to another member of his family." However, "he acknowledges, on re-reading his letter ... that it was rather tactless." And, by the way, he wrote, Cameron didn't recall saying he was a Communist.

Indeed, it must have seemed to Cameron and Newton sometimes that the university and its little radio station were fighting a losing battle against the forces of commercialism and popular taste.

A declaration of "Programme Principles for CKUA," dated June 24, 1943, listed the following:

1. The programme should always be worthy of a university station.
2. The service should be unique, not merely a duplication of service afforded by other stations in Edmonton.
3. A larger listening audience is desirable, and this should be built up on the basis of a reputation for consistently high quality entertainment and education features.
4. Swing music, crooning, and "thriller" plays have no place in our programmes. These may be quite legitimate forms of entertainment but they are already available in abundance on existing stations.
5. Light entertainment should, of course, be judiciously interspersed with heavier forms but should always be of such a nature that any

person can tune in at any time to the University station with full confidence that he will hear nothing incompatible with the dignity and purpose of an educational institution.

As young station operators, like Edward Jordan and Arthur Craig, who strayed from this path quickly discovered, CKUA's university management carefully guarded these principles, especially those against swing and crooning. Even the CBC wasn't immune from censure. In early 1944 Cameron, who was serving as CKUA program director at the time, wrote to the CBC regional program director in Winnipeg complaining that the national broadcaster had replaced a Toronto Symphony Orchestra broadcast regularly carried over CKUA with "a very poor type of dance programme" and on the same evening executed another substitution in which "some Winnipeg orchestra undertook to 'swing' the classics." CKUA operators were instructed in such instances to cut in and play records from CKUA's collection.

And that crooning! Handwritten notes in Newton's file from a CKUA program committee meeting in 1944 indicate there was a constant need for vigilance:

> Mr. McRae [Jim McRae—recently hired as program director to relieve Cameron] has been featuring the Boston Pop Orchestra during "Symphony Hour" (7–8 pm) when we should have really serious music; and jazz & crooning & "Music Hall" organ, on dinner music (6–7) when the Boston Pop would be about right.

Having come up empty-handed in his attempts to secure an agreement with the CBC in 1943, Newton took CKUA's financial problems once again to the provincial government. Cabinet suggested that the university turn the station over to the government. Newton put the proposal to the radio board in January 1944. This time the radio board agreed unanimously. There was no alternative. The university senate went on record with a resolution stating it preferred that the university retain control of CKUA, but if changes in administration were necessary, the university's requirements should be "adequately safeguarded."

In March 1944 Alberta's minister of telephones and acting premier, W.A. Fallow, wrote Cameron requesting that the university "prepare and execute a transfer of the existing licence from the University of Alberta to the Minister of Telephones." Newton read this letter at a special meeting of the university's board of governors. Board chairman Parlee said, "If it were to be a source of friction with the government, it should be advisable to accede to their request." Newton concurred, although he felt it was a "step backward" for the university to give up the station. The board of governors agreed to transfer the station to the Government of Alberta. But it wasn't going to be that simple. There were still Ottawa and the CBC to deal with.

The board of governors sent a draft Memorandum of Agreement, dated April 18, 1944, to Fallow spelling out their intent to apply for the licence transfer. In exchange, the agreement said, the government will "afford to the university all necessary facilities for continuing and improving their educational services over the Station, during a minimum period of three hours daily, advantageously distributed and entirely free of advertising."

A draft bill of sale between the board of governors and the minister of railways and telephones, dated June 15, 1944, turned over all of the station's transmitter equipment, valued at $26,477.23, to the government for the sum of $1.00. The list ranges from a "transmitter type 1–K" priced at $11,573.00, to a 36-cent cold chisel, and includes, literally, a kitchen sink. For another dollar, a second document transferred the land on which the transmitter stood.

The Alberta government quickly prepared two briefs to the CBC seeking, first, the transfer of CKUA's licence and, second, a private commercial broadcasting licence for the station it was planning to operate. On May 2 Premier Manning sent copies of the briefs to Auguste Frigon, acting general manager of the CBC, along with a letter from the university's board of governors to the controller of radio formally applying to transfer the licence. The letter stated that the Department of Telephones had agreed to give the university "all the time we desire for educational purposes" and pointed out that by transferring the station to the government, the university could "solve our immediate financial problem, while at the same time enlarging and improving our educational service over the station."

The first brief recounted the events leading up to the university's failure to secure a commercial licence and the misunderstanding with Gladstone Murray. It then explained why the provincial government hadn't given CKUA the funding it had requested for expansion: the government provided the university with a single annual grant, and to increase the grant by the sum CKUA required would "throw out of balance the per capita tuition costs of the University of Alberta as compared with those of other similar institutions of learning." The brief argued that the university "is concerned primarily with education leading to degrees, while the Government is and must be concerned with all phases of education" and that "the Government desires to extend and expand the educational facilities of CKUA to include all phases of educational effort from kindergarten to and beyond university and numerous other phases of vocational and adult education."

Anticipating the old arguments that Edmonton could not support a third commercial station, the second brief, seeking a commercial licence, made a compelling case based on statistics. Calgary, with a smaller population and fewer businesses than Edmonton, supported three radio stations: CFCN, CFAC and CJCJ. And Spokane, comparable in size to Edmonton, supported four stations. Calgary had only 59,000 "radio homes," compared with 83,600 in Edmonton. Calgary's population over the previous decade showed an average increase of 14.8 percent, compared to 62.2 percent for Edmonton. And "there is every indication that, after the war, Edmonton's radio listening population will be further greatly increased."

Especially interesting given the situation fifty years later, the brief said that "since the war Edmonton has taken a leading position on the entire continent as a centre of air transportation and there is every indication that it will continue to hold this lead after the war." These facts "substantiate the claim that Edmonton offers a greater market for three commercial stations than does Calgary."

Addressing the CBC's earlier argument that it couldn't allow a university-owned station to go into commercial broadcasting, the brief stated, "Station CKUA no longer belongs to the University of Alberta. It is now the property of the Alberta Government Telephones." And, of course, there was the Manitoba example:

It is respectfully submitted that all objection to the commercial operation of this radio station disappears in light of an examination of the
situation in the Province of Manitoba. The relationship existing between
the Alberta Government Telephones and Radio Station CKUA is the

same relationship which exists between the Manitoba Telephone System and Radio Stations CKY and CKX.

An undated report found in CKUA's files beside the brief says, "The radio department of The Manitoba Telephone System is operated entirely as any other privately owned station.... It appoints a Commercial representative to sell advertising on a commission basis which is a standard practise in Canada and the United States.... The department is showing a good net profit. The Canadian Broadcasting Corporation originates part of its national network programs from the CKY Winnipeg studios. They have their own program producing department but use the Manitoba Telephone System radio technical staff."

The brief made one more point. It referred to a meeting between Alberta's minister of telephones and CFRN's Dick Rice that supposedly took place the previous year "upon the suggestion made by one or more members of the Board of Governors of [the Corporation]." Describing the May 31, 1943 meeting, the brief said,

> The basis of Mr. Rice's views was that there was no room in Edmonton for a third commercial station and that even though CKUA be granted commercial privileges the station would probably fall short of paying its overhead and operating expenses, depending, as it must, on purely local advertising. Mr. Rice suggested that the Minister of Telephones consider utilizing the moneys required to operate CKUA in a radio broadcasting program through the facilities of CFRN Edmonton and CFCN Calgary. Such a program obviously would mean the virtual abandonment of CKUA.

And, perhaps, the opening-up of the coveted 580 frequency for CFRN? Interestingly, Edward Jordan said of Dick Rice that, although nominally a competitor, he "was often a friend in need in helping to keep CKUA on the air in the early days." Rice would also be among the well-wishers speaking on the station's thirtieth anniversary program in 1957.

The brief concluded that the Alberta government, "while confident that Mr. Rice's proposal was made in the best of faith, does not feel it should give the proposal further consideration. In the Government's view, the future of radio broadcasting is so great and capable of so much benefit to the people of the Province that it is the duty of the Government to retain and develop station CKUA limited only by such regulation, general or particular, which the Corporation thinks proper to impose." Surely, the government now had all its ducks in a row.

Fallow, the minister of telephones, and J.J. Frawley, a solicitor in the attorney general's department, presented the brief to the CBC board of governors on June 26, 1944. On August 16, Alberta had yet to receive word of the board's decision. Fallow wrote to CBC acting general manager Frigon, who referred his letter to Rush, the controller of radio. Rush wrote to Fallow on August 25:

> the Board of Governors have not recommended favourably on your application for a transfer of the licence of radio station CKUA ... for commercial operation, for the following reasons:—
>
> "Having noted that the present licence to CKUA was issued for educational broadcasting purposes, and having reviewed all circumstances surrounding the radio situation in Edmonton with respect to the commercial field, the Board feels obliged to recommend denial of this application for transfer of the licence."
>
> The minister has concurred in this recommendation and under the circumstances, the Department is not in a position to deal further with the application.

Fallow appealed directly to C.D. Howe: "It is very difficult for us to understand how the Board has arrived at such a conclusion particularly in view of the fact that radio facilities in Edmonton are so congested as to make it practically impossible to secure time of value during periods when any number of people are listening to the radio." Fallow asked for a further investigation into the matter "as quickly as possible."

Fallow heard on November 6 that his request had been referred back to the CBC board of governors and that they were standing by their decision. The case then moved to the topmost level. Premier Manning wrote to Mackenzie King outlining the situation. He called the CBC's refusal of a commercial licence "completely unwarranted and indefensible" and appealed to King's "sense of fairness":

> Naturally, the Corporation's refusal to grant a commercial license to this Government-owned station ... is a matter that will cause justifiable concern, and I feel, resentment, on the part of the people of this Province, especially in view of the fact that during recent months commercial radio licenses have been granted in other radio zones where, in our opinion, the need for an additional commercial station is not as great as in the Edmonton area. Furthermore, it has been intimated to us that if the station was owned by a private individual or company rather than by the Government of the Province, a commercial license would be granted.
>
> You will readily understand my concern in this matter, and why I have refrained from issuing any comprehensive statement on the situation until I had brought the matter to your personal attention.

King replied that while final authority for granting licences rested with the governor general in council, all applications must be referred to the CBC board of governors "to avoid charges of discrimination and favouritism in the important field of regulation of radio broadcasting." He added that he was sending the matter back through the appropriate ministers to the CBC for further consideration.

A month later, L.R. LaFleche, minister for national war services, wrote to Manning that "a careful inquiry" had been made and "we have been informed that the two Stations in Edmonton holding commercial licenses are not overloaded" and that both had hours available for commercial broadcasting.

Manning could scarcely contain his outrage when he wrote to King protesting this latest decision. He said that the CBC board members

> were outspoken in their determination to protect the private interests of radio station C.F.R.N., regardless of how adversely it might affect the rights of other citizens of this Province desirous of seeing a warranted expansion in radio facilities now available. The Government of Alberta regards this attitude as a most flagrant violation of the

fundamentals of Democracy, and it can only be interpreted as meaning that the Board of Governors intends to monopolize the commercial radio field for private interests for financial gain, irrespective of the interests and wishes of the people generally.

Surely, Mr. Prime Minister, you must realize that the attitude and the action of the Board in this matter will not be tolerated. In their most recent and final decision to deny our application the Board has maintained that the existing radio stations in Edmonton are not over-loaded and have ample time available to meet all reasonable requirements. This position, in the light of the facts, is so absolutely ridiculous that it could only have been designed to camouflage the real purpose of their refusal.

Manning said the government would continue to operate CKUA for educational purposes out of public revenues because "the need for increased educational facilities by radio [is] so great that we consider it in the public interest that we avail ourselves of the restricted sphere into which we have been confined by reason of the Board's unwarranted decision."

A week later, during the throne speech debate in the Legislature, Fallow publicly lashed out at the CBC, charging the federal regulator with "gross unfairness and discrimination" and warning the dominion government that "we will not tolerate impudence for long." He recounted the attempts to secure a private commercial licence for CKUA and read out loud Manning's letter to King, concluding, "and then the prime minister of Canada wonders why the disunity in Canada threatens to wreck Confederation. Let him examine his mind and he will find the answer."

Fallow's fulminations against the CBC that day must rank among the most colourful speeches ever heard within the walls of the Alberta Legislature. The Edmonton Bulletin said he "flayed" the CBC's board of governors, calling them "nothing more or less than a series of concrete pill-boxes forged around the federal government to shield them from attack while the board carries out the policies laid down by the federal authorities." Of the CBC itself, he said,

because of the power they wield over the lives and fortunes of the people, instead of being used to extol the virtues of all that is great and good, they have degenerated into a means of spreading vicious propaganda and the glorification of all the evils and vices known to the human race.

But he was only just warming up.

It [the CBC] has been so highly commercialized that the air groans with the admonitions of pill peddlers and peanut pushers, the wails of moaning mollies exhorting the fair sex to cover up their faults and imperfections with some gooey substance which will enable them to fool the unsuspecting male. The air reeks with putrid, sordid soap operas and now the employment of Hollywood stars for a magnificent consideration no doubt, who lower the dignity of a once proud profession and lend themselves to the humiliation of describing in detail how they rid their bodies of offensive smells and how they keep unmentionables so pure and sweet and clean.

Surely, Mr. Speaker, we have not degenerated into such a dirty race that we need to be plagued with this kind of cheap advertising.

CFRN did not escape Fallow's ire. Calling the CBC's objections to a commercial licence for CKUA "spineless," Fallow said,

They argued that the rights of one individual radio station, CFRN, should take precedence over the rights of 800,000 people. This in spite of the fact that it is openly stated by those who should know that this station is being operated under a gentleman's agreement to break the law.

Fallow charged that both CFRN and CJCA were "controlled by the Southam Press," which owned the *Edmonton Journal*. He said the CBC was allowing this to happen even though such an arrangement in a single market was against broadcast regulations. In its own story on Fallow's attack, the *Edmonton Journal* denied any interest in CFRN.

The Alberta government did not give up. On May 10, 1945 Fallow wrote to CBC chairman H.B. Chase that the circumstances with respect to broadcasting in Edmonton had changed. The CBC had opened a second national network, the Dominion Network, in January 1944. Fallow pointed out that CFRN was now affiliated with the new network. "With the Dominion network affiliation CFRN is financially secure, and any justification for opposing the granting of a commercial license to CKUA has disappeared." Fallow also informed Chase that the Alberta Legislature had passed a resolution expressing its desire that a commercial licence be granted to CKUA. Chase replied on May 15 that Fallow's "communication" would be placed before the CBC board at its next meeting.

Meanwhile, on May 1 the Alberta government took over operation of CKUA on campus, installing Walker Blake, a man with commercial radio experience, as manager. The transition was not smooth, judging from a memo Newton drafted to his executive assistant Clem L. King the next day:

> Since Mr. Blake has not yet come to see me, I shall set down here the points I should like you to take up with him.
>
> 1. Yesterday and today the station has occasionally made the following announcement: "This is CKUA, Station of the University of Alberta, owned and operated by Alberta Government Telephones." We need not concern ourselves with the legal point that Alberta Government Telephones does not in fact own the station yet, but we must request that the name of the University be not used in connection with any programme except those which we ourselves have organized and for which we take responsibility.

Newton also said he wanted all phonograph records belonging to the university removed from the station and stored. "These are mainly a gift from the Carnegie Corporation, and are in a number of cases irreplaceable. They were intended exclusively for educational use."

The "legal point" regarding ownership had to do with Newton's insistence that the transfer was not complete, on the grounds that he hadn't signed the April 18, 1944 memorandum of agreement because it did not include all the verbal promises the government had made. Newton had added a clause to the agreement to correct this deficiency and said he was told by Solon Low, then chairman of the government's radio committee, that it would be executed. But "I have heard nothing further to this day," he wrote to Parlee on May 1, 1945. "Consequently there has been no transfer of the Station or its licence to the Government."

On May 3 Newton shot off another memo to Clem King, clearly annoyed with the new management:

Last evening's experience made it plain that the station is continuing the policy of cancelling summarily and without consultation with us a number of long-standing university programmes, including the 7 to 8 hour of good music which has been a feature ever since the station was founded, and of replacing these with programmes we could not afford to have associated with the University in the public mind. In these circumstances I have decided, after consulting the Chairman of the Board, that we must dissociate the University from the station until a formal agreement with the Government, specifying our rights and hours, has been executed.

Will you please advise the Manager of the station that this action will be effective today, and that the name of the University must not be used in identifying the station.

King responded that Blake would comply and that the government would probably move the station "to temporary quarters over town as soon as the question of the commercial licence is settled." The station was moved two months later, even though the question of the commercial licence was still up in the air.

There was also some dispute over who owned what. On May 3, Cameron sent Newton a memo saying, "It is understood of course that all of our records and control equipment remain in the studios here." But a note in Newton's file says, "Miss Cowan [a university/CKUA employee] reports: (1) That AGT claim they own everything but Carnegie set, & are proposing to move equipment overtown within the next few weeks. Meanwhile they are using our records, apart from the Carnegie set, claiming they own them."

Over the next several months, a curious series of communications took place regarding the licence issue. CBC chairman Chase had assured Fallow the government's application for a commercial licence would come before the board at its next meeting. Fallow wrote Chase on July 19 inquiring as to the board's decision. On July 24, citing a provision in the Canadian Broadcasting Act, Chase replied:

> The Board makes its recommendations to the licensing authority, namely, the Department of Transport, and it then rests with that authority to approve or disapprove of the Board's recommendations.
>
> You will realize from the above that it would be inconsistent for the Board to advise any applicant as to its decision, for the reason that such decision may not be final. Your application was considered by the Board at its meeting on June 5th last, and recommendations with respect thereto have gone to the Department of Transport; therefore, may I respectfully suggest that you inquire from that Department as to what the decision may be.

Fallow waited until September 21 to write to Dr. J.J. McCann, the minister of transport. Meanwhile, CBC assistant general manager Donald Manson had been sent to Edmonton to investigate the local situation. On August 3, Manson wrote to Walker Blake asking him to spell out "on paper for me the eight points which you enumerated to me" and to send them by air mail.

Blake obliged. He argued that two-thirds of the population in northern Alberta lived in the country and that CKUA intended to program "more for the country audience than either CFRN or CJCA have been doing." He pointed out that "there is a wealth of musical talent in Northern Alberta" and CKUA intended to "develop and polish this talent and if possible originate the talent when ready, to the CBC. To provide lessons, amateur musicians must be paid." He then played the patriot card. If CKUA had a commercial licence, it would require a bigger staff "and these we would hire out of the armed services." He already had applications on file from army, air force and navy personnel. "A commercial license would create employment for these men." CJCA and CFRN were both secure because of their CBC network connections, so a CKUA commercial licence couldn't possibly harm them financially, he concluded.

Then a strange thing happened. Despite the fact that the requests for a commercial licence were coming from the Alberta government, the assistant controller of radio, G.C.W. Browne, sent notice of the CBC board's decision to Newton at the university. In a letter dated September 8, Browne told

Newton that the CBC board of governors had reconsidered the university's application to transfer the licence and operate the station commercially and

IT WAS RESOLVED

That the former rulings of the Board of Governors to deny station CKUA Edmonton a commercial license be confirmed and that no further consideration be given to this application for a period of at least two years by which time the situation may have clarified and the application may be reviewed again.

Newton was out of town when the letter arrived, so he didn't pass the letter on to Fallow until September 27.

Fallow was furious. On September 28 he dashed off a letter to Dr. McCann:

In the absence of the common courtesy of a reply to correspondence between the Government of Alberta and the Government of Canada, I take it that this [Browne's letter to Newton] is the means by which your Government seeks to terminate an important issue which it apparently has not the intestinal fortitude to face itself.

I can quite understand your timidity in giving your personal approval to a decision of the Board of Governors which could only be arrived at by process of reasoning utterly devoid of either principle or fact.

Fallow accused the CBC board of governors of caving in to pressure:

by individuals who are financially interested in Stations CJCA and CFRN ... no matter what injustice or unfairness it would mean to the people of Alberta.

The actions of the Board of Governors in their pathetic scramble to discover a peg on which to hang their flimsy excuses for denying our right to operate a radio station, in my judgment, reveals them either as a group of individuals wholly incapable of assessing a number of facts honestly or fairly, or who permit their opinions to be moulded by outside pressure. In either case, it reveals the depths to which power politics have descended.

Fallow added that he had been approached by people who told him they had been assured that if they could purchase CKUA from the government,

> they immediately would be granted a Commercial License.... I wish to assure you that Radio Station CKUA is not for sale, and will continue to perform the legitimate functions of radio broadcasting despite the discriminating actions of the Board of Governors. In the meantime, I can assure you that the matter is not going to be shelved for two years, as suggested by Mr. Browne.

McCann was unapologetic:

> The Board is convinced that the granting of a new commercial permit in Edmonton would very seriously affect the financial position of the two other local stations CJCA and CFRN....
>
> Let me say that the matter has come up for discussion at almost every meeting of the Board for the last couple of years and it was decided ... that it would not be placed again on the agenda for two years. I may add that no more pressure has been brought to bear on the Board of Governors by the individuals who are financially interested in Station CJCA and Station CFRN than by representatives of your Government.

McCann reminded Fallow that former U of A president Henry Marshall Tory's original application for a licence in 1927 promised that "the work carried on by us will be of a *purely educational character*."

"I think from the foregoing that it was clearly established that Station CKUA definitely had a broadcasting licence for non-commercial purposes," McCann concluded. "I approve of the action which the Board of Governors have taken in this application.

But the Alberta government was already embarking on another route to owning a radio station with a commercial licence. On October 2 Fallow had a letter drafted to CBC general manager Frigon: "The Government of Alberta in conjunction with the Alberta Government Telephones hereby makes application for a private commercial radio license for a 50,000 watt radio station to be located at Red Deer, Alberta."

After arguing the need for the station, he added, "Furthermore, it cannot be charged that the granting of this License would interfere with the radio monopoly presently existing in the City of Edmonton." (The letter was actually sent on October 15 to the Department of Transport under Walker Blake's signature.) On November 26 Fallow applied for a commercial FM licence in Edmonton.

The following March the Department of Transport advised Blake that the CBC board of governors "has not recommended favourably" on the Red Deer licence application. "Under the circumstances, the Department is not prepared to deal further with this matter." As it turned out, the CBC was reserving Red Deer for its own network.

Blake countered by renewing CKUA's application for a commercial licence. He had been carefully watching the national scene and noted that the CBC's interest in protecting CJCA and CFRN "is hardly sensible and not consistent with other CBC grantings." In fact, "many licences have been granted by the CBC in the past twelve months to radio stations in cities where other stations exist." He noted that a man by the name of Jack Blick "was not turned down in Winnipeg on the grounds that the financial positions of CKY and CKRC might be affected." There were similar examples of licences granted in Ottawa and Sudbury. Blake cited figures showing CJCA was taking in approximately $250,000 in annual revenue from its affiliation with the CBC's Trans-Canada Network, and CFRN was getting $125,000 through the Dominion Network. "You can see that with no commercial network affiliation we could hardly affect the financial position of CJCA and CFRN."

Once again, Blake was turned down. Political conflict involving the CBC on the national scene may have had something to do with CKUA's problems. Private broadcasters and their national association, the Canadian Association of Broadcasters (CAB), were still uncomfortable with the CBC's role as both their regulator and their potential competition, or as Conservative party spokesman John Diefenbaker called it, "cop and competitor." The CAB was highly critical of the CBC and was continually lobbying for a separate regulatory agency. The leaders of the CAB in 1944 were mainly from independent stations, including CFRN, and Rice was a board member.

Because it was under assault, the CBC was eager to be seen by private broadcasters as a partner and not as a competitor. In fact, Alberta MP and Social Credit leader Solon Low told the House of Commons in 1946 that the

CBC was motivated in the CKUA affair "not by the needs of the people, but by the financial appeals of the Edmonton station CFRN."

After the CBC's refusal in March 1946, Walker Blake shot back another volley, this time raising the issue of FM. "May I point out that FM, one of the most significant steps since the birth of radio, is about to come into being in Canada." Blake said he was concerned that if CKUA had to wait another year and a half to reapply for a commercial licence, it would fall behind other stations in FM.

"Will I be permitted a commercial license for FM when I have not obtained a commercial license for AM?" he asked rhetorically. "Will you kindly read this letter to the Board at their next meeting and appeal to their reason and common sense in this matter?"

This time, the CBC came up with a new reason for turning CKUA down: "The recently announced policy of the Dominion Government regarding the granting of commercial licences to Provincial authorities removes this question from the authority of the Board of the Canadian Broadcasting Corporation."

Where did this new wrinkle come from?

Alberta wasn't the only province in conflict with the CBC over broadcast rights. Quebec premier Maurice Duplessis had long opposed the CBC as a federal government instrument of centralization. In March 1945 Duplessis had flexed his muscle by introducing a bill to establish a provincial broadcasting service with the power to build and acquire stations. In Saskatchewan the CCF government had designs on a radio station coming up for sale in Moose Jaw.

In any event, Quebec was not going to be allowed its own broadcast mouthpiece. C.D. Howe stood up in the House of Commons on May 3, 1946 and announced a new government policy:

> The government has decided that, since broadcasting is the sole responsibility of the dominion government, broadcasting licences shall not be issued to other governments or corporations owned by other governments. In regard to the two stations in Manitoba, discussions are taking place with the government of that province which we hope will lead to the purchase of these two stations by the dominion government.

◆ CKUA football commentators at the broadcast booth on the University campus.
University of Alberta Archives 69–10–37; used by permission.

The Alberta government was stuck in the peculiar position of operating a radio station with a non-commercial licence held by the University of Alberta. This state of affairs was actually illegal because by CBC (and later CRTC) rules, a station must be operated by the licensee. Strangely, although the Alberta government continued to make periodic stabs at gaining a commercial licence, the national regulator turned a blind eye to this illegal situation for more than a quarter of a century.

At some point in the mid 1940s, there was speculation that the frustrated government would sell the station. But Fallow put a stop to the rumours, saying, "CKUA will not be sold. CKUA will remain the voice of the Alberta people. We regard CKUA as the last outpost of radio freedom in Canada—and CKUA will remain free."

While the licence battles played out, programming went on as usual. By the end of 1944 CKUA was on the air about fifty hours a week, seventeen of them devoted to CBC programs. Meanwhile, war was still raging in Europe and Asia, and the Americans were in the North building the Alaska Highway. In 1944, at the request of the American army, CKUA began sending regular 10:00 p.m. news and weather reports by telephone line to station CFWH in Whitehorse. These were the first radio broadcasts to Canada's north country, according to Joe McCallum, a CKUA announcer in the early 1950s. The reports tied up the phone lines each night so that no one was able to call in or out of the Yukon for the duration. CKUA continued sending the reports until 1950, when CFWH joined the CBC network.

After taking official control of the station on May 1, 1945, AGT moved CKUA on July 28 from the university campus to the Provincial Building in downtown Edmonton on the corner of 100A Street and 101A Avenue. During its reserved three hours per day, the university continued to produce its regular programs, including radio talks and an hour each afternoon and evening devoted to "good music." It also continued broadcasting the CBC's "Citizens' Forum" one night a week.

Provincial government school broadcasts continued, but other CKUA programs took on a more commercial cast almost immediately. The government had had a commercial licence in mind when it hired Blake, who came with experience as a sales manager at a Winnipeg station and most recently at CJCA; his management style would probably have reflected that culture. It's unknown what programs offended Newton so much that "we could not afford to have [them] associated with the University in the public mind." However, a 1946 program guide lists a number of shows that might have given him pause, including "Spotlite Bands," "Polka Time," "One Nite Stand," "Hits of the Week," and "Song Corral." And, in the early years of AGT ownership, Bing Crosby, the king of crooners, had an entire half hour devoted to his music every Sunday evening and appeared on the cover of more than one CKUA program guide. In fact, the program guide for November 1947 carried a front-page photo of Crosby. Inside was a copy of a letter to Blake from the man himself:

> How do you do it?
> We hear CKUA has fine programs, including some of our records—but no commercials.
> Congratulations.

(How had CKUA come to Crosby's attention? Perhaps he had heard the station on one of his pheasant hunting trips to the Brooks area—almost an annual event in the 1940s.)

It was well known that Newton's wife, Emma, kept a sharp ear tuned to the station and alerted her husband whenever it strayed from what she considered appropriate fare. In a brief University of Alberta archives biography, Emma Read Newton is said to have "participated actively in campus life"—too actively, for the liking of some CKUA employees. The young faculty wife who had played "God Save the King" at CKUA's debut in 1927 had become "a dictatorial force on campus" by the mid 1940s when her husband was president of the university, according to historian Tony Cashman, who was program director at CKUA during the 1960s. "No one could smoke in the campus cafeteria until after she had left each day."

Bill Pinko, who worked briefly at CKUA before the war and later returned, recalled the president's wife:

> Dear Emma Newton was like the KGB and always listened to the station when it was part of the U of A and GOD help you if you made any comment on air that she might find objectionable. I assure you the phone would ring and the president's office would let you know about it. I got my fanny in a sling a few times for an occasional comment (joking) that she felt was not of the high standards of the University.... It was a standing joke among the various people who were in any way connected with the station for the very short time that I was there, that she listened all the time we were on the air and if she was unhappy with anything she heard she called Dr. Newton and he did the dirty work of phoning the station with the complaint.

The university president seems to have taken a hands-on role with the station in other matters as well. In a letter to the station's program director Jim McRae, he cut short a hopeful announcer's career, writing that the man in question "has now had a prolonged test and seems to be definitely unsuited to radio announcing. I suggest, therefore, that you advise him to seek more suitable employment."

Was Emma behind that letter? The switch to AGT control seems to have caught her short, according to Cashman:

It was on April 1st, 1944, shortly past noon, when the lady got through on the phone to Jim McRae, the announcer on duty at CKUA. The lady told Jim the record he was playing—it was a frivolous record, perhaps by the King Sisters—was not appropriate for a university radio station. She was the wife of a university official, swung considerable weight in all campus affairs, and had often given Jim advice on radio, but no more.

In tones tinged with triumph Jim informed her that CKUA was no longer the university radio station; as of that date it was being operated by Alberta Government Telephones.

Nevertheless, when CKUA celebrated its twentieth anniversary on November 21, 1947, Emma was front and centre during the university's "Music Hour" at 7:00 p.m. Starting the anniversary program off with "God Save the King," Mrs. Newton reprised the role she had played at the station's debut. Following a brief recap of the station's history by her husband, she was introduced by H.P. Brown, who said she would "by request" play "a few of her own compositions." She played "two short chorales," then accompanied her friend Mrs. Helen Walker, a mezzo-soprano, who sang two songs for which Mrs. Newton had written the music. "Now Mrs. Newton will play a group of three of her short dance compositions, a Gavotte, a Bourrée, and a Jig," Brown announced. And finally, "Mrs. Newton will close this programme of her own compositions with a hymn tune which came to her, both title and music, in a dream several years ago. It is called 'And now with joy our parting hymn we raise to Thee'."

Emma's reputation at the university lived on long after her tenure. What else are we to make of a 1969 handwritten note from university librarian Bruce Peel to university archivist James Parker, attached to a brief history of CKUA: "The station apparently was turned over to the govt. because Mrs. Newton, wife of the university president, tried to run the station as well as many other things on campus."

Although in 1946 Blake was sending his correspondence on letterhead topped by the slogan "CKUA: *Voice of the People*, Owned and Operated by Alberta Government Telephones," the university and government were still sorting out details of the transfer of assets, which was not yet legally official. In fact, the issue was still unresolved in 1959, when U of A president Walter

Johns wrote to Newton for clarification, saying he was unable to find any document indicating the nature of the transfer. Newton explained,

> Mr. Fallow ... was not given to formality, and I do not think any formal transfer of CKUA assets was ever put through.... The Govt. looked upon U. property as essentially Govt. property and just took what they wanted. They did not even bother to notify us when they were moving the studio equipment, but just cleared everything out, including some things we did not want them to take. But the only thing we argued about, and finally got back, was the grand piano.

The extension department's 1946 annual report put it more delicately: "Pending the arrival of new equipment, the University studio equipment was borrowed temporarily."

For the next twenty-five years, the university dutifully renewed CKUA's licence with the federal regulator every year and invoiced the station for the licence fee. The government periodically applied for a commercial licence during that time and was routinely rebuffed. As for the FM licence application, Fallow mentioned it in a radio speech on the station's twentieth anniversary in 1947, taking the occasion for one more swipe at the CBC:

> To keep abreast of the developments in electronics, we have applied for a Frequency Modulation license. The Board of Governors of the CBC will meet in Ottawa on November 27th to consider the granting of this F.M. license. It is to be hoped that in this connection better judgement will be shown than has been apparent in the past.

The CBC obliged. On January 12, 1948 Blake received notice from the Department of Transport granting a private commercial FM licence for a 250-watt station with call letters CKUA-FM at a frequency of 98.1. The licence stipulated that the station was to simultaneously carry all programs broadcast by CKUA but no others.

While still in its infancy at the time, FM (frequency modulation) technology promised certain advantages over AM (amplitude modulation). These included a better ratio of signal to noise against man-made interference, less geographical interference between neighbouring stations, and well-defined service areas for a given transmitter power. The CKUA *Broadcast Guide* for February 1948 listed the benefits of FM as "static virtually eliminated," "station interference practically abolished," "fading almost impossible," "studio quality of tone, from the deepest bass to the highest overtone of flute or oboe" and "perfect realism, like having the artist in the same room with you.... When you listen to FM you hear programs recreated in unmatched fidelity against a background of velvety silence." However, FM also required considerably more bandwidth than AM and more complicated receivers and transmitters.

CKUA's February 1948 program guide shows a schedule from 7:00 a.m. to midnight packed with a wide variety of programs, most in fifteen-minute time slots, including BBC and CBC news as well as CKUA-produced local news, sports and weather. Other CBC programs ranged from "Church of the Air," "Vesper Hour" and "New York Philharmonic Orchestra" on Sundays, to children's programs, musical programs and a daily "Prairie Farm Broadcast." The university filled its allotted time with "good recorded music" on its afternoon "Music Lovers Corner" and evening "Music Hour," plus such faculty-delivered programs as "Chimney Corner" (selections from "good literature"), "Books at Random" (talks by university library staff), "Behind the Headlines" (talks on topics of current interest), "World of Science" (chats on scientific questions) and "The Alberta Farm and Home Forum" (presented jointly with the provincial Department of Agriculture.) The provincial government also provided French 1, 2 and 3 correspondence courses.

In addition to its own recorded music programs, such as "Hits of the Week," CKUA carried programs by the Junior Red Cross and Alcoholics Anonymous, the latter a first in Canadian radio. The Edmonton Stamp Club had fifteen minutes a week, "with a view of stimulating interest in this great hobby," in which "we in Canada lag far behind."

In his twentieth-anniversary talk, Fallow referred to CKUA's "live-talent policy" and the "Alberta Talent" program, through which many young musicians had been helped. "Now this program has been extended to include Calgary and Medicine Hat with CJCJ in Calgary and CHAT in Medicine Hat forming with CKUA a Provincial Network to widen the scope of the Alberta Talent Program."

Over the years to come, CKUA would remain a constant friend to Alberta talent.

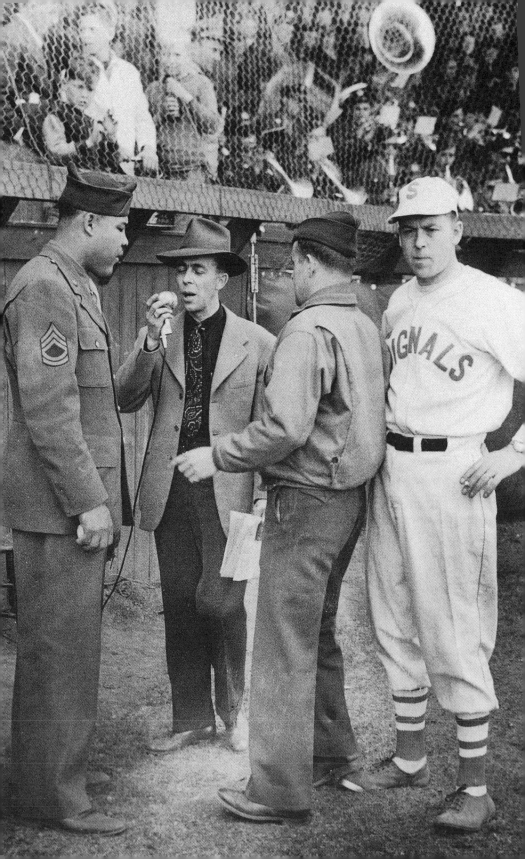

Asset or Liability? | 6

Jack Hagerman arrived in Edmonton in 1949 looking for a job in radio. He'd been working at a family-owned station in his home town, Saskatoon, but didn't see any future for himself there. Hagerman made the rounds of the three radio stations in Edmonton, all located downtown within a few blocks of each other, and was hired at CKUA for $175 a month.

"You couldn't exactly live like a king, but you could live on 175 bucks a month in 1949," he recalled. Chief announcer Bob Willson put Hagerman on the afternoon "Music for Driving" show, "which was fifteen minutes of records by some particular individual and another fifteen minutes of records by somebody else and so on. You could get five records into the quarter-hour. Mind you, we were not well researched. You just did it as you went along, catch-as-catch-can."

Owned by a frustrated government that didn't know what to do with it, CKUA was left pretty much up to its own devices, like a neglected stepchild. After the transition to AGT in the mid 1940s, the station had entered a free-wheeling phase characterized by a parade of relatively inexperienced but spirited young on-air personalities passing through on their way to jobs at the CBC or in commercial radio—or even to Broadway and Hollywood or other careers entirely.

"We developed good announcers and technicians who went on to better things, many to advance their careers in commercial radio," Walker Blake recalled.

One of those passing through was Arthur Hiller, who wanted to be a radio announcer long before the idea ever occurred to him that he might make a career in Hollywood. The Edmonton-born director of such films as *Love Story* and *The Americanization of Emily* said he still has rounded shoulders from listening to the radio as a young boy.

"I loved radio so much, I would sit on a footstool—because in those days the radio stood on the floor with the speaker in the bottom—and I would be on the footstool, bent over, with my ear right to the speaker." Hiller got a job as an announcer/operator at CKUA in the late 1940s during his first summer as an arts student at the University of Toronto. "I came in before 7:00 a.m. and had to turn on the station. You had to connect everything, and as you were connecting you also got the news coming out of a fax machine.... I'd have to prepare the morning news and then start with music.... Art Ward would come in and do the sports.... And I just loved it, except for the one day when I couldn't get the power going. I kept doing things and I was in total panic—I've got to get the station on the air!"

Hiller finally phoned a technician, only to discover "I'd just missed pushing a certain button that normally I didn't have to push, but because it was off I should have pushed it to 'on.'"

Blake tried to talk Hiller out of going back to university and even offered him a raise from $70 to $110 a month, "quite the salary in those days." Although he didn't stay, Hiller said his time at CKUA was "a wonderful period for me. At that time CKUA was doing programs ... that were for, let's say, audiences that were not in the mainstream.... It reached out to all sections."

Hiller said his CKUA experience gave him a leg up on sixty-four other people applying for a position directing a public affairs program for the CBC. That job led to another directing radio drama, setting him on a path that took him into live television drama, then film and stints as president of the Directors Guild of America and chairman of the Academy of Motion

Picture Arts and Sciences. Throughout his career, Hiller regularly returned to his home town and conducted workshops for theatre and film students at his alma mater, now the Victoria School for the Arts.

Another of CKUA's most famous alumni stopped at the station in 1951 on his way to Broadway. A native of Lawrence, Massachusetts, Robert Goulet moved to Edmonton at the age of fourteen with his mother and sister after his father died.

"My father on his deathbed told me I had to be a singer," the Grammy Award–winning baritone recalled in 1999 from his base in Las Vegas. "He said, 'God gave you a voice. He wants you to sing.' Those were his last words to me that night he died…. So when I left high school, I needed to be doing something to make a living."

While still a student at St. Joseph's High School, Goulet had been chosen by CKUA announcer Joe McCallum—only a few years out of high school himself—to contribute reports from his school for a program called "High School Highlights." After he graduated, Goulet made the rounds of the local radio stations. "CJCA said I didn't have enough experience. CFRN said I had a French accent. I went to the French station [CHFA, started in 1949 by a local group in order to bring French radio to Edmonton] and they said, 'You've got an English accent.' Actually, I had a Boston accent. John Langdon [who succeeded Blake as CKUA station manager in 1950] said, 'Beat it, kid.' But Jack Hagerman said, 'Give the kid a chance. He's got a beautiful voice.'"

Goulet got the job but almost blew it on his first day. "I didn't have a car, so I took the bus. And like an idiot … I took the bus I thought would get me there just in time. I mean—idiot Robert! You know you're going to be on the air, you should be nervous. You should get over there and prepare. Oh no, it's going to be a cinch. The idiocy of youth! I got there eight to ten minutes late because the buses were stuck in traffic…. Jack Hagerman had been sitting down in the control room and doing my show for me. And I said, 'Jack, I'm terribly sorry.' And he said, 'That's okay. It's all right.' And he walked away.

"About a week later, I was three seconds late. Same thing with the buses. Three seconds late is too late…. He just looked at me and walked away. And I said, 'I'm fired. I'm through.' But he never said a thing and kept me on. But I swear I learned from that. From that moment on, I've been three hours early for everything."

◆ *Robert Goulet (left), on a visit to CKUA in 1960, is interviewed by Gil Evans.*
Courtesy of CKUA.

Most of all, Goulet remembered the freedom he enjoyed at CKUA. "I was eighteen years old and I was in charge ... I could play anything—opera, jazz, pop. I had a great time." On Saturdays Goulet was in charge of a country-and-western show called "Saddle Serenade," a live studio program featuring local cowboy singers.

"People would come from all over the place with their cowboy gear and their guitars and their violins and they'd say, 'Me next, me next.' And I would point to one and say, 'You're on next.' I'd be in charge! They came in and they jammed in that place. And they all wanted to get on." One wonders how this show would have gone over with the extension department's Ned Corbett—he who had so abhorred those "cowboy yodellers" on the commercial radio stations twenty years earlier.

Goulet said his time at CKUA was "two years that helped me to grow up and learn a lot about this business." He left to study at the Toronto Conservatory of Music on a scholarship. Two years later he was host of a CBC television show called "General Electric's Showtime," and in 1960 he made his Broadway debut as Sir Lancelot in *Camelot*, with Richard Burton and Julie Andrews, a role that won him the Theatre World Award. Over the next forty

◆ Steve Woodman in the announcing booth, perhaps singing a "duet" with Doris Day, 1952.

Provincial Archives of Alberta PA 1631/2; used by permission.

years, Goulet acted and sang on stage, film and television; in 2002 he was running his own production company and performing out of Las Vegas.

One of the most colourful and memorable of CKUA's announcers in the late 1940s and early 1950s was Steve Woodman. "He really was 'Mr. Radio' in his day in Edmonton," recalled Jackie Rollans, who was CKUA station manager during the early 1990s and a young listener in the late 1940s. Woodman had a whole bag of tricks that turned conventional radio announcing on its ear. He would put on a record, open the microphone and sing along. CKUA still has a tape of Woodman crooning "Moonlight Bay" in a "duet" with Doris Day.

"Sometimes when he'd get a little bored, he'd say he was going to go in and play the piano in the studio," Rollans said. "He'd leave the mike open and you'd hear tromp, tromp, tromp as he went through the door into the

◆ After leaving CKUA, Steve Woodman (top) went on to CFCF in Montreal and later became a popular personality at NBC in New York.

Courtesy of Carol Woodman.

studio, and he'd sit down and play something and sing along." Woodman also did voice characterizations, creating a whole cast of personae, including Squeaky the Elf, that he would converse with in flights of whimsy.

"That kind of whacko broadcasting hadn't been heard before," said Tommy Banks, Alberta's "Mr. Music" and another CKUA alumnus. "He was completely berserk. Radio until that time was rather conservative."

Goulet and Woodman together got up to mischief on the air, not always maintaining a professional mien. Hagerman recalled one of those times: "Bob was reading the sports, and they both got to laughing. I was listening at home and phoned them. My wife-to-be was with me, and she said she'd never heard me use language like that before." Another, unsubstantiated, story has Woodman the helpless victim of a prank by other announcers who undressed him as he was reading the news over an open mike.

Woodman later moved to CFCF in Montreal and still later to NBC in New York, where Rollans once dropped in on him while visiting the city. "Here he

◆ Tommy Banks started at CKUA as host of his own teen show with his friend Barry Vogel.

Courtesy of Tommy Banks.

was in this immense studio and he's doing the drive-home show in New York, and guess what he's doing—the same program he did at CKUA. He was still doing all the voices ... but he was doing it to a sophisticated New York audience." Woodman also parlayed his talent for characterization into a successful television career in Montreal and later in New York as a puppeteer with his own show, "Stevio and His Friends."

Banks, a young musician and aspiring announcer during CKUA's early AGT days, had discovered the station as a teenager when he moved to Edmonton from Calgary with his family.

"My earliest involvement was listening to [CKUA] and realizing there was this incredible radio station that played really good music that other radio stations didn't play.... It was a wonderful discovery."

Banks was so taken with CKUA that late one night he was inspired to drop in on one of his favourite announcers. "I went up there at one or two o'clock in the morning to say hello, and I went up and rang the buzzer on the outside of the studio complex door, and Alan Hood, who was the drama producer of

CKUA at the time, came to the door and wouldn't let me in.... You know, when you're fifteen or sixteen, you think you know everything and you think you're entitled to everything. It annoyed me at the time."

But the man who would one day help save the station didn't hold grudges. Instead, he and a friend, Barry Vogel, pitched an idea for a variety show aimed at teens and succeeded. Banks and Vogel announced at a football game at Clarke Stadium that they were going to start a teen program the following week, and they had no lack of talent applying to be on the show. "We called it 'Teen Varieties,' 'Alberta's First T.V. Show,'" Vogel recalled.

"There was a remarkable [teen] scene here then," Banks said. "There was a teen newspaper in Edmonton. There was a central co-ordinating teen office for the activities of teenagers ... and there were several very active teen clubs in various parts of the city.... You went to the teen dances at the teen clubs on weekend nights, and to the concerts that they put on, and to the festivals they put on. It was a very busy and highly organized and well-structured scene to which everybody had access. So it wasn't hard for me to find out who was good."

Already an accomplished pianist, Banks sometimes played on the show himself, accompanied other performers and did interviews. At one point he auditioned with Hagerman for a full-time staff announcer job. "I failed the test miserably on general knowledge and pronunciation and foreign words and just about everything else." But he would be a strong presence on the station as a freelancer in many capacities over the next fifty years, even as he made a name for himself internationally in the entertainment world. Both Banks and Vogel, who went into law, have served on the board that guides CKUA in its present incarnation.

Another CKUA personality in the late 1940s and early 1950s was "singer/ announcer" Tony Biamonte, a tenor trained in classical music. Biamonte hosted some of the station's classical music programs, including a show on which he and his wife Dorothy sang opera arias. He earned his nickname "the Italiano cowboy" while doing shifts on the Saturday country-and-western show. Biamonte later moved over to CFRN and taught radio at NAIT.

Joe McCallum and Reg Shawcross ran a popular late-night request show called "Command Performance." "It seems nobody got tired of hearing 'My Happiness' by Ella Fitzgerald and 'Blueberry Hill' by Louis Armstrong,"

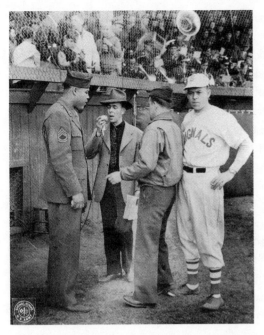

◆ Art Ward (with microphone) interviews world heavyweight boxing champion Joe Louis (left), at Edmonton's Renfrew Park, 1945.

Provincial Archives of Alberta; used by permission.

McCallum wrote in his history *CKUA and 40 Wondrous Years of Radio*. Two other announcers from the late 1940s—John O'Leary and Bob Willson—became part of the steady stream of CKUA people feeding into the CBC.

In 1945 Geoff Nightingale became CKUA's first news director. He not only covered local events but also expanded the station's coverage by travelling around the province for interviews.

Bryan Hall has told the story that as a young man he went to audition at CKUA one day when "I had some time on my hands." To his surprise, he was hired on the spot despite his lack of experience. He eventually hosted a Saturday afternoon jazz show, then moved on in 1955 to a career as a sports announcer, first as CJCA's "voice of the Edmonton Eskimos" and later as CHED's sports director.

In a reverse flow, sports commentator Art Ward moved from CFRN to CKUA in 1947 and stayed as CKUA's sports director until 1960. He was best known for his live broadcasts of Edmonton Flyer hockey games and of baseball games from Renfrew Park, and for his strong opinions and unique language. Don Rollans, who also arrived in 1947 and later became news director, said Ward "had a better command of the cliché than any man I've ever known. He had the widest assortment of ways to say 'puck'—such as 'biscuit' and 'rubber.' Nobody ever 'said' anything. They 'bantered' it."

Shirley Stinson provided another angle on sports in the late 1940s. A student at the University of Alberta, she wondered why women's sports weren't being covered on radio. "I was on the inter-varsity volleyball team, and it really distressed me that there was never any mention of what the women were doing in sports. This was way before feminism. I wasn't coming from a feminist point of view. There was just a logical gap—women's sports were not appropriately announced."

To correct that situation, Stinson joined U of A announcer Jim Redmond in reporting varsity sports from campus, thus becoming CKUA's first female sports announcer. She went on to earn a Ph.D. in higher education in nursing at Columbia University and racked up a host of other firsts in a long career as one of Canada's most distinguished nursing educators. She retired from the University of Alberta in 1993, having served as associate dean of graduate education and research development and as professor in the Faculty of Nursing and in the Department of Health Services in the Faculty of Medicine.

CKUA launched another first in 1947 when it sent Harry Carrigan to report from the Alberta Legislature. Carrigan provided the first direct reports from a provincial legislature press gallery in western Canada. CKUA's firsts were not always given due respect, however. According to Hagerman, others in the industry laughed when the station started broadcasting road and traffic reports in 1950.

In those days CKUA often did live remote broadcasts from events and locations around Edmonton. For example, station manager John Langdon's future wife Nelda Faulkner, an accomplished musician who had travelled Canada with the Young Artists Series, presented a weekly program of popular and classical organ solos from a downtown music store.

In the late 1940s North Americans were in the throes of a love affair with Hawaii and Hawaiian music played on the lap steel guitar. George Lake had taken the instrument up at age fourteen and by the time he was twenty-one had his own show, "Hawaiian Sunset," on CKUA. The show played for fifteen minutes three times a week from 1949 to 1952, opening with an invitation to "close your eyes for a moment as the surf rolls into the beach of Waikiki." A

◆ George Lake (in front) and the Hawaiians: (left to right) Dorothy Johnson, Dick Taylor, Con Ford and Joe Johnson. Courtesy of CKUA.

lot of listeners actually thought the program originated in Hawaii because they could hear the sound of the surf in the background. Lake picked up several other instruments and played in Edmonton's top clubs. After he finally set foot on Hawaiian soil in 1970, he was often invited to play his steel guitar in clubs and at luaus in the instrument's homeland.

One CKUA personality set a world record for his program's longevity. Gaby Haas immigrated to Canada from Czechoslovakia in 1939, carrying with him little more than his accordion and about forty recordings by great singers of pre-war Europe. He started his radio career that same year, playing his accordion on CKUA with other musicians.

In 1945 CKUA asked Haas to do a German-language program. Originally broadcast at the request of the government to assist German immigrants, the program consisted half of music and half of information about life in Canada. Although initially some listeners branded him a Nazi and complained about the show, Haas hosted the German program every Sunday for twenty-one years. He also did a live music show for CKUA called "The Sourdoughs," dedicated to the "pioneers of northern aviation."

In 1946 CKUA started "Continental Musicale," a program of European music to accommodate the great influx of immigrants after the war. Haas, who spoke six languages, hosted the program. On September 21, 1986 "Continental Musicale" went on the air for the 2,081st time, outdistancing a Wellington, New Zealand, radio program as the world's longest-running radio program with the same host and producer, on the same station, at the same time on the same day. "Continental Musicale" was a mixed bag of folk, pop and classical music from Haas' private collection, which eventually numbered more than fifty thousand records. These included some of his fifty-seven own recordings, such as the polka "Slap Your Maws and Clap Your Paws," and thousands of Swiss yodelling records. "Everybody likes our Swiss yodellers songs.... I could do the whole hour just of that," he once said.

CKUA expanded its ethnic language programming in the 1950s, providing airtime to several different groups. Erik Pedersen started producing the Danish portion of CKUA's Scandinavian program in 1952 with news and music from home. While his Norwegian and Swedish counterparts on the program received records from the national radio stations in their countries, Pedersen originally had to borrow records from his Danish friends. Later the local Danish community raised money through coffee parties so he could buy some 78s from Denmark. Among Danish program highlights over the years were Pedersen's interviews with the famous musician and comedian Victor Borge, who visited Edmonton several times on tour. In later years Norwegian consul Arne Johannessen and U of A Swedish instructor Marianne Morse co-anchored the Scandinavian program with him.

Carrigan, the legislature reporter, started an Irish program, which was later taken over by Sam Donaghey, a policeman and cartographer who had come over from Ireland in 1952. Well-known as "Mr. Soccer" in Edmonton and honorary chief of several Indian bands, Donaghey was named to the Order of Canada in 1981 for his contribution to amateur sports and his community service. CKUA also allotted fifteen-minute time slots to programs for the Ukrainian, Italian, Hungarian and Polish communities and aired a program of music from Great Britain for the English, Welsh and Scots.

◆ *Station manager John Langdon (left) and program director Ivor Roberts at the opening of the Athabasca Bridge.* Provincial Archives of Alberta PA 1631/8; used by permission.

"Many of the Europeans who did our ethnic programs had interesting, often traumatic backgrounds," recalled Kay Guthrie, who joined CKUA in 1969. She cited a Hungarian man who had defended Budapest's city hall with several of his countrymen for eleven days when the Soviet Union invaded his country in 1956.

School broadcasts continued to be an integral part of CKUA's programming. In the 1950s the provincial Department of Education was producing fifteen-minute broadcasts with both CKUA and the CBC, providing Alberta with the most extensive school broadcast program in Canada. Blake said that BBC officials told him that "our educational broadcasts were of a quality and excellence far superior to theirs at the time."

Many of the school broadcasts were dramas "and they were damned good," said John Langdon, who was station manager in the early 1950s. He had done some radio drama while a student at Wayne State University in Detroit, and wrote and directed many dramas during his time at CKUA. He recalled rehearsing the school broadcasts "in the middle of the night" and then recording them on sixteen-inch, acetate-coated discs. "Once you started them you couldn't stop, so you had to get it right the first time." Many Alberta schoolteachers were also involved in writing and producing the dramas.

In 1953 the provincial Department of Agriculture formed a radio and information branch and subsequently discontinued the "Farm and Home Forum" in favour of producing "Call of the Land," a ten-minute daily program of news and features for farmers. Interviews were taped in the department's offices and put together by CKUA, which then mailed copies to five other stations selected to distribute the program to rural Alberta. Fifty years later, CKUA was delivering the program by satellite and through its website.

The university continued its programs of "ideas and good music," including bi-monthly organ recitals from Convocation Hall and talks produced in its own studio in an army hut on campus under the direction, between 1945 and 1957, of Margery MacKenzie. Its most popular program by far was the daily "Music Hour," which by 1956 was believed to have had the "longest continuous career of a radio program in Canada." CKUA also broadcast music examinations live from the university, which proved a challenge, according to Langdon.

"It amounted to an awful lot of dead air when the examiners would write notes. I'd be trying to keep the dead air alive so listeners wouldn't think we were going off the air."

Langdon said the relationship between station management and the university was somewhat tentative during the first decade after the takeover by AGT. "They were afraid we were going to limit them, and we were afraid they would throw their weight around because they had the licence."

As a public service, CKUA regularly provided airtime—often in fifteen-minute segments—to a variety of organizations including the Red Cross, the March of Dimes, the City of Edmonton police department, the Canadian army, navy and air force, the Alberta Motor Association, the CNIB, Boy Scouts and Girl Guides, the federal and provincial departments of health and the Edmonton Symphony Society. The station also gave time to all religious denominations, including Jewish and Muslim, for special broadcasts, services and lectures.

Where CKUA's announcers in the 1940s and early 1950s were often inexperienced, the station's technical people were known to be among the best in the business. Almost legendary was Bill Pinko, who started as an

◆ Bill Pinko, *chief engineer—thrifty, resourceful and pure gold, ca. 1965.*
Courtesy of CKUA.

announcer/operator in 1937 and returned as radio engineer in 1946 after serving in the Canadian navy. At a station chronically short of funds, a man like Pinko, thrifty and resourceful, was pure gold. One time, in the late 1940s, he was driving to Saskatchewan on holidays when the station's only remote amplifier, at the Renfrew baseball park broadcast booth, was destroyed in a fire.

"Somehow they traced the place we had gone to, called me there and I was back on the road to Edmonton," Pinko recalled. "I was able to build another amplifier from an assortment of parts including some of my own out of my junk box. If my memory does not fail me we did not miss a game and I was back on the road to complete my vacation. As a point of interest there was no extra pay for my trip back, no overtime pay and I did not ask for payment for my parts that I had used. It was a tough time then with so many of us out of uniform looking for work and I was glad I was able to keep the broadcasts going."

Another time, Pinko returned to the station after taping a program at the University of Alberta using a portable generator only to discover the voices on the tape running at a high-speed squeak. He quickly assembled a three-storey length of power cord and ran it out the station's back window to the generator in the CKUA truck in the alley below. The program was broadcast on time and at the right speed.

"He [Pinko] was one of those Renaissance people," Hagerman recalled. "He used to just amaze me sometimes. He really hated, I think, to buy anything that he could build. If we needed a particular piece of gear, that was a real challenge for Bill."

Dan Key, who joined CKUA as a technician in 1952, said Pinko routinely custom-made his own capacitors and transformers, and maintained CKUA's FM transmitter well beyond the stage when parts were still available for it. "That little piece of machinery did yeoman service. Bill kept that thing together with bailing wire. He had it hooked up to a bicycle pump to keep the moisture out of the transmission line."

Langdon went so far as to credit Pinko with keeping CKUA on the air, calling him "probably the best technical man in the city." In fact, Pinko's counterparts at other stations sometimes called upon him for advice. Pinko served as CKUA's chief engineer until he retired in 1974.

Key operated CKUA's recording studio and was "a darned good recording engineer," Langdon said. The station had both microgroove and standard disc cutters and did virtually all the record cutting in Edmonton and for much of northern Alberta. This service was a revenue generator. Among CKUA's customers were figure skating clubs, which used the station's classical music library as a source for practice and performance music. Langdon recalled that every year at Christmastime, "we did lots of church choirs. It was quite a challenge fitting them into the studio." The station also recorded concerts and events on location around the city, including Edmonton Symphony Orchestra concerts.

In 1955, when the station moved into its present quarters in the Alberta Block on Jasper Avenue, Pinko designed the studios to fit the awkward space. The building was built in two halves, the back part six floors high and the front part, four. "All the floors slope," Hagerman said. "The higher you go in the building, the more they slope—not all the same way."

Five years earlier a move into a new building was the last thing the Alberta government had in mind for CKUA. In February 1950 a story in the *Edmonton Journal* said equipment from CKUA would be "on the block" shortly and "15 to 17 companies and individuals from Toronto to Vancouver are expected to submit tenders.... It is understood Mr. Blake is considering submitting a tender for the equipment." Blake, the station manager, had no comment to make. The net operating cost of the station was $58,650 a year, this at a time when the government had hoped to be making money on the station.

"They had finally given up on trying to get a commercial licence," Hagerman said. "And they figured, what the heck, they didn't need a radio station. So, dear old Ernie Manning announced that the assets were going to be sold. Of course, he got blasted from all directions. The whole thing just died a natural death. Nobody ever announced that they were not going to do it. They just didn't do it." The government had had its first run-in with a loyal and vocal CKUA listenership prepared to defend what to them had become something of a cultural treasure that was unique in Canada.

CKUA's listeners were "very possessive" of the station, Langdon said. Because of the station's emphasis on classical music, its listeners were different from those of other stations, he explained. For one thing, they were more knowledgeable. "Being more knowledgeable, they were more intense. The degree of classicism that we clung to was something that our listeners valued and were ready to protect—and at the same time ready to criticize."

One announcer tried to mobilize that protectionism to his own advantage and discovered CKUA listeners were not only passionately possessive but also reasonable. Alan Hood was outraged when management chopped five minutes off his classical music hour to accommodate an experiment in on-the-hour newscasts in 1952. At five minutes before the end of his hour, a few days before the new schedule was to go into effect, he identified the music he had just played: "'The March of David and His Friends against the Philistines,' from the *Carnaval* Suite by Schumann ... which music has a bearing on an announcement which now has to be made with regret that a proposal is on foot that the 'Music Hour' from one [o'clock] to two [o'clock] should be curtailed at five minutes to two for the reading of an additional news bulletin."

Hood urged listeners to protest this move by writing to the manager. The next day at the same time, he said, "I think the best thing to do is switch off now until two o'clock and let us consider in the four minutes that remain just what we are going to lose if our time is taken away from us. This is CKUA and the time is now three minutes to two." Three minutes of dead air followed.

Langdon said Hood also organized a protest rally at the station. "His fans showed up and they raved and ranted until—I think it was—Father Green

[Leo Green, the station's voice coach] told them that five minutes won't make or break the program if it's as good as they said it was. And the whole protest fell apart. People came to me later and apologized." Hood was subsequently fired. He went on to a successful career as an actor in Toronto.

Langdon had joined CKUA in 1947 as program manager in charge of school broadcasts and replaced Blake when the latter left in 1951 for a position with the Alberta Motor Association. He had a strong classical background and maintained good relations with the university.

He also set out to solidify CKUA's position with the government and correct long-standing areas of neglect that were due, he felt, to Blake's reluctance to "rock the boat." In April 1951 he presented "An Analysis of the Present Condition and Future Needs of Radio Station CKUA" to A.J. Higgins, the deputy minister of telephones, with copies to Premier Ernest Manning and Gordon Taylor, the minister of railways and telephones. His preamble got right to the point:

> It appears now that the uncertainty as to the disposition of Station CKUA has ended. As the manager, it appears to me that the next logical and immediate step should be to consider it a provincial radio station and operate it as such. The station costs approximately $60,000 a year at the present time and has been financed as an unofficial part of the Alberta Government Telephones budget. It has been the custom and the habit during the three years that I have seen the station in operation to cut expenses whenever and wherever possible for the very logical reason that the station is a liability. Treating it as a liability and operating it as such seems to have led inevitably to a minimizing of its potential value as a service to the people of the Province.

Langdon urged the government "to spend sufficient to make it one of the best stations in the Province." First, he wanted a new transmitter to improve reception in Calgary and the southeastern and southwestern parts of the province. The station also needed new tape-recording equipment because the machines it was using had been designed for home use. It also made sense, he pointed out, to purchase a car or a panel truck with the money the station was spending on taxis to cover "special events, concerts, church music and outside interviews."

◆ Vocal coach Bertha Biggs with Reg Shawcross in 1949. *Courtesy of CKUA.*

He also wanted an investment made in on-air staff:

> In the past, CKUA has looked upon itself as somewhat of a training school and it has been the custom to hire people for all kinds of radio station jobs who had no experience at all. Such people cost less, go into their jobs completely green and after a year or two, become quite capable. At this point, they are usually offered better jobs at correspondingly higher salaries than we are able to pay and many of them have gone on to distinguished careers in radio. The list of CKUA's alumni is a rather impressive one....
>
> It is very nice to be giving people a chance to develop their capabilities but the net result is that at least 2/3 of our staff is always made up of people who will someday be good in radio. I am afraid that listeners spend more time with their sets tuned to people who are already good.

As for his technical staff, Langdon said CJCA was offering a starting salary of $225 a month. "This is more than we pay our chief engineer (who incidentally is one of the best in the business) or our Program Director." And he had lost the services of "one of Canada's finest voice coaches" to other stations who could pay more. "This month we begin working with another very capable coach and certain members of the staff will improve ... or else." He was probably referring to Robert Goulet, who recalled Langdon reminding him, "Robert, there's a d and a t in 'Edmonton'." The new voice coach, Father Leo Green, tackled that problem after CKUA was no longer able to afford Bertha Biggs.

Langdon also tossed in a complaint about hand-me-down furniture from other departments. "There are few, if any, Government offices so shabbily furnished." He suggested an annual budget of eighty thousand dollars for the station.

Langdon got some satisfaction from the government, including modest raises for staff. During his four-year tenure, CKUA's annual budget went from $55,000 to $95,000. Even so, Langdon said he once felt compelled to moonlight and make himself a few extra dollars by scaling the transmitter tower to give it a new coat of paint. He had been acting manager for about a year without an increase in salary when Pinko recommended a coating of weather-proof paint for the transmitter and put the job out to tender.

"I figured the job didn't require any technical knowledge ... so I put in a bid a few dollars lower than the other bids, and I painted the whole darned tower myself. Of course, we didn't advertise the fact and AGT didn't know about it."

A former air force pilot, Langdon left CKUA in 1955 "to go flying," he said. "I got tired of CKUA, not that there was anything wrong with it—just that it pinned me down," he explained years later, after a long career in the North as a bush pilot working first for Max Ward and later for other companies. His letter of resignation suggests he was also dissatisfied with working under government control:

It has been made increasingly plain to me in the past few months, through personal interview and correspondence with the Honorable Gordon E. Taylor that the present government is not interested in a progressive radio station in which they can have pride of ownership.

The restrictions placed upon our operation and service to our listeners have produced conditions so stifling to imagination and ambition that I find them untenable. The type of operation which they have in mind is not for me.

Official correspondence shows that Taylor, whom Langdon didn't particularly like working for, had turned down two requests from CKUA in the months preceding Langdon's resignation. The first request was for authorization to hold a radio playwriting competition for Alberta's Golden Jubilee, and the second, for permission to interview the Social Credit leader of New Zealand. No reason for either decision was given.

However, "anything that was the slightest bit political was really *verboten* to us," Langdon said. "But if it was something in sports, we had no trouble getting co-operation." In fact, he said, Art Ward's remote hockey broadcasts were the largest item in CKUA's budget at the time. "We spent more money on sports and Art Ward than on anything else. Art himself had a loud mouth and banged on a lot of desks."

But in 1955 one of Ward's trips with the Edmonton Flyers apparently went too far. Taylor asked Langdon to explain how CKUA had financed hockey broadcasts by Ward from Montreal and Shawinigan Falls. Hagerman called the hockey episode a "schmozzle."

"The team [the Edmonton Flyers] did very well that year. By this time it was the farm team for the Detroit Red Wings ... and Art travelled east and we broadcast some final games.... There was some screaming going on in the Legislature that we were, in effect, being paid by the hockey club because they were paying the expenses to take Art down east ... that we were being paid by the hockey club to carry these broadcasts. And it was scandalous. That was the end of our hockey broadcasts."

However, Langdon's response to Taylor's query confirmed that "these [trips] were not sponsored nor was the cost defrayed by any group or individual." Ward transferred to the public relations department of AGT in 1960 due to a heart condition and died that year at age forty-eight.

Following Langdon's departure, Taylor appointed Jack Hagerman as acting manager.

The Joy of Benign Neglect | 7

Bob Rhodes remembers a young woman from Saskatoon by the name of Joni Anderson who came in to CKUA's studio sometime in the mid 1960s to record a song she had written called "Circle Game" to be played on his "Suddenly It's Folk Song" show. "She did many programs for us there, and we paid her nine bucks every time, mind you."

Herb Johnson, who was at CKUA between 1956 and 1968, called that period, only slightly facetiously, "the golden age."

Gil Evans remembered his thirteen years at CKUA, starting in 1956, as simply "magic."

"It was a *fabulous* place to walk into, the hippest place in town, absolutely the leading edge," Bill Coull recalled of the CKUA he found when he started working there part time in 1963.

Between 1956 and 1972 CKUA reinvented itself, taking on the eclecticism and intellectual playfulness that would become its trademark. In the process it began to attract announcers who saw CKUA as a home for their creative temperament rather than a gateway to greener pastures. In Jack Hagerman's words, "In the mid 1950s the station changed a lot.... During the late '40s and early '50s it had become something of a pale imitation of commercial radio."

When Hagerman took over the helm in 1955, CKUA wasn't quite sure what it was. In its quest for a commercial licence, the station had veered far off course from its arguably elitist extension department days. At this point it was a hybrid, providing classical music and educational programming not heard on other stations but also competing for audience share against commercial stations by offering a heavy dose of sports, news, pop and western music. This situation left it open to criticism from all directions. One disgruntled listener took exception to some of the popular programming at the time and wrote directly to Gordon Taylor, the minister of railways and telephones:

> We now have Western type music in the early mornings solidly until 7:30 a.m., followed by something called "Honky-Tonk Piano," after that things settle down into a normal course.... Why, oh why do we have to put up with news every hour (usually stale), and those appalling sportscasts which are shouted at us.... And of all things for the management to do, to cut down the restful dinner music "Candlelight and Silver" in order to make room for the 6:15 p.m. shouted sports which goes on for a solid 15 minutes. This is hardly helpful to digestion after a busy working day.

Asked to respond to this complaint and another similar one, Hagerman wrote that he also had letters on file from listeners who leaned in the other direction. "The policy of CKUA, since I arrived in Edmonton, has always been to attempt to please Albertans of all ages, types and persuasions." To accomplish this, the station divided its schedule into three approximately equal categories: classical and semi-classical music; popular music, "both western and otherwise"; and news, sports, talks and drama. A recent survey showed "we would please more people with popular music," Hagerman wrote, outlining the dilemma that would dog CKUA throughout its existence.

"Still we would be ignoring those who like classical music. The basic question is this: Do we want to reach a majority of Albertans or Do we want to provide only the services not provided by other stations." If the latter, "announcers would have to be of top calibre, to give the ring of honesty so

◆ Jack Hagerman had a hands-off management style that contributed to a "workshop" atmosphere when he was station manager.
Courtesy of CKUA.

necessary to the broadcasting of classical and information programs." (Hagerman's predecessor John Langdon recalled one announcer doing classical duty who, no matter how many coaching sessions he had, persisted in calling the composer Tchaikovsky, "Tichikowski.")

Hagerman provided *Maclean's* with the answer to the "basic question" in 1960: "Our policy is to please some of the people all of the time."

The decision to eschew the popular route was one pillar of CKUA's "golden age." Another was the move to hire announcers with a depth of knowledge and passion for music. The third was an external force: the social, political and musical revolution that was happening at the time. Folk music had taken on a political edge and was coming in for a revival on a wave of social and anti-war protest; a host of talented singer-songwriters and groups outside the mainstream were becoming available on recordings; and acid rock was bubbling up from underground. The last and perhaps most important pillar was what might be called an attitude of benign neglect on the part of management from the top down, starting with the Alberta government, which led to an unprecedented atmosphere of creative freedom at CKUA.

Hagerman said he had pretty much a free hand in running the station: "It was almost mine. AGT had really no interest. They would just as soon have been out from under it. They didn't really care, except that the general manager at AGT ... in my years usually took some pride in the radio station. They looked at it as something they were doing for the community that reflected well upon them. So, the end result was that they stayed out. The politicians were afraid of it—if they got involved in it, the opposition would be screaming 'political interference.' So they tended to tippy-toe. So, the end result was I ran it. And I ran it pretty much as my own kingdom."

This hands-off state of affairs came with one proviso, Hagerman said. "We could do all kinds of interesting things and nobody ever said nay. The only thing we had to remember was that we pretty much stayed out of politics. We didn't do much in the way of covering elections or anything like that in those years—basically because we had tremendous freedom otherwise. We didn't see any point in jeopardizing it. We didn't want to get into any schmozzles."

Hagerman himself had a hands-off management style, and he hired program directors—most notably Pat McDougall—who tended to trust the intelligence and taste of the announcers they hired. This attitude on the part of management exceeded even the wildest dreams of some of the idealistic young announcers who came into the CKUA fold during those years.

"Jack was a good manager," Herb Johnson said. "He had no rules that I can recall.... Those were the good old days. We were all young. Nobody paid very much attention to us.... We were sort of tucked away at the top of the Alberta Block.... We had a lot of freedom.

"Here's an example: Bob Rhodes and I decided we were too restricted. We were going to stay on after sign-off and do a program called 'The Program' and were going to play anything we wanted. We were just going to break loose and play anything we wanted. We did that three times—probably twice—then we stopped because we decided there wasn't anything we wanted to play that we couldn't play during the regular broadcast schedule, and there was really nothing to protest against. So we went back to just doing our job and having a good time."

Johnson was one of the announcers—along with Gil Evans—who "styled the station in the 1960s," according to Tony Cashman, who was program director from 1961 to 1969. Johnson had arrived at CKUA in 1956 at the age of twenty, realizing a long-time dream "to be a jazz disc jockey." He was chief announcer at twenty-two and stayed until 1968, becoming known as "Edmonton's Mr. Jazz." Years later, he looked back at that seminal time at CKUA and called it "probably the best job I ever had."

Cashman said of Johnson, "He had a tremendous taste. He had a tremendous knowledge.... He pretty well introduced jazz.... He had an intuition for it.... He also had a non-threatening delivery, so he could convey his knowledge and understanding to people." Johnson hosted, among other programs, a jazz show called "Five O'Clock Whistle" and a mixed music program called "Johnson's Wax." He also shared a two-hour Saturday program with Tommy Banks called "Music for Moderns," featuring "the newest and latest in jazz."

Regarding "Johnson's Wax," Hagerman recalled a visit one day from the regional Department of Transport radio inspector. "He was almost dictatorial—belligerent as hell—and he swung a lot of weight. He never ceased to ride our tails. He came in one day unannounced and said he'd had a report that we were carrying commercial content. I was puzzled as to what that could be, and he wasn't about to tell me. Then it dawned on me." Hagerman explained to the inspector that there was an announcer named Herb Johnson who did a program called "Johnson's Wax."

"Well, he became very embarrassed and excused himself and disappeared. And he never bothered us again."

Ed Kilpatrick was another of the new breed. Described by many as a Renaissance man, Kilpatrick had a deep knowledge of classical music and opera in particular. He arrived at CKUA in 1958 with no previous experience in radio, having come to Edmonton from Moose Jaw with an oilfield supply firm. He didn't get the first job he applied for at CKUA, but his keen interest in the station led to one of the most unusual job offers in CKUA history. He was driving to Calgary one day when an opening at the station came up unexpectedly. Hagerman phoned the number Kilpatrick had left and was told he was on the road. Hagerman then had Johnson, who was on the air at the

◆ Ed Kilpatrick was hired by "car radio" in the late 1950s.

Courtesy of CKUA.

time, broadcast a plea for Kilpatrick to phone the station. Of course, Kilpatrick had his car radio tuned to CKUA, and he reported for work the next day. He remained until his retirement almost thirty years later.

Many who listened to CKUA at the time say Gil Evans set the tone for the station. Hagerman had hired Evans in a Vancouver parking lot.

"I was working at Canada Dry [ginger ale] and I was going to university.... I had a friend ... Bill Wynne, who was the chief announcer at CKUA at the time," Evans recalled. "One of the announcers quit while Jack was on his vacation out here, and Bill told him about me, and Jack came out and interviewed me in the parking lot at Canada Dry during my lunch break." Hagerman hired Evans on the spot, and the new announcer was on the air before his boss returned from his holidays.

Evans already had a history with CKUA: he had been a choir boy singing in the All Saints Cathedral Choir on Vernon Barford's program in the 1930s. He had also been involved with the University of British Columbia Radio Society.

◆ Gil Evans in the main control room, 1960. *Courtesy of CKUA.*

A 1962 profile in *Edmonton Week* describes Evans as "the quiet morning man." Cashman said of Evans, "He had a very gentle outlook on life and a great taste and appreciation for a lot of things, which he could convey. He had a very nice, sort of non-threatening style. Most commercial announcers … were rather aggressive. Gil really established a kind of an atmosphere that mature people responded to. I think, before this, mature people were sort of turned off by the callow enthusiasm of amateurs at CKUA."

As CKUA reinvented itself, there was no longer a place for western music on the program schedule, Evans said. "We got rid of the 'Western Wagon' on Saturday night and turned that space into, eventually, a program that was my favourite: music for the mood of the season, 'Music for an Autumn (Winter, Spring, Summer) Night'…. The program had to have—like a story—a beginning, a middle and an end. The things you wanted to play, you had to figure out a way to have them make some kind of logical link. And when that worked, that was such a great pleasure…. I would start at 6:45, and at 8:00 I would finish and I'd say, 'The whole thing made sense.'"

An example was Evans' "Music for a Winter Night" for December 7, 1968. Listeners heard, in succession, Dave Brubeck, "40 Days"; Pro Musica, Spanish

◆ *Program director Tony Cashman in 1967. Courtesy of CKUA.*

medieval music; Joan Baez, "Annabel Lee"; Wes Montgomery, "Day in the
Life"; Don Shirley, "Waterboy"; Gabor Szabo, "San Francisco Nights"; Antonio
Carlos Jobim, "The Red Blouse"; and Blood, Sweat & Tears, "Without Her."

The program was typical of the eclectic mixed format that CKUA pioneered
in the late 1950s and early 1960s and that others would copy. Radio stations
in the 1950s adhered to a block programming style—thirty minutes of one
type of music followed by thirty minutes of another type. Then the familiar
"Top 40" format swept North America in the mid 1950s and stations went to
formats, playing a particular type of music twenty-four hours a day.

"The idea was you had just one program running 168 hours a week—
absolutely no creativity," Cashman said. "So, commercial radio became more
and more format radio, and CKUA became more creative, more searching."
Instead of a format, the station maintained what Cashman called "a kind of
workshop atmosphere."

Evans and Johnson credited Pat McDougall for paving the way for the
change. "I remember an announcers' meeting where Pat McDougall ... said,

◆ Pat McDougall had a
hand in designing the CKUA
mural on the side of the
Alberta Block on Edmonton's
Jasper Avenue in the
late 1950s.
Courtesy of CKUA.

'You think you could do a program without playing Stan Kenton and June
Christie and Frank Sinatra?'" Evans recalled. "So that was the start of it."

McDougall also wanted the general music programs, particularly the
morning program, to reflect the whole station, Evans said. "So that meant
that the music should be as wide an eclectic mix as you could possibly imagine
a way to fit it in." Johnson's "Club Matinée" in the late 1950s, offering "variety
music—jazz, classics, folk—in his own inimitable fashion," was an early
example of the new mixed programming. Of course, there always would be
blocks of a single genre, too, such as "Dixie Flyer," a Dixieland jazz program.

The changes didn't escape the notice of Sev Sabourin, a young Alberta
French-Canadian who aspired to a career in radio.

"I recall listening to CKUA in the '50s ... and CKUA had large blocks of
classical and jazz and pop music. Then ... I was going to university in '62–63
and I was getting up to CKUA in the morning, and Gil Evans had the morning
program and I noticed that he was playing a mix of music. At that time the
folk revival—the Joan Baez kind of thing—was just happening ... and he
started to mix the classical with the folk, and the pop sort of went out the door."

◆ *Announcer and producer Sev Sabourin, 1974.*
Courtesy of CKUA.

Sabourin took advantage of a training program for announcers that McDougall ran in 1959, but at the time his French accent kept him out of the running for a job. After more training he was hired in 1968, beginning what would be a thirty-year career in radio, most of it at CKUA.

When Alex Frame arrived at CKUA in 1963 from the CBC in Yellowknife, he found "a unique environment" where the programs were essentially vehicles of self-expression for an "extraordinarily diverse" mix of personalities. The personality who stood out as "the most inventive" was Bob Rhodes, Frame recalled. Rhodes, who was with CKUA from 1960 to 1967, had a passion for folk and roots music. His "Back to the Roots" program typified the increasingly alternative style of the station. For one program, to illustrate the origins of reed instruments, he managed to find a recording of two girls playing grass leaves.

Another CKUA announcer who brought a passion for music to the job was John Runge, a former colleague of Frame's in Yellowknife. Runge had come to CKUA in the early 1960s and was best known for his "House of Runge" show.

◆ John Runge is interviewed by Keith Watt, ca. 1988. *Courtesy of* CKUA.

"What was remarkable about him is [that] his love of music was very particular to him," Frame recalled. "You couldn't say that he loved just jazz or just this. But what really used to excite—when he found a piece of music that excited him, he was a missionary about it. And what he loved to do on that show ... was to develop a relationship between music. It was so important to him that one piece of music followed another piece of music, that every night that he was on that show he was actually creating a piece of audio art, and it was really wonderful to behold."

"Audio artist" and "missionary," rather than "disc jockey," may be the best terms to describe the new breed of announcer that populated CKUA in the 1960s. The announcers certainly saw themselves this way. Note how Johnson, for example, described the "fairly tricky" process of eclectic programming:

> If I may be so bold ... I think you have to have really good ears to do it and you have to understand—you have to listen to the music from an emotional perspective. That's what music is basically—it's a feeling.

Now, if you can get the same feeling from a piece of classical, a piece of jazz, a piece of folk, if it gives you the same feeling ... then you can put those pieces of music together.

You can't approach eclectic programming from the perspective that this piece of music is about rivers and so is this one and this piece of music has got "river" in the title, and all of these three pieces of music are about rivers, therefore we can put them on the same show.

Eclectic programming became an art form at CKUA long before it was adopted by other stations, most notably the CBC. When Alex Frame moved on to produce such programs as "This Country in the Morning" with Peter Gzowski for CBC Radio in Toronto (he would later become vice-president of CBC Radio), he hired Rhodes and Johnson.

"Herb and I had this idea of starting a program where we'd mix a lot of things up—a lot of different folk tunes, serious work, jazz and so on—something we'd been doing at CKUA for years," Rhodes recalled. "Herb came up with the title 'Eclectic Circus.' It was my idea to do the program. It lasted for twenty years—not too bad for a couple of guys from CKUA who just wanted to mix some tunes up."

As for missionary zeal, Johnson described how he and others approached their work at CKUA: "At the time I was: 'jazz is good for you, everybody should listen to it.' ... I mean, good music is good for you, and that was a very strongly held opinion amongst all the staff. We considered ourselves guardians of the faith, crusaders.... We may have got a little out of line from time to time—a little snotty about it. I don't know. It's possible."

Sabourin admitted that when he started at CKUA, "there was a certain kind of haughtiness, a certain kind of elitism, that really bugged me.... I mean, I was a country and western fan before I came to CKUA. In my teens, that's what I was listening to.... I have nothing against people saying we shouldn't have country and western on this station, but to say it's garbage and it's just a bunch of yokels who listen to it, well, I didn't like that attitude at all."

Nevertheless, the intensity of the programmers at the station in those days inspired the next generation of CKUA announcers. Bill Coull, who would be a mainstay of the station through the turn of the millennium, said that when he was very young, he heard Johnson and Banks on "Music for

◆ Bill Coull, host of "Coull Jazz," 1968. *Courtesy of CKUA.*

Moderns" and knew that radio was what he wanted to do for the rest of his life. A rock and jazz musician himself, Coull landed a part-time job at CKUA in 1963 at age eighteen while he was still a student at the University of Alberta, where he worked at the campus radio station. Within a few years, he and Runge took over "Music for Moderns," and by the end of the decade, he had his own daily show, "The Groove," playing rock, blues and jazz.

During the 1960s CKUA's crusading announcers introduced their listeners—who went along, sometimes kicking and screaming—to the exciting new influences in music that they wouldn't hear on commercial stations till later, if ever. Runge said CKUA was one of the first stations in Canada to expose listeners to the music of Charles Ives, Gustav Mahler and Eric Satie. The first Columbia recording of a young folksinger named Bob Dylan, he said, "brought more phone calls to the station saying 'Who is this guy? He'll never get anywhere. He's terrible.'"

Coull said that once in the early 1960s when he was filling in for Runge, he played "Michelle" by the Beatles. "This was so daring because CKUA never played any popular music.... It just was never done. It was absolutely insane. The phones just started ringing and they never stopped ringing ... complaint, complaint, complaint, complaint, complaint."

Cashman remembered a night when Evans did an hour-long program on the Beatles, providing analysis of "some of the more cerebral work that wasn't played on other stations. There were some complaints from listeners. Some listeners were offended. But [overall] it was well received. When things were presented in a way that mature people would accept, it made it possible to do a lot of things. People like Herb Johnson, Gil Evans and Bob Rhodes could do that."

CKUA listeners then, as always, provided checks and balances, appreciating the station's uniqueness—its sign-on was "You are listening to Canada's unique station, CKUA in Edmonton"—but keeping it from going off the creative deep end. The late Banff poet Jon Whyte, who worked as a summer replacement for various announcers between 1960 and 1964, wrote, "Our listeners then, like CKUA's listeners today [1978], had a benevolent proprietary interest in the station's welfare. They knew the formulas better than we did, and were keen to keep us in line."

Whyte recalled working as a replacement on Johnson's "Five O'Clock Whistle" jazz program: "I used to include my own small segment which I called 'Music for Mouldy Figs,' a one-track selection from Duke Ellington in his Cotton Club Days or 'In A Mist' by Bix Beiderbecke, and the outpouring of outrage was sublime. It was okay to be avant-garde, but not too avant-garde or derrière garde."

But CKUA didn't entirely forego the "derrière garde," and the music wasn't always edgy. The likes of Maurice Chevalier, Lawrence Tibbett and Ukulele Ike could be heard on "Music for Mom & Dad," a Sunday morning program of pre-1940s songs. "The Old Disc Jockey" made his first appearance on Cashman's watch, spinning his big band music from the late 1920s through the 1950s. Various announcers were responsible for the program, until John Worthington (a.k.a. Jack Hagerman) took it over in 1974. The program was still going strong in 2002.

A program called "Showtime" featured music of Broadway and London's West End. "Candlelight and Silver," to the dismay of purists on staff, was a venue for the lighter classical sounds of Mantovani, the Melachrino Strings and Percy Faith. Runge raged against "schmaltz" and wanted to drop the popular dinner program, according to Cashman.

"Some took it a bit too seriously. Some didn't respect the rights of listeners who liked the schmaltz. We didn't have that many listeners, so we couldn't afford to offend them." Cashman said Runge left the station "in a huff" at some point and that "it was all about schmaltz."

However, Bill Coull remembered Runge's departure differently. According to Coull, Cashman had a habit of micromanaging, sometimes revising scripts in mid-program for announcers who were live on air. One Saturday afternoon, Coull said, he received a call from Runge, who was on air. Runge said he had just put a record on and was walking out.

"He said, 'That's it. I'm walking out of here. You've got to be here in twenty minutes ... I've got a record that's playing here for twenty minutes.'" According to Coull, Runge said he had just phoned Cashman and told him off. "He said, 'I'm leaving .... I'm going to Bermuda.'"

After working in radio elsewhere, including the CBC, Runge returned to CKUA and was part of management when he died in 1990. Edmonton Journal entertainment columnist Alan Kellogg, who was a CKUA announcer for a while himself, wrote of Runge as "a genuine lover of music ... an approachable sort who always had an encouraging word for young, aspiring radio types."

A diverse collection of unique personalities was one key to CKUA's dynamic in the 1960s, Frame observed. Another was the station's connection with Edmonton's cultural and intellectual communities, in particular the university community. "CKUA always had a very small listening audience, but it had a connection with the cultural community and it had a connection with the intellectual community in Edmonton, where there was a frequent flow-through of people, coming in and out of the station.... In the early '60s, CKUA was part of Edmonton's intellectual environment—and those were days of great intellectual turmoil—and the relationship between the station and the university community was quite a remarkable one."

In 1956 the university had been experiencing difficulty filling its allotted time without undue pressure on its radio program staff. Consequently, it had reduced its scheduled broadcast time to six hours a week for its very popular "Music Hour" (often hosted by drama students looking for extra income) and "Saturday Evening Concert," plus fifteen minutes a day Monday through Friday for "University Talks."

But the intellectual influence of the university was very much evident in CKUA's own programming. In 1968, for example, two university psychology professors, Dirk Schaeffer and Kellogg (Kelly) Wilson, were hosting "Mainstream Plus," featuring unusual jazz records, and Bill Titland, a U of A teaching assistant, provided "A Guide to Understanding Progressive Rock Music." Schaeffer later did regular film reviews for CKUA. Many other university people were involved in CKUA features during those and later years.

Gil Evans, on his "Gil Again" and "Ten-to-One" shows, among the many music and talk programs he presented over the years, explored the nooks and crannies of contemporary ideas and issues. He featured local commentaries and interviews as well as imported recorded talk programs. Two Edmonton housewives, Jenny Bell and June Sheppard (later to become an *Edmonton Journal* columnist), contributed an interview segment called "Conversation Piece," which often explored controversial issues. Sheppard recalled the angry response to a program on wife battering and child abuse she aired with local environmental activist Mary Van Stolk: "A member of the Law Society said we were sensationalizing something for which there was no proof in Canada." But CKUA was no newcomer to controversy: in the early 1960s, a documentary on homosexuality had attracted calls from offended listeners.

A typical week of "Ten-to-One" in 1968 featured a conversation with Hagan Beggs, an actor with Edmonton's Citadel Theatre, including a tape of a "music-art experiment" with Beggs and five musicians "improvising reactions as a painter works on stage"; a preview of a play opening at the university's Studio Theatre, delivered by Frank Buechert, a U of A professor of drama; an interview with Alberta author Robert Kroetsch on his new book *Alberta*; Richard Frucht, an assistant professor of anthropology from the U of A talking on "Alternatives"; June Sheppard interviewing Stewart Boston of the University of Calgary on racial tensions in Kenya; and Ron Wigmore, assistant manager of Edmonton's Jubilee Auditorium, "Talking About Theatre" with professor Bernard Engel.

Thought-provoking imported material on Evans' programs included a series of conversations with C. Northcote Parkinson (of Parkinson's law fame) from the Academic Recording Institute, exploring "the inexorable burgeoning of bureaucracy, the phenomenon of war, and the cyclical progression of governments from democracy through dictatorship"; and a Broadcasting

Foundation of America program featuring Barbara Ward on "Poverty and the Problem of World Education."

Adding to the workshop atmosphere, Evans introduced a series on his show called "Thinking Out Loud," featuring free-wheeling gab sessions among himself, Van Stolk and two others active in Edmonton's media and cultural community—Reevan Dolgoy and Fil Fraser, both of whom would later become CKUA announcers. The group would get together after Evans finished his Saturday night show and start talking about various issues with a tape recorder running.

"The four of us—this was the '60s, right?—we all thought we could save the world," Fraser said thirty-five years later. "[We would] sit around the table and talk, sometimes for three or four hours, about all the stuff that was going on in the world.... We'd talk without a focus, then somebody would say something that would set us off intensely arguing.... And we'd deliver three or four hours of tape on Monday morning."

The following week, about half an hour of that tape would air on Evans' program. Although his subsequent career would include producing and directing feature films as well as positions as Alberta's human rights commissioner and as president of VisionTV in Toronto, Fraser said the time he spent thinking out loud for CKUA "was some of the most exhilarating stuff I've done—we were involved, committed young idealists."

Evans said the changes and additions to CKUA's programming in those days were "not made capriciously, casually or informally but came out of the endless bull sessions that the announce staff had amongst ourselves and with the station's freelancers ... and discussions with friends and others in the community. Working at CKUA gave us easy access to everyone in music, theatre, the arts, academia and beyond.... The program changes that we implemented were founded on a respect for why there was a CKUA—that it had been founded to 'Bring the University of Alberta to the people' ... [and] were predicated on returning CKUA to its original purpose but in keeping with the times.... "

Evans said that when he first started including talk in the morning schedule, Hagerman raised his eyebrows.

"Jack said, 'We can't have talk in the morning.' And I said, 'Why not, Jack?' I wasn't getting that much feedback from the audience but I was getting inquiries from people—young women who were stuck at home

◆ Tony Dillon-Davis in the 1970s. *Courtesy of CKUA.*

raising families—and they wanted something more than just music all the time. They wanted something for their minds, and so we changed that and we got rid of the western music [he laughs]...."

The talk was much appreciated by at least one young Edmonton mother. Bette Paterson recalled being delighted to discover CKUA when she and her husband arrived in Alberta in the early 1960s. "I didn't know anybody—I felt so isolated," she said of her first brutal Alberta winter spent housebound with young children. "CKUA was a lifesaver for me."

Tony Dillon-Davis, another Edmonton newcomer and CKUA listener in the mid 1960s, recalled being impressed hearing Evans and Sheppard talking in the mornings. "What was interesting about that was that they were talking about real stuff. They were talking about philosophical issues, they were talking about social issues, and they were discussing them. They weren't giving a news report on them—they were discussing the issues."

But something else that Evans did really astonished Dillon-Davis. "One of the first things I remember hearing on CKUA was Gil Evans coming on and saying, 'Now we're going to play this and this man is very persuasive, and I want you to sit back and listen to it, but listen to it with a very critical ear.'

And what he was going to play ... was Timothy Leary doing 'Turn On, Tune In, Drop Out.' And I remember he played the whole thing on the air. And I remember hearing that on a morning—it was a late morning—and it was an astonishing experience to hear that.... CKUA then impressed me as a place of possible intellectual activity, and that's what I *did* find."

He also found a new job, one that would last for the next three decades and beyond. Cashman hired Dillon-Davis in 1967, and the rookie quickly became a leader in CKUA's ongoing revolution.

"Tony came from Nanaimo and looked just like an English schoolboy, in a short jacket and skinny tie," Cashman recalled. "Tony was a real radical. I didn't realize it.... He was always playing songs about cops being pigs. I had to tone him down a bit."

Dillon-Davis started with Saturday night duty on a program called "Dance Time" that all the announcers at the time had cut their teeth on featuring what Dillon-Davis called "some of the dreckiest music of the period."

"It was designed for parties in the early 1950s among nice middle-class people who remembered Frank Sinatra with the Dorsey Brothers ... and it didn't work. ... It was one of those classic things where something had outlived its time....

"I didn't get the impression that anybody was listening ... I started running this new rock music and getting calls almost immediately from people saying, 'Wow! What is this stuff?' They loved it. Many of them were into the counterculture. They had the records, which weren't being played anywhere."

Dillon-Davis was mostly using his own records for the program—Jefferson Airplane, Moby Grape. "The acid rock and all that sort of stuff that I threw on Saturday night ... didn't fit in any program description that CKUA had ... I went completely out—took CKUA off the rails completely with it."

Program director Cashman eventually got some complaints, Dillon-Davis said. "They must have really got up his wick, because he called me up and said, 'Go from ten o'clock until one o'clock, and go into orbit!' ... And I'm sitting there, and I say, 'That's fine, Tony,' after hanging up the phone, not wishing to look a gift manager in the mouth....

"There's only one small problem: we have no music."

So Dillon-Davis appealed to his audience and managed to fuel his underground program with recordings loaned by avid listeners "bringing in their albums for me to play on the air, until we could order them. It was phenomenal. We always had the first ones." Dillon-Davis' program, "Mod Shop," ran from 10:15 p.m. to 2:00 a.m. and featured such performers as Jimi Hendrix, Country Joe & the Fish, the Beatles and Donovan.

When counterculture youth discovered a home at CKUA, their younger brothers and sisters already had a corner all their own. For almost the whole thirteen years he was with CKUA, Evans presented "Kiddies' Korner," Edmonton's only English-language children's radio program. Never talking down to his listeners, Evans encouraged them to call him "Ol' Gil."

A sampling of other programs during this era turns up a biography of Machiavelli, a three-hour summary of a royal commission report on education, a program produced in collaboration with CHFA on the "Quiet Revolution" in Quebec, and Kurt Weill's *Threepenny Opera* in the original German.

For a while, around 1960, Tommy Banks did a weekly live piano show, "The Solo Piano of Tommy Banks." "I'd lurch into the studio on Sunday morning and go and set up the microphone and turn everything on and then sit down and start playing," Banks recalled.

The station carried complete operas by the Alberta Opera Society from the Northern Alberta Jubilee Auditorium and the complete two-and-a-half-hour performance by the Edmonton Choral Society of Handel's *Messiah*. CKUA worked closely with such groups to publicize their performances, in line with its mandate to promote local and Canadian talent. On Sundays, Dan Key and Jon Whyte would hang a microphone from the ceiling of the Jubilee Auditorium and tape the Edmonton Symphony Orchestra's concert, then drive back to the station and present the symphony "almost live." This practice ended in the mid 1960s, according to Cashman, "when the union decided they had to get paid for doing the broadcast." When Runge and Coull were hosting "Music for Moderns," the program often featured music recorded live at the original Yardbird Suite, where Edmonton's jazz *aficionados* congregated.

In the 1960s CKUA had become the crossroads of cultural and intellectual activity in Edmonton. Well-known music and entertainment personalities who came to town, such as Stan Kenton and the Smothers Brothers, were often corralled into studio interviews and, while they were at it, into signing their autographs on the cover of the station's grand piano. Soon-to-be known entertainers, such as Joni Mitchell, came in and played live or recorded their music for the station's going rate of nine dollars a session, happy for the exposure. When American satirist and civil rights activist Dick Gregory spoke at the University of Alberta Students' Union Building in 1968, CKUA's technicians recorded his talk for the station's "Speaker of the Week" program. That same year, CKUA taped a "teach-in" at the university about student participation on arts faculty committees and broadcast it a few days later.

Sundays presented a mix of classical and semi-classical programs, including the long-running "Sunday Breakfast." In the early 1960s there was pipe organ music recorded by CKUA technicians in Edmonton churches, as well as religious programming such as "Sparks of Truth" by Rabbi Louis Sacks, selections by the Mormon Tabernacle Choir introduced by a local Mormon elder, and a program called "Showers of Blessing." The Sunday schedule was also peppered with ethnic programs along with Gaby Haas' "Continental Musicale." By 1965 every Sunday thirty remote Cree and Métis communities in northern Alberta were receiving news of interest to them from CKUA in Cree.

CKUA listeners in the late 1950s and early 1960s also heard programs produced in Paris by the French broadcasting system, including "French in the Air" and "Masterworks from France," and programs from the BBC, among them dramas on "World Theatre," comedy on the "Goon Show" and mental gymnastics on the popular "My Word" panel program. Listeners were also introduced to the intellectual satirical comedy coming out of Chicago's Second City and San Francisco's Hungry I, including routines by Shelly Berman, Mort Sahl, and Mike Nichols and Elaine May. But some listeners didn't get the joke.

The telephones minister received a complaint from an Edmonton woman in 1962 about "sick comic" routines, in particular "An Evening with Mike Nichols and Elaine May": "The sponsor was I believe Johnson's Wax. The dialogue was in the poorest possible taste, and verged on the blasphemous."

One unique program was "Operation Lift," for persons using wheelchairs. It was broadcast weekly from the home studio of Gordon Stewart, who was himself incapacitated by multiple sclerosis. Alberta nature writer Kerry Wood taped "Outdoors with Kerry Wood," an informed look at the animals and environment of Alberta, at his farm near Red Deer.

Some popular CKUA programmers didn't even live in Alberta. Matt Hedley, who started at CKUA in 1951, produced a classical program called

"World of Music" using his own enormous record collection. When his day job as a machinist took him to San Francisco in 1958, he continued the program, sending tapes from his home in California from 1959 to 1987. According to Brian Dunsmore, who came to CKUA later, Hedley was known for "accurate, informative, intelligent annotation to works not heard anywhere on the dial." Another popular announcer, known as DeKoven, sent his program of music of the baroque and rococo on tape from New York, adding "OTW" (out of this world) to the everyday vocabulary of his Alberta listeners.

Bucking the popular trend towards frequent, short news updates, CKUA ran its news reports in full, factual ten- to fifteen-minute segments. One news announcer was Jim Edwards, who later became general manager of CFRN and still later a member of Parliament and then head of Economic Development Edmonton. Cashman said Edwards had a flair for repackaging three-hour BBC dramas with appropriate music at intervals to revive lagging attention spans.

Jon Whyte admired Edwards for another ability that Whyte discovered after he had been working for CKUA "for precisely thirty minutes." Whyte had just turned off a tape recorder when "the air was filled with the Nike-like buzzing of the signal that screamed the transmitter was off the air. CKUA wasn't exactly put together with chicken wire in those days, but there were a lot of gizmos, whatzits, whachamacallits, and thingumabobs that had been developed by Bill Pinko and Dan Key that had no correspondence in other radio stations. One of them had chosen to fail as audaciously as a tumble from bed during a first seduction."

Jim Edwards had just arrived to read the news. "Edwards, sleek and professional as a TCA pilot, saw my face, a mask of terror, and knew, though he could hear nothing in the solitary insulation and isolation of his booth, that a catastrophe had occurred. In one swift flight he made it through both pairs of the double sealed doors from his booth to mine, cuffed the path-panel with the heel of his hand, and nothing happened. So he gave the whole panel a soccer-player's kick, and something clicked; the mike stopped screaming, and the station was back on the air. 'I'll explain later,' he shouted, as he headed back to the announce booth."

Overwhelmingly, the common theme among announcers who worked at CKUA during the years between 1956 and 1972 is the freedom they experienced. Decades later, Bill Coull still marvelled at the government's apparent disinterest in its radio station. He recalled a time in the early 1970s when film reviewer Dirk Schaeffer decided listeners needed to be "desensitized" to four-letter words and convinced Kilpatrick to let him purposefully insert them into his film reviews. According to Coull, CKUA's young rebels played "anything that had four-letter words, or religious references, anything that was offensive to the Pope or who the hell else wants to be offended—we offended them. A lot of the things that happened reflected a youth sensibility because we were youthful in those days. We were all around twenty to twenty-five years old."

Even so, he said, "Those guys [AGT] just basically sat in the background and paid the bills. Jack kept them at bay.... Hell, you've got a bunch of fundamentalist Christians ... running around, running the government and your life.... Somehow we managed to squeak by all this stuff. We were constantly at the vanguard, tilting at windmills, real guerillas."

Frame called those years at CKUA "an extraordinary time. I haven't been in a place since where I felt as free as I did there or as stimulated by my colleagues, and that was probably largely due to the environment but may also have had to do with my age." Frame was responsible for reading news and hosting a classical music program, but he also produced a series of programs out of the Banff School of Fine Arts. "As long as I worked my shift, I was free to do whatever else I wanted to, more or less." He credited his CKUA experience with providing the direction his career would take as a CBC Radio producer.

When Evans left in 1969, there was talk of his possibly going to the CBC, too. "But I'd done everything I needed to do in broadcasting. I'd had this golden opportunity of going to the station where I was allowed to do whatever I could imagine. So what else was there to do?" On a tape made for CKUA's sixty-fifth anniversary, he summed up his experience on what he called "the last of the steam-operated radio stations: I always regarded my time at CKUA as a privilege. Radio was, and still is, a magic space to me. My days at CKUA were almost always a delight."

Dillon-Davis cast a more critical eye on those free-wheeling days. "There was a lot of garbage on CKUA then, too. We had virtually nobody listening to us so we could do what we liked, and we produced some of the worst radio in the history of broadcasting—and some of the best, I think. But I'm not going to pretend that those 'golden years' were unmitigated pleasure or that somehow we were putting out all this wonderful stuff then. I mean, we put out some pretty awful stuff then, too. I did some of it myself."

Although few in numbers compared to commercial radio audiences, CKUA's listeners tended to be more forgiving. Looking back on the AGT years from the vantage point of an entirely different era in the mid 1980s, *Edmonton Journal* editorial writer and acid-tongued critic Bill Thorsell wrote,

AGT hardly knew it was there, and that was the secret of CKUA's delightful personality. CKUA lived on its own, like a club of moderate eccentrics who believed in a rare kind of radio—not too premeditated, and infused with a spirit of humanism and care for detail.

The Politics of the "Golden Age" | 8

While most CKUA announcers appreciated their freedom, some criticized Jack Hagerman's hands-off management style as no management at all. But Gil Evans saw it differently.

"I remember Jack being in there on weekends, preparing budgets and all kinds of stuff—what he was supposed to do.... He looked after making sure that we had the best equipment that we could afford, that was available. He made sure that we had an unlimited budget to buy records, which was incredibly important to us. I'd walk into Modern Music and Martin Bernstein [record shops], and I'd walk out with several hundred dollars' worth of records, and nobody ever said anything.... I think Jack knew what he was doing and that he gave people their head."

Behind the scenes Hagerman had his work cut out for him. Despite the listener uproar in 1950, CKUA still wasn't on secure footing with the provincial government, which kept pressing for commercial status and transfer of the licence from the university.

In 1953 then station manager John Langdon had made a submission to the CBC board of governors opposing an application by Hugh M. Sibbald to operate a commercial broadcasting station in Edmonton on the basis of the CBC's continuing refusal to let CKUA do the same. Around the same time, CKUA applied for a private commercial television broadcasting licence. The CBC board approved Sibbald's application and rejected CKUA's on the grounds that provincial governments could not own and operate broadcast stations.

Gordon Taylor, the minister of telephones, gave vent to the Alberta government's frustrations in a May 1956 submission to the Royal Commission on Broadcasting, struck to examine and make recommendations concerning the whole area of sound and television broadcasting in Canada. He called the existing situation, in which the CBC had authority to operate radio stations across Canada and to regulate its competitors, "a jumble of socialism and free enterprise with the socialist side having all of the authority.... The same Government has ordained that other Governments in Canada must not be given equal or equivalent opportunities to operate. It is well and good for the Federal Government; it seemingly is evil and bad for Provincial Governments!"

The Alberta government's submission took particular exception to a CBC regulation prohibiting network broadcasting, apart from the CBC networks, without CBC approval, and a regulation that disallowed broadcast appeals for donations and subscriptions by organizations other than universities, charitable institutions, not-for-profit arts organizations and "churches or religious bodies permanently established in Canada *and serving the area covered by the station* [emphasis added]," without written approval by the CBC. The submission points out that when the latter regulation was first proposed in 1953, churches were not listed in the exceptions.

"At that time the Government of Alberta made strong and strenuous representations and urged that, at least, churches and religious bodies be placed in the exceptions.... But, our recommendation was accepted only in part as the restrictive words at the end of this regulation, viz., 'and serving the area covered by the station' were added." Taylor's brief also objected to the fact that political parties were not among the exceptions to this regulation.

The brief concluded that "the great majority of Canadians find the type of regulation and control dealt with as nauseating and objectionable as we." The Alberta government's strenuous objections to the regulations and perhaps the inclusion of the restrictive words regarding churches and religious bodies might be explained by the fact that it was the only Social Credit government in Canada at the time, and the Social Credit philosophy embraced a concept of Christian democracy.

That same year, Hagerman received a series of queries from the minister of telephones regarding CKUA's operations. The station was under review. Hagerman dutifully responded. In a letter to Taylor dated November 13, 1956, apparently in reply to a question as to how the station's closing might affect the staff, Hagerman discussed the relative employability of various staff members and concluded, "In view of the above, disposition of staff would not prove to be too great a problem, particularly if our engineering staff could be absorbed by [the Ministry of] Telephones."

It appears that a few months later the government was toying with the idea of privatizing distribution of its radio broadcasts. A June 1957 letter from Hagerman to Taylor outlined the cost of distributing CKUA programs on a contract basis among commercial stations blanketing the province. Annual costs for airtime alone for a one-hour program six days a week would amount to $83,928, Hagerman pointed out. This was close to CKUA's annual budget for full-time programming. Production costs could easily double that figure, he added.

"In contrast, a capital outlay equal to the cost of one year's air time would enable us to continue a full-time cultural and educational service, something even the Dominion Government doesn't supply." CKUA was an absolute bargain to the government, even without a commercial licence.

Interestingly, when CKUA celebrated its thirtieth anniversary in November 1957, Taylor was front and centre, along with at least two other provincial government ministers, to promote the station's value to Albertans. One of its positive points, Taylor said, was that CKUA was one of the few stations that "does not operate on a commercial basis." CKUA also encouraged local talent and better understanding among ethnic groups and among religious organizations, he added. And "most of all," CKUA was "recognized as a station of good music, a place where you can find the very finest music that has been written throughout the ages."

While the government was contemplating the value of keeping CKUA, Hagerman was busy lobbying to upgrade the station's signal with a modern, remote-controlled 10,000-watt transmitter, a crusade begun by Langdon a couple of years earlier. If CKUA didn't act soon, Hagerman argued, stations in other provinces at or near the 580 frequency might "choke us off by raising power before us." When the federal Department of Transport lifted the power ceilings for regional and local stations in March 1958, Hagerman wrote,

It is my personal opinion this will be our final chance to expand a service that is unique in Canada. I think it can be proven the trend toward rock 'n' roll and give-aways in commercial radio is driving some of the listening public to us for better things. And, though the CBC is under continuing criticism from various sections of the public, the only public outcry about CKUA I can remember was when it was suggested the station be closed. Alberta is proud of her Jubilee Auditoriums, and could rightly be proud of a local radio service which supplements both the CBC and commercial radio while competing with neither.

Hagerman's persuasive powers finally won the day. Taylor gave him permission to go ahead and apply to increase CKUA to 10,000 watts. In March 1959 Hagerman and the government's lawyer went to Ottawa to argue the case before the Board of Broadcast Governors (BBG). After years of complaints about the dual role of the CBC as regulator and competitor, the BBG had been created in 1958 to assume the CBC's regulatory function. Hagerman felt pretty confident as he headed to Ottawa: the BBG's chairman was Andrew Stewart, former president of the University of Alberta.

On March 9, 1960 CKUA went on the air with a new 10,000-watt AM transmitter that, according to Hagerman, "pushed our signal to almost all points." In the following months the station received letters reporting reception as far south as Raymond and Montana. The signal reached Keg River and Fort Vermilion in the north, the mountains to the west and Saskatchewan to the east. A northern Alberta trapper was immediately won over. He wrote that he had been about to discard his radio when CKUA boosted its power. He was now an avid listener. However, reception in Calgary, Lethbridge and Medicine Hat still left something to be desired.

To coincide with the "switch-on" of the new transmitter, program director Pat McDougall had decided to go after some inexpensive, but much needed, promotion for the station. He had seen an article in the December 1958 issue of *Time* magazine on American satirist Stan Freberg and his controversial comedy record "Green Chritma," a wickedly satiric indictment of the advertising industry. Freberg, who had a show on CBS Radio, was pioneering novelty comedy records at the time. Many would come to know him for his single "St. George and the Dragonet," a take-off on the popular American television program "Dragnet." Freberg's spoof of the advertising industry and its commercialization of Christmas touched some nerves.

"The three commercial stations in this town, naturally, wouldn't touch it with a ten-foot pole—but as Canada's only full-time non-commercial station— we had a field day," Hagerman wrote to Freberg in early 1959. "The article in *Time* created a demand, and we leaped in to fill it. By promoting the disc for a couple of hours before each playing, we had people tuning us in—some of them for the first time—all over town."

Freberg responded:

May I extend a warm personal thank you for those kind words regarding "Green Chritma" ... In these days a satirist frequently has moments of depression regards whether or not he has gotten through to the people. After the first few hours in the life of "Green Chritma," I began to wonder if I should have sent my message by Western Union.

In November, several months before the new transmitter was to be switched on, McDougall contacted Freberg. He said that CKUA had worn out its original 45 of "Green Chritma" and claimed "the privilege of being the first Canadian radio worker to play 'Green Chritma' this season." He explained that the station's power was increasing from 1,000 to 10,000 watts and that he had a meagre budget with which to tell "several million people" about it. Would Freberg be willing to read the enclosed script onto a tape to be used on "electronic secretaries" attached to selected telephone lines? The script introduced CKUA and said, "They plugged my 'Green Chritma,' now let me plug them for a minute," and went on to explain the power increase. "They play only the best music—no rock-n-roll, no Hit Parade, no western ... ever."

Freberg recorded the tape. The electronic secretary was installed on March 24. The plan was to place an ad in the newspaper saying, "Phone Stan Freberg at GA 2 5163." When people phoned they would hear Freberg promoting CKUA.

CKUA never had to publicize the number, Hagerman said. "We just told our receptionist, who went home and told her mother. The line was plugged the next morning and nobody could get through." Six days later, the machine had registered 4,850 calls and a second machine was installed. But the lines were constantly tied up and the system couldn't take the pressure. By April 7 the phone company had disconnected both machines, but not before they had registered 21,129 calls. McDougall's frugal ad campaign was a huge success.

The day before the new transmitter was switched on, the new minister of telephones, Ray Reierson, responded to questioning in the Legislature regarding the cost of CKUA to taxpayers. There had been some complaints that AGT telephone subscribers outside of CKUA's broadcast area were subsidizing a service that was available primarily to Edmontonians, who received their telephone services not from AGT but from the city's own telephone company, Edmonton Telephones. Reierson pointed out that AGT customers enjoyed the lowest telephone rates in Canada and justified using AGT profits to operate CKUA on the grounds that the station performed "a valuable public service to a wide listening audience."

But the government was still determined to have its own broadcast licence. In September 1960 Reierson wrote to University of Alberta president Walter Johns requesting that the university apply to the federal minister of transport for a transfer of ownership of CKUA to AGT. The university complied, but the transport minister, Leon Balcer, replied that the government had decided to make no change in its policy that "since broadcasting is the sole responsibility of the Federal Government, broadcasting licences shall not be issued to other Governments or Corporations owned by other Governments with the exception that a licence may be issued in the name of an educational institution, where the station concerned is operated on a non-commercial basis only."

Notified of this decision, Reierson wrote Johns again in July 1961, pointing out that Cabinet was concerned that CKUA fell outside Section 103 of the Radio Act because it was operated by an entity other than the owner of the licence. Johns then took the issue up with the chairman of the BBG, Andrew Stewart, and reported back to Reierson:

He informed me that the matter had not been referred to the BBG for consideration and recommendation, but the decision was taken by the members of the Federal Government independently.... I understand ... that the position of the Federal Government is that they would be reluctant to set a precedent in this matter which, however reasonable it may be in this particular instance, could raise difficulties in subsequent applications.

Johns continued, "It is my own personal feeling that the Federal authorities prefer to ignore the failure to comply with Section 103 of the Radio Act rather than to approve a precedent about which they have some doubts. If this is the case, I believe CKUA's authority to continue broadcasting is not likely to be hazarded."

He closed by complimenting the quality of programs carried on CKUA: "It certainly does set a standard of quality which is unique in Canada. Dr. Stewart intimated to me that this was recognized by his Board and that they see no reason to change the present arrangement as between the University and Alberta Government Telephones."

In other words, it appears that by this point the federal government was also trying to benignly neglect CKUA, if only the Alberta government would let it—or the *Edmonton Journal*, for that matter. In June 1962 the *Journal* found out about the rejection of the licence transfer to AGT the year before and broke the story on its front page in the midst of a federal election campaign. The newspaper also felt compelled to point out, "While the Broadcasting Act stipulates a licence-holder must operate his radio station, AGT has owned and operated CKUA for the last 18 years. During this time the federal government has known its regulations were being broken, but turned a blind eye to the infraction."

When questioned on the situation, the deputy minister of transport would not comment on the legality of CKUA's operation, saying it was a matter for the Board of Broadcast Governors. But BBG chairman Andrew Stewart said responsibility for licensing fell under the minister of transport. "All he would say is that, 'CKUA is a good station,'" the *Journal* reported, pointing out that Stewart was previously president of the University of Alberta.

In a follow-up story the next day, the paper said Balcer, who was "electioneering in his constituency of Three Rivers, Que.," confirmed that he had asked the BBG the previous year to look into the operation of CKUA by the Alberta government but didn't remember if the BBG had ever reported back. Likewise, Marcel Lambert, seeking re-election as the Progressive Conservative MP for Edmonton West, said he knew the government had asked the BBG to investigate the operation of CKUA but did not follow up the investigation and "assumed everything was all right." Lambert was parliamentary secretary to the minister of national revenue, who reported to Parliament on the BBG. Lambert told the *Journal* that he had been assured that "while technically there may have been some difficulty about the holding of the licence there was no difficulty about the operation of the station."

Looking back, Tommy Banks said he didn't think the BBG would have wanted to see CKUA disappear. "There was a lot of wink, wink, nudge, nudge every time the licence renewal came up for CKUA ... because it was the only game in town for a long, long time—the only genuine alternative non-commercial broadcaster."

The issue blew over, at least temporarily. But that same year, CKUA made local headlines for another tempest, involving one of the rare times the Alberta government overstepped its hands-off stance with the station. The Sunday ethnic programs, including fifteen- and thirty-minute productions in nine languages, were a thorn in the side of CKUA management. They had been introduced after the war to help immigrants assimilate, but, according to Hagerman, by 1960 they had outlived their original purpose. What's more, the programs had been set up by a previous program director who had simply turned over the time to the various ethnic groups to use as they pleased.

"Really, what it amounted to was they set them up so the station had no control over them in any way, shape or form," Hagerman said. "So they wandered off into all kinds of odd directions.... We got to the point where we had transcripts essentially for all of them, because there was always the tendency to be a little politically inflammatory here and there.... I had to watch them like a hawk."

And for a station that was trying to become more professional, the ethnic programs, produced by inexperienced people from outside the station, no longer fit the image CKUA wanted to project. So Hagerman and McDougall decided to change the ethnic program setup, reducing the total foreign-language airtime from three and a half hours of individual programs to one hour-and-a-half CKUA-produced program of European music with announcements of interest to various ethnic groups.

Hagerman wrote to Reierson, explaining his reasons for wanting to make the changes and warning there could be repercussions. He pointed out that CKUA had originally taken on the programs because none of the commercial stations would do it, but now CHFA was offering programs in all the languages CKUA carried except the Scandinavian languages.

"It is perhaps not quite proper for us, as a non-commercial public service, to be broadcasting programs from which a commercial broadcaster could obtain revenue," he reasoned, in terms a government could appreciate. He also pointed out that the audience for the programs seemed to be dropping and that CKUA could fill those time slots "with professionally produced material of interest not only to language groups but to our audience as a whole."

Hagerman said he wasn't proposing to remove ethnic programming entirely. "We would still extend to the language groups concerned the opportunity to participate in the programs, but we would assume the responsibility for producing the programs themselves." He closed by warning that he expected "any number of specious arguments" for retention of the programs but that the time could be better used "to the advantage of all concerned."

Ten days later, Reierson formally notified Hagerman that "the Executive Council has approved the discontinuance of foreign language programming, in accordance with your request." He acknowledged that "certain groups of our new Canadians particularly, may feel slighted by this move, or disappointed" but said the general consensus of opinion "was along the lines of your own."

"Slighted" and "disappointed" don't begin to describe the actual reaction of the ethnic programmers to the change. "There was one person there who wasn't going to be muscled off the air—Eric Pedersen, who did the Danish program," Gil Evans recalled. "Eric went down to see the minister, and the minister gave orders that it was to be rolled back, and Pat [McDougall] said 'over my dead body.' ... There were others who took up the cudgel—it wasn't just Eric, but Eric, I think, took the lead."

According to Hagerman, "They [the ethnic programmers] appealed to Ray Reierson, the minister of telephones, and in effect he asked us to make some sort of accommodation. He was very reluctant to do it. Ray was a good guy, a good-hearted individual.... I thought, 'What the hell—this wasn't life or death. Sometimes you have to make compromises.'"

The minister had called a meeting among representatives of the ethnic groups and CKUA management and, to meet the objections of the offended groups, recommended that the station add an hour to the new program and allot fifteen-minute segments to eight groups in rotation. McDougall resigned on March 16, 1961, protesting that he couldn't take the fact—calling it "direct political interference"—that the minister had gone back on a change that he himself had authorized. A petition signed by sixteen of the eighteen CKUA staff members urged McDougall to reconsider, stating "we are in full sympathy with your stand on the issue." McDougall's resignation was to be effective April 16, but Reierson called his charge "utter nonsense" and decided his resignation should take effect immediately. Hagerman hired Tony Cashman, a former newsman with CFRN and CJCA and a respected local historian, as program director effective May 1. McDougall eventually went on to the CBC in Montreal. Pedersen continued to produce his Danish program until 1994.

One other incident of government interference occurred in the early 1960s. During the 1963 provincial election, news announcer Jim Edwards undertook a series of political commentaries on the campaign that attracted the attention of the normally hands-off government. Reierson queried Hagerman on the series and then sent him a "confidential" letter, notifying him that "Executive Council has determined that a better non-partisan attitude will be maintained by station CKUA, by having political news handled by the regular commentator in the same manner as any other news. Special emphasis on political news will in this way be avoided." He assured Hagerman this was "in no way to be construed as a reflection on Mr. Jim Edwards' very able work in this field."

In 1964 CKUA attracted some unwanted media attention when AGT was seeking to increase the rate it charged its telephone subscribers. An editorial read over CBXT by one Pat McDougall brought attention to the fact that AGT's budget "could be pared by a 150-thousand dollars or more every year by simply selling a radio station it isn't licensed to operate." The editorial called the money spent on CKUA "the least explainable item on A-G-T's budget" and pointed out that the station was heard best in Edmonton, "and worst, not at all, practically speaking, in Lethbridge and Medicine Hat. There is bitter irony in that situation, Edmonton's telephone subscribers don't help pay for CKUA because the city owns its own telephone system but residents of Lethbridge and Medicine Hat use A-G-T phones and thus help support a radio station they can't hear."

Edmonton Journal columnist Art Evans called the argument "as full of holes as a cribbage board." He pointed out that Edmontonians had to use AGT for their long-distance service and therefore helped pay for CKUA in their long-distance bills. "I happen to think CKUA is a bargain at an operating cost of $150,000 annually. I'd like to see the same kind of bargain obtained for every $150,000 spent by the province." J. Dickinson agreed, writing in a letter to the editor of the Edmonton Journal, "If all the expenditures of the Alberta government gave as fine a return as the measly $150,000 spent annually on CKUA, we wouldn't live in Alberta, we would live in Utopia."

There was growing opinion in southern Alberta, particularly in Calgary, that the government should spend even more on CKUA to improve coverage in that part of the province. Calgarians could receive CKUA's signals only in the daytime. Because radio waves travel farther at night, the station had to curtail its night-time reach to avoid interfering with US stations to the south.

There was even a suggestion that expanding CKUA's reach province-wide would be an ideal gesture on the part of the government to celebrate Alberta's Diamond Jubilee in 1965 and a worthy use for part of the government's $50-million surplus that year. Posing the idea in the Edmonton Journal, Cynthia Aikenhead said she was among the few in Calgary with "freak" reception making it possible to hear CKUA: "A real estate friend of ours recently confided that our ability to hear CKUA could be worth a few thousand dollars extra on the residential market."

One solution, some argued, would be to set up a satellite station for Calgary, but that would constitute a network, a class of radio service that was the sole domain of the CBC. Besides, the provincial government was concerned that a new station in Calgary would take away audience share from existing private stations in that city.

There was another argument against an expanded CKUA. Hagerman told the Calgary Albertan that he thought the chances of expansion were slim: "Because of Quebec's intentions to get a provincial radio service, the federal government is nervous about our situation here, and I doubt that a southern

Alberta station can be opened." A resolution was put before the annual convention of the Alberta Social Credit League in November 1965, urging extended facilities for CKUA in Calgary, but Reierson explained that under federal policy such a move was not allowed.

Meanwhile, "confidential" inter-departmental correspondence at the University of Alberta from May 1965 suggests that the kernel of an idea was being kicked around—to legitimize CKUA by taking it back into the university's fold. Guy Vaughan, director of broadcasting services at the university, wrote to U of A president Walter Johns on May 10:

> As per your verbal request and further to our conversation of May 7th on the status of CKUA ... may I make the following observations:
>
> As I understand it, the license is issued in the name of the University of Alberta and is retained by the University.
>
> Technically then, the University of Alberta is obviously responsible for the control and operation of the station....
>
> One method of rectifying this situation in order to make the status legal would be for the University ... to appoint ... a Director *fully responsible and answerable to the University of Alberta for the total operation of* CKUA.
>
> This could be done very smoothly with hardly any effect on the actual operation of the station since its current staff and equipment could be taken over intact....
>
> Admittedly it would take considerable tact and diplomacy in bringing this about but it could be done.

Vaughan then recommended that these suggestions "should be pursued through legal channels."

Johns responded on May 25 that he had discussed the matter with Reierson:

> As I suspected, neither Mr. Reierson nor, I understand, the Cabinet as a whole are disposed to interfere with the present situation and without their concurrence I feel it would be a mistake on the part of the University to seek to alter matters....
>
> I must agree with you that it does seem anomalous that the University should own the licence and Alberta Government Telephones most of

the facilities, but it does provide for a mutual sharing of responsibility which I honestly believe is not really a contravention of the intent of the agreement.

In any case I think we must leave the situation as it is for the present.

The *Globe and Mail* did a feature on CKUA in 1965, calling the station "a precocious orphan that has captivated Albertans and exasperated politicians for 38 years." The article mentioned the "highly unconventional licensing arrangement—one over which federal and provincial authorities tend to pull a thick cloud."

CKUA celebrated its fortieth anniversary in 1967 with an ambitious series, researched and hosted by Joe McCallum, reprising "40 Wondrous Years of Radio."

Then in 1968 the cloud started shredding.

The Birth of ACCESS | 9

As CKUA entered its fifth decade, political forces were at work in Quebec and Ottawa that would have far-reaching effects on the station and even threaten its existence.

Separatist sentiment was running high in Quebec. In 1967 Charles de Gaulle committed an astounding breach of diplomacy when he shouted "Vive le Québec libre!" from the balcony of Montreal city hall. A year later, Prime Minister Pierre Trudeau ducked bottles as he watched Montreal's St. Jean Baptiste Day parade while police battled enraged separatists. In 1970 Trudeau would proclaim a state of "apprehended insurrection" under the War Measures Act in response to kidnappings of a British trade commissioner and Quebec's labour minister—the latter found murdered—by the separatist Front de Libération du Québec (FLQ).

Around the same time, Quebec was involved in another dispute with the federal government over broadcasting jurisdiction. The province's nationalist premier, Daniel Johnson, announced on February 22, 1968 that he was dusting off the long-dormant Quebec Radio Bureau Act, sanctioned by the legislature under Premier Maurice Duplessis in 1945, to set up a broad-casting system. The new system would be called Radio-Quebec and would be operated by the Quebec Radio Bureau, which would act like a crown corporation. Asked whether the system would be limited to educational broadcasting or was the beginning of a state-operated broadcasting system that would include other forms of radio and television, Johnson said, "We haven't closed any doors." He said he was making the move to protect Quebec's rights in education and culture.

Educators and provincial governments were eager to get into educational television. But this powerful new tool for delivering knowledge straddled the federal–provincial jurisdictional divide. While education was a provincial responsibility, Ottawa insisted broadcasting was a federal affair. Secretary of State Gerard Pelletier provided a clue as to why the government was determined to keep it that way when he explained his refusal to give Quebec an educational broadcasting licence in 1968: "Suppose we grant permits to provincial governments. Then in Alberta for example, Premier Manning, a sincere believer in the Social Credit theory, could decide to broadcast two hours a day of political education on television and then broadcast exclusively Social Credit doctrine."

Nevertheless, the government was still looking the other way with regard to CKUA Radio. But Quebec wasn't going to let it get away with that any longer. On February 27, 1969, in response to a question in the House of Commons about educational television policy, Pelletier reiterated the federal government's stand that broadcasting licences could not be issued to provinces or their agencies. Martial Asselin, PC for Quebec-Charlévoix, shot right back, asking why a broadcasting licence had been granted to Alberta but not to Quebec. Asselin's question was ruled out of order on grounds that it was "argumentative." But that was the day "it hit the fan" for CKUA, according to Larry Shorter.

Shorter was another Renaissance man who would play a major role in CKUA's history. He first encountered CKUA when he moved to Alberta from Vancouver in 1953 to become General Motors' public relations manager for the province—the company's youngest such manager in North America. A jazz fan, he had started the first radio program in British Columbia aimed at teenagers.

◆ *Larry Shorter, founding president of ACCESS, ca. 1977.*
Courtesy of CKUA.

"So, when I first got to Edmonton, I looked to find out where the jazz was ... and it was at CKUA," Shorter recalled. He quickly connected with Tommy Banks, and the two started hosting a Saturday afternoon jazz show at CKUA. They also started an orchestra together, with a shy Banks providing the music and Shorter fronting the group.

During that time Shorter set up a business based on a new die-making process he had developed. In 1956 he sold the business and returned to British Columbia, where he became involved in television, earned an education degree, taught school and started Canada's first educational television system, in Kamloops. He also earned a diploma in television production at Ryerson Polytechnic, wrote numerous articles and CBC scripts, established a co-operative of BC Interior school boards, known as Inland ETV, and became its president—all before returning to Edmonton in 1967 as director of communications responsible for school radio and television broadcasts for Alberta Education.

The Department of Education had been collaborating with the school districts and universities in Calgary and Edmonton—and, in the case of

Calgary, with other post-secondary institutions—to form Calgary and Region Educational Television (CARET) and the Metropolitan Edmonton Educational Television Association (MEETA). Now these two educational television operations needed broadcast licences. One of Shorter's responsibilities in his new job was to handle federal–provincial relations with the Canadian Radio-Television Commission (CRTC—created in 1968 to succeed the federal Board of Broadcast Governors).

"[This] was really interesting because education was a provincial responsibility and broadcasting was clearly a federal responsibility, and what we were after was educational broadcasting," Shorter said. "It was like, say, if I have the franchise for sodium and you have it for chloride, who has table salt?"

The federal government introduced legislation in 1968 to set up a Canadian educational broadcasting authority but had to withdraw the bill when the provinces objected that it trod on their constitutional jurisdiction over education. During 1968 and 1969 a federal task force met with the provinces to resolve the issue. One solution floated by Ottawa was to have the CBC build and own the transmitters for educational television broadcasting, and the provinces operate them and provide the content. However, ultimate authority to pull the plug would rest with the federal government.

In Shorter's words, "Trudeau and Judy LaMarsh, the minister of communications, developed a scheme where they would define what education was and allow the provinces to be licensed to broadcast education, but the federal government would actually own the transmitters. So, one word about Social Credit or one word about Free Quebec and they could turn the switch off. That was their original idea of how they would handle the situation."

MEETA went on the air in 1970 under just such an arrangement, sharing a transmitter with CBC-owned CBXFT-TV, Edmonton's French station. TV Ontario followed shortly after, with the Ontario Educational Communications Authority, a provincial agency, providing programs for an educational station operated by the CBC. On June 4 of that year the federal government levelled the playing field between Alberta and Quebec with a directive to the CRTC that broadcast licences could not be granted to either provincial governments, their agents or educational institutions. This was the first time educational institutions were mentioned as being ineligible for broadcast licences. The CRTC would be permitted to renew existing licences up to March 1972. In addition to CKUA, the directive affected stations operated by

Queen's University, Ryerson Polytechnic Institute and the University of Saskatchewan. However, a news release announcing the directive quoted Secretary of State Pelletier as saying the government did not want the services provided by the affected stations to be jeopardized by the decision. "During the renewal period, and with the assistance of the CRTC, it is hoped that acceptable corporate structures will be devised."

In educational radio circles, some of the blame for this new state of affairs came down on the University of Alberta. Henry Mamet, the university's director of radio and television, reported to U of A president Max Wyman in September 1970:

At the Educational Radio and Television Conference at York University last month, the whole problem of recent Federal government action relating to educational radio was discussed. Those involved seemed to be unanimous in blaming the U of A for relinquishing operation of CKUA to AGT for recent developments....

All agree that CKUA is a key figure in the whole educational radio picture. They hope that the U of A can manage to re-assume operation of the station, even if it involves only a "paper" changeover....

The provincial government was already exploring ways to restructure ownership of CKUA. Renewal of the station's FM licence had gone before the CRTC in 1969 and been contested by the National Association of Broadcast Employees and Technicians (NABET). The union had made an application for certification as bargaining agent for CKUA employees and had been turned down by the Canada Labour Relations Board on grounds that the board lacked jurisdiction over employees of a provincial government. NABET filed its opposition to the licence renewal on September 10, 1969, on the basis that the licensee was not, in fact, the operator of the station. Pierre Juneau and Harry Boyle, chairman and vice-chairman of the CRTC, respectively, invited Alberta's telephones minister Ray Reierson, U of A president Max Wyman, CKUA general manager Jack Hagerman and AGT general manager J.W. Dodds to a meeting on December 11 at the CRTC offices to discuss possible changes in the operation of CKUA, but no conclusions were reached. On March 25, 1970 the CRTC renewed the station's FM licence to March 31, 1971.

News of the federal government's June directive against granting broadcast licences to provincial governments, their agents or educational institutions disturbed CKUA listeners. A woman from Hillspring, Alberta, sent a postcard to Reierson, imploring him to "Please save Radio Station CKUA Canada's best!! My daily life would only be barely worth living if I couldn't listen to their marvelous concerts, talks and lectures anymore." Under pressure by the public to respond to the directive, Reierson said the government was prepared to co-operate in setting up a new form of management for CKUA, "but we want some firm idea of what they [the CRTC] will accept." In a letter to the federal government quoted in the *Edmonton Journal*, he said, "We can't finance something totally remote from our administration. We can't just issue a blank check drawn on AGT."

Fears that CKUA was doomed spread as federal–provincial negotiations continued. In April 1971 a group called the Silent Majority of Edmonton, representing "a fair cross-section of Edmontonians," wrote to Reierson, urging him to take action to save CKUA. But by September, CKUA was no longer Reierson's problem. On August 31, after thirty-five years in power, Alberta's Social Credit party had been pushed aside by Peter Lougheed's Conservatives in a provincial election landslide. Leonard Werry was now minister of telephones and Don Getty, minister of federal and intergovernmental affairs, responsible for negotiating with Pelletier.

A briefing on CKUA from Education Minister Lou Hyndman to Werry, dated September 15 and copied to Getty, was found among Getty's papers. Next to a paragraph that says, "A fairly large number of Edmontonians are most concerned that the station continue to broadcast," Getty wrote, "Says who?" He soon found out.

The new intergovernmental affairs minister wrote to the CRTC in October seeking a one-year extension on the March 31, 1972 expiry date of CKUA's licence. Pelletier turned him down in a letter pointing out that the deadline already represented the only extension permitted under federal policy. He also wrote that affected stations "were encouraged to seek the advice of CRTC to establish suitable structures with a community service orientation if they wish to continue in general broadcasting after March 31, 1972."

News reports of this development triggered a rush of support for CKUA in letters to Pelletier vouching for the station's "community service" and to the Alberta government urging it to fight for CKUA. The board of governors of Alberta College, the Alberta Teachers' Association, the Edmonton chapter of the Committee for an Independent Canada, and the University of Alberta Students' Union were among those that registered their support.

One listener wrote, "Coming to Edmonton twenty-five years ago and finding C.K.U.A. on the radio dial was like finding a treasure.... You have given us such pleasure and delight which just cannot be expressed in words."

Another declared, "I can think of no station (radio or T.V.) which has given more community service and is still giving it than C.K.U.A.... You have provided us with hours of relaxation, learning and pure joy. You have become a way of life and we cannot do without you."

Still another told Pelletier, "This Station has been an integral part of the cultural life of this community for almost 45 years.... In these days of growing general interest in matters cultural, this Station stands out like a beacon in the night, and in this relatively remote area of Canada provides ... much appreciated educational and cultural programming."

Getty heard from a man who had recently come from Berkeley, California, and was "both delighted and surprised to find a radio station, CKUA, of comparable total quality to the best stations in San Francisco and the nation." One woman was so keen to save CKUA she proposed to Getty that listeners could support the station with contributions: "I had in mind a yearly, month-long drive for funds along the same lines as the United Community Fund, perhaps, but aimed at the broader listening community of CKUA."

Mick Burrs, a poet who had emigrated from California and hosted a CKUA program called "Stand Tall on the Rubble Pile," told Getty, "The Secretary of State would not kill culture in Edmonton if he cancels CKUA's broadcasting licence, but he would put it into a coma." Burrs, who later served as editor of Grain, wrote that his program was an outlet for creative writers in the region "who would probably have no opportunity to appear on this program's only equivalent, CBC's 'ANTHOLOGY' which is produced in Toronto and is more or less a closed shop, established writers only need apply."

Edmonton Journal readers registered their alarm at the situation in letters to the editor. "CKUA has been my lifeline to sanity for 23 years," wrote one woman. "It is almost a part of Edmonton's character as a city," another listener declared. "If it is taken off, many teenagers will find again something else to throw up to the Establishment for wrecking something which is truly doing a good job."

Meanwhile, Hagerman was quoted in the *Toronto Daily Star* on October 28, saying, "I wonder what the federal government would do if we refused to go off the air. Would they send in troops or something?" He was busy bringing the new telephones minister up to speed on the issues and exploring possible solutions.

Quebec had a bill in the works that would extend the Quebec Public Services Board's powers to include "in addition to telephone, telegraph, steam, heat and light services, all those whose main or accessory object is to transmit or broadcast sound, images, signs, signals, data or messages, by wire, cable, waves, or any electric, electronic, magnetic, electromagnetic or optical means." The bill had passed second reading on November 10. Hagerman wrote an analysis of the situation for the government, suggesting Pelletier was on shaky ground and would probably not want to have to take Quebec to the Supreme Court for a ruling on the legislation because even if he won, Quebec might forge ahead anyway.

On the other hand, he could "attempt to get agreement from the provinces, as a group, on a form of 'corporate structure' which will allow him to let Quebec proceed without himself appearing to have 'given in' to Quebec.... The second course would seem to be the safer for him both legally and politically, and I am sure that will be what he has in mind. He really needs to be taken off the hook."

Horst Schmid, Alberta's minister of culture, youth and recreation, sent Getty a memo responding to Hagerman's brief: "It seems to me that at the moment CKUA is a bystander in a Federal-Provincial fight for regulating information-carrying media; and the station stands a good chance of being hurt the most." Schmid, who was a friend of Gaby Haas and often appeared on his program, made a case for saving CKUA in a passionate appeal that, twenty-five years later, sounded quaint by the standards of the bottom-line Tory government of Ralph Klein:

CKUA, in my opinion, is more important now than ever before. It has never been interested in a mass audience because to do this, it would have to lower its standards. The station's function should not be to stimulate a "mass" audience—or even professionals. Instead it should appeal to the "thinking" individuals, those who are capable of asking the necessary and liberating questions by which humanity makes its way through time.

Since added costs (mainly increased postal rates) have caused the discontinuance of many high quality company and specialized magazines which were originated and edited by thinkers to stimulate thinking readers, CKUA's function moves from the area of being important to being necessary.

To sum this up as simply as possible, CKUA is communication. This is not to be confused with communications.

Education Minister Lou Hyndman submitted a formal request on November 23 for cabinet to decide "whether the government endorses the continued existence of CKUA after March 31, 1972," with an affirmative recommendation. Among the advantages of continuing CKUA, he cited endorsements by various education administrators including the opinion of the superintendent of Minburn County Schools that it would be "educational suicide to lose this valuable service."

He said that CKUA ranked eleventh or twelfth of twenty-two major AM stations in Alberta in audience size, averaging 58,000 listeners tuning in at least once a week. These were mainly housewives, students, managerial people and farmers, most aged eighteen to twenty-four and fifty to sixty-four and having a high school or university education. Hyndman pointed out that CKUA could be a "government information service" and could be used to broadcast legislative proceedings. As for disadvantages, CKUA cost $280,000 a year, had only a non-commercial licence and therefore little income, and was not clearly received in some places south of Red Deer.

Pelletier visited Edmonton at the end of November to meet with Getty and Werry. The meeting went so well that on December 22 Getty applied to the CRTC for a one-year extension of CKUA's licence. The federal government instead issued an Order in Council to the CRTC to extend the licence to March 31, 1974, in order to give affected stations a "breather" in which to restructure their management. Two other stations had already made the necessary adjustments. The University of Saskatchewan station was operated by the students' union, and the university was solving its problem by incorporating the Saskatoon Society for Public Broadcasting to hold the

◆ *Gaby Haas, host of the longest-running radio program in the world, with ACCESS president Peter Senchuk (left), CKUA general manager Don Thomas and Jim Woronuik (right), chairman of the ACCESS board, 1986. Courtesy of CKUA.*

licence. Ryerson let the CBC take over its transmitter while holding on to responsibility for programming.

By June 1972 Getty and Werry were assuring concerned listeners that the Alberta government not only was intent on keeping CKUA on the air, it was also "investigating ways in which more Albertans will be able to enjoy the unique broadcasting which it provides."

Then, on July 13, the federal government issued another Order in Council amending its original 1970 directive to the CRTC banning provincial governments and their agencies from holding broadcast licences. The new directive, made public on August 3, opened new possibilities for keeping CKUA afloat. It allowed a broadcast licence to be held by an "independent corporation" that is *not directly controlled* by a provincial government and whose programming meets a strict definition of "educational programming" already hammered out in earlier federal–provincial negotiations over educational television.

The matter of defining "education" had occupied a lengthy series of negotiations and resulted in a Byzantine formula that gave some CKUA supporters more cause for concern than relief. Larry Shorter said of the meetings, "We finally reached a definition ... a long, involved definition, which is in writing—boy, is it in writing! ... And this was really hard to do because the Feds have no education department. That's not their responsibility. So even to find anybody who knew anything about education in the federal government was hard.

"Of course, meanwhile the provinces are insisting that education was their responsibility, so they don't even deign to want to talk to the Feds about it."

The resulting definition was spelled out in the new Order in Council:

(a) programming designed to be presented in such a context as to provide a continuity of learning opportunity aimed at the acquisition or improvement of knowledge or the enlargement of understanding of members of the audience to whom such programming is directed and under circumstances such that the acquisition or improvement of such knowledge or the enlargement of such understanding is subject to supervision or assessment by a provincial authority by any appropriate means; and

(b) programming providing information on the available courses of instruction or involving the broadcasting of special education events within the educational system, which programming, taken as a whole, shall be designed to furnish educational opportunities and shall be distinctly different from general broadcasting available on the national broadcasting service or on privately owned broadcasting undertakings.

While this definition worried some, Pelletier said he thought the definition was "so broad you could roll a truck through it." For the Alberta government, the main problem was to devise an arm's-length corporate structure to hold educational television and CKUA broadcast licences that would satisfy the federal government.

All the while the CKUA crisis was playing out, a seemingly unrelated process was underway that would suggest a timely solution. In 1969 the Social Credit government had launched a royal commission on education, called the Commission on Educational Planning, under Dr. Walter Worth, a vice-president of the University of Alberta. The commission's task was huge and reflected the idealism of the times. Its mandate was "to investigate social, economic and technological trends for the next 20 years; to examine

◆ *Illustration from the* Worth Commission's *report* A Choice of Futures, 1972.
Courtesy of CKUA.

the needs of all individuals in our society; to analyse our total educational requirements; to recommend the future changes, structures, and priorities necessary for a comprehensive educational system."

Over three years the commission heard from nearly 100 expert consultants, sponsored or co-sponsored "dozens of research studies, held 36 public hearings, received 300 briefs, convened 14 large conferences and launched three major task force investigations." Larry Shorter was the education department's official liaison to the Worth Commission.

Alongside his work with the commission, Shorter had been piecing together the concept for a province-wide, integrated electronic delivery system for culture and education using radio and television and a time-sharing computer network. "There was an enormously strong atmosphere related to education and culture and the need to get it out to the people, the need for a delivery system," he said. "So I developed a plan, which was called ACCESS, in 1970."

The plan, in part, called for the expansion of CKUA and the use of extra bandwidth, gained by dividing the station's frequency into additional channels, to piggyback a fax network onto CKUA that would go to all the schools in Alberta. Shorter called it "blackboard by wire."

"The whole integrated idea of ACCESS was to develop that system—radio and television—so we could set up an electronic highway, so we could reach all the schools, universities, colleges and, indeed, people in their homes.... There were a whole lot of other people involved.... There were great pioneers in the Edmonton and Calgary school boards and the universities, and we were all involved in this dream we had.

"To make a long story short, the Social Credit government bought this plan." A corporation would be established to carry out the plan, and Shorter was designated president-elect.

When Lougheed's Tories swept Social Credit out of office, Shorter called upon the new premier and his two education ministers—the education portfolio was now divided into education and advanced education—to familiarize them with the Worth Commission's work and to secure support for it to continue. The commission had a high profile and was an easy sell. Shorter said he had assurances that the new government would back the commission's recommendations when they came out.

"The first thing we did is take all the work I had done on the development of ACCESS and referred it to the royal commission." Shorter was then seconded to the commission, where he served as staff writer and resident expert on educational technology.

The commission published its report, A Choice of Futures, in 1972. The 325-page report was a magnificent document, published in large-size book format and reflecting up-to-the-minute graphic design trends, complete with Yellow Submarine–style drawings.

At the time, the report was also at the forefront of liberal social and educational thinking, according to Shorter: "because Alberta had such a significant role in adult education, and because of where we are—this is 'burn, baby, burn'; this is 'school is irrelevant'; this is 'drop out'; this is hippie time; this is when the youth of the nation are screaming that education is totally irrelevant. So the Worth report is one of the most liberal educational documents you'll find in North America in the last one hundred years, because it was listening to all the screams.

"So not only is it educational technology, but it's gung-ho on cradle-to-grave education and further education in every way. And every citizen deserves more than just twelve years of school—he's going to have to retrain for his job; he's going to have to retrain and be educated for his leisure hours; the whole schmear.... This was a marvellous time for everyone who saw education as a way of life and believed that learning was important, and [for] all those people who wanted to bring enrichment to the province."

Shorter prepared a colourful *Reader's Companion to the Alberta Worth Report on Educational Planning* that summarized the commission's report and recommendations and invited Albertans to respond to the proposals. Copies were sent to every household in Alberta. The full Worth Report sold for five dollars a copy.

"I got involved with marketing it," Shorter said, "and we sell it for $1.62 a pound in Safeway stores—that's $5. We sold twenty thousand copies. No kidding. This was a best-seller."

The report called for the establishment of the Alberta Communications Centre for Educational Systems and Services (ACCESS) as the authority to develop the province's educational communications services. It would be a crown corporation and relate to the provincial government much as the CBC does to the federal government, and it would incorporate the facilities and personnel of MEETA, CARET and CKUA. However, the report allowed that "cost estimates associated with CKUA might continue to be borne by AGT in the event this station's operation by ACCESS is deemed inadvisable." On this score, the report acknowledged that current federal and CRTC regulations incorporating a strict definition of "educational" broadcasting would "prohibit CKUA from carrying on its present, highly desirable program format."

Many shared this view, especially at the University of Alberta. The Association of the Academic Staff of the University of Alberta (AASUA) had established an *ad hoc* committee on the status of CKUA. The committee met on September 13, 1972 and agreed that the Worth Commission recommendations for the future of CKUA "were not acceptable because under them it seems probable that the character of CKUA would be altered to a considerable degree." In its recommendation to the association, the committee said that radio was not an effective means of providing formal educational services and that CKUA's most appropriate role would be in the field of life-long learning, which is where it had already been functioning satisfactorily for almost forty-five years. It therefore recommended that there be no significant change in the operation of the station or in the nature of its programming.

Meanwhile, Getty's director of constitutional and economic affairs had sent him a memo in August sizing up the situation and recommending immediate restructuring of CKUA to make it eligible for a licence under the new CRTC directive, "not necessarily viewing the regulation as a threat to CKUA" but "as an opportunity to initiate the first step toward provincially controlled educational broadcasting, a step upon which a total educational communications system may gradually build." The memo recommended creating an independent agency responsible for the development of educational television and educational radio in Alberta.

In September a provincial government advisory committee on educational communications recommended setting up an Alberta Educational Communications Corporation to take advantage of the new federal policy. Among its responsibilities would be (in the order listed) the operation of CKUA, of MEETA and CARET, and of distribution services (ACCESS). Among four *Reasons for a Corporation*, the recommendation cited the first two as "1. The present licensing arrangement for CKUA ends in March, 1974; 2. Certain activities now being undertaken by MEETA and CARET should be centrally controlled and operated."

The concept provoked immediate controversy, raising fears that CKUA would be swallowed up by a monster bureaucracy. The *Edmonton Journal* cautioned, "As for CKUA, the question is not how to relate it to a larger provincial broadcasting policy but rather how to keep it just about the way it is. CKUA already has a reason for existence as a unique broadcasting institution and it could only suffer from inclusion in a larger organization with different objectives." Instead, the *Journal* and others suggested, CKUA might be better off with its own governing corporation.

The government was quick to assuage these concerns as it went ahead with plans to introduce a bill in spring session to establish the corporation. In response to concerns over control of programming expressed at a meeting of the University of Alberta board of governors, R.A. (Dick) Morton, planning director of the proposed corporation, said that the new corporation "will not be a monolithic monster doing everything for everybody." Ideas for programs would come from government departments, universities, school boards and other groups, he said.

Nevertheless, the AASUA was still uncomfortable with the proposal. In February 1973 it passed the final report of its committee on CKUA to the university's senate. The report contended that there were "distinct differences in the educational values of radio and television." It explained that "while television can be effective in a relatively formal educational sense, radio is better at providing a general community interest, meeting the needs of the community in the broad spectrum of activities which we call culture." Therefore, it said, "any organization of educational broadcasting must recognize this separation by function. Without such separation it is likely that radio broadcasting will become secondary to television broadcasting because television broadcasting must necessarily dominate funds available for educational broadcasting." In short, CKUA could become the poor stepsister to television.

On February 23 the University of Alberta Senate set up a fact-finding committee and resolved "That the Senate express to the Government of the Province of Alberta its strong concern for the continued independence and integrity of Radio Station CKUA."

The senate committee met at the station with Hagerman and Ed Kilpatrick, who was now CKUA's program director. In his notes from the meeting and an earlier lunch with Hagerman, William Thorsell, then executive director of the senate, commented:

> Mr. Hagerman appears to feel that CKUA has reached a point of stasis that can best be broken by its association with educational television. More money and more "resources" and "cross-fertilization" would be available.
>
> He reiterates that his personal interest encompasses television and that he has his own views on the development of television in Alberta. Presumably in the new Corporation he might be assigned responsibilities for television as well as for CKUA. This appears to appeal to him.
>
> Presented with the vision of a larger organization with more money, Mr. Hagerman has concluded that the advantages to CKUA of these arrangements outweigh the dangers....
>
> He has faith that, with the kind of people that are at CKUA, strong forces exist to assure the survival of the station's present character. Indeed, again, he suggests that the station would likely have more effect on the television operations than vice-versa.

In the same report Thorsell commented on a March 29 meeting with Dick Morton, in which Morton had indicated, among other points: "By stretching the CRTC definitions, almost everything CKUA is presently doing can continue to be done. We intend to protect its independent management status." Further, "insinuated into CKUA programming may be content more of a traditional educational nature."

CKUA staff signed a statement to the senate citing the station's "informative, creative and educational broadcasting service" for more than forty years. "Apparently, it could be maintained by the proposed Alberta Educational Communications Authority. However, if another organization or institution could better guarantee the future of C.K.U.A.'s unique style of broadcasting, we would prefer that alternative."

On April 9 the senate *ad hoc* committee released its report. It proposed a separate corporation for CKUA to better protect the station's character and programming independence while allowing it to operate within federal law. The corporation would be responsible to the same government authority as a parallel corporation for educational television. "As a footnote, we wish to record our concern that curriculum-oriented and continuing education programs might come to dominate the character of the station."

A week later, the government introduced Bill 45, the Alberta Educational Communications Act. The bill created a single corporation responsible for both CKUA and educational television—the Alberta Educational Communications Corporation (AECC, later known as ACCESS). The corporation would be answerable to a provincial authority representing the two departments of education—the Alberta Educational Communications Authority.

Hyndman, the education minister, said the transfer of CKUA to the corporation had CRTC approval, because the corporation's fifteen-member board would be as far away from government as possible, with no more than four board members being government employees. No board members could have any connection with broadcasting or with material supplies. CKUA would be first absorbed into the corporation. It would also be expanded and its transmission power increased to cover the whole province. The new setup would "not change the excellent type of radio that CKUA supplies," Hyndman told the *Edmonton Journal*.

Shorter, who had returned to the government as director of communications for both education departments, was named president of the new corporation in October 1973. The corporation's appointed board included Willard Allan, associate vice-president (academic) of the university. The next step was to convince the CRTC to transfer CKUA's licence to ACCESS.

The senate committee on CKUA was unhappy with Bill 45, partly because it did not put CKUA under a separate corporation. There were other concerns about "tight control by the proposed Provincial Authority," lack of safeguards to protect programming powers at the station level, and no definition of "educational broadcasting," raising fears that, in this context, the province might not define education as broadly as the federal government had.

On November 19, Thorsell, the senate's executive officer, wrote to Justice Michael O'Byrne, chairman of the new corporation, summarizing the senate's concerns and informing him that the committee on CKUA would remain standing "to monitor future developments" and "to offer any assistance that the newly constituted broadcasting authorities may find useful."

Shorter wrote to University of Alberta president Max Wyman seeking the university's support for the corporation's application to the CRTC for the licence transfer. The board of governors agreed to back the corporation. However, since there was still some question on the part of the CRTC about the independence of AECC from government control, the university filed a token application for renewal of its CKUA licence, just in case the CRTC turned the corporation down.

Meanwhile, Shorter set out to quell fears that the station might lose its character under the new regime. Explaining how the corporation would present CKUA's case as an "educational" broadcaster in the upcoming CRTC licence hearing, he told the media that programming would be altered only slightly to reflect more pre-planning, and that programs would be more carefully developed to ensure a "continuity of learning."

Much of the educational value of CKUA's regular programming was "accidental," he said. In the future it would be "on purpose." As an example, he pointed out that many of the jazz and classical programs offered background on the nature of the music, the artists and the circumstances under which the music was written. This could be considered a "learning experience" for the listener.

Shorter also hoped to develop programs that would lead listeners through various forms of music. People might hear a popular piece they liked on a mixed music program and then be exposed to other forms that they might learn to like, once they understood them. Shorter suggested that CKUA's "educational" programming might even be broken into categories, such as introductory, basic, higher and continuing, with fixed percentages of each. But he insisted that CKUA fans would notice little or no change.

Thorsell, now an editorial writer with the *Edmonton Journal*, was skeptical. "When anyone starts talking about improving CKUA, we get nervous.... [T]he success of CKUA as an institution, perhaps more than anything, is due to a happy accident resulting from an apparent policy of benign neglect on the part of its present sponsor, Alberta Government Telephones, which has allowed the radio station to develop in its own way."

Calling CKUA "this city's only serious music station," Thorsell wrote, "As far as programming is concerned ... AECC certainly has much more to learn from CKUA than vice-versa." He acknowledged that "indications so far about the future of CKUA are actually cause for some optimism. But, just in case, it might not be a bad idea for CKUA fans to keep letters of outraged protest handy—for immediate mailing at the first sound of *Peter and the Wolf*."

Shorter and AECC chairman O'Byrne presented their case to the CRTC on March 12, 1974 in Vancouver. Hagerman represented CKUA, and Morton, the authority. O'Byrne spoke to the independence issue, saying that while the corporation was responsible to the authority to follow its guidelines for establishing educational priorities, "it will be the prerogative of the Corporation to decide whether or not programs are of an educational nature." Funding for the corporation would not in any way be tied to program approval by the authority.

Shorter's presentation to the commission was inspired. "Getting the licence for CKUA was pretty tough, because we were determined not to make major changes from the music programming," he recalled. "And yet the licence was predicated on the fact that it would be used only for educational broadcasting meeting this definition. So, how do we do this? ... I did an education rationale, which was probably one of the best creative pieces of writing I've ever done in my life—proving CKUA was 'educational.'"

First, Shorter tackled the issue of how CKUA fit the federal directive's definition of "educational":

> once that definition is reduced to its essence, it says the following: the difference between entertainment and education is that education necessarily leads somewhere. Education must be profitable, it must

lead towards understanding and truth; entertainment must only pass the time pleasantly....

We would contend that the programming of Radio Station CKUA has always been educational. And when we examined CKUA's programming in the light of our interpretation of the definition of educational broadcasting, we found a very, very good fit. Oh—we may have to lengthen a sleeve here, take in the waist a bit and change a few pleats—but the tailoring is far better than one would expect off the rack....

CKUA has perhaps become best-known as a serious music station. This ... means that CKUA takes all music seriously and programs in every genre, but with catholic taste.

We would continue that policy. We would take music seriously. And when you take music seriously, it leads somewhere—to knowledge of terminology, knowledge of facts, knowledge of musical conventions, and on through interpretive skills, towards true appreciation, which really means to understand—not merely to like.

We would continue with programs of mixed musics, because only by learning to discriminate among musical forms can one be led to understand specific forms. The mixed music programs would then lead to programs specializing in, say, jazz or classics. And these programs would lead to certain kinds of jazz—say, blues—or certain kinds of classics—say, neo modern. And unlike the structure of a school, where you must enroll in September in order to understand what is happening in December, our programming would be open entry—you could start your musical education at any time.

Shorter made the case that other aspects of CKUA programming also fit the definition, asserting that news, film and drama reviews, public service announcements and even stock market reports aid in the development of social competence and social awareness, and enhance the ability to profit from leisure time and cultural pursuits—all of which "are vital to modern education."

We will program in accordance with the definition, Mr. Chairman. We will provide, in the words of the definition, "a continuity of learning opportunity." To do this, only a few structural changes will be necessary in the current CKUA format. But what about these "few structural changes"? After we make them will anyone be around to listen? Or will our programming be so dull, so insensitive, so schoolmasterish, so very, very structured that no one will bother?

Well, Mr. Chairman, I can only say that we believe that structure and grace are not incompatible and that education can be artful.

According to Shorter, as he spun his argument, CRTC head Pierre Juneau, who Shorter considered a friend of CKUA, "nodded wisely. Secretly, he told me earlier, 'That's a good piece of work. I think that shows the educational side.'" But CRTC staff lawyers started grilling Shorter.

"The CRTC has staff lawyers who cross-examine, and I guess Juneau hadn't got to John Hylton, who was the chief examiner, with the message to 'Cool it, we're trying to license to keep CKUA on the air.' But I guess he hadn't said that to Hylton. Hylton starts cross-examining me.... Finally there was this kind of high sign from Juneau."

CKUA squeaked through on Shorter's treatise on modern education. On March 29 the CRTC announced its decision to issue the AECC only a two-year licence for CKUA-AM and CKUA-FM. In explanation, the decision said, "The Commission remains concerned, however, by certain wording in the Act establishing the Corporation ... which contains a potential for lessening the independence of the Corporation thereby raising the possibility that the Corporation might not continue to meet the requirements of Order-in-Council 1972–1569 [issued July 13, 1972, allowing a broadcast licence to be held by an independent corporation not directly controlled by a provincial government]."

The university's board of governors received notice that its token application had been denied and that the licence had been transferred to ACCESS effective March 31, 1974. The board's summary of the issue ended with the statement "This closes the University's file on CKUA."

The station would from now on be called ACCESS Radio CKUA.

But Is It Education? 10

While politicians and bureaucrats presented briefs to each other, hammered out convoluted definitions of "education" and fashioned arm's-length educational broadcasting corporations, something completely different was taking shape behind the mikes at CKUA.

Bob Chelmick fondly remembers the night he had Bruce Cockburn in the CKUA studio for a recording session. "We decided to drink wine and make radio at the same time ... and I sat beside him with a mike on a stand and he had his guitar mike, and we were there for a couple of hours and just talked, rambled, and he played music and we drank wine from the bottle—you could hear it! I had so many requests for that program from people in the States who were presidents of Bruce Cockburn fan clubs.... That was a highlight of the 'Acme Sausage Company'."

The "Acme Sausage Company" was unique in Canada, and it cemented CKUA's position as a seminal force in Alberta's arts community. The program, which started in 1972, was the brainchild of Ed Kilpatrick, who took over as program director when Tony Cashman left in 1969. As the name

◆ Bob Chelmick cut his teeth in broadcasting at CKUA. *Courtesy of CKUA.*

implies, it incorporated just about "anything and everything"—folk, jazz, classical and pop music, by new, emerging and star-quality local, national and international artists, recorded live in concert or in studio all over the province. Interspersed with the music were down-to-earth interviews with the artists talking about their work.

The program was written, recorded, edited, engineered and produced primarily by Holger Petersen and Marc Vasey, and sometimes by Chelmick, "on almost no money and a lot of enthusiasm by everyone involved," according to Vasey. He and Petersen had been attracted to the increasingly alternative CKUA in the late 1960s.

"My tastes were eclectic, and there was nobody else doing what CKUA did," Petersen said. While a student at NAIT in 1968, he started phoning during Tony Dillon-Davis' late-night weekend show and making requests. "I told him that I was a radio-TV arts student, and he gave me an open invitation to come down and sit in whenever I wanted."

At that time, Petersen was interviewing visiting artists for the *NAIT Nugget* newspaper—Spencer Davis, Roy Orbison, Led Zeppelin, "virtually everybody that came through town. I just showed up at the gate and walked backstage

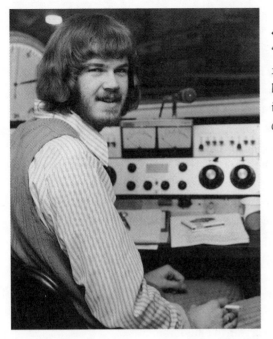

◆ Holger Petersen started "Natch'l Blues" at CKUA in 1969. In 2002 it was the longest-running blues show in Canada.
Courtesy of CKUA.

with the promoter's blessing. The artist would almost always say yes." Petersen eventually started packaging the interviews with music for Dillon-Davis to use on his show—for a princely ten dollars per interview, eventually raised to thirty-five dollars.

Chelmick, a classmate of Petersen's, landed a job at CKUA while still in school. "I must confess I fudged my interview a bit, because it was CHED I listened to in the morning," he recalled. "I needed a job, and I thought CKUA would be a good place to start.... I went in to see Jack Hagerman for a part-time weekend position ... and I said, 'Jack, if there's one radio station I want to work at, it's CKUA.' So he hired me, and as it turned out, it was the best place to learn my craft, to cut my teeth in broadcasting."

Chelmick invited Petersen, an avid blues fan, to talk about blues on his show. Kilpatrick, who had been looking for someone to do a blues program, was listening in. "He asked me if I was interested in a weekly blues show," Petersen said. "That was in 1969. That was 'Natch'l Blues'." In 2002 Petersen was fairly certain his show—featuring interviews with musicians coming through Alberta and artists that he sought out in his travels—was the longest-running blues program in Canada. (He also had a long-running blues show on CBC.) Kilpatrick gave Petersen another weekly time slot, called "H.P. Sauce," where he combined music with his interviews.

Vasey, hooked on jazz since he was a pre-teen, discovered CKUA "while flipping the radio dial and hearing this jazz music late at night." He started hanging around the station, volunteering time on the Saturday afternoon jazz program and talking about jazz with programmer Ron Durda on the latter's late-evening live jazz program.

"For me, it was an incredible resource of music that I was already deeply involved in.... [including the] library first of all, and a lot of people who had a lot of information about music and were very passionate about it at the same time." While Vasey was studying radio and television arts at NAIT in 1970, Kilpatrick approached him to produce a postmodern music program. He stayed with the station for twenty-five years.

Vasey and Petersen took turns producing "Acme Sausage Company" programs, bringing performers into the studio to play and talk about their music or taking recording equipment out to capture live performances. Often CKUA co-sponsored performances at venues such as the Hovel coffeehouse and Yardbird Suite jazz club in Edmonton.

"We'd go in and help the venue present the music, because we were putting money into those productions," Vasey said. "So somebody, instead of being able to make three hundred dollars when they came to town, could make six hundred dollars, because we were able to put resources in and work together with a whole bunch of different people all around the province."

CKUA had a particularly strong connection with the Hovel, originally located in a church at the edge of the University of Alberta campus and later in another building at the edge of downtown.

"It was a great place. The atmosphere was wonderful. It was packed on Friday and Saturday nights, and they had great corn bread," Chelmick recalled. "Bruce Cockburn would be there with some regularity.... He would roll into town, and we would take a suitcase type of recording device down there and we'd record the performance, and it was magic. Who would have known he'd become the star that he is? And Fraser and DeBolt—who else programmed Fraser and DeBolt? Nobody, except CKUA."

Ry Cooder, Stephane Grappelli, Sonny Terry and Brownie McGhee, Valdy and Bob Carpenter were among the many visiting musicians put through CKUA's sausage grinder. "Acme Sausage Company" also provided an outlet for Alberta musicians who would never have got a hearing elsewhere in the increasingly formatted and regimented commercial radio world.

"We recorded so much great local stuff," Petersen said. "I have no idea how many programs I did with Gaye Delorme, for example. The list goes on and on—so many exciting people." The program lasted five years. In 1974 CKUA released a compilation album from the show.

The "Acme Sausage Company" contributed to Edmonton's becoming "probably the most active recording community in the country" in terms of jazz, according to Vasey. "There wasn't as much activity on a per capita basis happening in Toronto or Vancouver—especially for some of the more interesting things that we were doing. A lot of commissioning was going on. A lot of original music was being written, a lot of challenging stuff. So much really great music was happening. And so many associations between local and regional and Canadian musicians in every genre and really great internationally famous people that Holger and I produced over those years."

A jazz recording session in the CKUA studio with Tommy Banks, P.J. Perry, Peter Thompson, Dale Hillary and two or three other jazz musicians stands out in Vasey's memory.

"We started recording around one o'clock in the morning. Of course, we had wine and beer and other stimulants available to us, and between every take of every tune, Tom would put his head down on the piano and sleep, because he was working about twenty-eight hours a day in those days. He had this ability to put his head down and sleep for five minutes and wake up refreshed like it was a brand-new day for him. Others of us were lying around on the floor. But out of this came some of the most amazing music. That was the cream of the crop of many of the very top jazz musicians in Canada in those days.... These guys were world-class....

"It [the "Acme Sausage Company"] was probably the most important programming that the station did because it actually brought the community—the local community, the provincial community, the national community and the world community—to the airwaves on CKUA. It wasn't happening anywhere else in the country, in North America, probably the world ... with the level of both the technical and artistic integrity and the information that the listeners were able to receive from this series.... It was really quite amazing."

CKUA's influence on the local arts and cultural community during the early 1970s was still being felt thirty years later. In the late 1970s Petersen and Vasey, both musicians, were movers behind Edmonton's budding performing arts festival scene. In 1973 Vasey started the Edmonton Jazz Society; in 1980 he founded the Jazz City International Music Festival, which has since spread to Calgary, Victoria, Vancouver, Saskatoon and Winnipeg. In 2002 he was still producing the Edmonton festival and had also started producing the Calgary festival.

Petersen was instrumental in starting the Edmonton Folk Music Festival and was artistic director from 1986 through 1988. He started his own roots music label, Stony Plain Records, in 1976. The company has multinational distribution and an international reputation, working over the past quarter of a century with such artists as Jimmy Witherspoon, Long John Baldry, Amos Garrett, Roosevelt Sykes, Ian Tyson (who switched from Columbia Records), Tom Russell and King Biscuit Boy.

During the turmoil over CKUA's licence in the early 1970s, listeners noticed nothing amiss at CKUA. In fact, the station may have become even more the CKUA they loved. An *Edmonton Journal* column listing the variety of jazz, blues and rock shows available on the station advised, "Listen to CKUA for just one month, and all your friends will stand dumbstruck before you in disbelief of your oracular wisdom." Chelmick recalled a poetry show called "A Soft Bomb Behind the Eyes": "We'd have a poet on each week—it was either Stephen Scobie or Doug Barbour—we had the best poets, CanLit giants, and we would get them from recordings."

While young jazz, rock and roots fans were finding a home at CKUA, the station didn't forget their grandparents. Chelmick, barely twenty at the time, proposed a program to Kilpatrick that would take him to seniors' residences around the province with his sports car and tape recorder, in search of prairie folk music.

"We'd go into old-age homes with a tiny little [tape] recorder. We just arrived—or sometimes sent out letters in advance—[at] little towns where the old-age homes were often the centre of the community, and we'd sit around the piano.

"I was hoping to do the Edith Fowke [a Canadian collector of folk music and folklore who brought her recordings to CBC Radio in the late 1950s and 1960s] kind of thing—field songs. Basically, I got English musical songs from people who had settled the West in the 1930s ... mostly the parlour songs they sang around the rare piano stuck in a farmhouse in the middle of nowhere on the Prairies.... We gave them a chance to talk about their lives."

CKUA was also doing creative programming in the educational area. In 1970 the station collaborated with MEETA "University of the Air" in an experiment in group discussion with a series called "Being Human." On one segment MEETA presented a television program on marital problems. CKUA followed with an open-line discussion featuring a marriage counsellor and a pediatrician in the studio. Several church groups used the "Being Human" broadcasts as a springboard for weekly discussions. In the late 1960s and early 1970s, the station carried a series on continuing medical education sponsored by the University of Alberta Faculty of Medicine. Doctors could call collect to ask questions on a special confidential phone line. An estimated two hundred doctors listened in each week, as well as two thousand lay listeners.

"Call of the Land," Alberta Agriculture's daily noon-hour information program for farmers, got a new host in 1970. Jack Howell was training as a district agriculturist at Ponoka when the job as host of the long-standing program came up. Having had some broadcast experience at the University of Alberta, he landed the job. In 2002 he was still bringing farmers the latest on agricultural issues and research.

Among CKUA freelancers in the 1970s, University of Alberta professor and poet Stephen Scobie, and later, Bill Beard, reviewed films and talked about the art of film; Dorothy Dahlgren conversed with authors and scoured the province for entertaining historical stories and anecdotes about people, places and events; and June Sheppard provided thoughtful commentary on issues of the day. Naturalist Kerry Wood educated listeners on such topics as how to beat the mosquito problem by setting out birdhouses to attract purple martins.

Talks by University of Alberta professors were an evening staple, and concerts recorded at the university were featured on Saturdays. In 1977 David Ragosin hosted both programs. CKUA also carried a program of gritty interviews by Chicago broadcaster and Pulitzer Prize–winning writer Studs Terkel. There was even a program called "Audio Ideas," about "the complex world of component audio equipment."

On Sundays Edmonton's ethnic communities could still hear programs in their native languages, while Gaby Haas brought them popular music from continental Europe. In the early to mid 1970s CKUA featured a home-produced comedy show—a series of half-hour programs produced and hosted by Steve Hannon and Andy Smith.

CKUA's music programming was heavily weighted towards classics and jazz. The university's "Music Hour" ran every evening; "Concert at Nine" each morning, "Concert at One" each afternoon and "Still of the Night" at midnight. "Candlelight and Silver" continued to provide light music, to aid digestion, weekday evenings at 6:00. "Shank of the Morning" mixed things up with classics, folk and jazz, while "Matinee" offered "a diversity of music."

Kilpatrick explained CKUA's music philosophy to RPM magazine in November 1977:

> The criterion for selection is based on the concept of the work's being motivated by a genuine or spontaneous artistic impulse, as opposed to being turned out to meet a commercial demand. Any work regarded as possessing intrinsic artistic value is automatically a candidate for broadcast on CKUA.

Radio plays came in for a revival on CKUA in 1972 with a series called "First Monday of the Month." The first play was *Dismissal Leading to Lustfulness* by local playwright Tom Whyte, featuring Walter Kaasa, Tommy Banks, Joan Francis, Jay Smith and Judith Mabey. Over a two-year period, Whyte and announcer-producer Don Gillis (later a CKUA technical engineer) produced more than 20 plays, providing work for 150 actors, writers and technicians. Whyte called their effort "Edmonton's third professional theatre," claiming that actors arriving in town called CKUA before contacting the Citadel, the city's major theatre venue.

CKUA was still treating its youngest audience with great respect. Three young women, Sharon Sinclair (then Vasey), Betty Gibbs and Cheryl Markosky, started a program in 1976 called "Just Because We're Kids" for a five- to twelve-year-old audience, using Sinclair's son Miles as "test kid." All had full-time jobs with ACCESS TV and put the program together in their spare time after work.

"We'd go into the studio (sometimes with the long-suffering Miles in tow) and try everything: short stories, music, jokes, snippets of interesting information, poetry, even smatterings of drama," Markosky recalled. "With

◆ Technical producer Alf Franke explains how sound effects are created during a school tour. *Courtesy of CKUA.*

a very low budget and admirable help from [technical producer] Alf Franke in the music library, the two of us put together what would be regarded today as a grass-roots, even homespun, children's radio programme. Miles, however, was the key. If he wrinkled up his nose and said 'boring,' or his attention wandered quickly, we'd move on—and try something anew."

Markosky, who went on to work as a teacher and freelance journalist and broadcaster in England, said of her time at CKUA, "Unlike many other broadcasting jobs that followed, I don't remember ever feeling particularly stressed or worried. Was this the *naïveté* of callow youth, or simply that CKUA was a relaxed and 'groovy' place to work? I expect both are true. The jazz 'n' blues meets the Bohemian chattering classes atmosphere certainly pervaded." Sinclair continued to produce the program until 1989, updating the format and travelling around Alberta taping stories, book reviews and interviews by kids themselves.

Many staff who worked at CKUA during the 1970s credit Ed Kilpatrick— as program director and later as station manager when Hagerman went over to ACCESS—for creating the atmosphere where new and interesting programs could flower. Sinclair said he tended CKUA like a gardener. "He watered and fertilized and then just let people's creativity blossom."

Marc Vasey said most of the interesting radio coming out of CKUA in those days was "stimulated by the generosity and the insight and love of the medium that Ed Kilpatrick had. It came from him because he was ... a Renaissance kind of guy in that he was so open to things, even though he was twice our age—he actually stimulated us to try a whole bunch of different things." However, Kilpatrick did draw the line at some point: "We cater to all areas of music except bubblegum and country," he told the University of Alberta student newspaper *The Gateway* in 1971.

The result was appreciated even beyond Alberta's borders. *Vancouver Sun* media columnist Ted Ferguson commented on the federal government's 1972 decision to allow provincial corporations to hold educational broadcast licences and suggested that the BC government use CKUA as a model for a radio system of its own:

> CKUA's chief asset is its diversity. On a recent day, for instance, the programs included a panel discussion on needy children, a lengthy talk on the origins of Stonehenge, an interview with Henry Miller, an open-line show hosted by symphony conductor Lawrence Leonard, and readings by local poets.
>
> Musicwise, CKUA isn't timid about mixing the works of classical composers with sounds of a more contemporary nature. It's not uncommon to hear the likes of Vivaldi, Bob Dylan or Roberta Flack sharing the same one-hour time slot with a batch of ethnic folk songs or an excerpt from an old Peter Sellers comedy LP.

A member of the British House of Lords, brought to Edmonton as a guest speaker, was also impressed with CKUA. According to June Sheppard, who interviewed him for her *Edmonton Journal* column, Lord Samuels was head of a committee to study broadcasting in the United Kingdom and took back copies of CKUA's program schedule, "so impressed was he by this 'distinctive' Canadian station, and by the lack of interference with it by the government which provided the funding."

The new corporation in charge of CKUA had every intention of keeping CKUA's distinctive character intact, according to ACCESS president Larry Shorter, except for asking programmers to pay a bit more attention to supplying contextual information with their music. His plan was "number one, to save the station, to maintain the musical programming, but also to graft onto it anywhere from 7 to 10 percent educational content—some of which would be hard-nosed education."

Shorter had big plans to use CKUA's additional bandwidth—a sideband or subcarrier, also called subsidiary communications allocation (SCA)—to deliver computer-assisted instruction and a fax network to all the schools in Alberta. "The idea was not to destroy the slightly dowdy programming—I often called it CKUA's catholic disregard for shallow popular taste—but to continue the quality of the station and add those other things."

During the corporation's first two years, ACCESS management concentrated primarily on expanding CKUA into a truly provincial radio station, mainly by adding transmitters and increasing the station's news coverage of the province. By the fall of 1977 CKUA had a news team of ten covering the province out of Lethbridge, Calgary and Edmonton.

Rather than compete with the CBC, which had fourteen people in Edmonton alone and primarily covered municipal and national affairs, news director Andy Smith (who later became director of CFRN-TV news) carved out a niche for CKUA on the provincial and international fronts. And on the high road. There would be no yellow journalism at CKUA. When Pierre and Margaret Trudeau's marriage started unravelling, Albertans didn't hear about Margaret's black eye or her dalliance with the Rolling Stones from this station. But they did get an intensive look at a land-use dispute between farmers and developers proposing a strip-mine operation in the Camrose-Ryley area. CKUA dispatched two reporters to the scene for two weeks, a luxury the station would enjoy for only a brief period during its long life.

CKUA put together its international news from a variety of sources such as the BBC World Service, Inter-News (a daily telephone feed from Berkeley, California) and the *Christian Science Monitor*. In 1977 Smith told RPM magazine, "We analyze rather than merely report the news. Our aim is to be a newspaper on the air." That year Smith began "The Bell Adventures," a phone-in public affairs program featuring controversial figures in the news. The

◆ Don Popein and Ed Kilpatrick (right) at one of the station's first FM stereo transmitters, 1975. Courtesy of CKUA.

next year CKUA began regular broadcasts of Question Period from the Alberta Legislature—another Canadian first for the station—with Warren Graves, a playwright and former clerk of the assembly, as commentator.

The expansion of CKUA's transmission coverage began almost immediately. Hagerman had already sold the corporation board on going with FM and with using the SCA. "Of all the things I've done, that's the thing I was proudest of," he said twenty-five years later. "FM was not widespread at the time, but I told them it would give much better coverage and it would be cheaper to set up. If we'd stayed with AM, CKUA would be dead by now."

The original plan was ambitious—to increase CKUA-FM Edmonton to 100,000 watts and add transmitters of the same power at Calgary and Lethbridge, Medicine Hat, Red Deer, Grande Prairie and Peace River by early 1976. A second phase would fill in with "step-outs" from these transmitters to ensure coverage to Drumheller, Stettler, Vermilion, St. Paul, Athabasca, Edson and the North Peace by the summer of 1977. A third phase would fill remaining holes in the network during 1977–78.

CKUA's broadcasting engineer Hugh Kroetch enlisted AGT in the project. In October 1975 Edmonton got its new 100,000-watt stereo FM transmitter. On February 27, 1976 Ron Yoshida of Lethbridge got his wish: he had written a letter two years earlier supporting CKUA's application to the CRTC for an FM licence to rebroadcast to the Lethbridge area.

"With a little luck, the proper radio, the proper weather conditions, and the proper time of day, I have been able to get some idea of what CKUA programming is like.... Night listening, of course, has been out of the question," Yoshida wrote. Yet most of the music he was able to hear on CKUA needed to be heard, he said. "It is a vital part of North American Culture and if it is left to ordinary commercial radio we will never hear it.... Southern Alberta in particular needs this programming. This is a nice area in many respects, but culturally it is a vacuum. The person who said that the tastes of Southern Alberta were formed by the Eaton's catalogue [was] not far off."

With Yoshida in attendance as a guest, ACCESS chairman Michael O'Byrne quoted his letter at the opening of CKUA's 100,000-watt FM stereo transmitter in Lethbridge. Medicine Hat listeners got their transmitter in June 1976; Calgary listeners, in September. The extended coverage brought CKUA nearly 20,000 new listeners between 1974 and 1976, when the station's weekly unduplicated audience was measured at 63,800.

Given these positive changes, CKUA got through its first few years under ACCESS relatively unscathed and in even better shape than before, putting to rest earlier fears that the station would lose its soul under the provincial corporation. "The pedagogues had not run amuck!" Shorter wrote, oddly enough, in a White Paper released in February 1977 explaining coming changes that would stir up those fears once again.

The Lougheed government was beginning to backpedal from the liberal educational philosophy it had endorsed by embracing the Worth Commission report. "The Conservative party became surprised to find what a liberal educational document they had bought," Shorter said years later. "They started toughening up their stance on education. Then they put the screws on to have more '3R' educational content on CKUA."

According to Shorter, even under ACCESS, CKUA had a tough time justifying its existence as an "educational" broadcaster in some quarters. "While the CRTC was prepared to give us a fair amount of latitude, the bottom line was a whole bunch of other people weren't, including commercial radio stations and other people who said, 'I tuned in the other night and someone was playing "I Hear You've Been Screwing my Old Lady" by the Stump Queens. Now tell me how that's educational.' So we were often under the gun to justify what we were doing. And especially if we ever got an audience for a program, the commercial broadcasters would say we were unfair competition—'What's educational about this?'"

Meanwhile, the federal government was concerned not only about CKUA's educational content but also about the length of the arm between ACCESS and the Alberta government. When the station's licence came up for renewal in 1976, the CRTC decided to grant the licence for only two years instead of the standard four years. It noted that the wording of the Alberta act establishing ACCESS had not changed. The act still gave the Alberta Educational Communications Authority—comprised of the two ministers of education—the power to give direction to ACCESS on programming. That meant the potential for decreasing the corporation's independence from government still existed, and the CRTC wanted to keep an eye on the situation. The decision also stated,

> The Commission wishes to remind the applicant that the programming in question must nevertheless be "designed to furnish educational opportunities" and must also be "distinctly different from general broadcasting available on the national broadcasting service or on privately owned broadcasting undertakings." The Commission considers that the "foreground format" as defined in section 12 (1) of the Radio (FM) Broadcasting Regulations, particularly as regards the following portion of that definition:
> (A) the intrinsic intellectual content of the matter being broadcast is entirely related to a particular theme or subject.
> (B) the duration of the presentation, including interruptions, is at least fifteen minutes ...
> ... is a format which is well suited to the type of programming contemplated by the order in council.

The commission's new FM broadcast regulations spelled out in great detail how FM stations must distinguish themselves from AM stations to qualify for a licence: specifically, "listeners should be able to hear on FM at various, regular, properly promoted times, programs with a sense of form and purpose." In general, FM stations would be required to devote twenty-five percent of their time to programs of the "foreground format" type, which "demands much closer attention from its audience," who have more time and "seek a more involved listening experience." As examples of "foreground format," the commission suggested magazine or documentary programs, staged presentations, seminars or meetings, or recorded music of a particular artist or composer or devoted to a particular musical genre. This was in contrast to the "rolling format" of AM, which consists of music without discussion by an announcer, plus time and weather. This format is "based on the assumption that listeners are 'on the go' and are only 'available' for limited and irregular time periods."

Provincially, the Alberta Educational Communications Authority had issued guidelines in February 1975 regarding appropriate percentages of various types of content for both radio and television. One guideline stipulated that overall programming should be twenty-five percent instructional, fifty percent educational enrichment and twenty-five percent special purpose. Further, instructional programming must be directly related to "a course of instruction offered by educational institutions or agencies." At the time, CKUA's "instructional" programming ranged between two and four percent. The guidelines recommended that "for the present" all ACCESS programming conform to the CRTC's definition of "educational" but then put forward a new definition for consideration that made it clear who the authority wanted to be in charge of programming decisions:

Educational programming is programming deliberately designed to fulfill clearly stated educational objectives derived from the needs of Canadians and expressed by those who by law or by reason of their professional responsibilities are recognized as being accountable to Canadians for educational activities.

Now the government was pressing its intent to put educators in charge of ACCESS with a set of ministerial directives affirming that the "principal role" of ACCESS—including CKUA—was to support Alberta's two education departments and their agencies.

ACCESS president Larry Shorter wrote a document, *Planning for Change: A White Paper on ACCESS Radio CKUA*, to diplomatically explain the situation to listeners and to seek their input but also to let them know that change was inevitable.

CKUA's licence is held by ACCESS subject to the regulatory control of two bodies, one federal, the other provincial. The federal body is the CRTC.... The second body is the Alberta Educational Communications Authority (AECA)....

Both the CRTC and the Provincial Authority have indicated that CKUA's programming should become more "educational" than it is now.

Anyone familiar with the CRTC will realize that the *suggestions* contained in the conditions of license are to be taken seriously.

Meanwhile, discussions between ACCESS and the provincial authority were "continuing," the White Paper said. ACCESS was proposing a gradual increase in instructional content of one and a half hours per week over each of the next five years, bringing instructional content up to between eight and ten percent. The White Paper mentioned certain mixed music programs, such as "Shank of the Morning," that might be shortened over the next few years, while "Candlelight and Silver" "might benefit from a more thematic treatment, so that it is not mistaken for incidental, background music. By the fourth year, it is likely that these programs would be eliminated entirely to allow a concentrated block of instructional programming."

The White Paper acknowledged this might not sit well with some CKUA listeners and included a questionnaire to solicit their reaction. "Mindful of its earlier pledge to maintain CKUA's 'uniqueness,' ACCESS is encouraging a listeners' forum concerning the proposed changes. This White Paper approach is an attempt to solicit listener opinions while plans are still flexible enough to accommodate some of the ground swells which could occur."

And they did occur. Coming so soon after the last crisis, the White Paper hit listeners in February 1977 like the second shoe dropping. They picked up their letter writing where they'd left off just three years earlier. More than seven hundred listeners responded to the White Paper, most of them against increasing CKUA's instructional content to ten percent. Edmonton-based filmmaker Tom Radford spoke eloquently on their behalf in an *Edmonton Journal* piece:

The wonderful thing about CKUA is that it has never really fit into any easy category. It has somehow escaped being "programmed" in the worst sense of that word. It has made its way with great freedom, been able to experiment, break the rules. Play Bach or Elgar beside the Beatles or Bruce Cockburn or Bob Ruzicka. Talk about local personalities in the same breath as those of national and international fame. You would hear a local musician or writer talking with a superstar in town on a one night stand—talking about what they had in common. Growing up listening to CKUA, I felt part of a much bigger world without ever doubting that Edmonton itself was an exciting place. I grew up an Albertan but never with a feeling that the outside world was cut off....

CKUA has always been a much better teacher than the educational system which now so self-righteously has come to stand in judgement of it. So much of what I learned—and very soon forgot—going through the school system here has later reappeared in my life through CKUA—but in a form that was able to hold my interest. You were much more likely to get to like classical music when you would hear it played between two of your favorite Top-40 songs. Much more than by hearing it analyzed by some expert. Now if we are to believe the white paper, more and more in the future we are to hear things one at a time in "themes" and have them explained to us. Why at this late date are we being returned to the classroom?

... I fear the future—driving home from a bad day, listening to a lecture on thermodynamics as a way to relax and regain faith in things; eating supper while listening to my old math teacher!

And what was the point of the White Paper anyway? Radford quoted a listener who had responded to a phone-in show on the station's future: "'It's like having some city officials arrive at your door to tell you a freeway is going to be built through your yard and ask about the best way to build it.'"

A Turner Valley listener wrote to the *Calgary Herald*, "Let us not stand idly by while a remarkable radio station is possibly mutilated by well-intentioned, but soulless officialdom."

Warren Graves, who had worked at ACCESS and would later serve as Question Period commentator for CKUA, wrote to the CKUA station manager:

As an employee in the television area of ACCESS, I found that educational television came to mean a bureaucratic growth of consultants and committees, checks and balances, the death of creativity, and, ultimately and incredibly, almost the complete loss of production capacity. The story of the brilliant concept of ACCESS appears to be turning into an extended tragedy....

Calling CKUA "an oasis in the desert of pop cult and commercial advertising," Graves continued:

It is a radio station for an audience and not for a sponsor. However, I feel the sponsors are gathering on the horizon and that they will consist of professional educators—those detached experts somehow manage to prevent the needs of teachers and students in the classroom from interfering with their work....

Just think how many consultants and committees could latch their parasitic tentacles onto a flourishing operation like CKUA? Enough to suck the production budget completely dry, you bet your arse.

A part-time CKUA announcer, Bill Jensen, was so incensed about the coming changes that he took matters into his own hands. On his mixed music program—presumably destined to disappear in favour of one taking a "thematic" approach—he complained to his listeners one Sunday afternoon in September about CKUA management's apparent indifference to the crisis and turned his show into a phone-in forum on the White Paper. In short order he was fired—for violating station policy by deviating from the stated objectives of an established program; that is, for letting editorial comment dominate a music program.

One of Jensen's listeners was so outraged that he wrote to the CRTC demanding that CKUA's licence not be renewed. Another listener wrote that the "mixed bag" music programs were "the most important part of CKUA's music education programming because they expose the listener to a wide range of musical forms." He concluded, "It is my belief that some of the White Paper proposals will result in a deterioration of music programming and certainly a loss of listeners."

Kilpatrick gamely responded: "A recent research study has shown that regular listeners to CKUA are strongly opposed to any major change in the programming of the radio station." He said ACCESS would send the results to the authority and press for only a "minor increase in instructional programs on CKUA. So we take a deep breath and learn to think of ourselves as educators. With an obligation to our listener's preferences, we can probably survive."

At the end of September, the *Edmonton Journal* revealed the contents of a confidential report, signed by O'Byrne for the ACCESS board, refusing to endorse the new directives from the province and suggesting they smacked of "one-sided, unilateral regulation." The board agreed with the authority that the "principal role" of ACCESS was to support Alberta's education departments, but it also wanted the new directives to spell out legitimate supplementary roles, namely, "support of educational objectives in other government departments including culture, agriculture, consumer affairs, environment and health"; and "advancement of cultural, artistic and recreational opportunities for Alberta residents." This would presumably legitimize CKUA as "educational." The board also wanted CKUA management to have a freer hand in programming decisions than that given to ACCESS television.

In addition to the restrictive directives, the government put a freeze on the ACCESS budget. As an immediate result, CKUA closed its Lethbridge news office and concentrated its news-gathering services in Edmonton and Calgary, using stringers in outlying areas.

Writing about the internal problems at ACCESS and the heavy-handed directives, *Edmonton Journal* television and radio columnist Jim Waters said that the ACCESS directors "seem more perturbed by government interference in programming which, after all, is the essence of ACCESS. If they can get it back on track, they'll be doing something. If not, we'll never know how good ACCESS could have been. Many Edmontonians who grew up during the formative years of alternative radio will never forget how good CKUA used to be."

In the midst of the White Paper turmoil, CKUA celebrated its golden anniversary on November 21, 1977 with a reception featuring an early radio play by Elsie Park Gowan, produced by CKUA announcer Chris Allen with members of the original CKUA Players. The event also featured a re-enactment of H.P. Brown's magnesium flash debacle on November 21, 1927. ACCESS marked the occasion by turning on the Peace River transmitter, located on a hill by the grave of "Twelve Foot" Davis, a gold prospector and fur trader who made his first fortune on a twelve-foot claim in the Cariboo gold rush of 1861. Grande Prairie's transmitter went on a month later.

At the time, CKUA's cumulative weekly audience was roughly 50,000, compared with 500,000 for Edmonton's top-rated CHED. But ratings were still not a big concern. On CKUA's fiftieth anniversary, Hagerman told the *Edmonton Journal*, "It [CKUA] was a chance to do the things you wanted and thought should be done without always having to worry whether it would sell. If it fell on its can, what the hell? You pick yourself up and try again. You could be fairly experimental without running the risk of going down the drain."

Describing CKUA's "educational" philosophy to RPM magazine, he said, "People sometimes forget how limited the world of the majority is—and how narrow their own world often is! If you can tempt a person into listening to something outside his own experience, even for a few minutes, that constitutes a genuine educational experience. If you can tempt him to come back again and again, that's continuing education."

But that wasn't good enough for the Alberta and federal governments. Once again, the times were changing for CKUA. After much deliberation over CKUA's instructional content, the ACCESS board resolved to increase the station's formal educational programming—which it called "principal role programming"—to ten percent. The remaining ninety percent would be devoted to "supplementary" programming.

While the emphasis on instructional content as CKUA's "principal role" made CKUA more palatable to government authorities, it would have far-reaching effects on the station's character and ultimately jeopardize its status with the very government that imposed it.

40 years of success!!
ACCESS NETWORK RADIO CKUA
HONOURS

GABY HAAS

for his dedication and enthusiasm in making

"Continental Musicale"

the longest running radio program in the world.

Sept. 21, 1986

ACCESS NETWORK

ACCESS NETWORK
CKUA

But Is It Entertaining? | 11

Nobody could argue that CKUA wasn't improving technically under ACCESS during the corporation's first decade. In 1981 four new low-power FM transmitter units extended the station's reach to Edson, Fort McMurray, Hinton and Whitecourt. By January 1983 Athabasca, Drumheller/Hanna and Spirit River had their transmitters. CKUA entered the space age in 1985 when ACCESS began beaming twelve hours of programs a day to cable-television companies and distributing CKUA programming to its network transmitters via the Anik B communications satellite.

On the news and current affairs front, CKUA stood out among its peers with its beefed-up resources and ACCESS mandate to cover the province. The station produced comprehensive news broadcasts throughout the day, plus half-hour news magazines and current affairs documentaries. It carried budget and throne speeches and the daily Question Period live from the Legislature.

"I had a very good sense that it was a place where you could actually practise broadcast journalism, and there weren't many places back then to do that," Ken Regan recalled. He had arrived in Alberta in 1982 after graduating from Carleton University's journalism program.

"Those were the glory days of CKUA. The newsroom was very comprehensive, well staffed, well financed—and frankly was one of the foremost news agencies in this province. No question about it. And it was recognized as such by everybody from the CBC to the *Calgary Herald* to the *Edmonton Journal*. People looked up to CKUA as the station of record for things Albertan, for what was going on in Alberta news."

Regan described his fellow news staffers at the time as "very accomplished people." Yvonne Gall, who reported from the Calgary bureau, eventually moved on to CBC Radio in Vancouver; Ron McDonald, CKUA's news director at the time, became chairman of the journalism program at Mount Royal College; Larry Donovan, another CKUA news director, went on to Christian Science Monitor Radio as London bureau chief; and Ian Gray, a CKUA reporter and news director, later freelanced for Reuters and the *Financial Post*.

CKUA also had a network of stringers reporting from Lethbridge, Medicine Hat, Red Deer, Grande Prairie, and even Toronto and Ottawa. "The mandate was for provincial coverage and we did—we covered the province," Regan recalled. "Whether it was a gas well blow-out at Lodgepole or whether it was something in Fort McMurray, we found a way to provide coverage for those events."

When it came to political reporting, the Alberta government kept its hands off, Regan said. "We were critical when it was legitimate to be critical and we were fair at all times.... Even in our dealings with ministers, we were tough but we were professional journalists, and the government people recognized that and they treated us as such, so there was never any interference or any hint of interference that I'm aware of."

The most significant change that came over CKUA under ACCESS was its increased emphasis on instructional—as opposed to merely "educational"—content, or to use the ACCESS bureaucracy's term for it, "Principal-Role Programming." In 1980 ACCESS took over responsibility for producing Alberta School Broadcasts from Alberta Education, and to meet ACCESS Radio CKUA's increased formal education responsibilities, the corporation hired CBC veteran Jackie Rollans as executive producer for Principal-Role Programming. Her first task was to set up a production department or "Principal-Role unit" to create the required programs.

Rollans had grown up in Vermilion and spent eighteen years as a producer with CBC Edmonton, where she developed and produced the station's first morning information program, "Edmonton AM," and for some time was in charge of the public affairs department. When she arrived at CKUA in 1980, Rollans had to move quickly.

"I advertised for producers all across Canada because a lot of [programs] were dramas and I really needed people from all over.... In that first year we had 93 dramas." She coaxed Fred Diehl, who had been with CKUA many years before, to take a leave of absence from the CBC to help set up the unit. "He had acted himself and produced drama and music ... and I thought, 'If anybody was an experienced drama producer in Canada, it would be Fred....' He stayed over six months, and we very hurriedly trained everybody."

A huge pool of freelancers complemented an in-house Principal-Role production staff of about six. The announcers were slow to accept the changes taking place and initially felt the new group to be interlopers. Their resentment was exacerbated by the fact that budgeting often favoured Principal-Role projects that came with co-production dollars attached. Dave Ward, who joined CKUA in 1982 as record librarian, said the library's previously generous budget had been cut back by the time he arrived.

Principal-Role programs replaced music programs in the 11:00 a.m. to noon and 7:00 to 8:00 p.m. time slots. Rollans' unit worked closely with Alberta Education to produce other taped materials intended for classroom use only. For example, the group created a series of eighteen ten-minute audio-tapes, entitled "All That I Can Be," for grades four to six, plus a French version of the series, to support the life careers theme of the department's new health curriculum. The Principal-Role unit also produced teachers' guides to go with the programs.

Alberta Education initiated many of the Principal-Role projects and attached budgets to them. Other projects received support from the advanced education department and from the province's universities, colleges and other educational institutions. ACCESS invited educators to contribute project ideas for consideration. Some of the instructional programs were funded completely by ACCESS; some were co-produced with other organizations.

Programs were produced in three educational categories: early and basic education, higher education, and further education. For example, a series of thirteen dramatized stories called "The Family of Stories" was conceived by

◆ *"Something for Seniors" hosts Peggy Holmes and Chris Allen, 1982.*
Courtesy of CKUA.

University of Alberta English professor Jon Stott for the elementary school English curriculum. Stott wrote the program outlines, freelance writer Andrea Spalding fleshed them out into scripts, and actors brought them to life for school audiences.

Tommy Banks hosted "Music Compositions" for grades five to seven, a program that deviated from customary methods of teaching children "what music is made of." Instead of using traditional folk songs with quaint pre-Victorian lyrics, the ACCESS approach engaged children with contemporary words and stories that were more "accessible" to them. Okotoks figured prominently in one ditty Banks composed for the program. CKUA also produced French-language programs and worked with Ukrainian-speaking teachers and actors to create several Ukrainian series in music and social studies for Alberta Education.

In addition to the formal instructional programs, CKUA expanded its traditional programming to include informal adult-education productions, drawing in the music programmers and news staff to help create general-interest documentaries and magazine-type programs. Over the next four years, CKUA annually produced more than four hundred half-hour principal- and supplementary-role programs.

Among the ambitious general-interest series produced during the early and mid 1980s were "Discover," with host David Suzuki; "Women in Science"; "Coping in the Eighties"; "Co-operation and Conflict Among Nations"; and "Listening to Literature." "Recombinant DNA and Beyond" surveyed the field of biological engineering and its moral, legal, economic and political implications for society.

In 1982 CKUA programmer Chris Allen teamed up with Peggy Holmes, who at eighty-five enjoyed a reputation as Canada's oldest broadcaster, to start "Something for Seniors." They delivered lively discussions on everything from housing to health, sometimes taking their mikes out of the studio to unusual locations—once even broadcasting from a hot-air balloon. A segment on sexuality was a groundbreaker at the time.

"Ask an Alcoholic," produced by Ken Regan and Principal-Role project manager Nancy Sherbaniuk, featured alcoholics talking about their struggles and experts answering questions from callers. A series called "For Single Parents" was co-produced with the Alberta Law Foundation and the Alberta Women's Bureau. "Preparing for Public Performance" took listeners behind the scenes in the piano master class at the Banff Centre School of Fine Arts and inside the personal studio of Alberta pianist and internationally known interpreter of Chopin's music Marek Jablonski. (When visiting Edmonton for a performance, Jablonski sometimes rehearsed on CKUA's grand piano.)

"Alberta People" profiled "interesting Albertans from all walks of life," while "Cowboy Capitalists" looked at Alberta's entrepreneurs. "The Chip and You" demystified computers in a thirteen-part series.

"Arts Alberta," hosted by Tommy Banks, played a big role in carrying out CKUA's mandate to promote Alberta artists. The program featured interviews, reviews and mini-documentaries on Alberta authors, sculptors, performers and other artists. Banks also hosted a "Celebrate Bach" series with Sandra Munn, a University of Alberta music professor, presenting young Alberta pianists playing the master's music in conjunction with the Tri-Bach events in the province.

The University of Alberta continued to supply weekly programs produced on campus by its radio and television department through the early ACCESS years. In 1980 these included "University Concert Hall," featuring composers and performers on campus discussing their music; "Legal Maze," dealing with everyday problems in Alberta society including controversial topics such as rape and sexual harassment; and "Extensions," a series produced by Jim Shaw of the U of A extension department. CKUA's formal relationship with the university ended in the early 1980s when the university discontinued its radio service.

Around that time CKUA began a partnership with Athabasca University, the province's fledgling "open university" experiment in distance learning. In 1980 the university broadcast twenty-four BBC-produced programs to its students over CKUA as part of its French 103 course, "Ensemble: French for Beginners." Later that year Athabasca University professor David Gregory decided to use radio to supplement the printed materials and telephone tutorials the university was using for some humanities courses. The result was "Writers and Thinkers," an ambitious spoken word series of seventy-four programs that ran for two and a half hours on Thursday nights for four years.

The series, which Gregory developed with CKUA producer Brian Dunsmore, turned into seven sub-series ranging from "The World of Ancient Greece" and "Shakespeare and His Contemporaries" to "Seminal Thinkers: Jesus to Nietzsche." More than half of the programs were dramas, such as Sophocles' *Oedipus Rex*, mostly produced by the BBC. The others concentrated on seminal thinkers or important topics in the history of ideas, including features on such intellectuals as Karl Marx and Friedrich Engels, Sigmund Freud, Bertold Brecht and James Joyce.

"I think my greatest achievement in the ... series, and probably the program that had the lowest listener count of all, was a feature on the philosophers Bertrand Russell and Ludwig Wittgenstein that took me an entire week to script," Gregory wrote in *Canadian Folk Music Bulletin*. "Well, it was definitely educational radio ... but was it entertaining? Except for a small minority of listeners who felt starved of serious ideas and good drama, I think not. Certainly the station manager at CKUA thought it was all a tad too heavy, a bit too intellectual even for the minority audience that the station was aiming to please." The program was retitled "Theatre of the Air" in 1984 and ran for twelve more years hosted by Athabasca University professor Anne Nothof.

◆ CKUA's 1981 Japan Prize-winning team: (left to right) Andrea Spalding, Alf Franke, Jackie Rollans and David Spalding. Courtesy of CKUA.

Meanwhile, Gregory and Dunsmore teamed up in 1981 to produce something equally ambitious but, Gregory hoped, a little more entertaining, to supplement his course on the history of popular music. "Ragtime to Rolling Stones" covered (mainly American) popular music from 1900 to 1970 in 104 1-hour programs. They included a chronological overview of musical traditions from ragtime to jazz-rock fusion and folk-rock, as well as programs on musical genres and individual artists from Appalachian hillbilly music to Bix Beiderbecke.

"Somebody, somewhere else, may have put together an even more comprehensive audio survey of the history of modern Western popular music, but if they have, I've never come across it," Gregory wrote. The early programs reflected an initial tug of war between Gregory's tendency towards painstaking explanatory commentary and Dunsmore's concern for the entertainment factor. But the pair—who, after regular workdays, worked through countless nights to record the programs when the studio was free—soon evolved a balance between education and entertainment that appealed to listeners. At its height the program had an audience of about ten thousand, according to Gregory.

ACCESS Radio CKUA put considerable resources into the huge volume of educational programming it churned out in the 1980s. The professionalism that went into those programs is reminiscent of the perfectionism Sheila Marryat brought to the task in the 1930s. Freelancers Andrea Spalding and David Spalding were part of the 1980s team, writing scripts and original music, singing, acting and creating just the right sound effects. Andrea recalled the attention to detail—and fun—that went into those productions:

> Once Colin Maclean was producing a script of mine for the program "Our Nearest Neighbour—the United States." The subject was the pilgrims.... I had set several scenes on board the Mayflower in a storm and I had written it as [a] sort of counterpoint choral speech scene with the pilgrims singing an old hymn interspersed with the shouts of sailors struggling with sails, and sound effects with wind and waves and a raucous sea shanty in the background....
>
> There we were in the studio rehearsing, singing this hymn as though our lives depended on it. Of course we couldn't hear the storm sound effects, as they were being added in the control room. We were placed in the center of the studio, pilgrims on one mike and sailors on the other.
>
> "Stop!" Colin Maclean came bursting into the studio. "It doesn't sound desperate enough, and it doesn't sound as though it's on a tossing ship." He moved the pilgrims to one side of the studio and the sailors to the other. We tried again.
>
> "Stop! Your voices are fine, but I don't get a sense of a swaying ship." He thought for a minute. "I need you to sing and do your lines while running from one side of the studio to the other. As though you are being thrown around a heaving deck."
>
> [CKUA technical producer] Alf Franke rolled his eyes, removed the mike stands and hung the mikes from the ceiling....
>
> We pilgrims sang, shouted, and ran in a mass from one side of the room to the other. The sailors did the same in the opposite direction.... The studio was small, there were a lot of actors, and several pile-ups

ensued. While mayhem took place, Alf added wind, rain and waves over the top. The final effect was stunning.

I should add this was taped on a hot summer evening and there was no air conditioning in the old building. At the end of the session we were exhausted, dehydrated and sea sick, just like the pilgrims. Unlike them we adjourned to the local pub for a beer.

Franke, who retired in 1990 after twenty-nine years with CKUA, is remembered with great respect by the people who worked with him. "He encouraged us to disrupt his studio many times, and helped create wonderful sound-scapes," Andrea Spalding said. "Never once did he tell us we couldn't try something, no matter how outrageous."

Once, Spalding found herself in front of a mike crumpling a foam cup to approximate the sound of a scorpion munching a grasshopper while her husband David narrated a natural-history script. The program was part of a basic life-science series, "Listen to the Prairie," that David wrote and narrated for CKUA. The subtle use of sound effects brought the prairie to life and helped earn one program in the series, "Prairie Rattlesnake," the prestigious Minister of Education Prize for Radio in the Japan Prize International Educational Program Contest for 1981. Perhaps as rewarding was the comment by an elementary school student that the program "made pictures in my mind."

Meanwhile, there was turmoil at ACCESS on the television side. Conflicts between ACCESS employees and management over contracting out, as opposed to in-house production, resulted in an exodus of staff. Many who left weren't replaced, while others were laid off in what one former employee called a "purge."

ACCESS founder and president Larry Shorter became frustrated that the provincial government was backtracking on its endorsement of the Worth Commission's liberal education recommendations. In particular, he was disappointed that the government didn't pursue his plan for reaching into the classroom with a vast educational technology network that included extensive use of CKUA's excess bandwidth for facsimile and computer downloads.

"The government ... would never give us a proper educational mandate and would never make use of the educational capacity we had built into the system with CKUA, turned down all the proposals for a computer download and facsimile and all these things we had up and running on an experimental basis. So we built this marvellous delivery system and the government decided not to use it.... We could never use the economy of scale that CKUA and ACCESS could deliver."

In the end, the government chose to use the excess bandwidth only for delivery of its Emergency Public Warning System. Shorter left ACCESS in 1982 after nine years at the helm.

Jack Hagerman left the same year. When he went over to the corporation as general manager of broadcast operations eight years earlier, he was put in charge of stickhandling budgets through the corporation and licence applications through the CRTC, a job he "didn't particularly care for." Looking back on those years he said, "I hated ACCESS. I hated it for a full eight years until I retired.... The stress level was very high in that place. You were banging your head against the wall most of the time. Not only was there a lot of politics, but ... educational administrators ... were just awful to work with."

Rollans, too, found it frustrating dealing with the ACCESS bureaucracy. Throughout her first three years on the job, she said, "We never had our own general manager at CKUA. It was always somebody from ACCESS who didn't know a damned thing about radio and it was frustrating as hell. Everyone who came in as general manager decided to change programming to their own personal taste—not for any other reason. They just thought, 'I don't like this program so it should go.' It was ridiculous."

Herb Johnson returned to CKUA in early 1982 and found a situation "noticeably different" from his earlier years. In particular, there was "a whole bunch of people giving orders." He said he didn't feel restricted in terms of the music he could play, because the musical programming structure that had evolved during his "golden years" at CKUA was still intact. But he did run into trouble when he took other liberties he was accustomed to in the old days.

"I changed the name of a program.... Back in the old days, we'd make up our own program names [but now] the original name was on all kinds of pieces of paper—program guides and things like that. I just got tired of calling it what it was called and so I called it something else, which was not a good idea under that kind of structure."

◆ Fil Fraser hosted or appeared on a number of CKUA programs between the mid 1960s and late 1980s.
Courtesy of CKUA.

Shorter's successor, Peter Senchuk, came from a private broadcasting background, most recently from fifteen years as vice-president and managing director of the local television and radio stations in Lloydminster. Before that he had spent a number of years in radio on the engineering side. Some say his Conservative party connections enhanced his qualifications for the position.

"The attractiveness to me was to create a new television educational service across Alberta," he said of his initial interest in the ACCESS position. Up to that point the corporation had been supplying tapes of its productions to educators and renting a couple of hours of time each morning on five Alberta television stations to carry its programs to the public.

Fil Fraser, who had been program director with MEETA and had worked with Shorter in the lead-up to ACCESS, said the transition from Shorter to Senchuk set a whole new tone for ACCESS.

"Larry [Shorter] had a view of educational broadcasting that was very different from the department's view. There was a clash between those who think it should be courses for students and teachers and those who feel it's a public service that should have a broad brush. And I think at the end of the day, Larry lost the battle. He was really the heart of the place when he was there. To go from Larry Shorter to Peter Senchuk... two absolutely diametrically opposed approaches, philosophies, styles ... You can sum up Larry Shorter [by the fact] that at his funeral [in 1998], at his request, we all sang the Louis Armstrong song 'What a Wonderful World'."

In 1983 ACCESS decided CKUA needed to broaden its appeal to mainstream Alberta and boost its ratings. "In light of that mandate, this year we are making changes, albeit moderate, in certain segments of CKUA's programming. We are moving out of the eclectic format, at least in the morning time period, to a more mellow sound, one that is upbeat, and more recognizable to Albertans," the corporation announced.

Calgary Herald columnist Patrick Tivy wrote of the upcoming change, "Listeners tend to switch dials when a Vivaldi concerto is followed too closely by an African thumb piano solo. But no more." The vehicle for the mellowing of CKUA would be a new program in the 7:00 to 10:00 a.m. time slot.

"Alberta Morning" started on September 1, 1983, heavily promoted as "The Talk of the Province." To host the program, ACCESS parachuted Fil Fraser in as "program consultant" and paid him a rumoured sum that was way out of CKUA's league. This didn't sit well with CKUA's on-air programmers. Fraser, a seasoned broadcaster and one-time feature film producer, had appeared often on CKUA since "Thinking Out Loud" in the mid 1960s. He'd also been an open-line host on CJCA and was most recently host of an innovative "journalistic information" morning program at CKXM-FM in which he phoned experts for live chats on current events.

With a hefty travel budget and research assistants, Fraser tried a similar idea on "Alberta Morning," including remote broadcasts from around the province. The laid-back Johnson was operator and "anchor," selecting and introducing the music, mostly jazz and classics. CKUA received numerous letters of complaint from listeners who didn't like this change on their morning radio. The *Calgary Herald*'s Tivy later pronounced the show "a dud." But Bureau of Broadcast Measurement (BBM) ratings in the fall indicated that the morning audience had picked up. Even so, after a little over a year, the show was cancelled.

Johnson said there was a clash of egos: "We had me with my ego sitting there ... picking the music ... and trying to keep things together and we had Fil and his ego in the other studio and they didn't always mesh. It was a very complicated situation." Ultimately it was Fraser's show. "He was the Lone

Ranger. I was Tonto." In hindsight, Fraser said he "came into CKUA like a bull in a china shop."

One of Senchuk's early moves was to launch a review of the ACCESS mandate. "One possible change (vis a vis CKUA) could be in a direction to attract a larger audience," he told the *Edmonton Journal*. According to CKUA insiders, Ed Kilpatrick was nudged out in the process. ACCESS had begun a search for a general manager of a newly created radio division and invited Kilpatrick to apply, but then left the post vacant and later advertised it again.

Kilpatrick, who had been acting in the position, retired in June 1984 after twenty-six years with CKUA. When he announced his retirement in January, he told the media it was not motivated by the corporate review or the search for a general manager. But insiders say there was a rumour that Senchuk wanted someone more "high-powered" for the job. A comment by Hagerman supports this version: "When it came to running the place, Ed was a little too gentle—he was too nice a guy for the job."

Kilpatrick was well loved by CKUA staff for his open mind as well as for his genuine kindness and respect for his fellow human beings. Files in CKUA's archives contain thoughtful letters he wrote in response to queries not only from listeners but also from others who couldn't possibly be listeners. One was to a schoolgirl from Birch River, Manitoba, who sent him a list of questions on all aspects of radio and wanted a response "as soon as possible" for a school project. She got a generous detailed response that probably saved her the trouble of doing any research of her own.

A young inmate in Georgia State Prison who had lived in Alberta as a child wrote Kilpatrick a plaintive letter asking him to broadcast an appeal to any relatives he might still have in the province. "My parents were both killed in an automobile accident when I was 16. I lived in a foster home until I reached the age of 18. I'm incarcerated in prison now and have never felt more lonely in my life."

Kilpatrick replied, "It would be useful to know where in Alberta you lived and attended school ... as well [as] the names of members of your family whom you think may still live in the province. Edmonton and Calgary have become the largest cities in Alberta, so I'll start here and do what I can to help." Kilpatrick sent the man the names and addresses of people in the Edmonton phone directory with the same last name. At his own expense he also ran a series of classified ads in the *Edmonton Journal* on the prisoner's behalf.

◆ *Don Thomas was appointed general manager of ACCESS Radio CKUA in 1984.*

Courtesy of CKUA.

After Kilpatrick left, Rollans became program manager for both the Principal-Role unit and CKUA's traditional programming group. In April 1984 Senchuk announced the new general manager for ACCESS Radio CKUA. Don Thomas was an Albertan with thirty-five years of experience in commercial broadcasting, most recently as vice-president and general manager of CFCN Radio in Calgary.

With his commercial radio background, Thomas felt CKUA was lacking in consistency and could be operated more professionally. That was also the conclusion of a 1979 report on CKUA that ACCESS had commissioned from Harry Boyle, retired chairman of the CRTC. Boyle, the first person with experience in both public and private broadcasting to head the commission, appreciated "some originality and much of what might be called 'worthy' programming" at CKUA. He also liked the "natural quality of many voices ... unlike the neutered tonality of voices that now seem interchangeable between

Memphis and Moose Jaw" and the "competent and at times engaging if uneven" announcers. But he noticed "at times a not unpleasant touch of amateurishness," on-air performances that were "inclined to be ragged"— "a lot of gasping on open mikes and rustling of paper that I found distracting"— and announcing that blurred the "difference between being casual and unstuffy and being careless."

Thomas said two things struck him when he arrived at CKUA: the "individualistic attitudes of the staff" and the "very political nature of the ACCESS organization." The politics "started at the top. Things were done that were politically expedient ... in my opinion, without reference as to whether or not what they were doing was going to ultimately reflect positively on the programming at CKUA." The station was suffering from day-to-day micro-management by ACCESS higher-ups more concerned with politics than with any consistent programming philosophy, he said.

As for CKUA's musical programming staff, "They were all very dedicated to their own little corner of the world and they felt that the world should conform to them. But, I'm sorry, that's not the way it is. It doesn't work that way.... It became obvious that the one person in the organization who had a global picture of the situation was Jackie [Rollans].... So I decided that, with her help, we would start to do some things that I thought were necessary."

The result was a totally different management–staff relationship from what CKUA announcers had experienced under Kilpatrick and Hagerman, and they resisted it. Reminiscing about that time, Rollans and Thomas sounded like parents recalling the trials and tribulations of raising rebellious teenagers.

"You have to have artistic freedom in a station like CKUA, but they didn't understand the difference between freedom and licence," Rollans said. "You still have to have some control—it has to be between certain boundaries— and it was the hardest thing to introduce them to the fact that they ... had to work within an overall framework for the station.... A lot of people at CKUA had never been anywhere else but CKUA, and they really had suffered from benign neglect—they were sort of left on their own. They ended up—it was almost like hobby radio."

Thomas and Rollans put their heads together and analyzed every program on CKUA's schedule. Thomas had no complaint about CKUA's basic music format. "I felt that what they were doing was all right. It was how they were doing it." But he felt the eclectic programming and even the sequence of programs were hard on CKUA listeners' ears.

"It was a hodge-podge of things. It's like sitting down to a meal and starting out with a salad, and then immediately having dessert followed up by bread and butter followed up by the main course followed up by something else—no semblance of order to it.... One of the things that jarred me—I'm sure it jarred a lot of people—was the juxtaposition of some of the music that was played. They would play a lullaby and follow it up immediately with some wild upbeat thing that was jarring."

Thomas and Rollans introduced the programmers to the concept of "day-parting," which they said was common in the broadcast industry. "It's parting the day into segments and then programming your music according to the time of day," Rollans explained.

Thomas elaborated: "You program to people depending on what they're doing.... When people get up in the morning, they seem to want something that's a bit up, because it takes them a little while to get up and rolling in the morning. And then as the day progresses, you can start to get into some more medium and then into some heavier stuff."

Thomas created a graph that indicated which hours of the day were to be "heavy," "light" or "medium." Each genre of music could also be divided into light, heavy and medium categories. "You can have heavy classical, heavy jazz, heavy country, as you can have light classical, light jazz, light country." Thomas and Rollans rearranged CKUA's programs to fit their day-parting model and asked the programmers to make smoother transitions between selections. "That was probably the largest basic change we made after I came to CKUA," Thomas said.

Thomas spelled out his ideas in a memo to the executive committee of ACCESS:

the action plan for CKUA must concentrate on the development of a program schedule which is designed to attract a larger number of people from not only the minorities served, but also from that portion of general audience who can be encouraged to appreciate the type of programming presented.

◆ *Sev Sabourin spent thirty years in radio, most of them with CKUA.*
Courtesy of CKUA; photo by Frank Gasparik.

Thomas saw CKUA's potential audience to be in the thirty-five-plus age bracket—"better educated, intellectually aware, mobile business and professional" types.

> We will be facing our largest challenge in the matter of changes which we contemplate in the music CKUA has played in recent time. I find ... that the narrow and limited and unorthodox approach to music ... has developed over a relatively short period ... and is the result of the lack of direction and discipline which has been allowed to develop. The "leading edge," or "avant garde," music plus the heavy emphasis on jazz has resulted from the fact that people addicted to these forms of music are very vocal, and our people have been able to get reaction from the audience by concentrating on them. This concentration has led some of the CKUA staff to believe that their purpose in life is to satisfy these narrow preferences....

Thomas recommended less emphasis on "leading edge," "avant garde" and jazz, and more on "popular" and "familiar" music—for instance, by artists such as Arthur Fiedler, Montovani and James Last—"without getting completely into the music types played by the commercial stations." He anticipated that "it is reasonable to assume that there will be pressures at the highest levels from the audience, and from staff perhaps, to prevent the change of emphasis. I am not suggesting that consideration keep us from doing anything."

Sev Sabourin recalled the effect Thomas had on the staff when he "came in and overturned the whole damn thing and said no more of this off-the-wall stuff." At the time, Sabourin was doing a night show called "All That and Jazz."

"I was doing English new wave and I was doing fusion music, because it was CKUA! And I was playing Depeche Mode ... and John McLaughlin, and Jackie was saying 'stir it down, stir it down, stir it down.' So then I finally changed the program and softened it up. I remember Cathy Ennis was operating at night, and I said [to her], 'Well, we're going straight mainstream now, mainstream pop. You'd better turn it off and listen to your own records,' and I was sort of joking....

"For me there was no problem because I like popular music, but that didn't mean I went Top 40, but I did take out the John McLaughlin screeching stuff and the weird new wave stuff from England and I went to a more folky format. I think everybody was forced to do that and I remember the complaining around here, about people saying, 'Oh, we gotta play pap now, Muzak.' ...

"Because it was not the kind of music we were playing before—we would never have played it before—but when we switched gears again, to suit this new format, that kind of music started to come in, and we started to get the so-called pop-jazz sound, with a quality to it."

The media weren't taking kindly to the changes at CKUA under ACCESS. Bill Thorsell, by this time an editor with the *Edmonton Journal* (later to become editor-in-chief of the *Globe and Mail*), took regular shots at ACCESS, "Alberta's disappointing educational communications arm," and what he called the "huge pile of useless provincial supervisors, bureaucrats and politicians" CKUA was labouring under.

Lamenting the "meddlesome change" ordered by the CRTC in the early 1970s, Thorsell said, "One of the peculiar romantic things about Edmonton used to be radio station CKUA," and complained that the CRTC's "'cure' was infinitely worse than the alleged disease. A lot of good things remain about CKUA, but the intrusion of interested busybodies all over the place has taken its toll—at least on the ears of many former listeners. It's a sad object lesson in management theory and government control. And that's not saying a word about the rest of ACCESS, surely the brightest dream in recent history that never came true."

Several months later he praised the University of Alberta student radio station CJSR, which had just gone city-wide, as "CKUA reborn." As for CKUA itself, he said that as a result of Ottawa forcing the Alberta government to take tighter control of CKUA and to produce more "educational" programming, "the spirit flagged, perhaps for other reasons too, and CKUA now has all the spark of a noodle in a steamroom."

CKUA was, however, getting some things right in the 1980s. *Edmonton Sun* columnist Ron Tibbett praised the "Mid-Morning" jazz show by Mary Lou Creechan as "the best two hours of daily radio this town has heard in some time."

Some lamented the taming effect ACCESS ownership had on CKUA's "alternative" style. A case in point was when the station nixed a documentary by freelance broadcaster Jars Balan, on the grounds that the program contravened the station's policy on obscene language by including comedian George Carlin's routine "Seven Words You Can Never Say on T.V."

According to *Edmonton Journal* columnist Bob Remington, "The program in question was a sober academic discussion that, if anything, erred on the side of caution. The situation does nothing to confirm CKUA as a source of alternative radio that historically has been bolder than its commercial counterparts." He quoted the miffed and rebuffed Balan: "'It would be truly unfortunate—for intelligent radio listeners and producers alike—if one of the few outlets for serious radio were to be castrated, so to speak, by the kind of policy that ACCESS seems to be determined to implement in such an ill-considered way.'"

Michael Skeet, who was part of CKUA's news team in the late 1970s and an announcer-producer in the early and mid 1980s, remembered the day "the record library suddenly sprouted a forest of red dots marking tracks we were no longer allowed to play." The incident that brought them about occurred when Bill Coull played a track from a new album during his afternoon show that turned out to contain several obscene words.

"Jackie was horrified, and insisted that all music would from thenceforth have to be audited and cleared before it could be played ... [and] tracks that contained obscenities would be marked with a red dot," Skeet said. He resented the new system, partly because "it broke with a long-standing CKUA tradition of announcer-producers choosing their own music."

But the red dot system had its own pitfalls. When Skeet found a new album by Jamaican reggae/dub artist Yellowman covered in red dots, he played the one cut that was not marked—"Get Me to the Church on Time."

"Well, about two-thirds of the way through the track Mr. Yellowman launched into a speed rap about how he didn't want to get married anyway because the ladies were all in love with his gigantic, throbbing... You can guess the rest. I just about had a heart attack—not because I was offended ... not because I was worried about the audience ... but because I was scared to death about what Jackie might do to me."

Nobody had bothered to vet "Get Me to the Church on Time," for obvious reasons. Soon blue dots also appeared to signify that a recording had been screened by library staff.

"Fifteen years later, of course, four-letter words air all the time on commercial radio in Toronto," Skeet observed in 1999. A speculative fiction writer and Toronto-based CBC movie reviewer, Skeet said that despite the "political rectitude" that crept in with ACCESS, "CKUA meant so much to the person that I became. Most of my current interests were either fanned by or started by CKUA. That dingy, unkempt suite of offices in Edmonton was the gateway to a much bigger world for me. It was like having the universe in a closet."

Listeners continued to have their say. An inmate who wrote to CKUA in the early 1980s from the Calgary Correctional Institute said he had to suffer the "cruel and unusual punishment" of listening to commercial radio—until his radio and headphones arrived. "Now this place recedes away from me as I escape into the world of CKUA daily. It is my solace. These next two years less a day will pass faster and better for me with 'Access'."

When the station dropped DeKoven's extremely popular "Barococo" program of seventeenth- and eighteenth-century baroque music in 1981, the act drew a flood of letters from irate listeners. The station explained that the garrulous, opinionated host wasn't producing new programs and the quality of the older tapes he had been sending from New York was no longer up to CKUA standards. In fact, the tapes sometimes broke during broadcast.

"What kind of nonsense is this?" a listener from Standard, Alberta, wrote. "You pride yourselves on being a 'different' radio station with a sophisticated listening audience. You have a program with poor sound quality and a guy with a big mouth. What more do you want to be different? A guy with a big mouth is a person to be prized today ... Bring back DeKoven to replace the other crap with the good sound quality. Professionalism run rampant is the curse of the communications industry today. Show us you care." Another DeKoven fan complained of the "homogenization" of CKUA's offerings: "The individual idiosyncrasies of your programs have been steadily ironed out."

But some new music programs introduced in the 1980s had staying power right into the next millennium. Dave Ward started "By Request," allowing listeners to "get a crack at" programming from CKUA's 50,000-piece record library—reputed to be the largest west of Toronto. An hour and a half before the new weekly program started, CKUA's phone lines were jammed with requests. Sev Sabourin introduced "Play It Again," a look back at popular music between the late 1920s and 1954. Tony Dillon-Davis later produced the program for many years.

Despite their differences of opinion over the changes taking place, CKUA listeners, media, staff and management would soon join forces under a common banner when the station's existence was threatened once again in 1987.

Saved Again | 12

During the mid 1980s Alberta's fortunes waned as oil prices plummeted and recession set in. Don Getty was now premier and under pressure to get a grip on the province's growing deficit. ACCESS was expected to do its share by trimming its $15-million budget.

Meanwhile, video and television had gradually replaced audio-tapes and radio in Alberta classrooms. Demand for CKUA's formal educational productions was drying up and with it, funding from Alberta Education. Alberta School Broadcast funding had dropped from a high of $325,000 in 1981–82 to nothing in 1985–86.

CKUA had to compete with the television side for a bigger share of ACCESS dollars to make up the shortfall, which was "a tough sell," according to Peter Senchuk, ACCESS president at the time. ACCESS also tried to enlist funding for specific projects from external groups such as the Alberta Teachers' Association in order to meet CKUA's commitment to formal instruction in its CRTC promise of performance. By 1987 CKUA was costing about $3 million a year to operate.

On January 13, 1987 Alberta's minister of technology, research and telecommunications, Les Young, confirmed that the government was considering selling CKUA. Young told the *Edmonton Journal* that the government was examining how ACCESS was fulfilling its educational mandate and "what is evident is that audio is not used very much in the school."

Asked if CKUA's news and music programming should be protected, Young replied, "What is the news (and music) that we would be protecting that isn't otherwise available?" He said his main commitment was to meet "the public concern that we have, which is to make technology work and complement the activities of teachers and school boards to the best that we can do that with the money we have available."

CKUA was in a catch-22 situation. There certainly was no case to be made that the station still played a role in the classroom. A spokesperson for the Edmonton Public School Board told the *Edmonton Journal* that neither the Department of Education nor the board included CKUA programs in their curriculum guidelines. An Edmonton high school principal said he didn't know anyone in the school system who used CKUA programs. But, as *The Advocate* (Red Deer) pointed out, "At the same time, [CKUA's] educational focus reduces its mass appeal." In the radio market CKUA commanded just four percent of listeners, according to figures from the Bureau of Broadcast Measurement (BBM).

Young took the brunt of the media and public outrage that followed, but several people close to the situation said the idea to get rid of CKUA came from within ACCESS. Fil Fraser, who had recently returned from two years in Ottawa working on the National Task Force on Broadcasting and was now director of development at ACCESS, said he was at a meeting in Peter Senchuk's office when the idea to close CKUA grew legs.

"The government put out a note to all of its departments asking, from my recollection, to give them a scenario based on minus-five percent of their budgets.... He [Senchuk] came as a political appointment ... so his agenda was to please the government. I was in the room—a meeting of his executive group—[when] he said, 'Well, the way we can solve this is just shut down CKUA.' He presented a budget in which ACCESS would just let CKUA go down and that would solve the budget problem....

"That's the point at which I exited ACCESS. I was furious. It was because of a lot of things, but that was the crowning insult.... That put into the air the notion that CKUA was expendable."

◆ CKUA staff in 1987 with ACCESS president Peter Senchuk (seated, left) and CKUA general manager Don Thomas (seated, right). *Courtesy of* CKUA.

Former ACCESS president Larry Shorter called it "throwing CKUA to the wolves so as to save the television side." Like "the Russians in the sleigh—the wolves are chasing along behind, so let's give them something to eat so we can get away."

When asked where the idea to cut off CKUA originated, Senchuk said there was a study of ACCESS underway, "but I certainly didn't expect it [CKUA] to be hived off and pushed away and it wasn't." Was there a movement afoot to privatize the station or sell its frequency, as media stories suggested at the time?

"I would say that was probably there to some degree at odd times.... CKUA had operated in Edmonton and Alberta with a very unique service that we all wanted to treasure and keep and keep enriched.... Through some tough years it was challenging to ensure that we would have enough funding to be able to continue to provide its network service throughout the province. There were probably more challenges in maintaining resources for its service than [there] would be [for] production for curriculum-related video for the classroom."

♦ The CKUA news team in 1987. Back row: (left to right) Bruce Corbett, Doug Morton, Ian Gray, Terry Beeler, Ken Regan; front row: Pat Barford, Bob Brace. Courtesy of CKUA.

Jackie Rollans and Don Thomas, who managed CKUA at the time, confirmed the idea came from within. "We knew what was happening internally because we were on the executive committee," Rollans said. "And we had to sit there, on the one hand, in those meetings and pretend that we were going along with it."

On the other hand, Rollans and Thomas were going back and sharing this information with CKUA staff. "We'd have been out on our ear if Peter had known we told anybody," Rollans said later.

Armed with information from Rollans and Thomas, CKUA staff "went underground," according to Sharon Sinclair. "We were all quite cloak and daggers about it.... Marc Vasey arranged for us to meet at the Yardbird [Suite] and we asked Ed Kilpatrick to come back and be our leader above ground and he did. Tom Banks was also a part of that." Shorter joined the fray.

The Committee to Save CKUA came together quickly. Its members represented a broad spectrum of Alberta's arts and cultural community: writers Sylvia Bough and Jon Whyte; musician/writer Sally Truss; publisher Mel Hurtig; CKUA's Irish programmer Sam Donaghey; Calgarian Anne Green; Robert Cook, director of the University of Lethbridge School of Fine Arts;

Keith Mann, music director at Red Deer College; Jack Mighton, chairman of the Department of Humanities and Social Studies at Grande Prairie Regional College; and Dorothy Zolf, acting director of the University of Calgary Department of Communications Studies.

The group organized a massive letter-writing campaign among CKUA listeners. And the letters poured in. Collectively they articulated what CKUA had come to mean to a significant community within Alberta's population.

"My husband and I moved to Alberta from Quebec in 1973 and lived south of Pincher Creek," wrote an Athabasca woman. "I remember the thrill of picking up a Holger Petersen program on a radio station in distant Edmonton. We listened to CKUA whenever reception allowed. In 1974 we purchased a farm and one of the qualifications that had to be met was good reception of CKUA, as well as good agricultural potential."

A farmer from Spirit River, who said he spent ten hours a day driving a tractor and listening to the radio, wrote, "As a rural Albertan, I am shocked and dismayed to hear that, with the stroke of a pen, you plan to sound the death knell of CKUA Radio, a service that I, personally have come to enjoy and depend on, for the last 15 years."

A Calgary couple described memories of listening to CKUA on a crystal set with earphones. A music teacher from northern Alberta said, "If it were not for this station, my musical background would thus far be severely limited." An Edmonton man equated listening to CKUA to "attending the academia within the home environment for the entire family." A "transplanted Nova Scotian" said CKUA helped him better understand his adopted province.

A Fort McMurray doctor called CKUA "one of Alberta's most valuable cultural resources" and a "major contributor to the quality of life for me and my family in Fort McMurray. For the people of Alberta, CKUA should rank right up there with West Edmonton Mall, the Calgary Stampede, and the Heritage Trust Fund."

Ernie Poscente, vice-president for programming with Shaw Cablesystems, said CKUA was "a constant and gentle friend introducing us to the artists, the musicians, the heroes and characters of this province.... As with other heritage pieces that we painstakingly preserve in this province, so should CKUA be maintained and nurtured." And this from a Calgary man: "Schools? Educational? The airwaves are the schoolroom, and wherever CKUA reaches is a school. Try to understand: CKUA is different, and many Albertans are indebted to it."

Letters to the editor were equally eloquent. Alex Kachmar, of Edmonton, wrote,

> As a longtime listener of this most unique radio station, I have witnessed its emasculation and bureaucratization over the last few years by this government. Despite all the tampering, CKUA still provides listeners with a real alternative to commercial radio.... I feel that CKUA should not only be retained, but its role as a cultural institution strengthened.

Douglas Lynass added, "Any successful attempt by a government and minister to destroy or diminish a unique resource like CKUA would only affirm the mediocrity of politicians unable to appreciate a long track record of excellence, diversity and performance in cultural matters."

Calling CKUA "very much a part of the cultural heritage of this province," Sylvia Bough wrote to the Edmonton Journal from Cold Lake: "Are we to accept his [Young's] narrow-minded view that education is something which happens only between 9 a.m. and 3:30 p.m. between the ages of six and 18? Are we to accept our lot as vegetating production machines, with no desire to understand what is happening in our province?"

The government's proposal "shows a crass disregard for the cultural life of the province," wrote A.F. Nothof, of Sherwood Park. "[CKUA] provides a sense of belonging and involvement in the life of the province to small communities which have little or no access to the arts.... It reflects the diverse social and political heritage, the broad spectrum of vocations and interests which constitute the lives of Albertans."

Edmonton musician Jim Serediak concluded, "Only a government with no foresight would dismantle what has taken 60 years to establish."

The arts and cultural community came out in force. Geoff Lambert, co-owner of the Sidetrack Café, one of Edmonton's most active live music venues, helped organize a petition to the Legislature. Edmonton's Walterdale Theatre printed an article in its newsletter calling CKUA "a good friend" and pointing out that "CKUA has for a number of years been very helpful to the theatre in terms of production assistance, advice on music and, more especially, in giving us free advertising." The Ukrainian Self-Reliance League of Canada, an umbrella organization for Ukrainian men's, women's and youth groups, wrote to the minister, "We have been using this radio station from its very early difficult beginnings, and now feel that our community is definitely a part of CKUA."

Patrick Slater, marketing and public relations manager of the Calgary Centre for Performing Arts, wrote a letter to the editor saying that CKUA "supports hundreds of amateur and professional arts groups in this province. This alliance goes far beyond strict aesthetics. Communication channels are essential to the survival of these arts groups, the same arts groups in which the province has made huge investments in capital and operating funds."

The media came down firmly on CKUA's side. In an editorial headlined "CKUA deserves more," the *Medicine Hat News* listed all the reasons why and concluded, "Beyond all this, however, is the matter of regional pride. CKUA is Alberta's radio station, run by Albertans for Albertans. So it would be sadly ironic if CKUA, a survivor of repeated attempts by the federal government to silence it, were to be undone by the Alberta government."

Just in case people agreed CKUA was expendable, *Edmonton Journal* columnist Helen Metella weighed in with a column that drew the distinction between CKUA and the CBC. She said she was impressed recently to hear a cut from a Kate Bush LP—"never a staple on popular radio"—on the CBC's "Primetime" program. But shortly later she heard the same cut again on another CBC show. This happened, she said, because few CBC producers were music programmers and often relied on a list of new releases prepared for them by one knowledgeable person—"sort of like buying sliced bread at Safeway. Over at CKUA, the chances of hearing the same song twice in two hours are remote. All announcers still do it the old fashioned way, choosing their own music for their own programs, based on their mood and memory. That's a nice alternative, like picking up warm buns from a baker who made them from his own special recipe."

Journal columnist Linda Goyette called CKUA "a sound stage for Alberta's musicians, writers, teachers, poets, actors and journalists. If we have a culture—and many Canadians think we don't—CKUA is its echo."

The *Journal*'s Alan Kellogg, who had been an announcer-producer with CKUA for a short time in the 1970s, was scathing in condemning the situation: "[With CKUA] stripped of much of its soul and intellect by managers with bad taste and dubious mandate, loyal listeners have dropped off, leaving a severely weakened target for the enemies of public broadcasting."

The *Edmonton Sun*'s Don Wanagas got down and dirty, calling the ACCESS board and upper management "a veritable who's-who of Conservative party yes-persons and butt-kissers." He said the situation came as no surprise to those familiar with ACCESS administration.

> Network president Peter Senchuk has never had any great love for the audiophiles on the CKUA payroll—primarily because ... [they] don't quite jive with his desire to run a television empire out of the board-rooms in Edmonton's west end.
>
> Neither do many of the radio types tend to have the kind of political affiliations which seem to be a prerequisite to survival at ACCESS.
>
> Senchuk, for example, was made president of ACCESS on the strength of little more than his long-time service to the Alberta Tories as a bagman in the Lloydminster area.

Wanagas said that if the government were sincere about getting value for money, it could also be considering privatizing ACCESS television. But, "such an action could jeopardize the livelihoods of all those Tories who are now finding sustenance there."

The *Edmonton Sun*'s arts columnist Dave Billington, who a decade earlier was broadcasting daily live reports from the Banff Television Festival over CKUA, blasted the "current gaggle of Tory hacks hanging out under the dome" for daring "to kill an institution as venerable as ACCESS/CKUA Radio.... If it is R.I.P. for CKUA, more's the pity—but where's the surprise?"

The CKUA Staff Association sent Young a letter addressing his concerns and pointing out that the station's 4-percent audience share compared favourably with the 1.9-percent national average for American public radio. The group also raised the point that CKUA never had the funding to promote itself properly, with the result that fewer than fifty percent of Albertans were even aware it existed.

Meanwhile, Shorter met behind the scenes with Young several times as spokesman for the Committee to Save CKUA and on February 18 drafted a proposal on behalf of the committee. The document recommended that CKUA be operated by a new, publicly accountable body "separated, but not divorced from ACCESS." CKUA's budget would be decreased to $1.8 million, with the group raising one-quarter of the necessary funds from private sources and corporate sponsorship and the government providing the balance. ACCESS would provide CKUA with free transmission, and the government would continue to provide free premises to the station.

The committee had been floating the idea of a community funding model to the media. At one point, Kilpatrick told the Edmonton Journal, "It would not be too dissatisfying to have corporations identified at the top and at the tail of programs, but not in the middle. That would destroy the format."

On February 19, Young backed down. His department's news release announcing the decision stated that "the government has always recognized CKUA's unique format and its role in lifelong learning, cultural development and musical appreciation. While ensuring the future of CKUA Mr. Young stated that ACCESS Network has been asked to develop financial support from listeners and to explore other funding sources." Young suggested the station could tap "financial support along the lines of public broadcasting" and said "the potential for greater volunteer community involvement to reduce costs will also be assessed."

The Edmonton Journal's Linda Goyette reported the next day that "sources suggest CKUA was far closer to the budget guillotine than anybody had imagined. Loyal friends delivered bags of mail to the minister's office."

Young received more than three hundred letters, but it was the quality of the letters as well as the quantity that impressed him. "Often we get barraged with letter-writing campaigns and they are photocopies or copies of a letter that someone has drafted somewhere," he told writer Reg Silvester in Broadcaster magazine. "In the case of the CKUA supporters, they were written by individuals, expressing their points of view and their interest. It was refreshing, from my position, to receive that kind of response." He noted, however, that the letters rarely mentioned CKUA's formal educational programming or its news and public affairs programming. What most people valued about CKUA were its music and its lack of commercials.

Senchuk sent a copy of Young's news release to ACCESS staff the day it came out, along with the statement "We are very pleased about the decision. We have concerns about the funding, but welcome the opportunity that has been provided for Albertans to show their support for the corporation's unique radio service." He later said, "There was no doubt in my mind that the audience of CKUA was such a loyal one that it would be there to support us whenever we were threatened."

According to Shorter, Young named him head of an advisory committee to look at ways CKUA could get more public support and funding. On February 28, Shorter sent Young a letter, with the salutation "Dear Les," suggesting the structure and terms of reference of the committee: "Although we [Shorter and Young] didn't discuss my contacting Peter Senchuk ... I thought it best to let him know what I was up to.... I phoned him on 20 February and offered to meet with him to discuss the committee. He thought it best to discuss the matter with you first. I briefed him a bit on the direction I was taking." The letter suggested eight nominees for the committee, including Ed Kilpatrick and Don Thomas, the latter to act as staff officer to the committee.

"So," Shorter said, "...the committee is established, but I am no longer its chair. I sit on it, but I only get to name two or three people from the public to it." Clem Collins, vice-chair of the board of ACCESS, was named committee chair, and instead of Thomas, Peter Senchuk sat on the committee for ACCESS. The group would report to Young within a year.

In the new budget year starting April 1, the government operating grant administered by ACCESS reduced CKUA's funding from $2.1 million to $1.9 million. The station was now expected to make up the shortfall with volunteer help, innovative programs and efforts to garner corporate support. Senchuk brought in a consultant from San Francisco with experience as a marketing executive in public broadcasting to give a workshop for the ACCESS board. The board subsequently gave its approval for ACCESS radio and television to start fundraising activities.

A public fundraising campaign for CKUA was set for May 1 under the theme "You've Been Part of Our Past, Help Us Be Part of Your Future." Thomas and Rollans flew to Toronto to pick the brains of Cam Finley, manager of CJRT, the former Ryerson station which was now operated by an independent board and funded by $1 million a year from the Ontario government and over $700,000 in donations from listeners.

During that first fundraiser, May 1–22, 1987, the station interrupted programs with four recorded on-air appeals each hour, including taped testimonials from such prominent Albertans as Ian Tyson and Ralph Klein (then Calgary mayor). The announcers themselves did not pitch for funds.

But on the last day of the campaign, Rollans said, she and Thomas decided to go live with the appeals. "I think we raised as much in that one day that we went live as we had raised the previous week by just doing pre-recorded cut-ins," Thomas said.

The campaign raised $53,000 from about 1000 donors, including pledges from Montana and Saskatchewan. A dollar came in from a welfare recipient who called CKUA "food for the soul" and said his contribution was his lunch money. Along with his donation he sent a poem that Rollans framed and hung on the wall:

If of thy mortal goods thou art bereft
And from thy slender store two loaves alone to thee are left,
Sell one … And with the dole
Buy Hyacinths to feed thy soul.

The *Calgary Herald*'s Patrick Tivy called it "a dirty rotten shame … that the government has put CKUA in a situation where it must beg for its very survival." Thomas said the station received only three letters of complaint about the on-air appeals—and each came with a donation. "They said the thing that annoys them is the fact that we have to do it."

Long-time CKUA fan Jean Greenough was moved to become one of ACCESS Radio CKUA's earliest volunteers when she saw the need during that first fundraiser.

"CKUA has been a part of my radio listening life since I was about 13 years old," she said. "It was mainly my earliest memories of CKUA listening to Herb Johnson and Tommy Banks on the jazz show 'Music for Moderns' that started my CKUA connection. Having just discovered jazz, becoming bored with the Top 40, CKUA was a veritable music heaven. Herb Johnson, being the wonderfully giving person that he is, inadvertently became my 'Jazz Guru.' He patiently answered all my dumb questions and sent me off to the Edmonton Public Library to check out the likes of Jelly Roll Morton, Billie Holiday, Bird, John Coltrane, etc."

Greenough later became friends with staff at CKUA while writing an English paper on the station. "I happened to drop into the station to see a friend and there was all the staff sitting in the general manager's office manning the phones for their first ever pledge drive. I volunteered to answer the phones for awhile, thinking if the staff is that committed surely I can at least do that too." Greenough, like many other CKUA volunteers, became a fixture at station fundraisers. She later became a staffer herself.

Fresh from the success of the first fundraiser, CKUA officially signed on its Banff/Canmore transmitter in June 1987 to coincide with Alberta Day at the Banff Television Festival. On November 21 the station celebrated its sixtieth anniversary. To mark the occasion, ACCESS published *A Sound for All Seasons*, a magazine-style history of the station. CKUA broadcast the 1938 classic H.G. Wells' *War of the Worlds* and a documentary-style "time capsule" of the station's history including highlights from past programs. CKUA had once again pulled through.

Listeners continued to support the station each spring and fall as programmers appealed on air for funds, always exceeding their goal. However, the ACCESS administration was uneasy about the first live on-air fundraiser in the spring of 1988.

"They were so afraid that we were going to say something that was going to embarrass the government, and so they were really, really touchy about everything we did and said," Rollans recalled. "We were supposed to ... emphasize the fact that we really needed the money."

But, Thomas added, "What they didn't want us to say was ... to in any way blame the government for lack of funding, which was why we were going to go fundraising."

Seeing tangible evidence of listener support was a heady experience for CKUA staff, who had originally approached the fundraising task reluctantly. "Fundraisers were so wonderful," Sharon Sinclair said. "Incredibly hard on announcers but a lot of adrenaline as listeners called and shared their CKUA stories (we'd tell the stories to announcers or put the calls through to them if convenient) and dropped by their pledges and we took them on tours and introduced them to the announcers and showed off the library.... It was a case of lemons turning into lemonade as listeners and CKUA connected like never before! We were all exhausted but ecstatic at the end of each one. It really pulled us together, too."

Among the donors were farmers who said they had their tractors rigged with sound systems so they could listen to CKUA through the long days of harvesting, and a university student who worked summers alone on a fire tower with nothing but CKUA to keep him sane. One day during the spring

1988 fundraiser, Premier Don Getty himself walked in the door, with no entourage, and dropped off a cheque with the words "my favourite radio station" written in parentheses on its face.

During the spring 1989 pitch for funds, CKUA staffer Bruce Evans took a call from a man who asked how much the station needed to reach its goal. Upon hearing that four thousand dollars would do the trick, the man wrote a cheque for the total and requested "Blue Bayou" for his wife. The man who had sent the "hyacinths to feed thy soul" poem along with his lunch money called a year later and pledged fifty dollars, saying he was now out of debt, had a job and was no longer on welfare.

Terry David Mulligan, veteran Canadian actor and music broadcaster, once phoned from a plane flying over Alberta from Vancouver to Toronto to make a pledge, according to Rollans. She also recalled "a little old lady from Lloydminster that came in one day with a little shopping bag and gave us a thousand dollars."

Meanwhile, the CKUA advisory committee had been meeting with a mandate to study five issues: (1) the cultural role played by CKUA in Alberta; (2) the feasibility of reducing to a solely AM or FM system; (3) community activity, with special focus on volunteers and the possibility of using some on-air volunteers; (4) new sources of revenue; and (5) possible cost-cutting measures.

Shorter focussed on CKUA's governance and pushed for distancing CKUA from government and from ACCESS. He was also concerned about accountability and the need to assure donors that their gifts would go only to CKUA. When the committee met on December 4, 1987 to discuss the recommendations they would make in their report to the minister, Shorter put a proposal on the agenda to the effect that ACCESS and the government should redefine CKUA's mandate so that the station would be responsible only for its traditional role with emphasis on cultural enrichment, ethnic diversity and public service. The station should continue to carry formal educational programs, but only if the station could demonstrate its effectiveness as a formal educational delivery system should that service become part of its mandate once again. Next, a separate, non-transferable money vote exclusively devoted to the costs of CKUA's traditional programming should appear in the 1988–89 Government of Alberta estimates. Then a sub-committee of the ACCESS Board of Directors should be struck with specific responsibility for CKUA and its accountability to the public. Finally, when new board appointments were required, consideration should be given to including two or three appointees from CKUA's constituency.

In the committee's final report, presented to the minister in March 1988, Shorter's proposal, signed by three of the eight committee members, landed in the appendixes. A fifth item was added: "Within ACCESS, efforts should be increased to establish greater autonomy, accountability, and a separate public identity for CKUA, either within the existing structure or through the establishment of a subsidiary corporation."

"This was embarrassing, because I was the guy who brought CKUA into ACCESS," Shorter said later. "But now it's obvious, if you follow the thrower to the wolf from the sled metaphor, that CKUA is the weak part. If you're working for a corporation whose mandate is education and you're having more and more difficulty proving that you're educational, then you're going to get thrown to the wolves. And under those circumstances, what's going to happen the next time you do this? Who's going to defend CKUA?"

Shorter said he had intended his proposal to be a minority report, but ACCESS rejected the idea of separating CKUA out as too costly. In the end, he said, his proposal was "railroaded" and buried.

The committee's report recommended against the use of inexperienced volunteers for on-air presentations but suggested that CKUA should use volunteers to assist in fundraising. "Volunteer efforts should not be regarded as cost-saving measures, but rather community-involvement activities." The report favoured seeking corporate underwriting for programs but not commercial advertising, although the CRTC was on the verge of easing its regulations to allow some commercial advertising as long as it didn't become a primary funding mechanism.

In another recommendation, the committee proposed a study of the role of news on CKUA, suggesting that the current service was not comprehensive enough to warrant the money being spent on it. It said either more money should be made available to beef up the news service—an unlikely prospect in those belt-tightening times—or the station should cut back the news budget and go to a syndicated news service, plowing the money saved into other programming. The FM system should be expanded to reach the last fifteen percent of Alberta's population not yet covered and when this was achieved, the AM assets should be sold to help finance the expansion.

Finally, the committee came up with a proposal that CKUA spearhead a partnership with private stations to provide Alberta artists with public exposure by making it possible for them to record professional-quality tapes to be played on participating stations. Called the Alberta Music Project, this CKUA initiative became part of ACCESS's three-year business plan released in the fall of 1988. Under "Radio Programming Directions," the plan said, "This direction is important in order to provide Alberta artists with public exposure and to expand the amount of CKUA's original cultural programming."

Directions for CKUA in the ACCESS three-year plan called for establishing the station as the "preeminent provincial FM radio service in two key areas: a) in adult cultural and information radio programming designed to display the talents of Albertans; and b) in the areas of classical, jazz, blues, and folk music programming." Gone was the formal education mandate.

A second direction was to review CKUA programming regularly and make changes "designed to expand CKUA's regular adult audience particularly among younger adults." CKUA had already begun what Thomas called a "judicious introduction of a type of contemporary music" in the "Alberta Morning" and "Afternoon Edition" programs, in order to attract a younger demographic. "Otherwise it is conceivable the CKUA audience will finally die off," he felt. The plan also called for expanding the FM service to underserved regions of the province. ACCESS would make marketing and promotion of both its television and radio services a priority in order to increase their audience numbers and raise revenue.

The Alberta Music Project was launched in November 1988. ACCESS Radio CKUA formed a consortium of Alberta stations, each contributing an amount in proportion to its market, to provide a number of new, unrecorded Alberta musicians with free recording studio and mix-down time, tape, a producer and even backup musicians. To avoid stepping on the toes of Alberta's recording industry, the tapes were to be good enough for broadcast but not for commercial recordings.

"This program is one that I like to think will search out the people who have the potential to be successful," Thomas told the media a year later when the first composite tape was released to stations for play. "The name of the game is to give professional studio time to people who may have the talent but may not have the money to do it." Stations would benefit by having an

◆ Folksinger Paul Hann (left) and CKUA announcer Cam Hayden, ca. 1979.
Courtesy of CKUA.

expanded pool of material available to satisfy the CRTC's Canadian content requirements. During the first year, nine performers benefitted and five more provided their own completed recordings to the project.

The Alberta Music Project was "highly successful," Rollans said. CKUA produced a CD from the project, printed in Japanese. The Alberta government handed out copies as gifts at Canada House in Tokyo.

CKUA's efforts to raise its profile in the community were starting to pay off. *Edmonton Sun* columnist Graham Hicks noted that a few years earlier the station had "crept under a rock, doing nothing in the way of promotion, nothing in the way of community involvement.... But now CKUA is front and centre, leading a consortium of CFRN, KEY-FM, MG 1200 and out-of-town stations in the Alberta Music Project.... You go to theatre and, lo and behold, CKUA is a media sponsor. In the libraries, CKUA bookmarks are everywhere." The station was also broadcasting concerts recorded live around the province; for example, Alberta blues great "Big Miller—Live in Athabasca."

The sound of CKUA in 1990 included a "bright" morning program hosted by Wayne Bezanson with music selected by Tony Dillon-Davis covering "the best of yesterday and today," followed by Mary Lou Creechan's "light, listenable" jazz. Chris Allen offered acoustic music in the afternoons and "All That and Jazz" late at night. Bill Coull presented "a potpourri of the best contemporary music" on "Afternoon Edition" and offered "Jazz" on Saturday afternoons. Marc Vasey's "Jazz Interactions" and Holger Petersen's "Natch'l Blues" and "H.P. Sauce" continued to run on Saturdays.

Other weekend fare included Cam Hayden with "a potpourri of blues, folk, reggae, and the newest and best of rock"; "Play it Again" and the "Old Disc Jockey" for nostalgia appeal; music from stage and screen on "Saturday Sound Stage"; listeners' choices on "By Request"; and Tony Dillon-Davis with Saturday and Sunday "Breakfast" classics. The ethnic programs were divided between "Old Country Melodies" of Britain, Ireland, Scotland and Wales on Sundays and music from the Ukraine, Poland, Hungary, Norway, Denmark and Sweden on Friday evenings. CKUA also ran "Windspeaker," a weekly program produced by the Aboriginal Multi-Media Society of Alberta. Imports included concerts by the Cleveland Orchestra and Boston Symphony on Monday and Wednesday evenings and BBC comedies.

As CKUA recast itself, the news team took a hit. "Invariably when budgets are cut back in radio, news suffers because it's expensive to do properly," Ken Regan said. "Around 1988 … we started to see layoffs, people being let go and some of the budgets being cut back." The station continued to broadcast Question Period live from the Alberta Legislature and Athabasca University's formal educational programs, including "Ragtime to Rolling Stones," "Theatre of the Air" and three French-language series.

Information programs ranged from "Pedal Power," a four-part series in celebration of the bicycle, and "Underneath it All," a series on archaeology in Alberta, to "The Hidden Handicap," a six-part series on learning disabilities, and "Trade Asia," six documentaries on doing business in the Pacific Rim, produced with the Calgary and Edmonton sections of the Hong Kong–Canada Business Association. In 1989 CKUA collaborated with the Alberta Law Foundation to co-produce "Great Alberta Law Cases," ten half-hour dramatizations, including the story of Raymond Cook, the last person hanged in Alberta.

On Sunday mornings teens aged twelve to fifteen were invited to write in "questions you're afraid to ask" on such topics as AIDS and relationships for response by experts. The program, "Teen Waves," had an advisory board of

◆ *Classical host Richard Moses often challenged CKUA management.*
Courtesy of CKUA; photo by Frank Gasparik.

six thirteen-year-olds and covered everything from "acne to zydeco." Another youth-oriented program, "Conference Call," produced by Sharon Sinclair and hosted by Fil Fraser, linked Alberta high school students by phone with their counterparts around the world to discuss issues that concerned them, from environment to poverty. The program attracted corporate sponsorship from AGT and PCL Construction.

In 1988 a new voice had joined CKUA from CJRT in Toronto. Richard Moses said he was serving as a media representative on a Blythe Travel Agency "Mystery Train" trundling across the country from Toronto to Vancouver in 1987 when he stepped into a gift shop on a stopover in Banff and heard Mozart playing on the radio.

"Wha—? was my reaction. In the middle of the mountains in the middle of the 'west,' a Mozart radio station?"

Seeking full-time employment after twelve years as part-time classical host at CJRT, Moses phoned CKUA from Lake Louise and talked with Rollans. Sev Sabourin had just left the station for Toronto—for the second time—and there was an opening.

Moses became CKUA's classical expert, hosting midday and dinner-hour classical programs. He immersed himself in the classical music community, initiating involvement with the Edmonton Symphony and Calgary Philharmonic orchestras and previewing their programs on his show. He also hosted a concert series for the Edmonton Symphony. His personable, talkative style made him popular with his audience, but an edgy, confrontational streak put him on a collision course with Rollans and Thomas. According to Thomas, Moses "didn't understand day-parting. He thought he could play a funeral dirge at any time of day and people would listen.... That's the height of arrogancy that the world will listen simply because I'm talking."

Moses said he was "summoned" to Thomas' office in January 1990.

I had played on the morning portion of the show, the Rutter REQUIEM. Jackie heard it. The rumor was that I was "playing too much heavy, somber choral music." ...

I was told in no uncertain terms that I was to cut way back on the human voice (period) ....

I went back to work, programming just as I had been, but cutting out all Passions, Masses, Cantatas, etc. Sometime in the ensuing months I was told by Sev [Sabourin was back again and serving as music director] that NO vocal or choral music could be played on my programs. Does this include the Beethoven 9th, the Debussy Sirenes, the Vaughan Williams Sea Symphony, I queried, and after some thought, he backed down....

On July 11, 1991, I received a memo from Sev enclosing a memo from Don [Thomas] stating that there was still too much voice music in the show and that henceforward I would be allowed 15 minutes a week of vocal or choral music to be played on Wednesday, and only after 12:30 p.m. (I had a friend, a composer and conductor, visiting from England when I received this memo. He was awestruck!)

In his memo setting out the vocal music edict for Moses, Thomas wrote,

I find it distasteful to have to set the restriction, but there is obviously a lack of appreciation of what research has told us, to whit ... Classical vocal music is the least liked of all Classical music, while the romantic, melodic Classical music is preferred by a majority. This doesn't mean that we play none of the former and all of the latter, it does mean that the balance in our on air programming take into account the wishes of our very knowledgeable audience.

The exchanges between Moses and management illustrated more than the obvious clash of personalities. The relative newcomer was voicing a viewpoint shared to some degree by many long-time CKUA staffers regarding a top-down management style that was the complete opposite of what they had experienced during their pre-ACCESS years. Cathy Ennis, who had joined the station as an operator in the early 1980s and hosted one of the classical shows before Moses' arrival, locked horns with Rollans and Thomas over announcer autonomy and left the station for a period as a result, according to Rollans.

In October 1991 Moses wrote a "job analysis," blasting the existing management style:

I have been here for nearly four years and have yet to be given any sort of job evaluation. There are occasional negative criticisms but virtually no opportunity for an exchange of ideas or an exploration of possibilities, etc. Communication in general is inadequate vertically and there appears to be little participative management of programming and station direction. There is little use of staff beyond the direct carrying out of specific job responsibilities. Decisions appear to be made at the top and passed down with little consultation or conference.

I feel the overwhelming need here is for somebody to pay attention. I can assume that attention is being paid to something, but all too often, it seems that that something is not the people who work here, their need to know, to be informed, to be included, nor does it seem to be the programming, its direction and its purpose. We seem to be languishing like a sailboat becalmed. There is no "wind," no driving force, no goals, no objectives, no participation, no communication. We do our jobs, the same for ever, and that seems to be enough. I don't think it is.

Moses also raised the perennial CKUA question: how broadly could the station safely cast its net for listeners and still maintain its alternative appeal? "In addition to providing that with which the listener is familiar and comfortable, we should perhaps also be offering a modicum of the new, different, unfamiliar and, yes, even uncomfortable." He disagreed with Thomas over the nature of CKUA's classical audience, claiming that it had changed considerably over the preceding decade and had become "perhaps more sophisticated than we believe."

Tempers flared often over the next couple of years with Thomas and Rollans, sometimes through Sabourin, calling Moses on the carpet for day-parting transgressions and Moses threatening to leave.

Kay Guthrie (then Wright), who came to CKUA in 1969 and worked as traffic co-ordinator, described Moses as a "fire-brand—always fighting for the rights of the staff. Management looked at him as a trouble-maker until the day he left."

Not all of CKUA's unique personalities were on air or in management. Janitors and even ghosts have left their stamp. Guthrie particularly remembered Sam, who was both: "[Sam] knew all popular operatic arias and sang along as he swept. He died on duty at CKUA and he loved the place so much, his spirit, many staffers avow, wanders the halls humming and opening doors."

Perhaps the most interesting CKUA personality of all—and by far the station's biggest single donor ever—is a senior citizen from Lloydminster whose name we will never know. The man appeared at CKUA one day to talk with station engineer Neil Lutes.

"He liked to listen to CKUA, but he had difficulty with the radio he had and was wondering if we had any plans to expand with a transmitter out in the Lloydminster area," Thomas recalled. "Neil gave the politically correct answer, saying, 'We don't have any money and we can't do that.' And he said, 'Well, how much would it cost to put a transmitter in Lloydminster?' And Neil did some quick mental calculations and said, 'Oh, probably as much as $70,000.'

"And so the old guy said, 'Well, I can't give you $70,000 but would $50,000 help you?'"

Rollans and Thomas visited the man on his farm shortly after. "He looked like he didn't have a cent to his name," Rollans said. "He had two stoves in the kitchen. He didn't want to use the gas all the time because it was too expensive so he had a wood stove.... He chopped his own wood.... His light in his kitchen was a soup can that he put a bulb in. And he actually had his refrigerator on a timer so that it wasn't on all the time, so it wouldn't use so much power.... He used to bicycle into Lloyd to get his groceries ... and he'd get day-old bread because it was cheaper."

The man had been listening to CKUA on an old mantle radio with an aerial. Lutes fixed the radio and replaced the twenty-year-old tires on the man's bicycle. Rollans and Thomas brought him a new stereo set. The transmitter, located at Lakeland College, began broadcasting in December 1992. But listeners would never know who to thank.

"He made us promise faithfully that we wouldn't tell anyone where the money came from," Rollans said. "So he never got any recognition at all. We would like to have put something on the transmitter, but he wouldn't let us.... His only concern was he had some friends that lived in Kitscoty and he wanted to make sure that they could hear."

Radio listeners in St. Paul were not so lucky. In 1994, just as they were about to get a CKUA transmitter, the station's fortunes took another drastic turn.

Cut Adrift | 13

On June 14, 1990 Peter Senchuk sent a memo to ACCESS staff announcing five new board members. Among them was Gail Ann Hinchliffe, a property developer and partner in Hinchliffe & Associates Realty of Calgary. Hinchliffe was active in Calgary's volunteer community and had good Tory connections. She chaired the first board of the Calgary Centre for Performing Arts—a government appointment—and was a fundraiser for the Conservative party. She was also a long-time fan of CKUA.

"I've lived in Alberta my whole life and have a strong sense of Alberta," Hinchliffe said. "Alberta is a culture, and CKUA has always been my link to that culture. So being a fan of CKUA, ACCESS had a lot of intrigue for me. That was why I wanted to be on that board." But she didn't find the same depth of interest among her fellow board members, Hinchliffe said.

"When I first joined the board, I thought that I would have lots of kindred spirits. But there wasn't really.... The ACCESS board had a lot of representation from the education field, so there were a lot of teachers and others from the education field that were there primarily for ACCESS television." Not a

◆ CKUA Radio Foundation
chair Gail Hinchliffe at a
CKUA promotion.
Courtesy of CKUA.

big television fan, Hinchliffe said she erroneously thought that CKUA "would be the centre of that universe." Instead, she discovered, "while it was important and appreciated it was far down the totem pole."

Hinchliffe joined the ACCESS board as vice-chair and was elevated to chair on June 7, 1991. She said she could "see the writing on the wall" for ACCESS right from the start. Despite inflation, the corporation's budget had remained stagnant over the previous decade. "When I took over as chair, Premier [Don] Getty was in office and Fred Stewart was the minister [science and technology] we were responsible to. And it was clear to me from my discussions with him that there was a great frustration on behalf of the government as to what to do with ACCESS.

"We realized that—not just realized—we were actually told there wasn't going to be any direction coming out of government for ACCESS, and it was really up to the board to make their recommendations as to the role ACCESS had to play. So then we started making some changes ... started doing a lot of strategic planning." The board started looking at ACCESS in terms of "business centres," Hinchliffe said, and determined that the corporation was in three businesses: educational programming, television and radio.

Indeed, Senchuk had told staff in a January 1991 memo that "status quo is no longer an option for ACCESS NETWORK." He talked of the need to face the "realities" of the 1990s and to "re-invent" the corporation, emphasizing "a stronger business and market orientation." ACCESS would have to "aggressively seek income from new sources" and undergo a review of "staffing requirements." Essentially, ACCESS was going to have to take a more entrepreneurial approach and rely less on government funding. On July 4 the other shoe dropped when Senchuk announced major "staff reductions," mostly in Calgary and on the television side but including some CKUA staff.

Senchuk resigned when his contract ended that year and subsequently took up an appointment to the CRTC. ACCESS started a recruitment process for a new president. But the person recommended by the board was unacceptable to the Alberta government because of his NDP connections, according to Don Thomas, CKUA's general manager at the time. Thomas was planning to retire soon, but Hinchliffe persuaded him to take over the position in the interim until they could find an acceptable candidate. "So there I am, rearranging chairs on the deck of the Titanic," he said. Around the same time, in December 1991, Jackie Rollans was named acting general manager for CKUA.

As one of his first tasks, Thomas was asked by Hinchliffe to find another home for ACCESS to move into when its lease came up for renewal the following December. In April 1992, at the direction of the minister, the search for a new president and CEO was put on hold in line with an across-the-board hiring freeze in the provincial government.

That fall Don Getty stepped down as head of the Progressive Conservative party. With the election of Ralph Klein as party leader on December 5, 1992, the Alberta government made an ideological turn down the path of privatization and take-no-prisoners deficit slashing. Klein was sworn in as premier on December 14 and would score a resounding victory in the provincial election held June 15, 1993.

In February 1993 Alberta's public works minister, Ken Kowalski, who was now responsible for ACCESS, had mused aloud that he didn't think the corporation was required to be a government entity any more. He complained that he felt restrained by both provincial and federal legislation with regard to ACCESS, the *Edmonton Journal* reported. "I've got a board of directors I've got to deal with and a piece of legislation which doesn't allow the minister to have much say in it. And then you've got the CRTC in it. It's almost sitting there, protected unto itself."

But not for long. Alberta's "Dr. Death" was waiting in the wings. Municipal Affairs Minister Steve West, a veterinarian who would earn his nickname in the mid 1990s for the massive downsizing he undertook in successive departments under his ministry, asked Kowalski during a briefing to caucus on ACCESS why the government was in the radio-television business at all when there already were private sector radio and television stations available. Kowalski replied that he was looking at the whole future of ACCESS.

Within months West's ministry was in charge of the corporation, and West was making a name for himself as the government's spear-carrier for privatization. At the time, the "Radio Business Centre" of ACCESS was costing $3,300,100 a year with revenue of $3,100,100, including the provincial grant of $2,890,100, plus $45,000 in corporate underwriting and $135,000 in listener donations. Because of amounts carried over from previous years, however, CKUA was still in a surplus situation.

Rollans called CKUA staff together to let them know layoffs were coming. When the axe was ready to fall, classical host Richard Moses found out his name was on the layoff list, to be activated in ninety days.

"I am nearly petrified with shock. Within the next day or two, I brazenly tell my listeners of the cuts to be made and the resulting staff layoffs, which appear to include 'your genial host.'... I go crazy. Yes. I do. Looking back on it, I see that the line between 'sanity' and whatever else there is, is not fixed, and that we probably all drift back and forth across it several times during a lifetime."

Before the "agonizing" ninety days were up, Moses said, he was offered part-time work that, cobbled together, would amount to thirty-five hours a week. "I was furious. They 'laid me off' to 'save money' and now they were offering me thirty-five hours a week and more, and just how did they expect to save money? ... What I really wanted to do was tell them to shove the whole mess to where the sun don't shine, but I told them I would think about it." In the end, Moses accepted the new deal.

But his on-air revelations had not fallen on deaf ears. Ric Baker, an intense CKUA and Moses fan in Calgary, was concerned. Baker had discovered CKUA as a teenager in Edmonton in 1967.

"One day [I] kinda happened onto this radio station ... and started listening to Tony Dillon-Davis' programs on Friday and Saturday nights.... And this group of us used to get together on Friday and Saturday night and drive around and listen to that program and listen to the new music that was coming on ... and we'd go to house parties and just listen to that program."

Gradually Baker started listening to other CKUA programs and soon was tuned in to the station exclusively. "It did a lot of good for me.... Sev [Sabourin] and Richard Moses would talk about classical music, and their enthusiasm was so infectious that when I moved to Calgary in '84, I started developing a real interest in other kinds of music." Soon Baker even had a radio in his bathroom tuned to CKUA and the bathroom light rigged so that the radio would go on automatically when the light was switched on.

So when Baker got wind from Moses that CKUA was suffering a funding crunch, he decided to do something about it. He wrote to Rollans suggesting that CKUA let Moses ask his audience for extra donations earmarked for his salary. But "Jackie Rollans never responded to my letter about Richard Moses. That would have been in early '93."

In the fall of 1993, Hinchliffe said, West asked to meet with her and two other board members, including Gerry Luciani, an accountant. Their time on the board was running out, but "he asked us if we would stay on and undertake a study of ACCESS and come back to the government with recommendations as to whether or not they should be funded by the government and if not what other options there were.

"And frankly, we weren't really too prepared to do that. We had really worked hard up to that point and really felt that we were—I can only speak for myself—feeling a bit discouraged at that point in time. I remember at the meeting we frankly told him that we don't have to do this. We're volunteers in this.... And I remember saying to him specifically that I wasn't prepared to be the grease on the slide if he'd already made up his mind about what was going to happen with ACCESS, and he could do this thing without us. And he gave us his assurances that that wasn't the case—that our recommendations would be considered. And so we decided to take it on, and he gave us very, very, very short timelines."

On November 30, fresh from launching the privatization of Alberta's liquor stores, West said the government's grant to ACCESS should be reduced from $16 million to "zero" and that he had instructed the ACCESS board to report back to him by January 31 with recommendations.

Meanwhile, Thomas had found new quarters for ACCESS—a state-of-the-art building with a twenty-year lease. But when the old lease expired in December 1992, the new building wasn't ready. So, part of the television side of ACCESS temporarily moved in with CKUA. The new lease took effect in May 1993.

"During that whole period of time when we were searching for a building, when we did our interim move, when we were finishing off the new building … not one person at the government level or at the board level phoned me up or came into my office and said 'Don, we'd better put a hold on this.'"

Two weeks before ACCESS was to move into the new building, Thomas had his first meeting with West, the new minister. "And as a sort of 'Oh, by the way' as I was walking out the door, he says, 'Don, you'd better put a hold on that new building.'

"It was like he had hit me in the face with a wet dishrag. I stopped and looked at him and I said, 'Steve, let me tell you, if that's your attitude, I'm out of here now.' And he didn't say anything. And I walked out, and we moved into the new building."

However, Thomas said West apologized at their next meeting, acknowledging that it was too late to abort the move. When it became obvious to him that the government wanted to back off funding ACCESS, Thomas submitted a proposal to West to reduce the government's responsibility to forty percent of the corporation's cost, with ACCESS responsible for raising a minimum of sixty percent. "He [West] said, 'That's not what we're going for. We want to get rid of all of it.'" Ideally, the government wanted to find private broadcasters who would buy the operation. Thomas said he asked West if he would accept a proposal from management. "And he said, 'Absolutely not.'"

Then, one morning in late November, Thomas was called to West's office. "It was a Monday or a Wednesday … and there's Gail [Hinchliffe]. And … Steve said, 'Don, I've been looking at all the reports that you've sent over and it's quite obvious to me that your plans for ACCESS don't conform to the government's plan. And therefore I think you should step aside.'

"And I said, 'How soon do you want me out?' And Gail said, 'What about tonight?' And Steve said, 'No, now just a minute. Don's been very good in all of this and he's not done anything that he shouldn't have done, and so if Friday closing time is all right, that's fine with me.' And so that was it."

Rollans said that when it became apparent that the government wanted to unload ACCESS and that private broadcasters were only interested in the television side, she asked the ACCESS board if she could come back to them with a plan to save CKUA separately. "And the board asked me to leave for a while and they talked about it and called me back in and said, 'Yup, you've got our permission to see what you can do. Come up with a plan.'" Rollans said Hinchliffe was out of the country on business and wasn't present at that meeting. Hinchliffe later said she didn't recall the meeting but had been present at all ACCESS board meetings around that time.

When West made his announcement on November 30, the fate of CKUA once again became a matter of public and media concern. The *Calgary Herald* said it made no sense to turn Alberta's public broadcaster over to the private sector, where programming would be

> dictated by the bottom line. This would be a terrible mistake if it were to happen to ACCESS TV. It would be a disaster if it also killed CKUA Radio.... To simply unload this rare operation on to the highest bidder and give some private operator the keys to a provincewide radio network would be dogmatic privatization for the sake of privatization. It would reveal even more clearly how enslaved the provincial government has become to the right-wing American point of view which attacks everything run by government as somehow interfering with the divine right of the private sector to make a buck. Public broadcasting in Alberta should remain in public hands and not be sold or dismantled.

Edmonton Liberal MLA Gene Zwozdesky later responded to a concerned constituent that he had raised questions regarding ACCESS during the fall sitting of the Legislature, "but the Government would not give any meaningful answers. In fact, it always appeared that information was being withheld." He accused the Klein government of "operating secretively, behind closed doors" and said Albertans "should have a say in this matter." (Zwozdesky later crossed the floor to join Klein's Tories.)

CKUA fans sprang into action and formed Friends of CKUA (FOCKUA). John Reid, executive director of the Canadian Music Centre at the University of Calgary, established a Calgary office and phone at the university, while public relations practitioner and former private radio broadcaster Randy Kilburn headed up the Edmonton drive with Tommy Banks, using space provided by Jazz City.

Banks later said he was "astounded" that the government would want to unload CKUA. "Floored! I am still floored.... The idea that a province that has, by the accident of time and geography, got its hands on a seventeen-station radio network that cost $3 million a year to run—giving it up is ludicrous! Ludicrous! It's beyond description.... Every time I think about it, I get angry. How could anybody be that shortsighted?"

Banks said he was on an airplane around that time with the premier of another province who had just heard that the Alberta government was going to divest itself of CKUA. "He was as astounded as I. He said, 'Give me that radio ... for $3 million a year? It's beyond belief that anybody would consciously do that.'"

Known to have both Conservative and Liberal connections, Banks said he appreciated that the government had to make substantive cuts in its expenditures but felt it could easily have made a case for exempting CKUA. "Hell, it's communications and this is the age of communications.... If I sat down with any reasonable person, broadcaster or not, in two hours you'd be able to find a thousand things that a government could do with a radio station that would be in the public interest....

"Alberta had that facility that no other province in this country could have ... and we gave it up. I mean, I'm stunned even sitting here, years after the fact, just thinking about it. It's mind-boggling."

FOCKUA's aim was to get listeners to lobby the government to "conclude that CKUA should be maintained—most practically supported by a CKUA Foundation" and to buy time for the station to come up with a solution that would keep the station on the air. CKUA staff threw their weight into the effort by "undertaking a massive re-assessment of their own wages, benefits, and fundraising measures in order to present some proposals to their board and to the government before its review is completed January 31st [1994]."

Ric Baker heard about the FOCKUA number in Calgary and phoned Reid to offer his help. Baker had had a lot of experience organizing people and raising funds. He was a founding member of the Calgary International Jazz Festival and had organized Alberta's first licensed beer garden as a fundraiser for the festival. Reid asked Baker to organize a meeting of concerned Calgary listeners who had phoned the number, and invited Hinchliffe to talk to them about the future of ACCESS and CKUA.

"And that's when I met Gail," Baker said. "I talked to her about what her interest was. And her main focus was 'Well, we'll see what happens with the TV station, but I'm not really interested in TV. I really want to keep CKUA on the air. I really want to focus on CKUA.' Of course, that's where my interests were as well."

Baker said Hinchliffe later phoned him and invited him to an informal meeting to focus on what could be done. Two people at the meeting were Corey Olynik of Haines Elliott Marketing Services and John Fallows of Ernst & Young Management Consultants. "So they decided they were going to focus on getting a business plan together ... and would I be interested in staying on and chairing our group in Calgary? And I said, 'Okay, we'll chair a group and call it Friends of CKUA.'" The Friends of CKUA was formed as a volunteer organization in April 1994 by Baker and four other CKUA listeners: Wayne Anderson, Cindy McLeod, Neil Campbell and Dick Cowie.

ACCESS television found a saviour in television entrepreneur Moses Znaimer, known at the time as co-founder, president and executive producer of Toronto's popular independent television station Citytv as well as Canada's music stations MuchMusic and MusiquePlus.

"And then there was CKUA," Hinchliffe said. "We tossed around all kinds of things. There were private broadcasters that came forward, and they wanted the AM tower. They wanted the big FM towers.... But there was no 'saviour' for [CKUA]." Hinchliffe said she figured that "probably the only way it could survive and maintain its integrity was to be a foundation."

On February 4, 1994 the ACCESS board submitted its recommendations to West. It proposed privatizing ACCESS television through a deal with Znaimer's Canadian Learning Television. The board also determined that "the Alberta government should not be involved in operating a radio facility." It said a "consulting team" of Ernst & Young Management Consultants and Haines Elliott Marketing Services had created a "strategic business frame-work plan" for separating CKUA from ACCESS and restructuring it into a self-sufficient operation under a charitable foundation. The board recommended that the government accept this concept and allow forty-five days to complete and submit a transition plan for the change "from a government funded operation to a self-funded foundation operation."

The board's recommendations included the steps required for CKUA to achieve self-sufficiency. It would "significantly reduce programming and operating costs while maintaining the core programming and audience base." Government financial support would be phased out over three years, with the government providing transition funding of $2,700,000 in year one, $1,400,000 in year two and $700,000 in the final year.

On February 10, the government issued a news release announcing the privatization of ACCESS television and radio operations. It had accepted the ACCESS board's report and recommendations regarding CKUA and requested a transition plan.

Meanwhile, Rollans said, she and CKUA staff "had come up with some plans," and "people were prepared to take a twenty-percent cut in salary" but they were rebuffed.

Hinchliffe fired Rollans in mid February, saying publicly only that "it is an in-house management change." Rollans, who by then had thirty-five years of experience in the broadcasting industry, told the *Medicine Hat News*, "I was told she didn't feel I had the talent to take the station through a transition period."

Later, she said, "I just can't understand the arrogance of anybody assuming that all of a sudden they can walk in and take over an operation like that— when they don't know a thing about the business." Rollans did extract some satisfaction: "The day she fired me, I said to her, 'Well, this is still my office until I've unloaded my stuff, and I'll thank you to get out.' And, boy, did she turn tail and leave. She was out of there like a flash."

On March 24 the ACCESS board endorsed the draft of a full *CKUA Radio Business Plan* detailing how the station would operate as a self-sustaining public broadcaster under a charitable organization, the CKUA Radio Foundation. The document was prepared by Ernst & Young and incorporated a revenue development plan written by Corey Olynik of Haines Elliott Marketing Services. The law firm of McLennan Ross assisted. The consultants analyzed all aspects of the CKUA operation, from audience research and a detailed analysis of the current program schedule to discussions with the CRTC and Revenue Canada on regulatory issues. They visited the station and sought ideas from management and staff on how to improve operations.

Around this time, former ACCESS president Larry Shorter approached Hinchliffe offering advice. He had been running his own consulting business designing distance education programs and providing strategic reports for such broadcasters as the CBC and Global Communications while keeping a paternal eye on CKUA. He had "some electronic highway marketing notions" for CKUA that involved using the sub-carrier capacity for a whole range of wireless applications to raise revenue.

"She blew me off, said all was under control.... She said, 'We've got a broadcast consultant we've already hired who tells us we can make it commercial.' ... But what she's talking about is some management firm.... And I'm telling her for free, by the way."

In April 1994 the Ernst & Young report was presented to the government. It began with a summary of the current situation: CKUA had a staff of 35 and was serving an audience of 69,400 with an annual budget of $2.8 million, of which $160,000 was raised from listeners. It concluded that "CKUA has far too few listeners, costs too much to operate, has no significant track record in raising funds, and has not been sufficiently focused on adjusting to changes in the province. The good news, however, is that there is a fundamentally sound, market-based position for the station to adapt to, which builds on its historic strengths and mitigates its weaknesses."

The plan called for CKUA to be owned and operated by a charitable foundation that had been set up a decade earlier by Larry Shorter and finalized by Senchuk, in case ACCESS might need to raise public funds. The Access Charitable Foundation of Alberta had already been taken off the shelf and had met by conference call on February 23. Its existing directors had resigned and were replaced by Hinchliffe, Gerry Luciani and Randy Lennon—all ACCESS board members. Ric Baker, representing Friends of CKUA, and Malcolm Knox, listed as acting manager, were included in the revived foundation's initial membership of five. Hinchliffe signed a Consent to Act as a Director of the Access foundation and was appointed chair to the foundation board on February 23. "As the Foundation evolves, it is expected that this Board will grow and include representation from major corporate and individual supporters, as well as CKUA Radio staff," the business plan said.

The foundation would have to get permission from Revenue Canada to change its name, revise its objects and continue its charitable tax status. CKUA would also have to get approval from the CRTC for a new licence under its revised structure—one that would allow it to seek corporate sponsorships and limited advertising and to change its promise of performance in case it had to reduce the scope of its programs during an initial downsizing period. The business plan stated that "the Commission [CRTC] does not appear to be aware that the station is carrying sponsorship messages at the present time." However, with Peter Senchuk, the former ACCESS president, on the commission, that's hard to believe. This may have been another case of the CRTC benignly turning a blind eye to CKUA's transgressions.

The business plan contained an organization chart showing "an independent Board of Directors, devoted exclusively to the governance of CKUA Radio"; an "external fund raising consultant," answerable directly to the board; a station manager "with particular emphasis on station marketing and development"; and marketing and promotion resources, responsible to the station manager. The highest salary would be $85,000, to be paid to the station manager.

A "Programming and Audience Development Plan" called for doubling the number of listeners and a "cost-benefit" analysis of each program. "The benefits of a program must be considered in terms of listenership and revenue," as opposed to CKUA's past "'production' rather than 'market' oriented" approach to programming. In line with this, the cost per program hour, which the consultants considered high at 7.6 hours of staff time, would be reduced. The plan also called for dropping the foreign-language and ethnic programs, because they "do not appear to be consistent with programming objectives and might be provided instead on the ethnic radio station in Edmonton." Key to increasing listenership, and therefore to revenue-generating potential, would be an aggressive promotional campaign, since ACCESS research showed that sixty percent of Alberta adults were still unaware of CKUA's existence.

Olynik's "Revenue Plan and Budget" pointed out that current corporate underwriting and sponsorship sales, at around $36,000, were "dismal." The plan claimed that sponsorship "packages" had been tested with "50–60 business people" and about a third of the firms contacted had shown potential interest in supporting CKUA, leading Olynik to conclude that $300,000 would be a reachable goal for the first year and double that amount by the third year. The station had already taken a more aggressive tack with its on-air spring fundraiser in March 1994 by upping its announced goal to $125,000 from the previous fall campaign's $75,000 and introducing the campaign theme "Help Us Build a Sound Future for CKUA." The revenue plan suggested that, with raised public awareness of CKUA, the annual fundraising efforts could raise $400,000 the first year and up to $600,000 by the third year.

The cornerstone of the revenue plan called for a Build the Foundation Campaign, "similar to a preservation fundraising campaign. Foundations, special names, corporations and Friends of CKUA will be asked to make a one-time five-year commitment to the station." The money, targeted at $1.2 million, would be committed in the first year and received over five years and used to provide any required bridge funding during the transition and to create a surplus to backstop the station. The plan saw the Build the Foundation Campaign bringing in $400,000 during the first year.

On the cost side, CKUA would have to immediately downsize from thirty-five to twenty-six or twenty-seven full-time employees. Those remaining would have to take an average twenty-percent pay cut; those leaving would receive standard ACCESS severance packages. The plan concluded with an assessment of the risks inherent in its projections, from annual fundraising at low risk, to regulatory approvals at medium risk for the CRTC and high for Revenue Canada, to the Build the Foundation Campaign at high risk. "However, the use of a professional external consultant to manage this campaign will assist in mitigating the risk."

Following submission of the business plan to the minister, Steve West, Cabinet approved the ACCESS board's proposal to transfer CKUA to a charitable foundation in mid May. West called it a "win-win arrangement for all parties" and said the plan removed government "from a business it should not have been in in the first place."

On May 19 the directors of the newly activated foundation changed its name to the CKUA Radio Foundation and amended its bylaws. The organization, registered under the Societies Act, would operate only on a non-profit basis. Membership would be subject to a majority vote of members. A quorum would consist of the lesser of at least ten members in good standing or fifteen percent of the members of the society—which is interesting, given that there were only five members. Members could participate by phone, but every question would be decided by a majority of votes from members present in person. The board of directors would consist of no fewer than three and up to fifteen people and must meet at least every six months. A majority of directors—in this case, that would mean two—would be a quorum, and meetings could be held without notice if a quorum was present. In the event of ties, the chairman would get two votes. Under the original bylaws, the president had one vote in case of a tie, and meetings could be held with no notice only if all directors were present. A membership quorum had required no fewer than three members.

The primary objective of the new organization would be "to use radio broadcasting on a not-for-profit basis to provide programming which makes educational instruction broadly available for post-secondary credit courses and enhances and promotes a better understanding and appreciation of the arts, music, literature, history and culture among the broadcast audience and to provide practical training and learning opportunities for students enrolled in radio arts and communication courses of study at post-secondary educational institutions."

On June 9, 1994 the ACCESS board approved the sale of the assets and operations of CKUA to the foundation, and on August 9 the CKUA Radio Foundation entered into an Asset Purchase and Sale Agreement with the Alberta Educational Communications Corporation (ACCESS) whereby the foundation agreed to purchase the assets and goodwill of the business operation of CKUA Radio for ten dollars. (The music library alone had an estimated replacement value for insurance purposes of $600,000.) ACCESS would provide the foundation with a transitional funding grant of $2,700,000 to March 1, 1995, $1,350,000 to March 1, 1996 and $675,000 to March 1, 1997.

ACCESS and the foundation also signed a management agreement covering the interim period between August 1, 1994 and the closing date of sale, subsequently agreed to be July 13, 1995. During the term of the agreement, the foundation was not to enter into any contracts exceeding $25,000 without prior written consent of ACCESS. The agreement also called for the foundation to provide its management services "in accordance with the Business Plan." Also, during the interim period the foundation was not to

make or undertake to make payments to any of its shareholders, directors, officers or managers, or to any corporation affiliated with their shareholders or to anyone dealing at arm's length with their shareholders, whether for drawings, fees, bonuses, dividends, redemption of shares, advancement or repayment of loans, forgiveness of debt or any other remuneration, compensation or payment either directly or indirectly or otherwise save and except as provided in the Business Plan or agreed to in writing by the Vendor (ACCESS).

At the time Hinchliffe was still chair of the ACCESS board. She would continue in that position until August 30, 1995.

On August 29, 1994 the board of directors of the foundation met by conference call at 9:30 a.m. Present were Hinchliffe, Luciani and Lennon (the latter via telephone), with John Gormley, the foundation's lawyer, also attending. Items of business included approving a management contract with Gail A. Hinchliffe & Associates, for three years effective August 1, 1994, and ratifying the appointment of Rick Lewis, a man with more than twenty years of experience in radio broadcasting, as general manager of CKUA, effective August 2, 1994. Hinchliffe diligently left the room to absent herself from the discussion while Luciani and Lennon voted to ratify her contract. They also named Hinchliffe the "nominating committee" for directors.

Then, at 9:45 a.m., the full foundation membership—Hinchliffe, Luciani, Lennon, Baker and Knox—met by conference call for the annual general meeting. They agreed to admit three new members: Rick Lewis, Tommy Banks and Larry Clausen, owner of Communications Incorporated, a Calgary advertising and public relations agency. Baker moved and Lennon seconded that "anyone donating $10 or more to the Society will be admitted as a member." The motion was carried unanimously. The membership resolved that twelve directors would be appointed, six to be elected "presently" and six to be appointed by the board. Hinchliffe, Luciani, Baker, Clausen, Banks and Lewis were named directors, with Hinchliffe as chair and Luciani as vice-chair. Lennon resigned as director.

In October the ACCESS board delegated Luciani, who was a director of both ACCESS and the CKUA foundation, the authority to approve any personnel contracts for the foundation. Hinchliffe's personal services contract, which called for remuneration of $120,000 in the first year, $135,000 in the second year and $150,000 in the third, plus all travel and living expenses out of Calgary, was signed for the foundation by Luciani on February 2, 1995, retroactive to August 1, 1994. Her duties would include strategic management planning; planning and execution of fundraising responsibilities; recruitment of members, directors, corporate sponsors and funding agencies; liaising with Alberta and Canadian arts and cultural organizations and foundations; developing public funding and corporate support for the Society and its radio broadcasting activities; liaising with the Provincial and Federal Governments and regulatory authorities; and the negotiating of contracts on behalf of the Society for the sale and sponsorship of radio programs and public fund-raising campaigns.

Hinchliffe had already drawn her first cheque in September for $10,000, covering August 1994, even though the foundation had hired Rick Lewis as general manager on August 29, effective August 2.

Although her contract specified that Hinchliffe provide "exclusive service" to the CKUA Radio Foundation, she had announced to the ACCESS board at a meeting on July 18, 1994 that, due to the workload involved in the process of privatization of ACCESS, she had been placed on a contract with the Alberta government. A 1997 forensic accounting review reported that between August 1, 1994 and September 1, 1995, she "appears" to have collected $31,216 from ACCESS in addition to her remuneration from the foundation. The existence of Hinchliffe's contracts and the inner workings of the foundation were not public knowledge during Hinchliffe's time at the CKUA helm.

Meanwhile, the foundation received charitable status from Revenue Canada after some difficulty, Hinchliffe said. "It took a lot of negotiation with the federal government to get charitable status.... It was really questionable whether [CKUA] fit the guidelines for charitable status, because at the same time we were applying to the CRTC for a licence that allowed selling of commercials. So, a little bit of a grey area there."

The application to the CRTC was sent out on September 9, with Rick Lewis, the new station manager, listed as the CKUA contact. The application included an item from the CKUA foundation's amended bylaws stating, "No Director or member of the Society shall receive any remuneration for his or her services." The application also stated,

The only officer or director of the Applicant who will become an employee is Rick Lewis, who has been retained by the Foundation as

General Manager. Lewis is a director of the Foundation and serves as Secretary to the Board.

Lewis was the only director of the foundation with significant radio broadcasting experience.

Once the foundation's management agreement was signed, Hinchliffe began hiring a series of management, consulting and marketing companies. (The forensic accounting review counted fifteen such companies hired by AECC and CKUA between May 5, 1994 and May 5, 1997.) Ernst & Young was hired to assist in accounting and with the CRTC application. Haines Elliott Marketing Services was brought onboard for strategic planning and fundraising. And Olynik was contracted on October 17, 1994, through his company Century Communications, to implement the revenue development plan he had written earlier for Haines Elliott Marketing as part of CKUA's business plan. Although the business plan called for an external fundraising consultant at a cost of forty thousand dollars a year, Olynik's contract called for remuneration of seven thousand dollars a month plus expenses.

Meanwhile, Lewis, who had been hired after an extensive executive search by Ernst & Young, was mysteriously let go by Hinchliffe on October 14 after only two months on the job. A hand-delivered letter from Hinchliffe to Lewis dated September 30, 1994 said,

> To confirm discussion of this afternoon, CKUA is changing the nature of its organization to operate on a management team approach. We agreed that you will be participating on the management team with a review to determine if this is an appropriate role for you. I suggest an interim discussion on Friday, October 14 where we can both consider the appropriateness of this structure for you.

Lewis later said, in the 1997 forensic accounting review of the foundation, that he was terminated after working for less time than it had taken to do the executive search. Clausen, who had been appointed a director at the August 29 meeting, later said, in the same review, that he didn't even know who Lewis was and was not aware of either his hiring or his firing. Records show that on October 26 the board of directors approved the removal of Lewis as station manager effective October 14. From that point on, Hinchliffe acted as *de facto* CEO, although it was never clear whether she was officially appointed.

Also in October CKUA held its first on-air fundraiser under the foundation and in nine days netted $135,000 from listeners. CKUA statistics indicate that 4,511 listeners contributed to the station in 1994. The following March, listeners responded to the foundation's spring fundraising campaign with $169,000 in 10 days.

The listeners were clearly doing their share. However, making a go of the station "certainly was far from being a slam dunk," Hinchliffe said later. For one thing, the CRTC licence didn't come through until the end of May 1995. When ACCESS Television had applied years earlier for approval to sell commercials, it had been turned down. Hinchliffe said that private broadcasters came forward to oppose CKUA's application for a commercial licence in 1994. "It [the licence the foundation applied for] was a restricted licence; it wasn't a full commercial licence. And we asked for so many [commercial] hours." Hinchliffe said the foundation then struck an agreement with the private broadcasters whereby CKUA would amend its application to request approval for fewer commercial hours if they would support the application rather than oppose it.

"We were doing a letter to CRTC saying that we had met with the Alberta broadcasters and that we had agreed to these concessions. But fortunately, when hearing time came, the CRTC granted our first application. I don't know how much influence he had, but Peter Senchuk was a commissioner on the CRTC.... You know, I think that across the country there is a great deal of empathy and support for CKUA, and they [the CRTC] didn't want to be the one to shut it down."

The new licence allowed CKUA to sell a total of 504 minutes of restricted advertising per week. As a condition of licence, the station was required to provide a minimum six and a half hours per week of formal educational programming.

Getting the licence was one condition of closing the sale of CKUA by ACCESS to the foundation. Another was to negotiate a new collective agreement with CKUA's union, the International Brotherhood of Electrical Workers. However, CKUA staff would question using the word "negotiate" in this context. "She [Hinchliffe] put a gun to their heads," said Brian Dunsmore, who was program manager at the time.

Hinchliffe had hired human resources consultant Rick Salt to prepare a human resources management plan and assist the foundation with labour relations. He submitted results of a survey showing that salaries paid to CKUA announcers were "significantly over market."

Richard Moses recalled, "It must have been just before the Easter holidays … when she [Hinchliffe] assembled staff in the big studio. Talks had been underway for some time, without real success, and at this meeting Gail told us, point-blank, that either we signed the deal NOW or she would close the station down in three days' time. Naturally, when the staff met together to discuss it, there was outrage. Both Chris Allen and I spoke strongly against caving in to these Tsarist tactics and urged calling her bluff.… But in the end, we two were the only ones to vote NO."

On April 1, 1995 staff ratified the new contract. According to Moses, it called for thirty-five-percent pay cuts and a fourteen-percent increase in hours as well as decreases in benefits. The previous summer staff numbers had been thinned to twenty-seven, as several CKUA employees chose to take what they characterized as "generous" severance packages from ACCESS.

Shortly after the foundation extracted a new deal from the union, Tommy Banks resigned from the board, effective April 11, 1995.

"The reason that I gave in my resignation letter—and it was true—[was that] I was never able to attend a meeting. Every time they had a meeting, I was on a gig some place or away.… What I didn't say in the letter was there were a couple of things that had happened in conversations that I had had—in casual conversations with a couple of other board members that I had just met—that I didn't like. Gail had never said anything to me that I didn't like, but a couple of other board members did, and I didn't like some of the things that they were saying and the direction I saw they were going that had to do with relations with the staff."

Banks said he realized that salary reductions were probably necessary to make CKUA self-sufficient, "but it had to do with the way that that was being gone about. Now, I was not party to any of the direct negotiations with the staff, but I am convinced that there are ways to do things that are okay and other ways to do them that are not okay.… There are ways of putting things with a degree of civility of approach no matter what a tough job is at hand … and I didn't like some of the things that I heard."

Behind the scenes, a very peculiar thing was happening. On March 31, 1995 the deputy minister of municipal affairs had approved the early payment to ACCESS, for transmission to the CKUA foundation, of the remaining $2,025,000 of the $4.7-million transitional grant payable to the foundation over three years under the sale agreement. While the original sale agreement signed in August 1994 did not require the foundation to submit accountability reports to ACCESS, on April 19, 1995 the ACCESS board approved amendments to the sale agreement requiring that the foundation provide a status report to ACCESS before October 31, 1995.

Inexplicably, the amendments also provided for ACCESS to immediately pay the foundation the $2,025,000 balance of grant money for the second and third years of the funding period. Hinchliffe and Luciani were still on the boards of both organizations, and Hinchliffe was still chairperson of both. On April 28, 1995 the foundation received the remaining $2,025,000 of the transitional funding grant, which the minister had advised could be drawn upon once the union had ratified the collective agreement and the CRTC licence was in hand.

On July 13, 1995 the sale of CKUA to the foundation was closed. That same month Luciani started receiving payment for accounting and management services, even though the business plan called for one accountant, who was already on staff. Without a written contract, over the next two years Luciani would receive more than $120,000 for his services.

And starting in March 1995, Clausen's company, Communications Incorporated, had been billing CKUA for advertising services and materials. The company would be paid $245,000 over the next two years. CKUA's advertising was never put out to tender, but Clausen later said, when interviewed for the forensic review, that the station had received better than fair value for his services.

During the foundation's first year, Ric Baker continued to build the Calgary Friends of CKUA organization. He raised some money for and awareness of the station by staging parties—including a Blues Boogie and a Caribbean Carnival—hiring local musicians at scale and charging admission.

"I did it all on a volunteer basis, got it all set up and was trying to start another business at the same time.... Then I finally went to Gail and said, 'Really what we need is ... a province-wide Friends of CKUA.' She said, 'Well, put it down on paper.' So I wrote a business plan for the Friends of CKUA ...

and I put in there what I thought it would cost to do it, remuneration for services rendered by me to do it."

Baker said he talked with other people who were performing similar functions in arts organizations and arrived at a figure of $40,000 per year. He formed a sole proprietorship called RB Consulting and was contracted for two years, starting in March 1995, to duplicate across the province the Friends model that he had created in Calgary.

By the end of August 1995, after CKUA's first year under the foundation, revenues for the station were falling seriously short of target. Funding from corporate sponsorships was only twenty-six percent of what the business plan projected, and the Build the Foundation campaign, projected to raise $400,000, hadn't even got off the ground. The only bright spot was the revenue from listeners, which came in at $93,000 more than the anticipated $400,000 for the first year. In spite of the big hit CKUA staff took with their new union contract, operating costs—not taking into account transition costs, which were lower than anticipated—were running nearly $500,000 over budget, mainly attributable to higher than forecasted salary expenses for marketing, administration and the senior management position.

Olynik's contract was cancelled, two months early, on August 31, 1995, on the grounds that his skills were no longer required because CKUA was shifting from a "corporate fundraising model to a more sales-oriented model." Between October 1, 1994 and August 31, 1995, his company had received $108,935 from CKUA, including $14,980 in termination fees for the last two months of his contract and $15,310 for travel and living expenses.

At the end of the CKUA Radio Foundation's first year of operating the station, there were four directors of the foundation—Hinchliffe, Luciani, Baker and Clausen—and all were receiving payments in some form or other, either personally or through their companies.

The Hinchliffe Years | 14

Ken Regan, CKUA's news director at the time of the transition from ACCESS to the CKUA Radio Foundation, figured out pretty quickly that he wouldn't be happy under the new regime. However, he gave the provincial government marks for "creativity" for converting CKUA into a not-for-profit private broadcaster.

"They could have just as easily shut it down and said, 'Turn out the lights, see you later.' But there was a political consideration in that, too, because they remembered what happened the last time when they tried to shut it down.... They were inundated with letters of protest from around the province, many of them coming from their own supporters. So closure was not the best option."

Indeed, in early March 1994 Premier Ralph Klein told CKUA's legislative correspondent, Ian Gray, that he'd just finished signing the last of two thousand letters to constituents concerned about ACCESS, and CKUA in particular, and said it was the greatest amount of mail on a single subject his government had ever received.

But Regan noted that when the government privatized ACCESS television, Moses Znaimer got a better deal than the one CKUA had got when it was cut loose. "So, they gave CKUA, which was this glorious institution ... with a proud history of public service in this province, $5 million for three years and said, 'Okay, go make your own way in life,' and at the same time turned over the provincial television network to one of the richest television people in the world and guaranteed him $8 million a year in revenue. I don't understand the economics of that. But ... it was a relatively creative solution, and it allowed CKUA to continue."

Regan decided not to continue with CKUA; he took the severance package. "Even though my heart remained with CKUA ... I knew, very soon after the change in the management team, that I was not going to stay—because of the people that Gail brought in. First of all, I didn't feel confident in their abilities to get the job done. Second of all, I knew that I was not going to be happy working for those people because I ... didn't agree with their philosophy of radio. I didn't think they understood public radio, and I didn't think that I was going to get along very well with them."

Brian Dunsmore stayed for several months and remembers that period as "the worst time in my life. It was terrible." He'd been involved with CKUA for more than fifteen years and had been on staff full time since 1987. He was hired as program manager by Rick Lewis shortly before Lewis was, in Dunsmore's words, "turfed off." There was speculation that Lewis, who was the only person on the foundation board with radio experience, was hired as a "straw man" to lend credibility to the CRTC application, Dunsmore said. "But I don't believe that. I think, from the meetings I was involved in at the time, that she [Hinchliffe] just realized that she wanted to be the general manager.... She was very hands-on, a controlling kind of person."

Hinchliffe, a Calgarian, flew up to Edmonton every week or so, often with Corey Olynik, the foundation's revenue development consultant. But, Dunsmore said, "Essentially I was *de facto* station manager on a day-to-day basis, not something that I'd ever wanted to do. There were all of the problems with the union. There was just a whole bunch of stuff that was dumped on me. Meanwhile, she was in Calgary and she'd be on the phone and making decisions.... So it just went into the ground."

Dunsmore said he was put in the position of having to cut programs and tell contractors there was no more work for them. He wanted out, but said

◆ Ken Davis, CKUA
operations manager under
Gail Hinchliffe and later
station manager.
Courtesy of CKUA; photo by
Frank Gasparik.

he didn't want to quit. "There's a certain zealousness about we CKUA people—
we feel strongly that we must help, do what we can until the bitter end.... I
really felt I had to be part of this ... but it was just awful, terrible. I knew it
wasn't working. I didn't have a clue what to do but I knew I couldn't leave my
station." Dunsmore was laid off in early April 1995, around the time that
Hinchliffe delivered the ultimatum to the union.

The previous fall, before Regan left, Lewis and Regan had recruited Ken
Davis as director of news and current affairs. Davis, who had worked with
Lewis at CJCA, came with more than fifteen years of experience in commercial broadcasting as a journalist, news anchor, producer, talk-show host and
prairie regional manager for Standard Broadcast News. He was also "avoca-
tionally" a musician and singer-songwriter and what he called a "selective
listener" to CKUA, which he said was "really the only choice when looking
for new influence."

But he thought CKUA during the ACCESS years was "stuffy and staid,
academic, ivory-towerish. Boring as hell, for the most part. But it still had
the redeeming virtue of being probably the only repository of alternative
music in Alberta. And I don't think I was really that different from a lot of
people that listened to it at that time."

Working at CKUA appealed to Davis for another reason: his anger at the Klein government, "which has privatized so much of what had once been public trust....

"We essentially watched the safety net disappear that had previously given all of us at least some comfort against adversity.... So I was angry enough at the Klein administration for a lot of its conduct ... that when CKUA was cut loose, I looked at it and said, 'Here's a chance for a little thing that's a jewel to fight for a new life.' It just appealed to me.

"I knew it was going to be a little dicey. Who knew what its future looked like? ... It was a long shot to even go there professionally.... If your life's going to mean anything at the end of it, once in a while you've just got to put it all out there and go for something that actually means something to you. And the fight appealed to me."

CKUA's news department was a "modest organization" at the time, Davis said. When Dunsmore was laid off, Davis was asked to add programming to his responsibilities, a job he found "daunting" at the start.

"To begin with, CKUA had its long tradition and its stable of announcers who had been there a long time, known to be strong-willed, independent people. And there was a job to be done to cast a new direction for CKUA—that, while preserving all the inherent qualities of the organization as a cultural icon, it still had to become more populist, because the numbers weren't there to financially sustain it.

"So, my initial duty during the entire period that Gail Hinchliffe assumed essentially CEO duties was that of retooling the programming." With the new title of operations manager, Davis became a member of the management team and was involved in certain senior administrative issues, he said. "But there was a distinction. There was a division. The fiscal management of the organization, all of those components, was very much held inside a smaller group of which I was not a part."

Richard Moses, who wasn't on good terms with CKUA's former managers, Jackie Rollans and Don Thomas, said he initially welcomed Hinchliffe's takeover:

and we all thought she might be the saviour of us all. In fact she was. For a while. She had connections political and connections financial and connections business, and betwixt them all she managed:

(a) to persuade the government of the day not to cut us off without a sou ...

(b) with some of her Calgary cronies, to work up a salable business plan almost overnight, a plan that looked really quite good on paper, and satisfied the government that we knew what we were doing. (A clear case of oversell.) ...

(c) to obtain from Revenue Canada and the CRTC all the paper that would allow the station to continue operating, and operating as a charitable organization. (no small feat).... Then it all began to fall apart, and our confidence with it.

Moses said that when Rick Lewis was dismissed, "it was announced that Herself would assume the duties of CEO. I, for one, was aghast, having had some experience with the non-separation of Board and CEO responsibilities." Following the union stand-off, "she knew she had us by the short ones and she never gave an inch."

On May 5, 1995 Moses gave Hinchliffe a letter:

As a member of the CKUA staff, one of whose duties it is to assist in raising money for the CKUA Foundation, I feel I am entitled to know the structure and budget of the Foundation including the top echelon management. This, in fact, is, or should be, publicly accessible information.

As you must be aware, several attempts, indirect and subtle, to be sure, have been made to gain access to this information or, to put it bluntly, to find out just what is going on around here. All to no avail....

It is painfully obvious that a good deal of secrecy exists.

I have this morning paid a visit to the Corporate Registry Office and, without mentioning any names, tried to determine just how we could break through this secrecy.

We all know the rules for non-profit corporations: "No Director or member of the Society shall receive any remuneration for his or her services," etc.

My questions are simple, and should be public knowledge: 1) Are you employed by the CKUA Radio Foundation? 2) If so, in what capacity?

3) Is there remuneration attached to this position, aside from reimbursement for expenses? 4) What is the range of this remuneration?

I am told by the Registry people that my concerns are justified and legitimate and that a simple inquiry should elicit answers. I was also told, somewhat to my alarm, that enforcement of corporate by-laws is a matter handled by the police.

Gail, I would like those answers and I want the entire staff to know them. I cannot imagine that there is anything untoward going on, but then why the secrecy?

...

Could we say May 12 for a response to my queries?

May 12 came and went. Moses never received an answer.

Bill Coull said that at the start he didn't know what to make of Hinchliffe. "She was very convincing. She could con me—maybe she didn't. Maybe she was really serious about that [closing the station] ... we weren't used to that kind of administration or management."

Listeners and media at the time were blissfully unaware of any troubles brewing behind the scenes. During the spring 1995 fundraiser, *Calgary Herald* editorial writer Charles Frank praised CKUA's focus on Alberta and things Albertan, and encouraged listeners to donate to "the closest thing we have to old-fashioned radio." The campaign achieved its goal, bringing in $169,000.

Around this time, according to Moses, a slick five-colour program guide was printed and then quickly scrapped before it could be sent out. The reason given was that it told listeners that they could become members of the foundation with a donation, which was in line with the motion Ric Baker had made, and the board had passed, at the August 1994 general meeting. Now it appeared the board was back-pedalling on that policy. Staff shook their heads over the waste and the abrupt change in rules.

Staff were also concerned about money going out the door for what they considered ill-advised marketing and advertising campaigns. One, billed as a "teaser" campaign, featured ads placed on the backs of buses with alliterative messages such as "Radio Vivaldi would value" and "Radio Dizzy would dig."

"There were no call letters, no frequencies to identify CKUA, nothing," said one staff member. "There were five or six of these stupid slogans and then the ads disappeared. It was a huge waste of money."

On July 13, 1995 the CKUA Radio Foundation issued a news release announcing that the sale between ACCESS and the foundation had closed and the CKUA Radio Network was now owned by the foundation. It also gave a rosy picture of the financial situation: "Corporations are quickly coming on board to support CKUA and sufficient commitments are in place to ensure that the station remains on the air for the next 18 months." The foundation threw a reception that same day, at Jazz Beans coffeehouse in Commerce Place in Edmonton, celebrating the closing of the deal. CKUA staff stayed away.

Four days later Larry Clausen sent Hinchliffe a letter in which he referred to the reception:

I was excited to meet so many people who are supporting CKUA! The event at Jazz Beans was full of enthusiasm and people who really care about the future of the network were bubbling with ideas.

As a new Board member, I had hoped to meet the people of CKUA at this event. I was very disheartened that most of the employees of the network did not attend....

Certainly change is difficult to embrace and I am sure that CKUA people have many apprehensions about what is next. But my experience with other not-for-profit organizations enforces the view that we can only make CKUA survive if we are all working together.

You can count on me to encourage a team approach. I am also interested to ensure that we remain as open as possible with the team so that all of us can work effectively together.

On the day following the reception, the board held a workshop/retreat on audience development and sponsorship. Clausen raised the issue of staff being conspicuously absent from the reception. Ken Chapman, an Edmonton lawyer active in the Progressive Conservative party who later became a board member, participated and wrote a summary report. In it he said, "Special attention needs to be placed on giving staff a chance to decide if they are 'into the new CKUA' or merely on the side. There is not time or energy or resource base to allow for anyone to be a bit player or an observer. CKUA staff must be in the game or off the field. It must be their choice to make."

Moses struck again on July 20, responding to a letter from Hinchliffe to staff reporting on the retreat and other developments. He commended her and the board for establishing a staff task force to help re-examine the program schedule. But he took issue with her announcement that the foundation had a "limited membership" that would not be increased. "I find this quite alarming," Moses wrote.

It seems to be contrary to everything both staff and listeners have been led to believe since the whole transition began and can hardly lead to meaningful audience involvement and input or staff/board teamwork. It apparently changes the Board—which appears now to actually BE the Foundation—from a "Management Team" into an exclusive, self-perpetuating autocracy, bereft of any sort of checks and balances.... It is a situation unheard of in the modern age, certainly somewhat arrogant in concept and, if I may say so, most likely doomed to failure. The problem is, of course, that that failure will take the radio station with it. ...

You ask for our continued dedication to CKUA, and make use of that overwrought word "team" in relation to "our" efforts. Surely you must realize—even if our declining to attend the Closing Reception didn't tell you—that "dedication" is not now a particularly significant term around CKUA.... I cannot speak for others on the staff, but it is apparent that morale is, as they say, sucking canal water, and that anger and despair, at being repeatedly and continually treated as gratuitous presences with nothing to contribute except, incidentally, our talent, are constant companions.

As to that much vaunted "teamwork," there must be a new definition of the word in use by the Board. Try as we might, we, the staff, cannot seem to get on that team. We aren't even the last to be picked—we aren't picked at all. Your chosen few just march away and play the game all by themselves.

Moses mentioned a number of grievances, including the pay cuts and the recent printing and scrapping of the expensive program guide.

On top of all this comes your letter which just sort of screws down the lid: to paraphrase "The Foundation is the Board and the Board is the Foundation and the Board is going to run things without any help from anybody—the staff, the listeners—anybody. There is no democracy at CKUA, so get used to it."...

Let me suggest that this teakettle is just simmering now, but it could reach the boiling point and some teakettles have those little whistles that blow when the pressure gets high enough....

...things must not continue this way. I sometimes find myself wondering how long I will be able to go on the air, beseeching our listeners to give us money when I know so little about how that money is spent and often suspect the worst....

...I cannot help but wonder what those generous, attentive, devoted—innocently naïve—listeners would think if they knew what was really going on here.

Moses copied his four-page letter to the whole board and management team. He got no response, in spite of the thinly veiled reference to whistle-blowing. A year later he was, remarkably, still employed; staff relations weren't any better. More remarkably, when Hinchliffe was interviewed in 1999, she commented, "I loved Richard Moses. I thought, 'Nobody can do a classical program like Richard Moses.'"

Just before Moses wrote his second letter, a consulting group, Turner Associates, had been brought in. Following an initial "team investigation" meeting, they reported that "trust (top-to-bottom and vice versa) is low in the organization." The report noted a "strong sense of 'ownership' in the employee group, especially those that are long-term ones," but also found that "fear and insecurity is evident." The culture of the organization "is presently based in Protective Parentalism vs. Innovative/Entrepreneurial Mentality." Tacked onto the end of the report was the motto "If your ship hasn't come in perhaps you should row out to meet it."

Hinchliffe brought in a number of consultants to reconfigure CKUA into a business model. They bandied about terms like "value-added" and "entre-preneurial attitude," which had become buzzwords as government strove to become more like business and executive development consultants like William Bridges made fortunes telling individuals to think of themselves as a business called "You & Co."

A draft of an operations plan dated July 19, 1995 had this item under a section entitled "Audience Development—Programming":

Progress to model of each program being its own business…. Each program will have its own budget with a designated producer/ announcer who is prepared to provide value-added attitude.

This shift to a business paradigm set up a clash of cultures with staff. "It's basically a corporate world that she came from, and that's basically how she tried to deal with CKUA," Bill Coull said. "It's not really helpful here." According to staff, there were workshops with facilitators where staff were encouraged to provide input, but nothing ever came of them.

Employee relations wasn't Hinchliffe's strong suit. She got off to a bad start by hiring Rick Salt to negotiate with the union. Staff already knew and disliked Salt for his hard-ball negotiating style when he had been employed by ACCESS. After years of dealing with unions for ACCESS, Salt had left the corporation and was working as a human resources consultant when Hinchliffe hired him to provide a human resources management plan and negotiate for the foundation.

Unlike previous station managers, who had broadcast experience and had come up through the ranks, Hinchliffe operated at a different level altogether, Ken Davis said.

"Gail's difficulty was, in my humble opinion, she came across as rather aloof, rather aristocratic in her dealings with staff, and that's not how these people wanted to be talked to…. At a certain level, Gail preoccupied herself with the upper echelon business and government and arts community of Alberta. That's where her focus was, that's where she networked, that's where she wanted to play. And she didn't necessarily want to be particularly preoccupied with a more egalitarian, democratic body that was underneath all of that, that also was a part of the CKUA community."

Nevertheless, Coull remembered a woman who "genuinely liked blues…. She'd go down to the … bar and drink beer with the guys and listen to blues. She was a surprise. She was an anomaly. I treated her as a curiosity, and there were lots of times when we were in accord." But, Coull said, "I didn't keep my mouth shut. Neither did Moses."

Coull credited Ken Davis with intervening on their behalf when they were in trouble with management. "It was incredible what this man was able to pull together and save…. He saved my ass. He saved Moses' ass…. Whoever was a naysayer, whoever happened to have ideas that were somehow reasonable and she didn't like it, Ken was there to save them.... He made this place reasonable in a time of unreasonableness.... He walked us through that very difficult time."

When interviewed in 1999, Hinchliffe declined to speak about her employee relations or the matter of her own salary, citing a pending court case in which she was being sued by, and was counter-suing, the current CKUA Radio Foundation. However, she did talk of the reasons for the pressure on the union.

"A new deal with the union had to be negotiated by a specific date or the deal wasn't going to go through with the government, so that's what was driving the urgency.... A committee had been struck to do the negotiation and they just couldn't come to terms."

Hinchliffe said the existing salaries "were the highest in the broadcast industry" and "were based pretty well on what was under the government scenario—you got paid for how long you were there, not for what you did or what kind of audience you had. So if you were there for twenty years and had a late-night show that [only] your mother listened to, you got paid more than the morning person who really could carry a lot of programs that were selling ... where there really was a lot of responsibility.... So the model that was presented was more along broadcast lines where the pay is tied to performance."

Hinchliffe acknowledged that "there was an awful lot of trauma" among the staff at the time, which she attributed to loss of the security afforded by a government job and general reaction to change.

In the climate of the times, CKUA staff felt they had nowhere to turn, Dunsmore said. "This was a time in history when going public wouldn't have meant anything. I don't think the union could have done anything. The day after I left, another two thousand nurses were laid off. That was the kind of profile of cutbacks and pain and paranoia that was going on in the province at that time. So what was happening to these twenty-three people at CKUA wouldn't have meant diddly-squat."

However, it's clear that whatever else Hinchliffe did, she bought CKUA a few more years of life at a time when the Klein government was ready to choke it off, Dunsmore conceded. "Had she not been there, CKUA would have been dead.... CKUA is on the air largely because of what Gail Hinchliffe did through that period. It's true."

But, Dunsmore added, in the process she lost "the good will, the passion, the love of the employees. She didn't kill it, but she put it into hibernation or cold storage in many ways, and it was very difficult."

Dunsmore felt that Hinchliffe and her consultants were mistaken in trying to apply a pure business model to operating the station. For one thing, he said, the "traditional broadcast yardsticks" don't apply.

"CKUA is a one-off operation [and] it always has been.... Why [do] listeners feel such a strong proprietorship sense? ...You can't measure that stuff....

"John Fallows [of Ernst & Young] ... put together a pretty common-sense view of how CKUA could go about organizing itself ... but even he didn't understand how announcers go about picking music for shows and how much time that takes and the kind of personality you have to have to do that.... These people take years to develop...."

While CKUA employees were feeling more and more distanced from management, Hinchliffe's memos to staff were enthusiastic and punctuated with exclamation points. "WOW—WHAT A JOB!" she wrote to staff after the spring 1996 fundraising campaign. "To everyone working on the Spring '96 campaign, a sincere THANK YOU for your efforts."

In August 1996 she issued an upbeat message to employees saying, "Our collective efforts to cast away the past and to seek a creative and positive future are now paying off." In the same report she wrote,

> The Board was ecstatic with what programming has planned and thanks the many people involved in the process for such a fine job. I believe we have the most dynamic schedule ever! ... Personally I am excited about the direction of CKUA and hope you will share the same enthusiasm.

The message included the basic outlines of the board-approved budget for the coming year. Interestingly, although a 1997 auditor general's report on the CKUA radio foundation later revealed that the revenue earned in advertising and sponsorships in the year ending August 1, 1996 had fallen significantly short of projections—$292,685 actual as opposed to $450,000 projected—the budget for the 1996–1997 operations projected revenue at an ambitious $1.2 million for advertising and sponsorships. Listeners were still pretty much keeping the faith, falling short of the projected $500,000 for 1995–96 by only $10,000.

On the other hand, expenditures were still vastly exceeding amounts forecast in the business plan. This was mainly due to salaries, benefits and fees—coming in at $362,000 more than anticipated in the plan—and marketing and fundraising costs—at $135,000 more than planned.

Modest savings were achieved in news and public affairs. A July 1996 report by the staff news and public affairs work group said a significant upgrade of CKUA's news-gathering capability was needed in order to live up to the station's promise-of-performance commitment to the CRTC. In response, Hinchliffe's August 1996 message announced "a major shift in news programming. News will be aired as surveillance only and the BBC news service will be expanded."

With their thinner paycheques, disgruntled staff were taking note of what they considered extravagances on the part of management. In the early days, Hinchliffe often flew into Edmonton and stayed at the elegant Hotel Macdonald. Her expense claims for the period between January 16 and February 9, 1995, for example, showed four trips involving stays of one to three days, including room service, at the hotel. (Years later, when in Edmonton on business as vice-president of a development company, Hinchliffe said that she always drives or takes the bus, given "the cost of airfare these days.") After the first several months, CKUA paid for an apartment for Hinchliffe to use during her visits to the city.

When details of Hinchliffe's expense claims became public in 1997, her predecessor, Jackie Rollans, was incensed. "All those years that I was there, I'd take people out to lunch at my own cost because ... I was trying to save money for a transmitter, putting it away. I don't think I spent more than a couple of hundred dollars a year in expense funds. I even went to the WAB [Western Association of Broadcasters meeting] at my own expense because I was trying to save. And when I saw what she had spent on her expense account, I just about was sick."

Gerry Luciani, who also lived in Calgary that first year, submitted numerous invoices for airfare between Edmonton and Calgary, many for return trips on consecutive days. For example, he filed expense claims for Calgary–Edmonton return trips at $233.11 for both January 10 and 11, 1995. He also filed claims for return trips on each of April 5, April 6, July 13, July 14, August 15, August

16 and August 17. However, Luciani showed some restraint, often staying at the Mayfair Hotel at half the price of Hinchliffe's rooms at the Macdonald. Luciani also filed huge expense claims each month for all kinds of day-to-day station expenses, which were routinely charged to his personal Canadian Plus Visa card. (The buildup of frequent flyer points on that card, at one point per dollar spent, would have been impressive.)

Baker's contract, like Hinchliffe's, also called for payment of all travel and living expenses out of Calgary. His expense claims show a little more frugality: $33.17 for a Greyhound bus ticket to Edmonton for a board meeting in January 1996; $41.50 for a room at the Eastglen Hotel in Edmonton in the fall of 1995.

Foundation director Larry Clausen's Calgary company, Communications Incorporated, invoiced the CKUA Radio Foundation for various advertising and marketing services—from "general consultation on various issues," preparation of a "speech for the CEO" and attendance of management meetings, all at ninety dollars per hour, to the purchase of balloons for a fundraising campaign. Clausen was seen often in CKUA offices for meetings of the management team. He also stayed at the Hotel Macdonald. Between December 1995 and June 1996, Communications Incorporated was given advertising spots on the Saturday and Sunday "Breakfast" programs in a contra deal in exchange for some of the company's services.

Although she kept an apartment in Edmonton, Hinchliffe spent little time there. She moved CKUA's Calgary office out of the modest space it rented for four thousand dollars a year from Mount Royal College to tonier, more expensive quarters in the downtown Burns Building and operated out of there, hiring an executive assistant to handle day-to-day affairs for her out of the Edmonton office.

Hinchliffe later attributed the financial difficulties of the foundation largely to forces beyond the board's control and said there was nothing in retrospect that she would have done differently. The Build the Foundation Campaign was doomed, she said, because of the tight fiscal atmosphere in Alberta during the mid 1990s.

"To do a campaign like that is a huge undertaking, huge. And when we had done the first test of feeling ... we weren't getting a lot of support for our ideas because we were talking big dollars. Remember, at that time—that was in the early stages where everything was cut. Education was cut. The arts were cut. Hospitals were cut. CKUA in terms of getting donations was far down the list. And everyone was asking for the same dollars. So, we just found it really an extreme uphill battle, and it would take a lot of resources to do and we didn't have much time. We just didn't feel we could put all our eggs in that basket."

Likewise, the year it took to get CRTC approval of a limited commercial licence cost CKUA dearly, she said. The business plan had anticipated earlier CRTC approval.

"So, in that first year we couldn't sell any time. So we endeavoured to raise money strictly through philanthropic sponsorship of programs. And they were a kind of PBS-style program structure—no tag lines. And again, we found that very tough. First of all, we were starting from scratch.... There was no track record. So it took a lot of time to sell those, which we didn't have a lot of. And we had a lot of competition for these kinds of dollars from health and from education. So, if companies before were getting a hundred requests a month, they were now getting a thousand."

Eventually, there were some corporate sponsorship successes. When members of the Alberta Roundtable on Environment and the Economy approached CKUA to do a radio series that would "monitor a variety of environment and economic indicators" and provide information on "issues related to sustainable economic growth in Alberta," CKUA got Chevron to underwrite it. The program, called "Chevron Ecofile," was hosted by environment writer, editor and educator David Dodge and won the 1997 Communications, Media & the Arts Award from the Emerald Foundation for Environmental Excellence. In 2002 the program—now called simply "Ecofile"—was still going, sponsored by Destination Conservation, an environmental education project of the Edmonton-based Tomorrow Foundation.

Syncrude, a prominent supporter of the arts in Alberta, signed up to sponsor "Arts Alive," a six-minute program on Alberta's arts and culture scene featuring interviews by host Chris Allen. Telus also became a CKUA sponsor. Hinchliffe said an industry-sponsored Alberta business program was on the drawing board. "We were talking to people like Xerox, IBM, the *Globe and Mail*."

Listener donations were another, happier story. Hinchliffe brought in a fund development consultant, Joan Laurie of Laurie Works, to help develop

CKUA's fundraising office, train staff and install the donor-profiling systems and software that CKUA was still using in 2002.

"She felt … compared with other charities … [that] we had a very high response rate, but that there would obviously be a ceiling because of the listener numbers," Hinchliffe said. "Her plan forecast a half a million sustainable dollars. There would be times it would go up or it would go down, but with the right amount of work and the plan that she helped us put in place, that was something you could almost take to the bank."

With the new limited commercial licence in place, CKUA started going after advertisers in mid 1995. The move to advertising proved another "trauma" to the staff, and to listeners. Hinchliffe said there was a concern about "losing the essence of CKUA. What kind of control are we going to have over the commercials? Are we going to do those screaming things like you hear on all the power stations?"

CKUA librarian (later morning man) Dave Ward recalled the first ad that CKUA ran. "We had taken an agency ad for Ford. It was something you could hear anywhere—Power 92, CFRN. The first morning Cam [Hayden] had it scheduled to play at twenty to eight…. He must have had ten, fifteen phone calls: 'What the heck is going on? I thought my kid had changed the station.' We pulled it right away."

After that CKUA controlled the tone of commercials to least offend listener sensibilities. Selling advertisers on CKUA was a challenge because the first thing they wanted to know was how many listeners the station had, Hinchliffe said.

"It's not *how many* we have but who they are and how they listen. And they *listen* to CKUA. You could buy twenty-five spots on any other station and that's going to be as effective as five spots on CKUA. I mean, the power of the on-air people and the influence they have—it was just mind-boggling. I mean, if Bill Coull said, 'Go to McBain Cameras and tell them that CKUA sent you,' they do. It was really quite amazing."

Record retailers could see immediate cause-and-effect results of CKUA advertising. Mike Pleau from Megatunes in Calgary sent programmer Cathy Ennis a note in December 1996 about a run on a world music recording she had featured on her "Listening Room" show:

Within 20 minutes of your feature on Wasis Diop on Tues. Dec. 3rd, we sold 12 copies of his CD! It went on to be our No. 1 BEST SELLER of the week! Just about everyone who bought it last week mentioned your name, and the fact that you mentioned it was available at MEGATUNES.

There was a similar run on an album that host Andy Donnelly played on "The Celtic Show."

"Our phone lines were swamped that night and the next morning with people asking how to buy the disk," Ken Davis wrote in a memo to CKUA advertising rep David Fraser. "That's nothing—the U.S. supplier was swamped with phone calls all the following week—to the point that he started ordering special shipments into Alberta just to meet demand."

Volvo became an advertiser after noting that a high percentage of radios on cars brought in for servicing were set at CKUA.

Hinchliffe noted that CKUA was equally good at putting "bums in seats" for arts organizations and quickly moved to exploit that avenue. "There were a lot of things CKUA had just been giving away for nothing. So we were looking at those areas—what are we already doing that we could be getting money for? And one of the things, obviously, is promoting concerts." For example, Hinchliffe pointed to cases where a well-timed CKUA promotion had spiked lagging ticket sales for the Calgary Centre for Performing Arts. "So we started kind of brokering our position."

The station worked out partnerships with various arts organizations, in some cases becoming the official media sponsor by exchanging on-air publicity for having its logo displayed on event brochures and ads. "We were looking for those kinds of partnerships throughout the province, and we were really receiving a lot of success on it."

Another kind of partnership—with CADVision Development, a Calgary Internet service provider—gave CKUA another Canadian first. On February 29, 1996 CKUA became the first radio station in Canada to go online, broadcasting live on the Internet via RealAudio. "As of this evening, our audience will be the world," Hinchliffe told the *Calgary Herald*.

While CKUA was broadening its financial base, it was also "retooling" its programming to broaden its listener base. The ethnic programs had been unceremoniously dumped in the changeover from ACCESS. In 1996 CKUA discontinued co-producing original "Theatre of the Air" programs with Athabasca University, and that program disappeared. Athabasca University's French-language programs were also dropped.

◆ *Celtic show host Andy Donnelly with Bushmills. Courtesy of CKUA; photo by Frank Gasparik.*

However, to meet its CRTC promise-of-performance requirements, CKUA purchased broadcast rights to several formal Open College series from CJRT in Toronto, including "The Global Economy," hosted by economist Dian Cohen, "Sexuality: Contemporary Issues" and "History of Espionage," all of which served as supplementary material for Athabasca University courses.

The connection with Moses Znaimer opened up by the sale of ACCESS to his company led to CKUA landing MuchMusic's Terry David Mulligan to produce his weekly "Mulligan Stew." Described by some as the Dick Clark of Canadian broadcasting, Mulligan was still recording the show—a mixture of classic and new pop, rock, R&B and soul music—in 2002, working from the basement of his home in Vancouver.

Donnelly's weekly Celtic show was another specialty program added to CKUA's line-up during the retooling. A native of Gourock, Scotland, Donnelly came by way of the University of Alberta campus radio station CJSR, as did many CKUA announcers. With his thick Scottish accent and "Tell Your Mum" tag line, Donnelly quickly developed a following for his show, which ranged from "head-banging Celtic music to a wee ballad that would bring a tear to a glass eye."

Largely through the eclectic tastes of "Listening Room" host Cathy Ennis, CKUA became increasingly a conduit for the exotic sounds of world music, from Tuvan throat singing to the didgeridoo.

Meanwhile, Ric Baker was busy building a province-wide listener support network of Friends of CKUA organizations, with the goals of creating revenue for the foundation, increasing awareness of the station and expanding its audience, and helping CKUA extend its community involvement. Using the Calgary chapter as a model, his business plan called for setting up chapters in Edmonton, Lloydminster, Red Deer, Medicine Hat, Lethbridge, Athabasca and Fort McMurray in the first year (April 1, 1995–March 31, 1996), with a total of seventeen satellite chapters, one for each frequency transmitter in the province, within two years.

"I spent a lot of time phoning people, talking to people, asking them how they could support us.... If they were an artist, would they be willing to do a poster for us? If they were a musician, would they be able to play something for us? And if they knew somebody in a community, well, could we get that community hall? Or, do you know how to cook, or ... would you be a volunteer? If not a volunteer, would you be able to support us with some kind of financial support?"

By March 1996 Baker had the eight chapters in place right on plan. In May 1996 the foundation board determined that the role of the Friends chapters would be "to assist revenue generation activities through the Fund Development Office and audience development through promotion activities." On June 10 Hinchliffe terminated Baker's two-year contract with a letter:

It is anticipated that the activities of the Chapters can be met by the volunteer core you have established and further investment in this area is not warranted for the coming year. Accordingly, as we have discussed, your Independent Services Contract dated October 16, 1995, will be terminated effective August 31, 1996.

While Baker had delivered on creating a grassroots province-wide organization, it was becoming evident that his vision for the Friends of CKUA was at odds with that of the rest of the board. At the August 18, 1995 annual general meeting of the foundation membership, he moved to rescind his resolution from the previous year's meeting granting full foundation membership to anyone donating ten dollars. In its place, the members present—Hinchliffe, Luciani, Clausen and Malcolm Knox (by phone)—approved a resolution

> That anyone donating $10.00 or more to assist the CKUA Radio Foundation will be admitted to the Friends of CKUA and that membership in the Society will continue to be on the basis of new Members being admitted in each Annual Meeting by an election of the Members.

The new resolution flew in the face of Baker's own democratic plans for the Friends groups. But he later said he was convinced by other members that it was necessary to prevent "special interest groups from taking over and then executing their agenda." Baker said the concern came from Clausen, who was chairman of the Alberta Ballet Foundation and who said he'd experienced problems with volunteers trying to exert power. Baker also said he was told that certain Christian groups were lobbying to buy the morning show and were threatening to become members in order to get their way.

"I hadn't realized that perhaps because of my motion a special interest group could come in and change that [CKUA programmers' freedom], because I hadn't thought it through that far. I just thought that the people that volunteered their time and dedicated their time, they should have a say."

Baker's two-year term on the board of the foundation ended in August 1996. At the August 26, 1996 annual general meeting of the membership, which was held by conference call, the members present—Hinchliffe, Luciani, Clausen, Knox and Chapman—passed a motion by Chapman that no new members be admitted and "for the better and more effective administration of the society, that Ric Baker, having completed his term as director, resigns from the Society."

Baker said he hadn't seen the cancellation of his contract coming. "They cancelled my contract when I had just bought a new house, had a wife that was pregnant.... They restructured the Friends right out of the organization chart, and there was absolutely nothing I could do about that."

Baker said his main concern was building the grassroots support for CKUA, and he had trusted the rest of the board to take care of other aspects of CKUA governance. "I just thought they basically knew what they were doing there.... I trusted Gail simply because from the very first moment I met her ... she said, 'All I want to do is pour my effort into making sure that CKUA stays on that air. That's my goal.'...

"She sounded very sincere and I believed she was sincere—that she just was very interested in the radio station and very interested in keeping it afloat and keeping the music that we'd all grown up listening to playing. And that was the topic of conversation around a lot of our board meetings: How do we keep this going?"

Hinchliffe later said she didn't recall the motions regarding membership in the foundation. "I can't remember that. We considered ourselves to be in transition. There was an enormous amount to be done in a very short period of time. So, I guess it was picking the priorities and getting the foundation blocks in place and then letting it go to other areas....

"I know we had discussions about the long term for the foundation and, certainly, as it evolved it should become a foundation where you could buy a membership.... So, if there was any resistance to that at that period of time, it was because everything took a lot of energy."

In the spring and summer of 1996, Moses became openly confrontational at staff meetings. At one of them he demanded a flat yes or no answer from Hinchliffe as to whether she was getting paid. Staff said Hinchliffe was adept at deflecting inconvenient questions. After this particular meeting Moses received a letter from Davis expressing concern with his conduct:

It is my view that you allowed yourself to reach a point where your manner was openly rude and disrespectful to the Board Chairman and negatively impacted the intent, spirit and direction of that meeting. I refer specifically to the point in a conversation in which you adopted a prosecutorial manner and demanded a 'YES' or 'NO' answer from the Chairman....

You serve CKUA best when you concern yourself primarily with providing this company with excellence in the execution of your own assigned duties.

The letter was copied to Hinchliffe.

Moses said he liked Davis and believed Davis was simply "doing his duty" in defending management. He finally chose to leave CKUA and, at the end of September 1996, retired to Salt Spring Island. "I began to realize that I could no longer, in good conscience, go on-air and beg people for money which I knew would go ... into the pockets of this ... board. It was this realization that cemented my decision to leave."

Davis said he had to devote a large part of his time to keeping peace at the station. "When I look back on it, that's where I spent most of my bloody energy—just trying to make peace with everybody so they ... don't squabble over this and lose the prize. I felt like I was dealing with my kids."

CKUA's fall fundraising campaign in November 1996 drew a record $260,000 in pledges, well over the $227,000 goal. "The future has never looked brighter," said a *Calgary Herald* story reporting the results. Plans were well underway to celebrate the station's seventieth anniversary the following year. In January 1997 *Herald* columnist Bob Blakey reported, "Hinchliffe says fund-raising is slightly ahead of target and she's confident the station, which has trimmed staff severely since its days as part of the Access network, will stay healthy. 'There's no reason not to be optimistic,' she says."

Communications Incorporated, Clausen's company, invoiced CKUA in January and February 1997 for more than three thousand dollars in consulting fees for work on the station's seventieth anniversary plans. On February 18 the directors held a meeting at the Ranchman's Club in Calgary and heard Clausen review the plans. The theme of the anniversary celebration would be "Seventy Years of Being First," and the objective would be to "establish confidence in the future of CKUA." In other business, the directors moved to operate annually on a balanced budget and to valuate the CKUA music library to be included in the foundation's assets. A new director, Les Brost, was appointed to the board.

Five days earlier, on February 13, CKUA had sent out a news release announcing the upcoming anniversary over Canada NewsWire to the attention of business editors. It quoted Hinchliffe saying, "This year will be a fundamental year for CKUA. The impact we create in the province will carry us into the future." The release ended with the promise that "CKUA will announce unique 70th anniversary initiatives during their spring fundraising campaign in March, 1997."

The statements were ironically prophetic. A month later, on March 20 at 8:00 a.m., the directors met via conference call. Hinchliffe reported that if all operating costs were maintained at current levels, projections showed the foundation would have a deficit of $400,000 by year-end. She recommended that the station cease operations. The foundation's existing reserves would cover salary and termination liability of $270,000, for which the directors could be personally liable. Clausen then moved to terminate all employees and to authorize management to sell the assets of the foundation as necessary to satisfy outstanding obligations.

Shortly after, Ken Davis received a call telling him to lay the staff off and shut down the station. The first thing he had to do was to line up a host for the last radio show.

Shock and Aftershock | 15

On the afternoon of March 21, 1997 Larry King rode up the elevator to the fourth floor of the Alberta Block and stepped into an eerie scene when the doors opened on to CKUA's offices.

"I think I was still slightly in shock.... I could hear the tone we put on the air after sign-off. I'm used to hearing it but only in the middle of the night, so middle of the day was weird.... The fourth floor had a couple of people on it, but 5 and 6 were deserted. Everything left waiting for staff to come back....

"The BN [Broadcast News] tape recorders had run their reels of tape through and had not stopped so the tape was making that flapping noise that only tape can make."

King was engineering supervisor and had been with CKUA since the early ACCESS years. Gerry Luciani had phoned him the night before and asked him to come in. When King arrived, a security guard escorted him to the accountant's office. Luciani asked him if he was willing to do the job of shutting down the network.

◆ Bud Steen, chairman of the board that brought CKUA back to life in 1997.

Courtesy of CKUA; photo by Frank Gasparik.

If not he would hire someone from the outside to do it. I made the decision to do it so that things did not get screwed up and it was done properly so it could be restarted if the chance presented itself....

I went through it all and shut things down. When I was done there was just the silence broken only by the [off-air] tone from the speaker in the hall. My footsteps going up and down the stairs seemed much louder than usual....

I talked to one of the security guards some time after ... and he mentioned that they had difficulty with locks staying locked and a couple of other strange things (our friendly ghosts giving them difficulties?).

Bud Steen's first clue that something was wrong came when his clock radio went off on the morning of March 21. "All I got was that God-awful screech. And then seeing it in the newspaper that morning—that CKUA had signed off—was a real shocker to me." A prominent Edmonton lawyer, Steen had been a fan of CKUA since 1969, when he and his high school friends had discovered Tony Dillon-Davis' Saturday night show.

"CKUA was really the only place that you could get introduced to new music and new music coming out of Britain.... I thought that what they were doing was extraordinarily hip.... I've listened virtually exclusively to CKUA ever since."

Steen's ambition when he graduated from high school was to work for CKUA. He says he was turned down by the radio and television arts programs at NAIT and SAIT on the grounds that his grades were more suited to university. "I shelved all of that and just went on with the rest of my life."

In an ironic way, Steen's early ambitions were about to be realized when he picked up the paper on March 21. "That weekend I talked to my family and my friends about my frustration with what had happened—and the fact that there were probably hundreds of people like myself who had loved CKUA but hadn't done a damn thing about CKUA during the most recent transition period. And basically I said to myself, 'I'm not going to sit on the fence anymore.'" Steen said he immediately "took a fully operational, crazy, flat-out legal practice and parked it."

Tommy Banks, who had been on the CKUA Radio Foundation board in its first year, was as surprised as anyone to hear that the station had been shut down. "I think they forgot what their principal asset was. They had a radio station over which you could say things to people. Even if somebody went on the air ... and said, 'Look, people, if you don't send us a bunch of money tomorrow, we're going to have to turn it off....'

"Nobody knew ... that the station was going to go off the air, so nobody could do anything about it. It just wasn't there one day."

Now that the station was down, Banks became one of a growing throng of people who decided to do something about it.

Calgary businessman Lindsay Hood also sprang into action. Twenty years earlier, while working in the oilfields, he had become a CKUA "groupie," listening to the station while criss-crossing Alberta in a pick-up truck. He had also volunteered with a public radio station in Houston while living there "and really appreciated CKUA even more."

Hood had been concerned three years earlier when there was talk of privatizing the station, and had contacted Alberta treasurer Jim Dinning, whom he had met when both were serving on a board together. He had later sat in on a meeting with Dinning and Steve West where CKUA was discussed. "I just couldn't see, right off the bat, how they were going to be weaned off public funding and survive. I just ran the math.... I just didn't understand that.

"They told me how that would be, and they were very businesslike and professional. But, of course, at that time CKUA was a minor blip on their cultural horizon—they had other issues going. So I just filed it."

Hood had later contacted Gail Hinchliffe. "I could see where CKUA was going to have problems.... And I said, 'I can probably help you.'... And she offered very cordially a series of platitudes which I took as such and really felt that she was dismissive of me." Between careers at the time, he was wearing long hair and jeans and wondered if that had anything to do with his reception.

Hood, senior vice-president and director of ARC Financial Corporation, said he was "just appalled" when the station went off the air. "I was outraged, entirely outraged that they could have done what they'd done without any public consultation, without any attempt to try and have a dialogue on it. I mean it was just the most abusive, pathetic situation I'd seen for an institution that had been around for seventy years." Hood told his partners at ARC he was taking a leave of absence. "They were unbelievably supportive.... They let me operate right out of my office there."

CKUA staff were already mobilized. After Chris Martin had finished playing "The Last Waltz" and switched CKUA to the off-air signal at midnight on March 20, he rushed over to join the other CKUA staff members at Lee Onisko's house.

"Everyone was already planning how we could possibly take over the radio station and get it back on the air.... We decided to have a press conference the next day."

Martin called the night manager at the Sidetrack Café to see if staff could meet the media there. "They were behind us 100 percent." The next day he opened a post office box for the group and set up an e-mail address through Freenet. "Within a matter of days, letters started coming in and the e-mail was inundated with about one hundred entries a day sometimes." At the news conference held on the afternoon of the day following the shut-down, Dave Ward, who would become unofficial spokesperson for the group along with news staffer Katherine Hoy, said, "This is not a wake; this is not the end."

Bradley Odsen, a lawyer and president of the Edmonton chapter of the Friends of CKUA, got to work organizing a grassroots movement to save the station. Larry King had contacted the CKUA staff union, the International Brotherhood of Electrical Workers (IBEW), and secured the use of their headquarters for the staff and volunteer effort. "The union let the ex-staff and other volunteers use the meeting rooms, had a phone system installed and paid for a security guard to be there whenever there were no union staff on premises," King said. "I am not sure that we could have organized and got CKUA back on without the assistance the union provided."

By the end of their first weekend of hearing the droning off-air signal coming from CKUA, employees, Friends, people from the arts community, and other outraged listeners had launched a Save Our Station coalition, using the IBEW headquarters as their war room. Among them were Banks, publisher Mel Hurtig and Terry Wickham, artistic director of the Edmonton and Calgary folk festivals. On the Wednesday following the station shut-down, they held a standing-room-only public rally at the City Media Club and had to set up outdoor speakers for the more than three hundred people who couldn't be accommodated inside. Another rally packed the Calgary Media Club. Similar events were also held in Lethbridge, Medicine Hat and Red Deer.

Alberta artists, including k.d. lang and Jann Arden, who owed early career boosts to CKUA's playing their music, threw in their support. Arden agreed to chair the group. Some international artists who got frequent play on the station, such as Englishman Martin Simpson and American Christine Lavin, also contributed.

By March 27 the coalition had incorporated as the Save Alberta Public Radio Society (SAPRS), with Tommy Banks, Holger Petersen, Peg Barcelo, Bill Coull and Brad Odsen as founding directors, and started to sell memberships. Meeting daily at their makeshift IBEW office, SAPRS volunteers co-ordinated a province-wide campaign to pressure the government to help them wrest control of CKUA from Hinchliffe's board and to raise funds for a resurrected station under the control of a new, more representative board.

Terry Gray, who was one of the first on the scene the night CKUA closed down—carrying a lighted candle and a sign saying "No fat lady sang"—and Les Thompson, who had hosted the university's "Music Hour" when he was a student in the mid 1960s, devoted full time to co-ordinating SAPRS activities. Daphne Bain of CKUA's Calgary office co-ordinated activities in that city.

Lee Onisko organized a phone tree—a pyramid in which each person at each level phones five others—to reach CKUA's listeners and past donors.

◆ *Lee Onisko joined Dave Ward on the Touch the Transmitter tour of Alberta to help restore CKUA in 1997. Courtesy of CKUA; photo by Frank Gasparik.*

Ric Baker said that, although the terms of his cancelled contract with the foundation precluded him from communicating with anyone involved with CKUA for a full year after his dismissal, he couldn't stay totally on the sidelines. He surreptitiously turned over the eighteen-hundred-name Friends database he had created for CKUA to Tom Coxworth, the Calgary-based host of CKUA's "Folk Roots" program, for the group to use. By April 7—even without the benefit of airwaves—SAPRS had raised $120,000, including membership dues and pledges from more than 2,200 people from all over Alberta as well as proceeds from benefit concerts held by Friends groups throughout the province.

SAPRS also took its cause to CKUA's advertisers and corporate sponsors, and quickly gained support from a number of them—including Syncrude, a major coup—for a reconstituted CKUA under a new board.

The media, sniffing a scandal, leaped on the CKUA story. Some found it significant that the shut-down had come just nine days after a provincial election. Some suspected that Hinchliffe and her board, with their Tory connections, had protected Ralph Klein by maintaining that all was well with CKUA until after the March 11 election, which gave the Tories an even bigger majority than they had going in.

While Hinchliffe became the focus of media and listener outrage, the government still took a lot of the heat. "The dead air at 93.7 on your FM dial is starting to raise many loud questions that need an answer," columnist Geoff Taylor, a CKUA listener, wrote in the *Crossfield/Irricana Rocky View/Five Village Weekly*.

> And it's one more indication that privatizing everything in sight, despite the neo-con propaganda, is not always better and cheaper.
>
> The fact that the radio station went off the air, ending 70 years of continuous broadcasting, also again raised the argument regarding the government's cost-cutting measures which left some wealthy corporations untouched at the expense of struggling small enterprises like CKUA.
>
> ...
>
> There are rumours that her [Hinchliffe's] salary is in the $100,000-a-year range, plus an apartment in Edmonton. If true that means all the loonies raised during the last fund-raising event went towards paying her salary.... It also places her in the same salary league as the chief administrative officer for the MD of Rocky View, but he doesn't get an apartment.

Edmonton Journal columnist Liane Faulder admitted she'd never been a CKUA listener, "but what's happening at that station matters regardless. The demise of CKUA is just one in a slow series of contractions, belt-tightening and out-and-out excision of those parts of Alberta which are about the imagination and the spirit of the people who live here."

A *Journal* editorial pointed to the government's "flawed decision ... to entrust the station to a hand-picked board with deep connections to the provincial Conservative party."

Former ACCESS president Larry Shorter wrote a letter to the editor from his base in Canmore: "I find it curious that CKUA's pending closure was not made public by the station's toady board of directors during the just completed election campaign. Said closure is the direct result of Tory slash-and-burn tactics. After 70 years of proud integrity, does CKUA die a Tory hack—covering Klein's uncivilized ass?"

Even right-wing *Alberta Report* magazine's Ted Byfield, writing in the *Financial Post*, had tough questions for the government. Pointing out that all the CKUA board members were "recognizably Tory," he asked, "And what about Steve West? Had he actually sold off one of the biggest communications properties in the province to a group of Tory loyalists for a buck?"

CBC television news anchor and former CKUA announcer Bob Chelmick had been one of the first reporters on the street outside as Martin was broadcasting the last show. "I took a camera guy down and talked to people who were milling about on Jasper Avenue.... We had the door open, listening to Chris Martin. It was like a death-watch. Dave Ward was on the street, and other people were just spontaneously coming, and that's where the groundswell began."

Chelmick kept the story going almost nightly. "There was really no problem at CBC talking up the value of CKUA. Public broadcasters tend to stick together. I think they took our enthusiasm for saving CKUA as good community involvement. So they were fine with it."

Ironically, former CKUA news director Ken Regan was now producing the CBC evening news. He said he was able to point the CBC's investigative team in the right direction in their sleuthing, leading to an I-Team report that confirmed what had been, up until then, merely strong suspicions about CKUA board members receiving payment. On April 3 the CBC reported that records showed Hinchliffe took home more than $162,000 in 1995—$146,000 in salary, $10,000 in expenses and $6,000 to pay for her Edmonton apartment.

Media were also reporting that documents filed with Revenue Canada showed three executive officers of the foundation had received combined pay and benefits of $221,530 in 1995, or nearly ten percent of CKUA's overall budget.

Hinchliffe did have some friends in the media. David Rutherford invited her to appear more than once on his phone-in show, broadcast on Edmonton's 630 CHED and ITV, and deftly deflected hostile questions for his guest.

Unrepentant in the face of blistering media attention, Hinchliffe tried to head off her rivals, announcing within two days of the shut-down that she planned to put a scaled-back version of CKUA on the air in as little as a week's time. "While we are happy that so many people want to support us, that support must be directed to us—we're the party that can and wants to put CKUA back on the air," she said. She proposed to accomplish this by getting some employees to come back on a volunteer basis. She also would launch an immediate appeal to listeners for financial support. Hinchliffe claimed "98 per cent" of the calls she was getting were from people asking what they could do to help. She refused to answer media questions about how much money she was earning as CEO and dismissed calls for a new board, saying, "It is a private foundation. It was never set up as a public body."

The *Edmonton Journal* greeted her announcement with an editorial cartoon showing voice balloons coming from behind a door marked Board of Highly Paid Directors. "We can't possibly ask our laid-off employees to work for free," said one. The other replied, "You're right! How much should we charge them?"

On March 27, yielding to growing public outcry, Municipal Affairs Minister Iris Evans ordered an audit of the foundation's books.

Meanwhile, at Athabasca University, "when the axe fell in March 1997, courses, professors and students were all left high and dry," according to professor David Gregory. "It was a brutal way to terminate a partnership." However, Dan West, the university's multimedia co-ordinator, had been working with CKUA to create a website that would make the university's courses available to a wider audience. So when the station went down, Athabasca University arranged to make recorded versions of CKUA programs available by RealAudio technology through its website.

But even more important, West added conferencing software and started a forum on the website that would play a huge role in CKUA affairs over the next two years. Kicking off the forum on March 21 at 2:15 p.m., West wrote, "This morning I was stunned to find CKUA gone from my radio dial. What happened? I don't know, but I would like to hear if others are as upset as I and my friends are about this. I'd also like to hear ideas for what can be done now."

His first response, from Chris Hortobagyi, came just forty-five minutes later: "Please say it isn't so! Do you think e-mailing our MP or even the Premier would help?" Then Carla Gannaw registered with, "I too am totally devastated. I feel like I've just lost my best friend. I think we all must be very vocal with our objections. If we don't speak up the powers that be won't hear us.

My letter is half composed and I have a long list of politicians I plan on sending it to."

Over the next five weeks, hundreds of CKUA supporters checked in with the forum almost daily, making a total of more than 2,500 contributions. Among them were former ACCESS president Larry Shorter, who provided ideas and counsel from the vantage point of his long experience with CKUA, and Lindsay Hood, who had undertaken to try to reason with Hinchliffe and reported that he had her ear, urging participants to reserve judgement.

A call on the website forum for a campaign to inundate the provincial government with handwritten letters resulted in more than one thousand letters landing on the Legislature within a twenty-four-hour period. Online observers from other parts of the world were fascinated. One wrote, "Watching your discussion from St. Vincent and the Grenadines—so interested to see the Internet being used in this constructive way."

Writing in the *Globe and Mail*, West called the result "valuable data for any sociologists wishing to study the evolution of a social crusade. CKUA supporters moved swiftly from shock and outrage to anger, strategy and the eventual formation of a plan. They reminisced about moments in CKUA's history, and expressed dismay at the void listeners would feel in its absence. A sense of community emerged, as did ideas for restructuring its operations. This exchange was influential in the station's survival."

Behind the scenes, Steen, Hood, Banks and Odsen were playing out a parallel campaign. Steen called it "the dance." On the Monday following the shut-down, Steen said, "I started calling around to find out what it was a person like me could do." He contacted Ken Chapman, who had resigned from Hinchliffe's board the day the station closed, and asked if he would help resurrect the station. Chapman arranged a meeting between Steen and Hinchliffe for Wednesday.

"He was pretty helpful," Steen said. "I know he was sort of the bird on Gail's shoulder talking about me and the people that I was involved with during the six-week period that we were doing the dance."

Steen also phoned Holger Petersen, who had been at Lee Onisko's house the night CKUA went off the air. Petersen told him there would be a meeting of CKUA staff and Friends at the Media Club the next day [Tuesday] and put him in touch with Brad Odsen. That same day Lindsay Hood also got involved, after a friend suggested that he, too, get in touch with Odsen. But the first call he made was to Hinchliffe. In fact, he literally camped on the doorstep of CKUA's Calgary offices until she appeared.

"I said, 'Gail, I'm just really interested in trying to help the station—can we get together?'... At this time she was in such a defensive posture, and she was so completely incapable of reading the situation that I felt we had a very good opportunity of getting the board to resign. And the key thing was not to alienate her." Hood said he contained his anger and met about four times with Hinchliffe and Clausen. "But it became very clear that we were at an impasse and that ... she was not going to resign from the chair."

In Edmonton, Steen went to the Tuesday evening meeting of staff and Friends at the Media Club. "I'd been at the office on the phone basically up to the time of the meeting, so I showed up with a suit on and rather stuck out.... Because of my discussions during the day with Gail and Ken Chapman, I was dealt with with a fairly high degree of suspicion by the staff.... Banks had been informed that there was going to be a lawyer there other than Brad Odsen, and I think he spotted me coming in the door because he parked himself at my table and introduced himself to me....

"I told them what I'd heard on the phone that day and told them that there was a meeting [with Hinchliffe] planned at my office the next day.... Everyone at that point was paranoid.... I liken them to a bunch of beaten puppies.... They just really didn't know what to do and who to trust. At one point in the meeting, one of the staff members ... called the meeting to a halt and said, 'Look, I know who this guy is'—pointing to Odsen—'and I know who this guy is'—pointing to Banks—'but'—and she points to me and says—'who the fuck are you?'

"It's something I'll never forget. Banks just leaned out of his chair, put his hand on my shoulder and said, 'He's with me.' And everybody just kind of backed off at that point."

On Wednesday Steen, Odsen and Wickham met with Hinchliffe and Luciani in Edmonton. Steen said it was clear that Hinchliffe "was bound and determined to get CKUA back up.... She even gave us glimpses of what her plan was." Steen's group wanted Hinchliffe's board to resign, but they would ask Hinchliffe and Luciani to remain for a while. "We didn't know everything that we had to know to be able to operate.... We just felt that we needed somebody around for a couple of months to help us through the start-up again."

Steen said the meeting did not go well. "She wanted to know what our credentials were, basically telling us that we had no credibility, [that] she was the only one able to bring the station back up again."

Two days later, following the public rallies, Municipal Affairs Minister Evans ordered the audit. Over the next two weeks, she came under increasing pressure from the public and from SAPRS for the government to intervene and force Hinchliffe's board to resign. But she resisted going that far, even though Odsen pointed out that the government still had control of the station because the three-year term of the original sales agreement for the station would not expire until August.

Steen said taking the station back was the last thing the government wanted to do. "The government said to me on a number of occasions, 'We just don't want to be in the radio business. We're finished with it.'... But in some conversations with the deputy minister, I asked him to please not say that to the other side....

"I felt that over at the Leg we were among friends, that they were very sympathetic to our cause." Steen said that as the media kept the story going daily, "the heat on the government got crazy. We had a meeting with the minister at one point.... Iris looked across the table at me and she said, 'Bud, can you make it stop?' I said, 'What are you talking about?' And she said, 'The mail. Can you make it stop? I can't get into my office. It's coming in two bags or more a day.'

"CKUA became a bigger thorn in their side than the problem with the hospitals and doctors and health cuts."

Evans insisted publicly that the best solution to the crisis would be reconciliation between SAPRS and Hinchliffe's group. "That ain't going to happen," SAPRS spokesperson Katherine Hoy said.

Throughout the crisis, Hinchliffe and Luciani continued to collect their paycheques, and the media pointed out this fact. They had taken care to close the station while there was still money left to meet all of the foundation's contractual agreements and financial obligations—including to themselves.

The government was getting more embarrassed by the day. Edmonton Liberal MLA Laurie Blakeman publicly asked pointed questions regarding the circumstances of the original agreement signing CKUA over to Hinchliffe's foundation, in particular, the criteria used for appointment to the board. She attached a list of CKUA Radio Foundation board members with their PC party activities and donations. A member of Blakeman's staff at the time later said that during the crisis their office had regularly received leaked information from Evans' office, indicating turmoil within the government over the affair.

Edmonton Journal provincial affairs columnist Mark Lisac discovered that the foundation had not been filing financial records with the province's corporate registry, as required under provincial law. Further, he uncovered a previously unreported decision by Steve West, made when he was minister of municipal affairs, that groups would not have to comply with that part of the Societies Act. "Philip Mulder, communications director for the department, describes the decision as 'an administrative procedural change, I guess.' He says he can not find anything written down on paper. The head of corporate registry was simply told it was good enough for societies to keep financial statements available at their offices." Lisac concluded, "The official (although secret) laxness in the name of reduced paperwork helped undermine the credibility of the CKUA board."

As the media gradually exposed details of CKUA Radio Foundation business and minutes of foundation meetings, calls for Hinchliffe's resignation grew louder. However, she remained resolute. "I love CKUA. I would challenge anybody to be a keener listener and supporter," she told the Edmonton Journal. "If you want to cry about CKUA, I can do it with the best of you, but that's not going to take us where we want to go."

While CKUA listeners, and many non-listeners, who were following the scandal vilified her, Banks and even Shorter publicly gave Hinchliffe credit for good intentions. Shorter told the Edmonton Journal, "I think she is an honorable and well-intentioned woman. But what happened was, I don't think she knew how to run a broadcast station and put together fundraising."

While the station was off the air, there were concerns that CKUA could lose its licence. Steen said his group was in touch with the CRTC and kept former ACCESS president Peter Senchuk, now a CRTC commissioner, apprised of what they were doing. "[The] CRTC wasn't about to do anything to prevent CKUA from going back on the air. Peter Senchuk ... was of great assistance to us, gave us ideas. He certainly made sure that the people in Ottawa that had to know what was going on got good news stories.... He was quite helpful."

On April 7 Steen's group got a call inviting them to a meeting of the foundation board on April 10 in the office of the board's law firm in Calgary. Steen, Odsen and Banks flew down from Edmonton. They found Hinchliffe, Clausen, Luciani and two other board members there, plus representatives from Iris Evans' office and Chapman acting as "bridge."

"The meeting wasn't going particularly well," Steen said. "Gail had asked us, essentially what our plan was. And we told her that our plan was that, in conjunction with SAPRS and staff, we would begin operating CKUA as a strictly volunteer operation for a few weeks. We would mount a fundraising campaign and then sort of crisis-manage the thing for as long as it took to get it back going again.

"Larry [Clausen] then launched into a lecture about how we really didn't have a very credible plan or a credible organization. It didn't sit very well with me, so I felt that I had listened long enough, and I looked at Mr. Clausen and I said, 'Mr. Clausen, there is something you have to understand'—that he'd been in the fundraising business for the period of time that he had been on the board and was in breach of the Alberta legislation that regulated the collection and expenditure of charitable donations. That they had indicated that monies that would be coming into the station would be used for things that, in fact, they weren't used for.

"And in my somewhat aggressive style, I remember pointing my finger at him, saying, 'Mr. Clausen, you must immediately resign as board of directors in our favour, or on Monday morning I will sue you for a million dollars.' And then I turned to Gail and I said, 'And I will sue you.' And every board member in the room—I pointed at them and I said, 'I will sue you, and I will sue you, and I will sue you, and we will make sure that you are all punished for the manner in which you conducted yourselves in the direction of CKUA.' That basically shut Clausen up....

"The one deputy minister I'd been speaking to most on the phone did his best to keep from grinning. They weren't aware of what our card was going to be.... Odsen and I had done some research on the legislation. We were satisfied that we probably had a good cause of action and felt that only the threat of litigation would cause these people to at least listen to us, and they did.... Within a short period of time thereafter, Gail adjourned the meeting, thanked us for our attendance and asked us to leave. And we did."

The next morning, Chapman called Steen. "He said, 'Well, you did it, Bud. They're all resigning.'"

When word reached the troops in the SAPRS war room, euphoria erupted. Hinchliffe issued a news release on April 11, headlined "CKUA board decides on restructuring," which said, "The CKUA Radio Foundation Board of Directors has concluded its review of restructuring opportunities and selected an option for CKUA."

The release stated the board had met with a group represented by Tommy Banks and

> decided this last opportunity to bring CKUA back should be imple-
> mented, despite the lack of assurance that it is financially feasible.
> Board members felt the spirit of accord was such that if there is a
> chance to put CKUA back on the air, this is likely the best option....
>
> The Board and Mr. Banks mutually agreed that they would need
> considerable help with developing a business plan and Gail Hinchliffe
> has agreed to continue in her capacity as Chief Executive Officer to
> provide transitional counsel.

The release ended with a quote from outgoing vice-chairman Larry Clausen: "In 1994 she [Hinchliffe] championed a plan to save CKUA and in 1997 through her strong will and management has again provided CKUA with this opportunity to move forward."

Hinchliffe would continue to receive her salary, which at this point was up to $150,000 a year but still not publicly confirmed. She told the Edmonton Journal she would concentrate on fundraising: "My first task will be to fill the bag with money. A bottle drive's not going to do it. It's got to be big time."

The existing board and membership of the CKUA Radio Foundation had one more item of business. Before resigning, they had to admit the new group as members in order to keep the foundation viable. For a number of reasons, including the fact that the foundation already held CKUA's broadcast licence, the new group decided to take over the foundation from within rather than try to transfer the station from the foundation to SAPRS, which was the original intent of SAPRS's founders.

On April 14, 1997 the foundation's members met and admitted Banks, Steen, Odsen, Hood and Diane Allen to their ranks. Then the existing members resigned. Those who were directors then resigned from the board. The new members next appointed Banks, Steen and Odsen as an interim board.

To get the station back on the air, the newly constituted foundation had a monumental task ahead. Despite listeners' impatience with the off-air signal coming from their radios, Banks told the media that CKUA might not be back on the air before the end of April. Commenting on that prospect, Hinchliffe was quoted as saying, "That's too bad. I think there'll be a lot of people unhappy with that. I would have thought they'd be better organized than that."

The next day Steen suspended Hinchliffe's contract. Before she shut down the station, Hinchliffe had purchased a table for CKUA at the Calgary Mayor's Luncheon for Business and the Arts, scheduled for April 15, for five hundred dollars. Steen found out that Hinchliffe was still planning to attend the event on behalf of CKUA. He ordered her to stay away and not to speak for the station in any context again.

"I had sort of remained with my concept of having her involved in some fashion through the transition," Steen said. But when he saw Hinchliffe's comment in the *Journal*, "I was just—she's got to go. We can't have her around. She's just absolute poison. I also hadn't received a copy of her contract yet, and if her comments hadn't have been the straw, certainly the contract would have been. The camel's back was getting pretty weighted down at that point."

Also, SAPRS was finding it difficult to collect on pledges while Hinchliffe was still receiving a handsome salary from CKUA. Hinchliffe, who still wouldn't divulge her salary, was adamant that she should receive a severance package or pay-out of her contract and said she had referred the matter to her lawyer.

Two days later the CKUA Radio Foundation's new thirteen-member board, cobbled together by Steen, Hood and Odsen, met in Red Deer. Steen was named chair and Hood, co-chair. "We had a real eclectic, experienced, honest, interesting board," Hood said. They included a cross-section of lawyers, representatives from Friends groups, and arts administrators.

Larry Shorter, who had been active on the CKUA Internet forum, was drawn in. "We would have been absolutely screwed without Larry, because he really understood CKUA," Steen said. "He understood the history of CKUA. He understood the philosophy.... He was a very political animal, too, and had been extremely helpful in keeping the street organized, so to speak, keeping people focused, going in the right direction." Dave Ward was included as a bridge to CKUA staff.

The interim board had asked Ken Davis, who Hinchliffe had laid off the day after he finished the job of laying off the CKUA staff, to come back as interim station manager, and he had agreed. He talked with staff and prepared a tentative budget for a new CKUA and brought it to the meeting. But at the same time, he resigned as interim manager, citing personal and family reasons.

Now the board had to scramble for a manager. Banks called Holger Petersen, who had played a role on the executive of the group trying to rescue the station. It turned out that both were going to be on the same flight to Toronto that day, so they agreed to meet at the airport.

"When we ... went to the gate," Petersen recalled, "I said to the woman there, 'We're not travelling together and one of us is in business class. Is there any way that we can sit together? We have a lot of stuff that we have to go over.' And she said, 'Well, as long as you're working on saving CKUA ...'

"We didn't know this person, but she knew Tommy.... So, we ended up sitting together on this flight to Toronto—in business class, thank you very much!"

Banks wanted Petersen to step into the station manager's shoes for a few months. "But there was no way I could do it.... Tommy said, 'You've got to do this.' So, I realized the only way I was going to get out of this was to come up with somebody else.... Tommy is a very convincing person—you can't say no to Tommy Banks.... So I said, 'How about Jack Hagerman?'"

Banks phoned Hagerman when he got to his destination. Hagerman was taken by surprise. "I said, 'Geez, Tom, that's something I'd have to think about. I'm pushing seventy here.'"

Banks wasn't about to take another no for an answer. "I dragooned him. We had to have someone with authority and with respect who knew where the ketchup was.... [Hagerman] was the obvious and right choice."

After a second call from Banks, Hagerman agreed. But he had one problem: before he could tackle running CKUA again, he had to finish his basement in time for guests who were arriving shortly for an extended stay.

That same day Steen attended a social event where he was introduced to a carpenter who happened to be a big fan of CKUA. "And I said, 'Look, are you interested in helping us out?' 'Yeah.' 'Will you hang a door for me?' And so he said, 'Sure.' So, bingo, we got Jack working for us by getting his basement finished for him."

By 9:00 the next morning Hagerman was back as a volunteer in the general manager's chair he had vacated almost a quarter of a century earlier. But while there were a couple of familiar faces among the staff, there was a very important difference between the CKUA he encountered now and the station he had managed under AGT.

"The one thing I hadn't really understood in all of this was just how distrustful the staff had become of any kind of management. Because during my tenure here, I was used to being able to talk freely with people, and we all understood each other and we knew where we were at. But the paranoia that I encountered at that first meeting just floored me."

Hagerman met individually with each staff member and said he was able to arrive at "a meeting of the minds. And then everybody went to work. And, lo and behold, as close to the old schedule as we could get, we had her up and going." Staff volunteered to perform their regular programs for a month without pay, even though at the end no one was guaranteed a job.

CKUA came back to life at 6:00 p.m., April 25, on Andy Donnelly's "The Celtic Show." Chris Martin, who had signed the station off a month earlier, signed back on with the declaration: "None speak louder than those forced to shut up." Donnelly launched the party with Dougie MacLean's "All Together."

Those who had worked towards this moment were gathered for a re-launch party at the City Media Club. "People were almost in tears because we felt like—to us, in our little world—that we had overcome the wicked witch of the east and that everything in Oz was beautiful again," Hood recalled.

Another party was happening at the station. "We loaded up the station with friends and hard workers during the campaign, and six o'clock came and we just let 'er rip," Steen said. "God, that was a party. I showed up with my largest briefcase full of single malt scotch and a pocket full of Cuban cigars.... We just sat there with our glasses of scotch and cigars and just kind of reminisced about the last thirty years and the last thirty days of insanity and just prepared to sort of face where we were headed with CKUA and where we were going."

A two-week fundraiser kicked off on May 2 with a goal of teasing $500,000 out of 10,000 donors. "You have never seen nor heard such a catch-as-catch-can setting up of a pledge drive in all your life," Hagerman recalled. "A pledge drive normally takes a couple of months to set up to run properly."

The drive kicked off with a full-blown ad campaign and slogan, put together at no cost to CKUA by Karo, a Calgary marketing, design and communication company. Karo partner Michael Dangelmaier had become involved in the crisis after a phone call from Ric Baker. Karo's slogan—"Radio Worth Fighting For"—captured people's imaginations and lingered long after the crisis had passed.

Telus volunteered its Calgary phone centre to help handle the expected deluge of calls during the campaign. On the day the campaign began, the phones started to ring at 5:30 a.m. In no time the phone centre lines were jammed.

"At six o'clock we opened the [pledge] lines and blew our switch in Edmonton," Steen said. "The operators in Calgary had never been hit with a blitz of calls like that before.... Our engineering staff spent the next few days just keeping our telephones operating. It was just absolute bedlam. We got some incredible donations. We had people phoning fairly regularly with donations of a thousand, two thousand, five thousand. And it was steady."

It didn't hurt that a few days into the campaign, on May 5, the Alberta government released Auditor General Peter Valentine's report on the financial management of the CKUA Radio Foundation. For the first time, the amount of payments made by the foundation to Hinchliffe and other board members or their related corporations—totalling $772,166—was made public. Gail A. Hinchliffe and Associates had received $355,000 of that amount, the report said.

As to what went wrong, the auditor general said, "The simple answer is that the Foundation ran out of cash because its revenues were less than planned and its expenditures were more than planned." He noted that, "Most expense overruns related to payroll costs.... [T]he Chair of the Foundation's Board functioned as *de facto* CEO with remuneration considerably in excess of that for the station manager position budgeted for in the Business Plan."

The report stated that

ACCESS, and later the Department of Municipal Affairs, did little to help the situation, probably in part because they lacked in-depth knowledge of the Foundation's situation. This was because the accountability information obtained from the Foundation during the past three years was minimal.

The report faulted ACCESS for not establishing an "appropriate accountability framework" for measuring the foundation's performance. "In my view, the failure of ACCESS to require the Foundation to be properly accountable for the ongoing performance of the goals and objectives contained in the Business Plan allowed a bad situation to become critical and Provincial funding to be wasted."

The auditor general said the fact that three people—Hinchliffe, Randall Lennon and Gerry Luciani—were directors of both ACCESS and the foundation when the transition agreements were signed "created conflicts of interest during their involvement in decisions relating to the sale and subsequent operation of CKUA Radio."

Evans called the findings "shocking," according to a government news release accompanying the release of the report. But Hinchliffe told the Edmonton Journal, "They shouldn't be shocked, nothing was secret. They just don't want their fingerprints on it."

On May 6, Evans announced that her department had hired Deloitte & Touche Financial Investigation Services to conduct a forensic report to determine if the $4.7-million government grant to the foundation was used for the purposes set out in the business plan and whether the foundation was in default of its obligations under the sales and operating agreement with ACCESS.

Evans was quick to say the CKUA debacle was "not an issue of failure of a privatization initiative," but a failure of the foundation's board to follow their own business plan. But Edmonton Journal columnist Mark Lisac wrote, "It was like NovAtel—the failure of a political culture used to running any public business as if it were a private social club."

The Edmonton Journal called for the government to consider a lawsuit. "The amount is staggering. The selfishness is sickening. This was supposed to be a small non-profit station serving its loyal band of listeners, not a cash cow for people looking for big corporate salaries."

Hinchliffe and Clausen, whose company Communications Incorporated had received $259,077 from the foundation for marketing and communication services, publicly blamed the government for CKUA's problems. "They didn't really follow their investment very carefully," Clausen told the *Edmonton Journal*. "I think they should have more closely monitored what we were up to. I think the government should have recognized board members may not have come with a broadcast background."

The auditor general's report added fuel to a raging fundraiser. Midway through the campaign, Ward and Onisko decided to tour all of CKUA's transmitter sites in the province, taking the campaign to the listeners on a more personal note. On Friday afternoon they announced on air that on Monday they would begin their Touch the Transmitter Tour. By the time they left Edmonton for their first stop, Fort McMurray, someone had already paid for their first tank of gas. They phoned in progress reports to announcers on air several times a day.

"Before we knew it, people were offering us places to stay, people were feeding us," Ward said. "They fixed our car in Athabasca.... It really wasn't about Lee and me because we'd never really been on the air a lot. We just represented CKUA, and we were doing this crazy thing."

The tiny community of Daysland, southeast of Camrose, wasn't on their original itinerary, but when Ward and Onisko heard there was a local campaign collecting pennies for public radio, they decided that "with some creative driving," they could fit it in.

"We pulled into this little town on Main Street, and you could see this group sort of hanging out by their cars ... and they saw us coming and ran down the street.... There were about twelve, fifteen people—high school kids primarily—but they had made these signs and had collected all this change, and they were so happy to see us."

At each stop, Ward and Onisko collected donations, sold CKUA T-shirts and taped listeners' endorsements to play later as station IDs. By Friday night, with just hours to go before the fundraiser closed, they headed home from Lloydminster. Total donations stood at more than $975,000. Ten minutes before the 1:00 a.m. deadline, Ward and Onisko ran into the station with the cash they had collected—pushing the total over $1 million.

CKUA was back in business.

www.ckua.com | 16

Even with a million dollars in the bank, a new board and untold goodwill generated by the crisis just passed—not to mention perhaps thousands of new listeners drawn to the station by curiosity during the fracas—CKUA was not yet out of the woods.

In the midst of euphoria following the successful fundraiser, Jack Hagerman had the unpleasant task of telling some staff, who had just volunteered a month of their time, that there would be no jobs for them in the new, downsized CKUA, and others that their jobs would be only part-time. "Not nice, not nice at all," Hagerman said. "I feel very emotional about that period." After five weeks of fourteen-hour days, he decided to step down and recommended that the board approach Ken Davis again.

"Ken was the obvious choice and ... he was the only choice," Hagerman said in the fall of 1997. "They didn't have time to train anybody.... Besides, I think Ken's the best manager the place ever had."

The CKUA Radio Foundation's new chairman, Bud Steen, had noticed the toll the job was taking on Hagerman. "I could see that the job was just killing

Jack. He was working himself far too hard…. So we started looking for another general manager, and in my view, the only person for that job was Ken Davis."

The choice was less obvious to others. Some CKUA board members and staff wanted to start with a clean slate and felt that Davis, in Dave Ward's words, was "tarred with the brush—he was Gail's right-hand guy." Despite Davis' defence that Hinchliffe had kept him out of the loop with regard to the station's finances, some still suspected he knew what had been going on. The fact that he seemed to flip-flop regarding his agreement to take over as interim manager also bothered some people. Davis later explained that in the week leading up to the Red Deer meeting, where he had resigned as interim manager, he had had to devote time to a family crisis resulting from a sudden death that had occurred just before CKUA went off the air. But the suspicions would dog him for the rest of his time at CKUA.

Lindsay Hood, vice-chair of the foundation board, was one of those against rehiring Davis, although he harboured no suspicions about Davis' motives. "Ken was just a good guy in a bad situation…. We absolutely had to have a clean slate…. I was completely angered by the fact that we would bring him back…. And what it led to was another year of yippity-yipping and back-biting and snapping."

Steen pressed his case for hiring Davis and prevailed. A reduced staff of sixteen was hired back, all taking pay cuts, along with Davis, of between ten and fifteen percent. Most of the staff cuts were in administration and the news department, leaving CKUA with primarily a "rip-and-read" news service. To meet the station's drastically reduced budget, Davis also cut arts and cultural programming and current affairs.

Then he set about making some changes in CKUA's programming to appeal to a wider audience. He struck a staff programming committee, and over the summer the station conducted a series of demographic surveys with the help of Stanley Varnhagen, an evaluation researcher with the University of Alberta Department of Extension who had worked in planning and research at ACCESS. Friends and SAPRS volunteers contributed by participating in focus groups. The audience surveys got "huge" response rates, Varnhagen said. "What's remarkable is we didn't just get one-word answers."

Karo, the company that created the "Radio Worth Fighting For" campaign, produced a new campaign on a *pro bono* basis. The new theme, "A World of

Difference," was carried through on a raft of CKUA merchandise, such as coffee mugs and T-shirts, that would become another source of revenue for the station. Local Friends groups continued to hold fundraising events, while Alberta artists such as Jann Arden, Ian Tyson, Bill Bourne, Lester Quitzau and Oscar Lopez paid CKUA back for years of support by putting on benefit concerts or offering other assistance.

Meanwhile, CKUA remained in the headlines. On July 29, 1997 the Liberal opposition leaked a draft of the Deloitte & Touche forensic accounting review, charging that the Klein government was sitting on the results while deadlines expired for launching a lawsuit against the foundation's former directors. Among other details that came to light with the review was the fact that between April 5, 1994 and January 5, 1995 Hinchliffe was in personal bankruptcy—while she was a director of both the CKUA Radio Foundation and ACCESS, and while her business was being paid for services to both. The review suggested that by not disclosing her bankruptcy to ACCESS and the foundation, and by "engaging in business or trade" with them, Hinchliffe was in violation of the Bankruptcy Act. It also found that "the former directors of CKUA breached their fiduciary duties when they entered into contracts with CKUA, first because they received remuneration from CKUA without prior court approval, and second, because those contracts were neither fair and reasonable to CKUA nor in CKUA's best interests."

The review cited numerous problems including conflict of interest on the part of board members, poor record keeping and missing expense claims, and contracts given to board members even though payments to directors— and contracts in excess of $25,000 with anybody without prior written consent from ACCESS—were explicitly forbidden in the management agreement between ACCESS and the CKUA Radio Foundation.

The report said the foundation might sue its former directors for breach of fiduciary duty and claim back the money that had been paid to them under their "illegal contracts with CKUA." It also said it might be possible for the attorney general of Alberta to sue but that such an action would be "less certain than one by CKUA and is unprecedented in Alberta." The Klein government ruled out such a suit, but the premier conceded that Hinchliffe made a "valid criticism" when she charged that the government should shoulder some of the blame for not monitoring the privatization more closely. He said the government would use the lessons learned from this case to be more vigilant in the future and make sure it didn't happen again, but he resisted calls to make amends to CKUA.

To outraged listeners who wrote demanding government action—at the very least, refunding CKUA the lost money—Municipal Affairs Minister Iris Evans replied, "Privatization of CKUA was the right decision in 1994 and would be the right decision today."

When the draft report was released, Hinchliffe argued that she had interpreted the management agreement between the foundation and ACCESS to mean that directors could not receive funds for their board work, as opposed to operational work for the station. She also corrected the report's finding that her company was paid $388,325 between August 1994 and April 1997. In fact, she said, she actually earned $405,000 over the contract period. Later, Hinchliffe told *See Magazine*, "In hindsight, I was underpaid. I devoted 160 per cent of my time. I lived and breathed the whole thing.... It was extremely good value for what we got."

This was typical of the statements Hinchliffe made to the media throughout the crisis—unrepentant and often flip. Ironically, the more outrageous Hinchliffe's words and actions during the crisis, the more they contributed to CKUA's survival. Alberta political economy writer Larry Pratt observed in *Alberta Views*, "By shutting down CKUA in March 1997, she made it a *cause célèbre* and almost certainly saved it. As everyone's favourite scapegoat, Hinchliffe unwittingly galvanized her opposition behind a revitalized foundation and station, deflecting the criticism away from a government that rightly deserved it. If CKUA ultimately survives, part of the credit will have to go to her."

Meanwhile, if the government wasn't going to sue Hinchliffe, CKUA fans were pressuring the new board to do so. But CKUA chairman Steen said he was interested in pursuing legal action only if it could result in returning funds to CKUA without great cost to the station. "I'm personally not supportive of a pound-of-flesh type of legal action," he told CKUA listeners. Within days of making this statement, Steen told the *Edmonton Journal*, "My phone has been ringing off the hook for the past week from law firms that are prepared to assist us."

In the fall of 1997 Hinchliffe returned to the real estate business with a development company, United Inc., as vice-president of a division responsible for developing assisted living communities for seniors. On April 28,

1998 the CKUA Radio Foundation filed a statement of claim against Gail Hinchliffe, Gerry Luciani, Ric Baker, Larry Clausen, Gail A. Hinchliffe & Associates Ltd., and Communications Incorporated (Clausen's company), seeking judgement in the amount of the money paid to them by the foundation while they were directors, plus damages and costs. Hinchliffe and Clausen countersued for money they claimed was still owing to them from the foundation. Among her defences, Hinchliffe said a tense work environment contributed to the problems, claiming "the staff at CKUA Radio was resistant to change."

Steen said the decision to file the suit was prompted by a need to "say to the public once and for all: 'We don't agree with what our predecessors did, so let's see if it was legal or not.'... We had to close the chapter."

The case was settled out of court in September 2001, but details were not disclosed. In the press release announcing the settlement, Hinchliffe was quoted as saying, "I realize the court of public opinion questioned our intentions, but I can assure you they were honourable. At the same time, I recognize that the contracts between directors and CKUA were not handled as well as they could have been and as chairman of the board at the time, I accept some of the responsibility for that." Judging from her public attitude up to that point, the statement represented a major concession.

In an interview about midway between the start of the lawsuit and its conclusion, Hinchliffe said in retrospect she wouldn't have done anything differently. She still felt the government had been in too big a hurry to privatize CKUA and had given her too short a time frame in which to succeed. "All the things were moving in the right direction. It was just really a matter of time." She said she had no regrets, "but it is nice to be back in real estate."

Over the three and a half years it took the case to come to a conclusion, CKUA had some rebuilding to do—of financial and human resources, but primarily of trust—before it could put the trauma behind.

After the reconstituted foundation's annual general meeting in August 1997, Steen announced, "We've now moved from the emergency ward to a general ward. We hope to soon be discharged from hospital to home care." He added, "I figure that if we're still here in 24 months, we'll be here 10 years from now."

However, CKUA management and staff approached the 1997 fall fundraiser with some trepidation. The million-dollar outpouring in May was almost certainly a high point fuelled by the emotion of the moment and not likely to

◆ Dave Ward in front of the CKUA building on Jasper Avenue in Edmonton during the station's 1997 fall fundraiser. Courtesy of CKUA.

be seen again in the near future. To increase the station's chances of achieving long-term stability, management adopted a strategy to convince listeners to become "subscribers," viewing CKUA not as a charity but as a service in the same class as other communication/entertainment services they subscribe to, such as cable television, magazines and newspapers. The fall drive raised an amazing $511,000. On the station's seventieth anniversary in November 1997, Davis announced a deal with Telus to sponsor part of CKUA's news coverage.

But behind the scenes, unrest was brewing. Factions were forming among staff and Friends over unresolved issues having to do with management and governance, accountability of the board, and communication of the board's business. The larger part of the community that had rallied spontaneously to the common cause of saving CKUA faded into the background, their task accomplished. But a small minority switched their focus to the day-to-day operation of the station, casting a critical eye on management's every move. Purists groused about having to listen to more commercials and threatened to pull their financial support. Some demanded nothing less than a fully democratic community radio or campus radio model for CKUA. Others complained about staff and program changes.

The Internet forum began to degenerate into bickering, rumours and name-calling. Considerable vitriol was directed at Ken Davis and his perceived motives and at the new board, which some suggested was as much a closed circle as the previous board.

"Well, I suppose the fact that we're allowed to discuss CKUA issues on this forum is a small element of democracy, but I have to remind everyone that CKUA is still as much an oligarchy as it was when GH and her cronies were running it," James Bowman wrote in one forum discussion.

"I ain't saying we should all bow down and not ask for better from our station, but that we can do so without personal attacks on staff and board members, without second guessing their motives, and without rude and hurtful language," a contributor who signed as "Louise" commented in the midst of another heated discussion.

Unique personalities emerged, such as Megan Fulton, a passionate, evangelical CKUA fan who signed herself "from_the_ heart, megan_cgy," urging others to follow her example: "Tell AT LEAST one *NEW* person a day about CKUA !" and "TAKE_RESPONSIBILITY for CKUA_PERSONALLY!"

Davis recalled that time: "All of those who had gathered around CKUA in any intense way to help it become renewed and restored entered into that period with a highly charged sense of ownership, and there was no agreement that was universal about how the organization should proceed. Everybody was jockeying for position at a very delicate time in the organization's re-evolution." Davis monitored the forum and sometimes jumped in to defend his decisions or correct misconceptions.

The board was sensitive to the need to communicate with CKUA supporters, Steen said. "We had said all along that we were going to be open and accessible.... In one of my meetings with Ken [Davis] ... we were trying to figure out how we get information out. We were talking about mailers and newsletters ... and I said, 'We run a bloody radio station. Why don't we just go on the air?'"

The result was the "Bud and Ken Show," a monthly program in which CKUA news staffer Katherine Hoy interviewed Steen and Davis on what was happening with the station, including issues of governance, finances and program changes.

◆ CKUA depends on its huge, loyal volunteer base. Above: (left to right) Karen Fraser, Trea Schuster, station manager Ken Regan and Martin Schuster. Lower left: Jenni Feldman. Lower right: Sandra Worabec. *All courtesy of CKUA; photos by Frank Gasparik.*

At the August 1997 board meeting, Larry Shorter and Lindsay Hood had not stood for election, Shorter because he would be spending most of his time outside of Alberta. Hood later said he was frustrated at the cumbersome process of reaching consensus on the board. "I just couldn't get used to the consultation, dragged out meetings.... I'm a private-business guy; I'm not looking for consultation." Both Hood and Shorter remained strong CKUA supporters.

The foundation invited SAPRS to help appoint two members from the volunteer community to the board. Dave Gibson, founding president of the Lethbridge Friends of CKUA chapter, joined the board at that time along with SAPRS president Ralph Henderson.

After the crisis the foundation had organized a Futures Committee to make recommendations for an organizational structure for volunteers and supporters of CKUA and for ensuring accountability of the foundation board. The committee included representatives from SAPRS, Friends of CKUA, the CKUA Radio Foundation, and station management and staff. They met in Red Deer and filed their final report and recommendations on September 18.

The committee recommended that SAPRS and the provincial Friends organization merge into a new Friends of CKUA organization to operate as a support group driven by needs identified by CKUA and working under a CKUA volunteer co-ordinator. It also recommended that they "provide democratic representation of a meaningful number of Friends of CKUA" to the foundation board.

The two volunteer organizations merged at the SAPRS annual general meeting in the fall of 1997 to form the Friends of CKUA Society. In a Memorandum of Understanding between the Friends and the CKUA Radio Foundation signed in December 1997, the foundation agreed to draft new bylaws laying out qualifications for membership and provisions for selecting board members to make the foundation a more representative group.

But for some, progress was too slow. Les Thompson, one of the SAPRS volunteers who worked full time on the front lines during the crisis, was pushing for a totally democratic, elected board. On February 22, 1998 he also posted a message, on the Internet forum calling the agreement "a mere sham, a delaying tactic to further entrench their 'temporary' Board." He also complained of the "incremental commercialization" of CKUA and concluded that "another uprising is needed." He said he had put a motion on the agenda of an upcoming meeting of the Friends that "the Friends of CKUA Society withdraw and withhold all support, financial or otherwise, from the activities of the Foundation," until the board changed its bylaws "to ensure a broad listener and supporter membership in the Foundation" and "to implement democratic elections for the Foundation Board."

Davis responded to Thompson's posting, defending the time it was taking to "ensure that we do not end up with a clumsy and unwieldy structure and set of bylaws which might serve to paralyse CKUA's effectiveness down the road." He cautioned, "You are pushing for radical surgery that could well kill the patient."

James Bowman entered the online discussion in Thompson's defence: "If the Board is concerned that an organized 'boycott' could result in a financial crisis, let's hope they take some CONCRETE steps toward establishing a democratic governance structure for CKUA." He said, "The first time I contributed to CKUA, in 1993, it was implied that I would be given a membership and a vote in the Foundation. I felt burned when that didn't happen. I don't want to be burned again."

Thompson continued his campaign, posting a call to action to Friends/SAPRS members on February 26: "We can wait while more and more unfulfilled promises delay, distract and defer our hopes. Or … we can seize the opportunity to turn the Foundation around into the kind of democratic, egalitarian organization we dreamt of last spring."

Shorter leaped into the fray. On February 26 he posted a message calling the statements by Thompson and Bowman "balderdash of the lowest manipulative order." He argued,

> When you contribute to the Heart Fund, need you govern it? When you help the Sally Ann, must you ascend the pulpit? There are 600 public broadcasting stations in North America and fewer than three per cent are run by cooperatives…. Yes, the present board has not communicated properly, and it has not been transparent as it promised…. [T]he cause is not because the foundation is not controlled by donors. The cause is because the present board has erred, albeit with good intentions. Come on, listeners. The station is back on the air, with money in the bank and is now putting its act together. And every one of those directors who are ridiculed by the likes of Thompson and Bowman

signed their names and assumed personal responsibility for the debts of the previous, profligate, administration. And posters to this forum belittle those same directors for risking their own assets to bail out CKUA.... the present board has been accountable in one very large respect—the members of that board (until the appointment of SAPRS's members, who are subsidized by donors' dollars) paid every penny of their own travel, their own accommodation, their own communications costs, and their own meeting costs—in short, they spent thousands of dollars in out of pocket expenses without thought of recognition, and certainly with no thanks from the Bowman's and Thompson's of this world....

Shorter then revealed that part of the reason he had resigned from the board was "because it didn't deliver the way I had promised in this forum—but I will be damned if I will sit back and watch the likes of Bowman and Thompson make a mockery of the very positive things this board accomplished. I know what it is to contribute to CKUA—over fifty years, at considerable personal cost to my health and my modest resources. Who are these bloody carpetbaggers?"

Within a few months members of the forum community would be mourning Shorter's sudden death of a heart attack on June 2, 1998.

In an earlier interview, Shorter had said that he favoured a mixed board in which a "significant number" would be elected democratically. "But I also want to have a structure where you know you'll have some people in there who know a little about broadcasting."

A year after the crisis the foundation was still "just a group of self-appointed people who actually own the radio station," CKUA librarian and foundation board member Dave Ward told See Magazine at the time. Now the board was promising revised bylaws for no later than June. The Friends organization did not follow the rump group into a boycott and instead committed to raising at least $200,000 for the station. The spring 1998 fundraiser raised just over $500,000 from 13,000 donors, about 3,100 of them subscribers. Advertising revenue was expected to be triple the previous year's total, rising to $750,000.

The "Bud and Ken Show" gradually petered out to be replaced with a quarterly newsletter distributed to all donors. Meanwhile, Davis and the

◆ *Lark Clark, part of the "new generation" of CKUA. Courtesy of CKUA; photo by Frank Gasparik.*

programming committee were adding and subtracting programs to fine-tune CKUA's sound.

When the popular Cathy Ennis left her 9:00 a.m. to noon "Listening Room" program after the crisis, Davis made a controversial move and filled the time slot with newcomer Lark Clark. While inexperienced as a broadcaster, Clark exhibited the trademark CKUA breadth of knowledge and passion for music. She had travelled widely, studied South African music extensively and had founded the a cappella group Juba, which sang southern African material in African languages.

Davis knew he was taking a chance by parachuting Clark into the daytime slot without putting her through the usual late-night apprenticeship. "I thought she was one of the most brilliantly intuitive programmers we've seen in years.... She wasn't ready, she wasn't a broadcaster *per se*. But I heard something in her that said, you've got part of what's got to be the new generation of CKUA. You've got a creativity, a sensitivity, a risk-taking [attitude] which this organization needs."

When Clark's "Radio Mondo" program hit the air in mid 1997, a wave of snide comments flooded the Internet forum. "They got nasty on the news groups; they phoned in; they left her in tears certain days with the messages they left on her voice mail; and some of the announcers were definitely sitting back and saying, 'Show me,'" Davis said. "She learned fast, and she started winning people over one by one. She ended up being one of the most popular and effective announcers that CKUA has had in a long time."

On the forum, a listener who signed himself "Ron" wrote, "When it ["Radio Mondo"] first came on I thought it was the lamest thing I'd ever heard, but my opinion is not that any more." Another forum participant ventured, "It is truly amazing that the more I listen to Lark, the better she sounds." And yet another wrote, "I am sitting here in my office having my ears opened yet again by Lark—this time with some traditional Chinese lute music followed by some contemporary Brazilian! Thanks, Lark! Keep it up!"

An existing program, "Night Music," which had an eclectic character leaning towards soft jazz, came in for a make-over when Davis and veteran CKUA programmer Tony Dillon-Davis put their heads together. "Tony is a unique character ... eccentric as hell in his own way, and brilliant," Davis said. "He used to come to me and just lay all these discs he was into on me— they were new age this and aboriginal that. And I started hearing this show....

"Tony and I conjured up the idea we were going to go new age. Now, *new age* is a dirty word to a lot of people, but it was new age applied our way. It was taking that beautiful cross-over, kind of meditative and contemplative kind of music, with soulful jazz tracks, with aboriginal compositions that were coming into vogue at that time. And we evolved a brand-new sound for 'Night Music' that was perfect for late night. It was ethereal; it was innovative; it was calming; it was creative; it was cross-over—and Tony was the master."

The board and management recognized, especially after the support the station had received from Calgary during the crisis, that CKUA's on-air personality had to broaden to reflect its provincial nature. In the spring of 1998 John Rutherford was brought in to host a weekly program, "Deuces Wild," from the Calgary studio. The show featured "contemporary folk" music and a celebrity co-host each week.

Throughout 1998 Davis and Cathy Ennis worked on a major project that was part of a strategy to earn CKUA a new revenue stream through syndication of some of its unique programs. "The Folkways Collection" was a big financial risk, the first big project undertaken by the station since it was

◆ Popular "Listening Room" host Cathy Ennis introduced CKUA listeners to a wide range of world music.
Courtesy of CKUA; photo by Frank Gasparik.

privatized. The 24-part documentary series explored the collection of nearly 2,200 recordings produced and acquired over a 40-year period by small independent label Folkways Records, founded in 1948 by New York music producer Moses Asch. The collection reflects the visionary character of Asch, who saw it as something of an encyclopedia of the sounds of the world, containing American field and roots music, ethnic international field recordings, poetry and even political speeches. The recordings range from the music of Bob Dylan, Woody Guthrie, Pete Seeger, Leadbelly and Ella Jenkins, to Martin Luther King Jr.'s "I Have a Dream" speech, the sounds of central African tree frogs and Appalachian cloggers, and songs of the Spanish Civil War.

After Asch died in 1986, the Smithsonian Institution in Washington, DC, took over Folkways Records. But there was an Alberta connection. His son, Michael Asch, was a professor of anthropology at the University of Alberta and had secured a complete set of Folkways recordings for the university. A decade earlier he had approached CKUA with the idea of doing something with the collection, Davis said.

◆ Celebrating "The Folkways Collection": (clockwise from left) Brian Dunsmore, Ken Davis, Robert Wiznura, Cathy Ennis and Dan Cherwoniak.

Photo by Walter Tychnowicz; used by permission of the Edmonton Sun.

"For a variety of reasons that I've never totally understood, different administrations had never decided to bite on it. And when I took over as programming director, I inherited that file, and when I looked at it, I was excited.... When I became GM ... I thought, 'I'm going to do one great project that should have been done a long time ago.'"

Davis brought in Cathy Ennis as initial producer and host. Michael Asch served as creative consultant; U of A postgraduate student Robert Wiznura was researcher on the team; and Folkways-Smithsonian curator Tony Seeger provided assistance on the project.

Michael Asch had grown up in Greenwich Village and knew many of the people Ennis wanted to interview for the series. "Michael was able to make things happen," Davis said. "He could open doors for us." Ennis and technical producer Dan Cherwoniak went to New York for the celebration of Folkways' fiftieth anniversary at Carnegie Hall and taped interviews with Pete Seeger and others who knew Asch. Brian Dunsmore later joined the team as producer.

"I kept feeding Folkways every discretionary buck I could find," Davis said. "There was something in me that ... told me it was right, that we needed to do a great work in that era and to do a definitive piece to show how for real we are.... I think it was a great project, and it was there to remind CKUA's community we can dream big; we can execute big; we can be definitive."

"The Folkways Collection" took almost a year to complete. It would be launched on January 31, 1999. By that time, Davis was gone and CKUA had weathered another crisis.

In July 1998 Davis discovered he had made an error interpreting accounting statements for the previous three months and that the station's deficit for the year, originally thought to be around $61,000, was in fact nearer to $200,000. On July 14 he sent a memo to CKUA staff explaining the situation:

> As General Manager I am responsible for what happens inside this company. This problem is mine and I take full responsibility for it. My resignation is on the table for the CKUA Foundation Board to pick up if it wishes. But I have no intention of simply quitting on you guys and leaving you high and dry. I take responsibility for getting us into this mess and I'm going to do everything in my power to get us out.

Davis explained the station would have to tighten cost controls and eliminate as many as seven staff positions, "on at least a temporary lay-off basis." He cautioned staff to keep the details of the current problem in-house. "I must stress that if you really want CKUA to go under, just start talking on the street about our difficulties. This will get a media swarm going and in no time will only serve to reduce the confidence of business and donors once again, potentially reducing our revenues yet further and thus forcing yet more reductions—at this point we'd likely be in a downward spiral from which we could not escape."

Steen supported Davis, and the board didn't act on his initial resignation. "For all of Ken Davis' strengths, one of his weaknesses was in translating financial information," Steen said. "And unfortunately, it came as a bit of a surprise to him and me and the rest of the board that we were about 175,000 bucks in the red for the year.

"The fact of the matter is—it was worse than a start-up business. It was essentially a bankrupt company that we were trying to clean up and make profitable. So, to think that in the first year of operation we would break even, I think is a fallacy; it's just lunacy. So, a $175,000 loss in the first full year of operation I don't think has been a bad thing.... Yes, I was concerned, but from where I sat, it wasn't the end of the world.

"[But] it was a point where Friends and some staff members, I guess, focused their frustrations, and it took Ken right off the deep end."

A faction on staff had resented Davis' hiring from the start and had been openly disputing his decisions ever since. After the revelation concerning the accounting error, things quickly came to a head. Davis reacted to the stepped-up criticisms by tendering his resignation again on July 23 in a lengthy memo, a copy of which he hastily tacked on to the CKUA staff bulletin board before submitting it to Steen. In it he wrote, "I feel like a bonehead for having made such a rookie mistake and I have been totally prepared to pay for it with my career if necessary, but it is still a very fixable mistake." Then he revealed his frustrations with staff opposition, saying that he was resigning "because too many staff think the inmates should run the asylum and will use all sorts of foolish and poisonous tactics to keep things going their way." His resignation would be effective October 21.

On August 7, after the board had approved a reduced budget for the coming fiscal year, Davis laid off six staff members—some on a temporary basis. Among them were Dave Ward, Katherine Hoy and Daphne Bain, all of whom, because of the leadership role they had played as spokespersons for SAPRS during the station's shut-down, had become almost folk-heroes to the volunteers who had rallied to save the station. They also happened to be part of the faction on the CKUA staff which had been critical of Davis. Some accused Davis of using the deficit crisis to get rid of the people who opposed him. In response to a critical posting on the Internet forum, Davis defended his decision: "I went after positions, not people. I sought to protect programming, technical services and revenue-generating areas of the company—and that meant I had to go after the volunteer co-ordination department, the marketing & promotions director, the Music Director/Librarian [Ward] and two positions in the News & Current Affairs division [Bain and Hoy]." He also pointed out that he had himself taken a salary cut.

In the second week of August, following the layoffs, details of the situation hit the street, and Davis' predicted "media swarm" materialized in full force. CKUA Radio Foundation board member Dave Gibson, who was also president of the combined SAPRS/Friends organization, had leaked confidential board information and Davis' letter of resignation to the media and the Internet forum. CKUA was in the headlines again, with media speculating over the station's financial health and its apparent state of "disarray."

Staff loyal to Davis contacted the media to voice their support. One, who prefers to remain anonymous, called it a "gang rape." Don Bell, CKUA news director at the time, told the Edmonton Journal, "I have worked other places for other bosses, and I have had other bosses here, and Ken is the best boss I have ever had." Several staff members told the Journal that if Davis had a fault, it was that he was too accommodating of those who opposed him.

A message string on the forum, headlined "I Protest," drew accusations and innuendo. "It would seem to me the spirit of a certain former chairperson is alive and kicking at CKUA," wrote one participant. "Not only do I protest too, but I demand an exorcism."

One Edmonton business decided not to renew a sponsorship contract "out of support for the people who got the station back on the air." Gibson, who left the foundation board after leaking the confidential information, admitted the publicity would have some impact on the next fundraising campaign but said the troubles could have a positive result if they forced the foundation to hold democratic elections for the board. Gibson had been one of the Friends pushing for a democratically elected board. "You should start to question the real agenda of the Foundation's executive.... CKUA deserves better," he wrote in a forum posting. "And so do you."

Steen said of that period, "It was really an ugly, ugly time. We had a faction on the board. We had the staff forming camps. It was really all we could do to keep our heads down and carry on."

Gibson later said he had leaked the documents because he felt he had to "make a statement for the friends [Ward, Hoy and Bain] who supported me.... It wasn't about Ken [Davis]. I was anxious to see change in many different ways.... So, maybe I was commenting on a management decision. I felt these were the resources we could not let go."

Gibson, in retrospect, called the turmoil of that year "an evolutionary process that had to run its course. There were a lot of expectations for immediate change, and when that didn't happen right away, it roused suspicions." He said that after the Hinchliffe board closed the station, CKUA supporters felt "once bitten, twice shy."

"The society that was SAPRS, renamed Friends, needed to step aside and allow a professional approach as opposed to an idealistic or activist approach," he admitted. "They had to let go of that and put their trust somewhere." A year after the 1998 crisis, Gibson was still a CKUA listener, supporter and donor but was no longer officially involved in the CKUA volunteers' organization.

The provincial Friends organization became inactive, and in 1999 CKUA received a grant from the Wild Rose Foundation to hire a staff person to co-ordinate the activities of local volunteer chapters in Lethbridge, Canmore, Grande Prairie, Peace River, Red Deer, Calgary, Edmonton and Fort McMurray. Members of the local chapters would act as ambassadors for the station, represent CKUA at local events and put on special CKUA-authorized fundraisers. In 2001 the Bow Valley chapter started a campaign to raise $25,000 to upgrade the Banff FM transmitter. Volunteers assumed responsibilities at CKUA headquarters to help staff with such tasks as cataloguing and filing CDs and records in the music library, contacting donors and running the station's music information line, not to mention doing telephone duty from 6:00 a.m. till past midnight during the semi-annual fundraisers. In 2002 volunteer co-ordinator Maureen Workman had a "staff" of nearly eight hundred to call upon.

The CKUA Radio Foundation board revised its bylaws in the fall of 1998 and established a more democratic structure. Steen said he had been concerned at the start—when the Futures Committee was trying to sort out the role of the support community with respect to station management—that "we could be opening up a can of worms that could kill CKUA.

"One of the problems with the board that I recognized very early on, of course, was that we were well-intentioned but ill-experienced individuals in directing the affairs of a charitable foundation/radio network. And here was another group of well-intentioned but very naïve individuals [a faction of the support community] who, frankly, wanted to play in the wrong sandbox, in my opinion. One of the things the board said to its interim manager very early on was that we would not play in his sandbox. He had the business of running CKUA. It was our business to try to get some money together so that he had something to pay the bills with. We weren't going to be talking to him about programming; we weren't going to be talking to him about staffing."

The new membership rules said, "Any person, over the age of 18 years, wishing to become a member of the Foundation, shall submit to the Board an application, in a form approved by the Board, to become a member of the Foundation, and the Board shall approve same if, in its sole discretion, it determines that such approval is not detrimental to the best interests of the Foundation." A membership fee of twenty dollars would be required.

According to Steen, this meant "you can for all intents and purposes purchase a membership, so to speak, and be allowed to attend the annual general meeting and participate in the election of the directors." Between fifty and sixty CKUA fans seized the opportunity, and eight to ten of them kept up an active interest in CKUA affairs by attending annual meetings, Steen said.

The bylaws stipulated that "the Board shall be comprised of eight (8) Directors who are elected by the membership as herein set out, and up to a maximum of twelve (12) additional persons who the Board in its sole discretion considers capable of making a valuable contribution to the Foundation and Network."

Steen said the decision to go with a partially elected, partially appointed board was to ensure that there would be people with the skills needed to function effectively—"the thought being [that] you need people who can get their calls answered on the board so that they can do the fundraising kinds of activities."

In late 2001 the board commissioned a complete review of CKUA's governance structure and bylaws. Steen said the review would also look at ways to empower CKUA's local chapters to apply for casino licences and "raise big funds." He expected the board would receive recommendations and make appropriate changes before the station's seventy-fifth anniversary in November 2002.

After Davis' resignation the board began a search for a new general manager. During the turmoil of 1998, Ken Regan had been in Vancouver producing a series for the Discovery Channel. When the CKUA position was advertised, some former colleagues urged him to apply.

"At first I wasn't the least bit interested, because I was involved in this wonderful project at Discovery Channel.... At the last minute ... I thought maybe I should contribute because it's [CKUA] a very important institution.... It's part of the history; it's part of the culture of this province; it's part of the fabric of this province; it's part of the people of this province...."

"It was a clarion call. This thing that was so important to this province, and important to me, was in trouble.... It's the strangest thing. I gave up an inordinately prosperous career and salary, but you know, money is not everything.... It was an opportunity for me to make a contribution to something that I love, and it was a critical time in the station's history.... This will sound goofy, but it was sort of like, this is the Alamo and I'm going up there with Davy Crockett.... So, I applied for the job.... and here I am, at the Alamo."

Regan read the situation CKUA had just come through as an understandable result of everyone—staff, board, volunteers—operating in emergency mode for so long while trying to keep the station afloat. It was a case of group burn-out. "So after a year and a half of working flat out in that kind of environment, people started—basically, it started to come apart at the seams ... through no one's fault or negligence.... It's just what happens in the midst of that kind of a situation....

"In a way, I'm the beneficiary of someone else's great misfortune.... My predecessor was a very talented guy and absolutely devoted to making this thing work, and he worked himself half to death trying to do it."

Regan started a healing process, urging staff to get whatever was bothering them off their chests and then put the past behind them. "I made it very clear to people that I would hear them out and I would do whatever I could to address their concerns.... But once it was over, it was over, and we were going to move forward."

A few months later CKUA got some good news. Telus had commissioned Environics to conduct a listenership survey for CKUA. The results were exhilarating. The station could claim more than 300,000 listeners. Other surveys suggested a more modest, but still impressive, 150,000. Steen believed the high figures were partly due to new listeners attracted by the crisis publicity and partly to the fact that traditional Bureau of Broadcast Measurement (BBM) surveys had measured only Edmonton and Calgary audiences. For decades one-third of CKUA's audience had been in rural Alberta.

"It was a real boost when we got it," Steen said. "It certainly helped our sales department because now all of a sudden they can, with some credibility, walk in to potential advertisers and say, 'If you want to get a message out to Albertans, instead of Edmontonians or Calgarians [only], we're the medium you should be using.'"

At the start of his watch in the spring of 1999, Regan said his goal was, within three years, to have $750,000 of CKUA's total $2-million budget coming from donors on a subscription basis. After the spring 2002 fundraiser, CKUA was generating about 60 percent of its revenue—or $1.8 million— from its listeners. Of the station's 13,000 donors, more than 6,000 were subscribers annually contributing over $1.3 million in regular monthly install-ments. The remainder of the network's annual budget of approximately $3 million was fed by about $400,000 in commercial sales, $100,000 in media partnerships, and more than $400,000 in fee-for-service revenue, primarily from a major contract with the provincial government to operate and expand the province's Emergency Public Warning System.

The new CKUA was also turning out to be resourceful with managing donors' dollars. "If we want something, we go out and contra it," Steen said. "If we want some print, we'll trade. The new CKUA seems to be, in my view, a hell of a lot more resourceful than our predecessors.... I believe we're doing a hell of a lot more for a lot less money."

In August 2000 CKUA took the first steps towards opening a new revenue stream. The station completed negotiations with Radio New Zealand for syndicated broadcast of "The Folkways Collection." However, syndication of CKUA music documentary programs would be a long-range goal because copyright clearances are required for music included in a syndicated program—a very costly, time-consuming process.

In 2002 CKUA had one of the few Group 3 Specialty broadcast licences in Canada. The licence, renewed in March 2001 and good through August 31, 2007, required CKUA to broadcast a minimum of six and a half hours of formal educational programming per week and allowed up to 504 minutes of advertising per week, or an average of four minutes every hour. It also allowed the station to broadcast twenty-four hours a day, an option that was being considered in 2002.

Despite the sensibilities of purists, advertising would be a permanent characteristic of the new CKUA, Regan said, "because the more reliant on one revenue stream we become, the more vulnerable we are. So we need a diversity of sources of revenue, and the commercial stream is one of them.

"That's not necessarily a bad thing as long as we retain the integrity of the product. And that means that if we are going to do commercials, we must try consistently to do them tastefully and to respect our audience because our audience is primarily still a public alternative radio kind of audience.... There is a lot of good faith that goes on between CKUA and its audience and vice versa, and I think as long as we commit to that, people will take us on our word."

In fact, the station was using only about seventy percent of its commercial allocation. "It may sound strange to say we're not really trying to fill it up, because that would obviously mean more revenue," Regan said. "And I suppose if the revenue came in, we wouldn't necessarily turn up our noses at it. But we're not really going hard to try to sell all of that commercial time."

CKUA was turning out to be, in Regan's words, a "broadcasting hybrid. One of my staff put it very succinctly.... He said it has a commercial-radio structure but a public-radio format ... but the commercial component is only of necessity, and it's only a very small portion of CKUA's persona.

"There's still a significant component of our audience that tolerates the commercials but doesn't like them.... So we walk kind of a tightrope there." Besides, Regan said, "I think it's important that CKUA retain as much of its public broadcast persona as possible. I think it makes us distinctive. I think it makes us more of an alternative for people and I think it will ultimately garner us more listeners."

But being commercial-free was becoming less and less a distinction as more and more non-commercial choices were becoming available via the Internet and digital satellite. As consumers moved away from commercial radio, CKUA wanted to capture as many of them as possible—which raised the age-old question of how widely CKUA could cast its net to haul in listeners without dumbing down its content.

Regan preferred to call it making CKUA "more accessible." Comparing the post-millennium CKUA to the CKUA of the 1980s, he said, "The fact is when we were fully funded by the provincial government, we could afford to be pretty elitist, and we did a lot of things in radio that were pretty narrow in terms of their audience potential.... Some people might say that it's been watered down.... I think it just was made more accessible, and I think in broadcasting that's what it's about.... The whole idea is to reach people."

But Marc Vasey, veteran fan then programmer from CKUA's edgier days, said the attempt to make CKUA "more acceptable to more people" could backfire and lead to a "lack of importance in the music community."

In 2001, from his perspective as producer of the Edmonton and Calgary jazz festivals and program manager for jazz at the Banff Centre, he observed

◆ Folk-roots musician Lionel Rault, host of "Lionel's Vinyls."
Courtesy of CKUA; photo by Frank Gasparik.

that on the CKUA of the late 1960s and early ACCESS years, "there was avant-garde classical music; there was avant-garde jazz music; there was leading-edge pop music and leading-edge blues.

"From what I'm hearing now, I don't think that programming is happening at that level.... You just don't hear something that sets you on ear. You may hear something that's nice, sort of noveltyish, a nice blend of this and that, but nothing that really kicks you in the butt—like, 'Wow, what is that? That scares me.' I think that's the function of radio: it's supposed to scare people. I think it's supposed to kick you in the butt and in the head and everywhere else and make you sit up and take notice. Make you angry, make you sad."

But as CKUA approached its seventy-fifth anniversary in 2002, Regan felt CKUA had finally struck the right balance. "We have changed our programming philosophy ... but I don't think that we have sacrificed the principles upon which CKUA was founded—the principles of integrity and intelligence, as well as providing something that will engage the audience and entertain them."

In 2000, nearly half a century after the Saturday country show was banished, CKUA once again had a country program, in response to listener demand. Increasing CKUA's provincial profile, "Wide Cut Country" was hosted in the Calgary studio by Allison Brock and "cut a wide swath" through the genre, from traditional hillbilly to contemporary pop country. "A Bluegrass State of Mind," hosted by Dave Ward, who had returned shortly after the 1998 layoffs, quickly gained a following after it made its debut in 2000. Another specialty program added in 2000 was "Lionel's Vinyls," hosted by Alberta folk-roots musician Lionel Rault, who played recordings "from the past 60 years of popular music that have stood the test of time" by artists ranging from Frank Sinatra to the Beatles. Rault also presented "The Rhythm and Blues Review."

Regan admitted that management made at least one mistake in CKUA's programming make-over, and listeners didn't let it pass. "Bel Canto," a program of choral and opera music, had been hosted by Sev Sabourin for years. When Sabourin died suddenly in March 1998, classical host Mark Antonelli was parachuted in to carry on. Station management later decided that with Sabourin gone, the program may have run its course, and they cancelled it.

"People were incensed," Regan said. "To be honest, our classical music audience is not as vocal as some of our other audiences.... This generally reserved audience just erupted. We got e-mails and phone calls, and people were cancelling their subscriptions to CKUA. Oh my God, it was crazy—and we knew instantly that we had made a mistake. He [Mark] is a brilliant classical programmer.... People love the show and they love him for it." "Bel Canto" was reinstated.

In addition to program changes, there were major staff changes between 2000 and 2002. Chris Martin and Lee Onisko left. Cathy Ennis returned and left once again; Lark Clark left but returned to revive "Radio Mondo"—both women carrying on a long tradition of CKUA programmers. Tony Dillon-Davis—a veteran who, like Bill Coull, never left—once jokingly demanded that staff who left be required to return their going-away gifts when they came back.

Long-time CKUA morning person Cam Hayden, also host of the popular "Friday Night Blues Party," left in 2001 to devote his attention to the fledgling Labatt Blues Festival, which he had co-founded three years earlier. By the summer of 2002 the Blues Festival had become a staple of Edmonton's summer festival scene, along with the Edmonton Folk Music Festival and

◆ Monica Miller, host of "How I Hear It." *Courtesy of CKUA; photo by Frank Gasparik.*

Jazz City, which owed their birth years before in a large part to efforts of CKUA programmers Holger Petersen and Marc Vasey, respectively. Dave Ward took over as morning host, while Hayden continued his "Blues Party" program. Lisa Robinson, who toured Alberta—from the Star Trek convention in Vulcan to the gopher museum in Torrington—to bring back audio postcards called "Travel Treasures," left in 2002, to be replaced by Tamara Nowakowsky.

Mindful of developing its next generation of listeners, CKUA was also developing its farm team. In the late 1990s, Todd Gray had become CKUA's youngest program host when he launched "One Drop Rhythms," a program of reggae, dub, roots, rap and dancehall, which he hosted until he left in 2002. Relative newcomers in 2002 were Tony King, hosting "Music for a Sunday Night," Brian Golightly, presenting the Saturday and Sunday morning classical "Breakfast" shows, and Jacqueline Janelle offering "Electric Jello," described as "a sophisticated oasis of everything that grooves: funk, acid jazz, electronica, trip hop, even a little disco." The latter was a conscious attempt to attract a younger audience in the fifteen-to-twenty age group—denizens of the underground scene the station hadn't

◆ *Long-time classical programmer Mark Antonelli.* Courtesy of CKUA; photo by Frank Gasparik.

courted since the late 1960s. Gray, Golightly and Janelle were veterans of CJSR, a traditional source of new CKUA talent.

Meanwhile, newsman Don Bell and technical producer Dan Cherwoniak moved over to the CBC, a traditional beneficiary of CKUA talent. One new voice came from within CKUA. Monica Miller started with CKUA in 1977 as a part-time record librarian and worked as producer and project manager for numerous spoken word programs before taking over the early afternoon time slot with her own music program, "How I Hear It."

Old standbys were still in the mix. As ever, "Old Disc Jockey" John Worthington was playing Glenn Miller, Tommy Dorsey and Benny Goodman. Other long-time listener favourites—Bill Coull's "Coull Jazz," and Tony Dillon-Davis' "Play It Again" and "Night Music"—were still on the program schedule. Holger Petersen's "Natch'l Blues" was in its thirtieth year, while Andy Donnelly's "The Celtic Show" continued to attract a large following.

Mark Antonelli's "Classic Examples" carried on the tradition, started by the University of Alberta seventy-five years earlier, of "good music"—that is, classical music—during the evening. And CRTC formal education content requirements were being filled with the right mix of education and entertainment by Athabasca University's David Gregory and CKUA's Brian Dunsmore with "The Long Weekend," featuring a study of popular music in Western culture between the great wars; "From Bop to Rock," covering music from World War Two to 1960; and "Rocky Road," documenting the trip from Presley to punk.

Four CKUA programs were taped out of their far-flung hosts' homes— Terry David Mulligan's "Mulligan Stew" in West Vancouver; former "Breakfast" host and jazz singer Dianne Donovan's "Voices in Jazz" in Austin, Texas; Tom Coxworth's "Folk Routes" in Calgary; and Loran Fevens' "The Music Box" in Milton, Prince Edward Island. John Rutherford still broadcast his show live from CKUA's Calgary studio.

For a while, CKUA was also importing "The Woodsongs Old-Time Radio Hour," a folk music program produced live to tape out of Lexington, Kentucky. Regan and program director Brian Dunsmore were keeping their ears open for other programs the world over that might intrigue CKUA listeners.

Veteran CKUA announcer Chris Allen covered Alberta's arts and cultural scene, on "Arts Alive" and the "Arts and Culture Guide" with the assistance of southern Alberta arts correspondent Jayme Johnston. Andy Posthumus and Scott Stevenson provided news reports out of CKUA's Edmonton and Calgary studios respectively, while freelancer and former CKUA newsman Ian Gray chaired a public affairs panel on "Sunday Magazine." David Dodge informed "Ecofile" listeners about environmental issues, and Jack Howell entered his thirty-second year of bringing Alberta farmers "Call of the Land."

This was the sound of CKUA as it approached age seventy-five. And judging from the response, it was working. In 2001 CKUA won a third consecutive Prairie Music Award as Media Outlet of the Year and was named Edmonton's Best Radio Station in the annual *See Magazine* readers' poll.

Perhaps some of the acclaim had to do with the fact that CKUA was showing its face more in the Alberta community. To promote the station, Regan encouraged staff to get out of the studio and travel beyond Edmonton and Calgary to host local concerts and fundraisers. During the 2001 spring fundraiser, a group of CKUA programmers hosted a live broadcast from Fort McMurray showcasing local musical talent. Harking back to the station's earlier, more ambitious community activities, CKUA began broadcasting live from music festivals around the province. In 2002 the station had a series in production called "Live From Festival Place," broadcasting live performances of Alberta musicians at Festival Place in Sherwood Park.

In April 2000, with funding from the Wild Rose Foundation, CKUA launched a dynamic new website. The site added to CKUA's awards, picking up a silver medal the next year for innovative design in the *National Post*'s Design Exchange Competition. The site was packed with services from program playlists and staff biographies to an ever-expanding catalogue of CKUA's 100,000-plus-piece record library and a calendar of upcoming events on the Alberta arts and cultural scene. It also archived CKUA's informal educational programs for easy downloading, including "Ecofile," the environmental issues program; "Innovation Alberta," freelance producer Cheryl Croucher's series on science, research and technology in Alberta; and "Heritage Trails," Croucher's five hundred vignettes on Alberta history made available online through a partnership with the Heritage Community Foundation. "Travel Treasures" programs were archived on the site along with links to a wealth of Alberta travel resources, from maps and trail reports to Alberta's museums and historic sites, and the Alberta Bed and Breakfast Association.

The website was intended to be another revenue generator. CKUA had forged several partnerships with such online businesses as britannica.com, BBC Online and RollingStone.com, whereby the station would receive a commission on every sale made through a CKUA webpage link. For example, listeners could consult CKUA's "Top 30" charts of CDs selected by staff, click one that interested them and be transported to the Edmonton Public Library site to borrow it or to the site of a CKUA retail music affiliate where they could purchase the CD online. In November 2001 the station doubled the number of audio-streams available from its website from one hundred to two hundred. Within two weeks they were consistently filled as listeners from more than sixty countries tuned in to hear CKUA via Windows Media Player technology. Many sent money during station fundraisers. If the future of radio was on the Internet, CKUA was getting in on the ground floor.

Commenting on the state of the station in January 2002 as it approached its seventy-fifth anniversary, Steen said, "I think it's a fair statement that the ship's floating pretty well right now." CKUA was no longer running a deficit and was even salting away a little bit of money towards a capital fund to address its most pressing concerns—aging infrastructure and a looming eviction notice.

Many of the transmitters were reaching the limits of their reasonable life expectancy. Although CKUA technicians maintained the infrastructure as best they could after CKUA was privatized, upgrading was pretty much out of the question financially. "As a result, this infrastructure, which is the backbone of CKUA, was left deteriorating," Regan said. "A transmitter—to replace it—is a $150,000 hit. To replace an antenna is anywhere from $30,000 to $60,000. And we have seventeen of those to take care of around the province, so it's an expensive proposition."

In 2001 CKUA received a grant from the Edmonton Community Lottery Board to replace the Edmonton transmitter. It also received a casino licence from the Alberta Gaming Commission to raise money to invest in new antennae. Calgary was set to get a new antenna in 2002, a prospect that would cheer that city's CKUA fans, who had traditionally put up with "dead spots" due to Calgary's challenging geography.

The biggest challenge for CKUA in 2002, however, was to find a new home. Its Edmonton landlord, the provincial government, was preparing to sell the Alberta Block building, which had been CKUA's home for nearly half a century. Not only was the station's generous dollar-a-year lease coming to an end, CKUA was also facing a move that would cost, according to Regan's estimate, about one million dollars. Perhaps the solution Regan, Steen and the CKUA board were pursuing was the most significant indicator of CKUA's health in 2002. Rather than move into another lease situation, they had decided to look at building a new station from the ground up.

"Yes, it may cost money," Regan said. "But we can't afford to do this more than once ... so we need a solution that's going to be a long-term solution.

"We're in a position now of relative strength in terms of our finances.... We have control of our operational costs and our product. We're in a position to, I think, start thinking this way as opposed to in the past when [management] were forced to think in terms of crisis management because we were really just lurching from one situation to another.... We don't have to think in terms of crisis. We can plan appropriately."

As the CKUA board, management and staff began planning the seventy-fifth anniversary celebrations, announcing a capital campaign to create a new home for CKUA was at the top of the wish list, along with an alumni reunion. Early in the year, Steen was talking with three levels of government and potential corporate partners to build support for the project. "There's a part to play for everybody."

He felt he had a pretty good case for getting the provincial government to play its part.

"A couple of years ago we got a call from a fellow in Calgary [who said,] 'I've been transferred here from Toronto. My wife almost left me when we were transferred. I almost left the company—a major international company.' And he said, 'I decided to try it, so we moved to Calgary. Soon after getting here I discovered CKUA. Without you, I think I would have lost my sanity. What can I do for you?'

"Those kind of stories I like telling to the government because basically what they say is that we're part of the Alberta Advantage."

Steen had no doubt that CKUA listeners would play their part in securing CKUA's future. They always have. "It's quite amazing the reaction on the telephones when we make certain 'asks.' Those asks are quite typically fulfilled.... It's really quite mind-boggling....

"I think that unless we make a very serious mistake with our audience or with our donors—we must never take our audience for granted; we must always satisfy our audience's needs and wishes—if we do those things, then I expect our audience will be there for us with all of our reasonable requests.

"There's a relationship between CKUA and its audience that doesn't exist in other broadcasters—if we can maintain that relationship, then I think CKUA will reach one hundred."

EPILOGUE
What Makes CKUA Tick?

Turning seventy-five in the radio world—where the eldest of the elders among North American radio stations can't be much more than eighty—is a remarkable feat. How did CKUA do it? Started on a shoe-string, often living on the edge at the mercy of sometimes indifferent, sometimes reckless—some would even say hostile—caretakers, how did CKUA manage to survive so many near-death experiences? Why have listeners been willing to fight rather than let CKUA go out of their lives?

One word—"passion"—comes up whenever people talk about CKUA's longevity and what the station means to them. Mela Pyper, publisher of the *Rossland Record* and a former Albertan, summed it up this way: "Driving back to B.C. once, I got the CKUA afternoon show and realized what a loss it was not to have that informed and pleasant voice and person picking music I could listen to in my own house—someone without apparent ego.... CKUA was making music a gift rather than a presentation.... There was a passion for the music on the station, and maybe passionate people were responding to that. Passion cannot be faked."

Others call it "spirit," almost on the verge of religiosity. Dave Ward said the idea occurred to him on his and Lee Onisko's Touch the Transmitter tour of Alberta after the station's shut-down and rebirth in 1997: "This isn't a radio station; this is a religion. The way people reacted to what happened was more like what they would do if a church burned down. They'd rally around and put it back up again."

Station manager Ken Regan made a similar observation while talking about listener reaction to programming changes: "Our audience is incredibly loyal. I've described it to people sometimes as more like a religious congregation than an audience because they are so passionate.... When CKUA makes a change, it's kind of like the equivalent of changing the tenets of the Anglican church ... from the audience's perspective."

Former CKUA programmer and retired CBC television news anchor Bob Chelmick compared CKUA listeners to a spiritual community: "When you see a bumper sticker that says 'CKUA,' you have an immediate affinity.... I would imagine to a degree there's a similar sense of community when a born-again Christian sees somebody with a '930 The Light' [today's CJCA, a Christian gospel station] bumper sticker—there's a warming of the heart towards them. And maybe that which defines the CKUA community has a very strong spiritual versus religious element to it.... It's cliché and sappy to talk about the 'spirit' of CKUA, but if there's ever a group that has commonality of spirit outside a religious organization, it must be a CKUA listenership."

CKUA program director Brian Dunsmore said the CKUA community is almost a cult. "The religious element is the wild card in the thing. It is a strata of society—not a white collar–blue collar kind of thing—that has to do with, I think, open minds, people who are interested and engaged in our society."

The fact that CKUA cuts across socio-economic lines is a big factor in its longevity, according to fan and former CKUA Radio Foundation board member Lindsay Hood, one of the rescuers of CKUA during the 1997 shut-down. "I don't know what you call people that listen to CKUA. It just crosses any spectrum ... from artists to doctors to ... a housewife in Forestburg to a rig worker in Girouxville.... It's just an amazing, eclectic bunch of people who are independent-minded, but community-minded.... It's a microcosm of the beauty of Alberta."

Chelmick defined that community by a certain "broadness of appreciation. If you say you are a CKUA listener, you usually have a broad sense of taste, a broad sense of openness to various musics. And when you say that, you can't have that broad sense without an openness to cultures and peoples, and less narrowness of vision on many levels, emotionally and otherwise."

Not that loyal listeners love everything about CKUA. Dunsmore said, "You get people who love different aspects of the station. Some people love the blues show, or love classical and not much of anything else.... CKUA has always had different constituencies."

But they all take a sense of proprietorship in the station. And, it seems it was always thus. Writing in the introduction to a booklet celebrating CKUA's fortieth anniversary in 1967, Jack Hagerman, station manager at the time, said, "I have never seen a broadcasting station whose listeners have such a proprietary interest in what the station does and how it does it. And from conversations with some of the *real* CKUA old-timers, I gather it has always been this way!"

The passion started with CKUA's founders, those educators at the University of Alberta who had almost a religious sense of mission about taking the university to the people. In some sense, you might even call them radio evangelists of a different stripe than their contemporary, "Bible" Bill Aberhart. In his book on the struggle for control of adult educational broadcasting in Canada in the early days of radio, Ron Faris called the Radio League, of which the University of Alberta's Ned Corbett was a member, the "passionate educators." Corbett, Donald Cameron, H.P. Brown, Sheila Marryat and all the volunteers who worked with them to build CKUA in the early days had a sense of mission about bringing "good music" to Albertans.

And while the definition of what constitutes "good music" has broadened over the years as CKUA and its listeners and Alberta itself have broadened, that sense of missionary zeal and passion for quality has been a common thread from CKUA's founders to its present custodians. It runs from Donald Cameron's complaint to the CBC over substitution of "some Winnipeg orchestra" swinging the classics; to Herb Johnson's assertion that "jazz is good for you, everybody should listen to it"; to Ed Kilpatrick's pronouncements that "any work regarded as possessing intrinsic artistic value is automatically a candidate for broadcast on CKUA" and "we cater to all areas of music except bubble gum and country." It ties the enthusiasm of Lark Clark introducing a new world music find, or of Allison Brock bubbling over with excitement about a Dwight Yoakum or Johnny Cash (yes, country!) CD; to Sheila Marryat's "slave driving" of the CKUA Players with rehearsals into the middle of the night and the striving of sound technician Alf Franke and docudrama creators Andrea Spalding, David Spalding and Colin Maclean to approximate the sounds of pilgrims desperately singing hymns on a dangerously tossing ship. The passionate regard for "good music" and quality has been a constant. Even during CKUA's brief flirtation with becoming a commercial station in the mid 1940s and early 1950s, the University of Alberta, within its own three hours a day, valiantly maintained the station's standards.

CKUA's founders had a passionate regard for informal education, or "lifelong learning" in today's buzzwords. And when people talk about what they like—most say "love"—about CKUA, the common theme is that it has always educated as well as entertained them.

Ric Baker, a passionate CKUA fan and original organizer of the Friends of CKUA network, got caught in the undertow when the CKUA Radio Foundation sued certain members of Gail Hinchliffe's board. Even so, in the midst of it all, he could say, "I still love CKUA. It's still the best radio station on the freaking planet. And the music that I learn and the education that I get ... I carry that with me every day.... I don't want it [CKUA] to go away. I want it to be here for my kids. I want them to have the same opportunity to listen to a broad spectrum of music so that they can learn about different cultures from all over the world. I want to give them that. CKUA helps me get that so I can pass that on to them."

It's the same sense of enrichment Alberta filmmaker Tom Radford said he felt growing up in Edmonton and listening to CKUA: "I felt part of a much bigger world without ever doubting that Edmonton itself was an exciting place." Or that experienced by George Vaitkunas, who remembered as a child in the 1960s hearing a "Candlelight and Silver" program

> that came out of the car radio helping to reveal a starry Alberta winter sky out the rear window on a drive back from the "big city" to my home town of St. Paul. To have that kind of urbane, non-commercial, cultural experience available in a rural setting was truly enriching. It put me in touch with real music; it enlarged my world and actually offered hope that civilization did exist out there, somewhere.

Vaitkunas grew up to be a CKUA announcer-producer himself for a few years. In 2002 he was a graphic designer living in Vancouver. And although he took graduate studies at Yale, he said, "CKUA is my real alma mater. Its lessons were about more than music. It taught me the meaning of quality."

One other constant throughout CKUA's history has been its support for Alberta talent. Whether cramming a thirty-strong local choir into its university extension department studio, recording the Edmonton Symphony Sunday concerts live, bringing Alberta artists into the studio to talk about their music on "Acme Sausage Company," or providing the essentials for Alberta artists to record their first CDs on the Alberta Music Project, CKUA has consistently provided a showcase and home for Alberta talent.

"The fact that CKUA was airing performers like Triple Threat, Oscar Lopez, Crystal Plamondon, James Keelaghan and Bill Bourne long before they became Juno nominees (and, in some cases, winners) is important enough—in my mind at least—to justify our unconditional support," wrote *Calgary Herald* editorial writer Charles Frank in 1995. In 2001 Juno Award-winning saxophonist P.J. Perry told *Alberta Views*, "CKUA has been instrumental for me. It [my success] would have been impossible without it. The station sticks its neck out, playing longer tracks than would ordinarily be played on commercial radio."

Alberta's "Mr. Music" Tommy Banks, who hosted a teen show on CKUA near the start of his internationally successful music career and who was named to the Canadian Senate in 2000, said, "Just ask any reasonably successful Alberta recording artist where their record first got played, and the answer is CKUA, always, just always.... Most of them would lay down in front of a train for CKUA.... It was the first place that many, many Alberta artists got their first substantive airplay to a discerning audience that understands what's going on and who will either like it or not with some reason to their opinion."

The station's influence goes beyond listeners and individual artists who got their boost there, Banks said. "It's been important to everybody who has been involved in the arts in Alberta." That's because CKUA created "a fertile base on which other things have been able to grow," Banks said. "It's in no small measure responsible for the happy existence of the sort of reasonable infrastructure of arts support and knowledge about the arts in Alberta."

Holger Petersen, CKUA "Natch'l Blues" host and head of Stony Plain Records, agreed. "I think right now we're culturally at a really good place in this province. Visual artists, musicians, theatre and film people—those people tend to really love CKUA and I think that provides a connection for all the arts organizations—CKUA seems to communicate to all these people."

By providing a platform for Alberta artists and ideas throughout its existence, CKUA has mirrored Alberta to Albertans, and in the process it has become, in the eyes of many, a cultural institution in itself—comparable to, say, the Provincial Museum of Alberta. As Linda Goyette pointed out in an *Edmonton Journal* column in 1997, "not all cultural institutions have walls and ceilings." Former CKUA classical music host Richard Moses once described his sense of CKUA's role as "not unlike a library, an art gallery or a museum (in the best sense): we are preserving and bringing to the attention of folks, the very best that human beans [*sic*—Moses' irreverent humour showing here] have created and are creating."

As CKUA was turning seventy-five in 2002, Alberta itself was approaching its one hundredth birthday, in 2005. Essentially, CKUA and Alberta grew up together. And Alberta would have been a "lot different" place had it not been for CKUA, Holger Petersen felt. "I think it just makes life more interesting in this province that we have CKUA here."

Perhaps CKUA's influence is best summed up by Bob Chelmick: "The quality of life that issues from listening to CKUA over time cannot be denied.... Listening to CKUA over time changes everybody, not just everybody working there but everybody listening to it.... It changes your whole outlook...

"Your boundaries fall away, which is the whole idea of spiritual growth—letting the boundaries fall away."

REFERENCES

◆ **Published Sources**

"ACCESS Announces CKUA-FM Network." *ACCESS Magazine*, Summer 1975.

"ACCESS Has a Place." Editorial. *Calgary Herald*, 6 December 1993.

"ACCESS President Resigns from Job." *Lethbridge Herald*, 1 December 1993.

"Across the Atlantic, Sig. Marconi Receives a Message from England." *The (Toronto) Globe*, 16 December 1901.

Aikenhead, Cynthia. "Let's Expand CKUA to Mark our Jubilee." *Edmonton Journal*, 27 May 1965.

"Alberta Radio Stations Join to Boost Local Musicians." *Calgary Herald*, 14 December 1989.

Allard, T.J. *Straight Up: Private Broadcasting in Canada, 1918–1958*. Ottawa: Canadian Communications Foundation, 1979.

"Backstage in Radio." *Maclean's*, 7 May 1960.

"Bad Air Day for Hinchliffe." *Edmonton Sun*, 30 July 1997.

Bambrick, Kenneth. "The Evolution of Radio." In *The History of Canadian Broadcasting* [online]. Canadian Communications Foundation [cited 11 August 2002]. <http://www.rcc.ryerson.ca/ccf/stations/radio/evltnrad.html>.

Banford, Doug. Letter to the Editor. *Edmonton Journal*, 30 November 1971.

"BBG Was Asked for CKUA Report." *Edmonton Journal*, 10 June 1962.

Billington, Dave. "Nature Radio." *ACCESS Magazine*, June–August 1984.

Bird, Roger, ed. *Documents of Canadian Broadcasting*. Ottawa: Carleton University Press, 1988.

Blaxley, John D. Letter to the Editor. *Calgary Herald*, 16 March 1977.

Breuer, N. and J. Rollans. "The Longest-Running Radio Program in the World." In *A Sound for All Seasons: CKUA's 60th Anniversary*. Edmonton: Alberta Educational Communications Corporation, 1987.

Brown, H.P. "Pioneering Adult Education in the West." *Food for Thought*, January 1955.

Brown, Percy. "H.P. Brown Gets an Idea." *Strathcona Plaindealer*, Winter 1988.

Byfield, Ted. "View from the West." *Financial Post*, April 1997.

Byrne, T.C. *Alberta's Revolutionary Leaders*. Calgary: Detselig Enterprises, 1991.

"Cabinet Plans Seize People's Radio in Propaganda Scheme." *Spotlight*, 2 December 1940.

Cashman, Tony. "CKUA Joins ACCESS." *Alberta Calls*, 17 May 1974.

"CKUA: An Orphan Voice." *Globe and Mail*, 6 December 1965.

"CKUA Bounces Back." *See Magazine*, 19 March 1998.

"CKUA Chair Says Remedies Are Possible." *Edmonton Journal*, 8 August 1997.

"CKUA Could Be Back on the Air as Early as Friday, Director Says." *Edmonton Journal*, 25 March 1997.

"CKUA Firing Reveals Cuts Agenda – Foster." *Medicine Hat News*, 21 February 1994.

"CKUA Foundation Bylaws [online]." [cited 31 January 2002]. <www.ckua.com>.

"CKUA GM Slams Staff on Way out." *Edmonton Journal*, 13 August 1998.

"CKUA May Lose Licence." *Red Deer Advocate*, 9 June 1970.

"CKUA May Yet Survive." *Edmonton Journal*, 10 March 1972.

"CKUA Mismanaged, Auditor Says." *Edmonton Journal*, 6 May 1997.

"CKUA Nears 70." *Calgary Herald*, 25 January 1997.

"CKUA Parties Must Reconcile, Evans Says." *Edmonton Journal*, 8 April 1997.

"CKUA Radio Goes Live on Internet." *Calgary Herald*, 29 February 1996.

"CKUA Radio Staff Petitions to Keep Program Director." *Edmonton Journal*, 20 March 1961.

"CKUA Radio to Become Independent Charitable Foundation." *Edmonton Journal*, 14 May 1994.

"CKUA Replays Board Lawsuit." *Edmonton Journal*, 21 August 1997.

"CKUA Sale Is an Option for Tories." *Edmonton Journal*, 13 January 1987.

"CKUA Settles out of Court." *Edmonton Journal*, 11 September 2001.

"CKUA to Serve Province with Repeater Stations." *Edmonton Journal*, 17 April 1973.

"CKUA: Wide Ranging Programming Rewarded with Wide Support." *Calgary Herald*,
9 November 1996.

"CKUA's Chances Were Squandered." *Edmonton Journal*, 7 May 1997.

Clark, Ralph J. *A History of the Department of Extension at the University of Alberta,
1912–1956*. Toronto: University of Toronto, 1985.

"Communications Corporation Critics Reassured." *Edmonton Journal*, 8 January 1973.

"Community Funding Proposed for CKUA." *Edmonton Journal*, February 12, 1987.

Corbett, E.A. "Says CKUA Leads Canada in Radio Education Work." *Edmonton
Journal*, 20 November 1937.

———. *We Have with Us Tonight*. Toronto: Ryerson Press, n.d.

Cormack, Barbara Villy. *Beyond the Classroom: The First 60 Years of the University of Alberta
Department of Extension*. Edmonton: University of Alberta, 1981.

———. *Perennials and Politics: The Life Story of Hon. Irene Parlby, LLD*. Sherwood Park,
AB: Professional Printing, 1968.

Davis, Harry P. "The Early History of Broadcasting in the United States." In *The Radio
Industry: The Story of its Development, as Told by the Leaders of the Industry*. 1928.
Reprint, New York: Arno Press, 1974.

Day, Moira, ed. *The Hungry Spirit: Selected Plays and Prose by Elsie Park Gowan*.
Edmonton: NeWest Press, 1992.

Dickinson, J. Letter to the Editor. *Edmonton Journal*, 10 October 1964.

Douglas, George H. "Early Radio in the USA: The Story of Westinghouse Electric."
In *The Early Days of Radio Broadcasting*. Jefferson, NC: McFarland, 1987. Reprinted
in *Adventures in Cybersound* [online]. Compiler R. Naughton. Australian Centre for
the Moving Image, 2000. [cited February 2001].
<http://www.acmi.net.au/AIC/RADIO_WESTINGHOUSE.html>.

Editorial. *Edmonton Journal*, 3 October 1972.

"80 Per Cent City Homes Now Are Radio Equipped." *Edmonton Journal*, 11 January
1937.

Evans, Art. "Sell CKUA?" *Edmonton Journal*, 30 September 1964.

Evergreen and Gold, 1922–23 [Yearbook]. Edmonton: University of Alberta, 1923.

"Ex-Director Blames Government." *Edmonton Journal*, 7 May 1997.

"Extending CKUA Said for S.C. Use." *Edmonton Journal*, 8 November 1940.

"Fallow Flays CBC Governors for Refusing Station CKUA Private Commercial
License." *Edmonton Bulletin*, 7 March 1945.

"Fallow Raps C.B.C. Refusal to Issue License to Station." *Edmonton Journal*, 7 March
1945.

Faris, Ron. *The Passionate Educators: Voluntary Associations and the Struggle for Control of
Adult Educational Broadcasting in Canada, 1919–52*. Toronto: Peter Martin
Associates, 1975.

Ferguson, Ted. "Leisure's Television Highlights & Schedules." *Vancouver Sun*, 18 August 1972.

50 Years on the Leading Edge of Broadcasting: CKUA Golden Anniversary, 1927–1977 [brochure]. Alberta Educational Communications Corporation.

"Former CKUA Directors Defend Policy." *Edmonton Journal*, 10 July 1998.

"Frank Conrad." In *The Conrad Project* [online]. National Museum of Broadcasting, 2002. [cited 11 August 2002]. <http://trfn.clpgh.org/nmb/nmbcnrd.htm>.

"Future of ACCESS up in the Air, Says Kowalski." *Edmonton Journal*, 19 February 1993.

Gasher, Mike. "Invoking Public Support for Public Broadcasting: The Aird Commission Revisited." *Canadian Journal of Communication* 23, no. 2 (1998). [online]. [cited March 2001].
<http://www.cjc-online.ca/~cjc/BackIssues/23.2/gasher.html>.

"Gil Evans: The Quiet Morning Man." *Edmonton Week*, 29 September 1962.

"The Good Old Days: CKUA Gets off to a Blazing Start." *ACCESS Magazine*, Summer 1975, 4.

Government of Alberta. *A Choice of Futures: Report of the Commission on Educational Planning*. Edmonton: L.S. Wall, Queen's Printer for the Province of Alberta, 1972.

Government of Canada. *Report of the Royal Commission on Radio Broadcasting*. Ottawa: F.A. Acland, 1929.

Government of Canada. *Report of the Task Force on Broadcasting Policy*. Ottawa: Minister of Supply and Services, 1986.

"Gov't May Be to Blame – Klein." *Edmonton Journal*, 31 July 1997.

"Gov't Too Overbearing, Claims ACCESS Board." *Edmonton Journal*, 1 October 1977.

Gregory, David. "In Memoriam R2RS, 1981–1997." *Canadian Folk Music Bulletin* 32, no. 3 (1998): 6.

Hardie, Mrs. H.M. Letter to the Editor. *Edmonton Journal*, 30 November 1971.

"He Was King of Hawaiian Music in the Fifties." *Edmonton Journal*, 12 June 2000.

"History of Broadcast in Edmonton." *Edmonton Journal*, 4 October 1979.

"Image an Issue for CKUA." *See Magazine*, 27 August–2 September 1998.

Jordan, Edward. "Recollections of CKUA." *New Trail*, Summer 1987. Excerpted in *Alberta Past*, December 1987.

Letters to the Editor. *Edmonton Journal*, 20 January–5 February 1987.

Lisac, Mark. "CKUA Audit Uncovers Novatel Look-alike." *Edmonton Journal*, 6 May 1997.

———. *The Klein Revolution*. Edmonton: NeWest Press, 1995.

———. "Points to Ponder in CKUA Shutdown." *Edmonton Journal*, 4 April 1997.

"Many of CKUA's Staff Rally Around Their Resigning GM." *Edmonton Journal*, 14 August 1998.

Marryat, Sheila. Letter to the Editor. *The (University of Alberta) Gateway*, 27 March 1923.

———. "Music Plays Leading Role Air Program." *Edmonton Journal*, 20 November 1937.

McCallum, Joe. *CKUA and 40 Wondrous Years of Radio* [booklet]. 1967.

———. "CKUA and 60 Wondrous Years of Radio." In *A Sound for All Seasons: CKUA's 60th Anniversary*. Edmonton: Alberta Educational Communications Corporation, 1987.

Milne, W.S. "Drama." *Letters in Canada: 1937*; *University of Toronto Quarterly* 7 (April 1938): 367.

"New Board Says CKUA Fine Tuning May Take a Month." *Edmonton Journal*, 15 April 1997.

"New Board Takes over CKUA Radio." *Edmonton Journal*, 12 April 1997.

"No CKUA Here but Nickel Phone Calls." *Calgary Albertan*, 16 July 1965.

"No Profit in Privatized CKUA—Employee." *Edmonton Journal*, 14 January 1987.

"On the Scene." *Edmonton Journal*, 12 March 1971.

Ottewell, A.E. "University Radio Station CKUA Celebrates Tenth Anniversary." *Edmonton Journal*, 20 November 1937.

Peers, Frank W. *The Politics of Canadian Broadcasting: 1920–1951*. Toronto: University of Toronto Press, 1969.

Planning for Change: A White Paper on ACCESS Radio CKUA. Edmonton: Alberta Educational Communications Corporation, 1977.

"Planning to Sell CKUA Equipment." *Edmonton Journal*, 13 February 1950.

Pratt, Larry. "Privatization & the Radio Station." *Alberta Views*, Winter 1998.

"The Privatization of CKUA." *Edmonton Journal*, 6 April 1997.

"Provincial Bid Fails To Legalize CKUA." *Edmonton Journal*, 9 June 1962.

Radford, Tom. "CKUA: Letter from a Friend..." *Edmonton Journal*, 7 May 1977.

"Radio and the University." Editorial. *Manitoba Free Press*, 13 February 1928.

Selman, Gordon, and Paul Dampier. *The Foundations of Adult Education in Canada*. Toronto: Thompson Educational Publishing, 1991.

Shorter, Larry T. Letter to the Editor. *Edmonton Journal*, 25 March 1997.

———. *A Reader's Companion to the Alberta Worth Report on Educational Planning: A Choice of Futures*. Edmonton: Queen's Printer for the Province of Alberta, n.d.

Silvester, Reg. "CKUA Review." *Broadcaster Magazine*, April 1987.

Slater, Patrick. Letter to the Editor. *Calgary Herald*, 9 February 1987.

"Sources Differ as to Finances in Wake of CKUA Layoffs." *Vue Weekly*, 13–19 August 1998.

"The Station That Started with a Bang." *Edmonton Journal*, 19 November 1977.

Statistics Canada. "Wages and Working Conditions." Series E4–48. In *Historical Statistics of Canada*. 2nd ed. Ed. F.H. Leacy. Ottawa: Statistics Canada, 1983.

"Stress on Education in New CKUA Format." *Edmonton Journal*, 31 January 1974.

"Supporters Rally to Save CKUA Radio." *Advocate*, 21 January 1987.

Takach, G.F. "Ears a Little More Open." *Alberta Views*, September–October 2001.

Thomas, Lewis H., ed. *William Aberhart and Social Credit in Alberta*. Toronto: Copp Clark Publishing, 1977.

Thorsell, Bill. "Notes from the Overground." *Edmonton Journal*, 14 January 1984.

"246 Interference Troubles Eliminated in Edmonton." *Edmonton Journal*, 18 October 1930.

University of Alberta, Department of Extension. *Annual Report*. Edmonton: University of Alberta, 1930-32, 1934, 1946.

"Vaughn De Leath: The Original Radio Girl." In *Edison Restored Recordings* [online]. Tracer Technologies. [cited 12 August 2002]. <www.tracertek.com/vaughn.htm>.

Vipond, Mary. *Listening In: The First Decade of Canadian Broadcasting, 1922–1932*. Montreal & Kingston: McGill-Queen's University Press, 1992.

Waters, Jim. "Television and Radio." *Edmonton Journal*, 1 October 1977.

Weir, E. Austin. *The Struggle for National Broadcasting in Canada*. Toronto: McClelland and Stewart, 1965.

West, Dan. "The Crusade to Revive CKUA." *Globe and Mail*, 29 April 1997.

Whyte, Jon. "Confessions of an Ex-CKUA Broadcaster." *ACCESS Magazine*, Spring 1978.

◆ **Archival Sources**

Board of Governors Papers. Record Group 75–86–4. University of Alberta Archives, Edmonton, Alberta. Includes "A Summary of the Issues, Re: CKUA," 3 May 1974.

Brown, Percy. Personal files, including a scrapbook of clippings.

Chancellor and Senate Papers. Record Group 82–113. University of Alberta Archives, Edmonton, Alberta. Includes minutes, CKUA staff statement, correspondence (L.A. Desrochers, Louis Hyndman, Michael O'Byrne and William Thorsell), the "Report of the Senate *ad hoc* Committee on the Future of Radio Station CKUA," CRTC Decision 74–67, and other documents relating to the AASUA Committee to Review CKUA and the Senate Committee on the Future of CKUA (1972–73).

CKUA archives, Edmonton, Alberta. Collections include correspondence (originals or copies) and memoranda between government, university, ACCESS and CKUA officials (Perren Baker, Ric Baker, Larry Clausen, Ken Davis, Brian Dunsmore, Cathy Ennis, Neil Evans, David Fraser, Stan Freberg, Don Getty, Warren Graves, Jack Hagerman, Gail Hinchliffe, Ed Kilpatrick, Rick Lewis, Harry Mamet, Pat McDougall, John V. Montour, Randy Morse, Richard Moses, Corey Olynik, James Parker, Bruce Peel, Mike Pleau, Michael Plumb, Jackie Rollans, John Schmid,

Peter Senchuk, Larry Shorter, Don Thomas, Ukrainian Self-Reliance League of Canada, R.C. Wallace, M. Wyman, Ron Yoshida, Les Young); expense claims, invoices and other financial records; summary report by Ken Chapman; documents relating to the CKUA Futures Committee; minutes of CKUA Radio Foundation Annual General Meetings and Board of Directors' Meetings; copies of news releases and editorials relating to CKUA; scripts and other materials relating to CKUA programming; Walterdale Theatre newsletter; ACCESS Network, *Transitions: The Next Three Years*, Fall 1988; Harry J. Boyle & Associates, *Report on CKUA-Edmonton to Alberta ACCESS*, 11 May 1979; ACCESS Network financial statements; Minutes of directors' meeting, ACCESS Charitable Foundation, 19 May 1994; Rick Salt, "Focusing on the Future," Salary and Benefits Survey Results, 23 November 1994; Contract between CKUA Radio Foundation and Gail A. Hinchliffe & Associates Ltd., 2 February 1995; Operations Plan, 19 July 1995; Contract between Richard Delmer Baker (for RB Consulting) and the CKUA Radio Foundation, 16 October 1995; Turner Associates, report on June 6, 1996, CKUA Initial Team Investigation meeting.

CKUA audio archives, Edmonton, Alberta. Collection includes taped reminiscences of Walker Blake, H.P. Brown, Elsie Park Gowan, Dick MacDonald, J.W. Porteous, Gordon Taylor and Harry Taylor on the occasion of CKUA's 30th anniversary (CD 2; 1957); taped reminiscences of Jack Hagerman, Don Rollans, John Runge and others on the occasion of CKUA's 50th anniversary (CDs 2.3a, 2.4; 1977); taped reminiscences of Tommy Banks, Robert Goulet, Jack Hagerman, Edward Jordan, Dan Key and June Sheppard on the occasion of CKUA's 60th anniversary (CD 2.4a; 1987); taped reminiscences of Brian Dunsmore, Gil Evans, Herb Johnson and Bob Rhodes on the occasion of CKUA's 65th anniversary (1992); recordings of programs and speeches at CKUA's 30th anniversary (CD 2a; 1957)and 60th anniversary (CD 2.4; 1987).

CKUA Internet forum. Archived by Dan West, Athabasca University, Athabasca, Alberta.

Draft contracts, correspondence, CKUA. Record Group 69-135-112. University of Alberta Archives, Edmonton, Alberta. Includes Government of Alberta documents relating to the 1944 Agreement between University and Province; correspondence and memoranda between G.C.W. Browne, Donald Cameron, C.L. King, J. McRae, Robert Newton and H.H. Parlee.

Getty, Don, fonds. Accession No. 79.60. Provincial Archives of Alberta, Edmonton, Alberta. Includes documents relating to CKUA; correspondence and memoranda between CKUA, Don Getty, Lou Hyndman, Peter Knaak, Gerard Pelletier, Carol Pettigrew, Horst A. Schmid and others; and Jack Hagerman's 1971 briefing for the Alberta government, "CKUA and Federal Policy on Provincial Broadcasting.

Gowan, Elsie (Young) Park. Papers. Record Group 88–63. University of Alberta Archives, Edmonton, Alberta. Includes a scrapbook kept by E.H. Gowan for "Science Question Box."

Hagerman, Jack. Personal files, including copies of government and university documents relating to CKUA and radio broadcasting; submissions, reports, memoranda and briefs relating to CKUA and its licensing and transmitter power; *Votes and Proceedings of the Legislative Assembly of the Province of Alberta*, No. 19, 1st Sess., 14th Leg., 8 March 1960; Order-in-Council P.C. 1972–1569, 13 July 1972; correspondence between Leon Balcer, Walker Blake, G.C.W. Browne, Donald Cameron, H.B. Chase, M.B. Corah, A.D. Dunton, W.A. Fallow, A. Frigon, Jack Hagerman, A.J. Higgins, C.D. Howe, Walter Johns, Mackenzie King, L.R. LaFleche, John Langdon, Ernest Manning, Donald Manson, James J. McCann, Rene Morin, Gladstone Murray, Ray Reierson, Walter Rush, Gordon Taylor, Wayne M. Vleck and Mrs. Frank Willis; CKUA scripts; and Broadcast News transmissions.

Moses, Richard. Personal files, including correspondence from Ken Davis and "Job Analysis Outline," 2 October 1991.

Newton, Robert. Papers. Record Group 71–161–44. University of Alberta Archives, Edmonton, Alberta. Includes CKUA programming material.

Office of the President and Vice-Chancellor Papers. Walter A.R. Kerr Papers. Box 3, Record Group 68–1. University of Alberta Archives, Edmonton, Alberta. Includes memoranda and correspondence by Donald Cameron, Walter Kerr, Gladstone Murray, H.H. Parlee, G.R.A. Rice and J.A. Weir regarding CKUA.

Office of the President and Vice-Chancellor Papers. Robert Newton Papers. Box 20, Record Group 68–1. University of Alberta Archives, Edmonton, Alberta. Includes CKUA-related correspondence between William Aberhart, Dan Cameron, Donald Cameron, C.D. Howe, H.G. Love, E.H. McGuire, Robert Newton, James A. McKinnon, H.H. Parlee, Bill Rea, James S. Thomson and Walter Rush; documents relating to CBC–CKUA relations and to CKUA programming.

Office of the Vice-President (Academic) Papers. Record Group 69–123–948. University of Alberta Archives, Edmonton, Alberta. Includes correspondence between Walter Johns and Guy Vaughan.

Porteous, John Wardlaw. Papers. Record Group 69–27. University of Alberta Archives, Edmonton, Alberta. Includes Porteous' technical notes on CKUA's first transmitter, and MA theses by Porteous and W.E. Cornish.

Record Group 68–1–2243. University of Alberta Archives, Edmonton, Alberta. Includes correspondence between Walter Johns and Robert Newton, and Guy Vaughan's "Brief History of Radio Station CKUA."

Record Group 69–116–3. University of Alberta Archives, Edmonton, Alberta. Includes documents by H.P. Brown relating to the early years of CKUA.

Shorter, Larry T. Personal files, including remarks at Alberta ACCESS–CRTC Hearings, 12 March 1974; correspondence with Gail Hinchliffe; and minutes and reports of CKUA AM-FM Advisory Committee

Shorter, Larry T., fonds. Accession No. 90.157. Provincial Archives of Alberta, Edmonton, Alberta. Includes documents relating to CKUA.

Tory, Henry Marshall. Papers. Record Group 68–9–198. University of Alberta Archives, Edmonton, Alberta. Includes CKUA programs; correspondence between Tory and Alex Johnston; copies of news articles about CKUA.

Walters, Marylu [author]. Personal files, including copies of CKUA memoranda and correspondence by Richard Moses, Don Thomas and Gene Zwozdesky; copies of news releases; 1997 circular to donors; B.G. Parlby, "D. Sheila Marryat," family history; David Gregory, "From Radio to Real Audio: A Changing Partnership," 1998; *The ACCESS Network Board of Directors Recommendations*, 4 February 1994; Ernst & Young, *CKUA Radio Business Plan*, April 1994; Management Agreement between the Alberta Educational Communications Corporation and CKUA Radio Foundation, 9 August 1994; Peter Valentine, report on CKUA Radio Foundation, 30 April 1997; Deloitte & Touche, "CKUA Radio Foundation Forensic Accounting Review," 7 August 1997.

◆ **Interviews and Correspondences**

The following individuals consented to conversations, taped personal interviews, or telephone interviews, either with the author or with Sharon Sinclair, during the research period from 1997 to 2002: Ric Baker, Tommy Banks, Tony Cashman, Bob Chelmick, Bill Coull, Arthur Craig, Ken Davis, Tony Dillon-Davis, Brian Dunsmore, Gil Evans, Alex Frame, Fil Fraser, Dave Gibson, Robert Goulet, Jack Hagerman, Arthur Hiller, Gail Hinchliffe, Lindsay Hood, Herb Johnson, Eve Keates, John Langdon, Clarence Laverty, Chris Martin, Holger Petersen, Ken Regan, Jackie Rollans, Peter Senchuk, Larry Shorter, Bud Steen, Shirley Stinson, Don Thomas, Lawrence Twigge, Stanley Varnhagen, Marc Vasey and Dave Ward. In addition, a conversation between Sev Sabourin, Bill Coull and Tony Dillon-Davis was taped by author and Sharon Sinclair on 18 November 1997.

The author and Sharon Sinclair also corresponded with the following people during the research for this book: Gil Evans, Iris Evans, Jean Greenough, Kay Guthrie, Larry King, Cheryl Markosky, Richard Moses, Bill Pinko, Mela Pyper, Michael Skeet, Andrea Spalding and George Vaitkunas.

INDEX

Marylu Walters is a professional writer and editor based in Edmonton. She is the co-author of *Pottery in Alberta: The Long Tradition*, published by the University of Alberta Press. Her feature stories on topics ranging from travel and business to science and health have appeared in numerous magazines and newspapers. She is a graduate of the Syracuse University School of Journalism and holds a Master's degree in communication from the S.I. Newhouse School of Public Communications at Syracuse.